P9-EDH-317

Socio-Economics

Toward a New Synthesis

Studies in Socio-Economics

MORALITY, RATIONALITY, AND EFFICIENCY
NEW PERSPECTIVES ON SOCIO-ECONOMICS
Richard M. Coughlin, editor

SOCIO-ECONOMICS
TOWARD A NEW SYNTHESIS
Amitai Etzioni and Paul R. Lawrence, editors

Socio-Economics

Toward a New Synthesis

EDITORS
Amitai Etzioni
Paul R. Lawrence

M. E. Sharpe, Inc.
Armonk, New York • London, England

PROPERTY OF
CLACKAMAS COMMUNITY COLLEGE
LIBRARY
WITHDRAWN

Copyright © 1991 by M. E. Sharpe, Inc.

All rights reserved. No part of this book may be reproduced in any form without written permission from the publisher, M. E. Sharpe, Inc., 80 Business Park Drive, Armonk, New York 10504.

Available in the United Kingdom and Europe from M. E. Sharpe, Publishers, 3 Henrietta Street, London WC2E 8LU.

Library of Congress Cataloging-in-Publication Data

Socio-economics : toward a new synthesis
/ Amitai Etzioni and Paul R. Lawrence, editors.
p. cm.—Studies in Socio-Economics
"Product of the first International Conference on Socio-Economics
conducted at the Harvard Business School,
March 31–April 2, 1989"—CIP pref.
Includes index.
ISBN 0-87332-685-7
1. Economics—Sociological aspects—Congresses.
I. Etzioni, Amitai.
II. Lawrence, Paul R.
III. International Conference on Socio-Economics
(1st : 1989: Harvard Business School).
IV. Series.
HM35.S625 1991
306.3—dc20
90-40462
CIP

Printed in the United States of America

The paper used in this publication meets the minimum requirements of American National Standard for Information Sciences—Permanence of Paper for Printed Library Materials, ANSI Z39.48–1984.

MV 10 9 8 7 6 5 4 3 2 1

Contents

Figures

Tables

Tables

Preface

This volume is the product of the first International Conference on Socio-Economics conducted at the Harvard Business School, March 31–April 2, 1989. The program committee included Alfred Chandler, Paul Lawrence, Amitai Etzioni, Pankaj Ghemawat, and Michael Useem. The conference was sponsored by the Harvard Business School Division of Research and we are grateful to Jay Lorsch, director of the division, for his guidance and suggestions. It was during this conference that colleagues coming together from numerous fields and countries sensed that a shared perspective and paradigm was emerging and that there existed, for many years in effect, an invisible college of people dissatisfied with neoclassical economics, and working in complementary ways to develop alternative conceptions, theories, and methods for the study of economic behavior and choice in general. The conference made the invisible college visible. It led, among other developments, to the formation of an international society, the Society for the Advancement of Socio-Economics; a series of books of which this is but the first; and to annual meetings (March 1990, Washington, DC; June 1991, Stockholm School of Economics).

The topics covered by socio-economists are well illustrated in the parts of this volume. The first part discusses several of the historical, philosophical, and conceptual sources of socio-economics. The second part deals with the all-important question of whether people can be productively perceived as dealing with one overarching utility or whether the concept of a more complex and nonreducible set of overarching goals is more accurate. Once goals are set, leaders are often a tool that affects implementation, the subject of the third part. Individuals, however charismatic and powerful, are but one source of social change and order, and often function in the context of institutions, which they also affect (part four). Institutions, in turn, are not only structures of relationships, they are formed according to guiding principles, which are embedded in corporate cultures (part five). Finally, socio-economics recognizes that the question, "What is the right unit of analysis?" is far from self-evident. At first glance it might seem, for instance, that firms are a clear unit of analysis. Socio-economists show, however, that the picture is considerably more complex: firms are woven into larger entities. Recognizing this complexity, without unduly overloading analysis, makes for a more explanatory and predictive social science.

Amitai Etzioni and
Paul R. Lawrence

February 1991

Contributors

Mitchel Y. Abolafia, Professor
Department of Public Administration & Policy
SUNY, Albany

Joseph L. Badaracco, Jr.
Associate Professor of Business Administration
Harvard Business School

Nicole Woolsey Biggart, Professor
Graduate School of Management
University of California, Davis

Richard M. Coughlin
Professor of Sociology
University of New Mexico

Daniel R. Denison
Assistant Professor
School of Business Administration
University of Michigan

Nancy DiTomaso
Associate Professor
Graduate School of Management
Rutgers University

Amitai Etzioni
University Professor
George Washington University

Robert S. Goldfarb
Professor of Economics
George Washington University

George G. Gordon
Assistant Professor of Management
Rutgers, The State University

Mark Granovetter
Professor of Sociology
SUNY, Stony Brook

William B. Griffith
Professor of Philosophy
George Washington University

Jose Carlos Jarillo
Professor
International Institute for Management Development

F. Thomas Juster
Research Scientist
Institute of Social Research

Rosabeth Moss Kanter
Professor of Business Administration
Harvard Business School

Paul R. Lawrence
Professor of Organizational Behavior
Harvard Graduate School of Business

Ian C. MacMillan
Professor of Management
The Wharton School

Robert D. Miller
Doctoral Student in Economics
George Mason University

Paul S. Myers
Doctoral Student in Organizational Behavior
Harvard University

Drazen Prelec
Professor
Harvard School of Business

Lee E. Preston
Professor of Business
University of Maryland

Harry J. Sapienza
Professor
University of Baltimore

Jennifer A. Starr
Research Fellow
The Wharton School

Howard H. Stevenson
Professor of Business Administration
Harvard School of Business

Richard M. Swedberg
Professor of Sociology
University of Stockholm

Ted H. Szatrowski
Professor of Quantitative Studies
Rutgers Graduate School of Management

John Oliver Wilson
Professor
University of California, Berkeley

I

Introduction

1

Amitai Etzioni

Socio-Economics

A Budding Challenge

Neoclassical economists view man as a two-legged calculator, efficient and cold-blooded. But truth reveals him more often as muddleheaded, part morally conflicted and selfish, part morally dedicated and caring, and prone to moving in herds. Socio-economics was born of a need to understand man and how hard he works, how much he saves, and what he purchases. This new science challenges the basic assumptions at the root of neoclassical economics, including the assumption that people are basically rational beings, interested in maximizing their personal interests, unswayed by friends and outsiders alike.

Neoclassical economics assumes that because people are rational, they ought to invest in their IRAs (at least until the 1986 tax law went into effect) on the first possible date, so that their money will earn the maximum tax-deferred interest. Socio-economics points out that most people are not that rational. They have poor memories; they invest in their IRAs when their accountants remind them, or when the subject is discussed in newspapers or advertisements; they buy insurance without understanding the policy and pay stockbrokers for advice that does not improve their investment performance.

People, according to the neoclassicists, are largely focused on improving their lot. Indeed, James Buchanan just received a Nobel Prize for arguing that politicians, just like the rest of us, are out to maximize their self-interest. Nevertheless, neoclassical economists are puzzled by the fact that people make contributions to public TV or bother to vote, for which each individual gets nothing in return personally. Socio-economists argue that these behaviors are the result of dual personalities. Men, they say, are part debased (drawn by a quest for pleasure and self-interest) and part noble (in search of higher moral purposes).

Men ought to be viewed, say the neoclassicists, as free-standing individuals, "decision-making units" standing alone. Socio-economics assumes the decision-making units are individuals integrated into one or more social groups, ethnic groups, classes, and subcultures. Individuals do render the final decision, but usually within the context of values, beliefs, ideas, and guidelines installed in them by others, and reinforced by their social circles.

While neoclassical economics is well entrenched, socio-economics is a young upstart. Its foundations may be ancient, found in Kantian philosophy, humanistic psychology, and traditional sociology, but its application to economic issues is recent. In effect, most people who do socio-economics are not identified by that name or by any other common label. And, as is often the case in a rising, challenging group, they hardly ever fully agree with one another. But, published in journals such as the *Journal of Economics and Psychology, Economics and Philosophy,* and the *Journal of Behavioral Economics,* and a series of books, scholars such as Herbert Simon, Albert Hirschmann, Amartya Sen, Mary Douglas, Amos Tversky, Daniel Kahneman, Aaron Wildavsky, David O. Sears, as well as the contributors and editors of this volume, and many others are fashioning the new approach.

The Elements of Socio-Economics

Behind the mathematical equations, the grand theories, and the technical jargon of various social sciences are many powerful images of human nature. Thus, all attempts to answer questions such as why Americans save little, why they pay most taxes when due, and why they intake less hard liquor than they used to as recently as five years ago, reflect basic conceptions of what people *basically* are like. What is the nature of their goals? How efficiently do they go about pursuing them? And are they individual nomads, part of a herd, or do they stand out in a crowd? Neoclassical economics (most economics taught in American universities, used by corporations and government, and inoculated into MBAs) sees individuals as out to get as much as they can get for themselves (greed is the implied creed), quite able to set goals clearly and find the most efficient means to implement these goals (even if this involves a complex "search," complicated gathering and processing of information), and above all, willing and able to make their own decisions (individualism). The socio-economist's image of the decision makers is fundamentally more complex: goals are not neat but confounded; people both seek to serve themselves and care about others and their community; people are poor thinkers but often are sensitive to other considerations than efficiency; and as a rule they move in step with their fellow persons, while they are also able to strike out on their own.

The Conflicted, Judging Self

Although few of the thousands of neoclassical economists remember or care, at the root of their discipline lies a particular brand of utilitarian ethics, the notion that people are out to maximize their own happiness. Typically, neoclassical economists have argued that people will not act out of altruism or love of others, but get up in the morning and do their chores because they expect to get something they want in exchange. Because people have basically one overarching motive, they are assumed to know clearly what they want and to arrange their "preferences" into neat consistent patterns. (This feature makes mathematization much easier; God, it is assumed, wired people in ways that make it easier to do neoclassical economics.) Socio-economics, in contrast, draws in effect on deontological ethics: people are seen as torn between their urges and their values; they differ from animals in their capacity to judge their inclinations; individuals stand above themselves and examine what they are seeking to do. Sometimes their urge wins, sometimes their conscience.

Take, for example, saving. One major neoclassical economic theory assumes that people save money all through their working days so that when they retire, they can spend the money, aiming to pass away about when their savings book is exhausted. Actually, many people miss the mark by very large amounts. (True, the poor die without assets, but then they had few to begin with. Others often reduce their assets surprisingly little after retirement.) Socio-economists argue that people save for *additional* reasons: because they believe they *ought* to help their children (even if those children are in their thirties or forties), because they believe it is not "nice" to be dependent on the government or on their kids, and because of other such beliefs. For similar reasons, many thousands of people who are entitled to welfare do not sign up; they internalize societal notions that it is morally abhorrent to be on welfare. Studies of the extent to which people pay taxes show that they calculate the benefits from cheating and the "costs" of being caught, *and* are influenced by how legitimate they consider the government and its goals for their tax dollars. Vietnam and Watergate thus explain in part the rise of the underground economics, as does the rise of "Me-ism" as a social philosophy.

Poor, Caring Thinkers

Herbert Simon received a Nobel Prize for showing (among other things) that people are unable to think through most questions. Long before they reach the maximal solution, they stop collecting more information or processing what they got. They often grab the first satisfactory solution that pops up. (Not just consumers and investors but governments too.) In recent years, a group of psychologists led by Daniel Kahneman and Amos Tversky has shown that people's minds contain *systematic* biases that prevent them from thinking right. For example, they may "raise" in poker if they have won or lost a lot, even though the odds in favor of winning are rather poor.

While Simon, Kahneman, and Tversky focused on what are called "cognitive limitations" (those of the mind), Janis and Mann highlight the emotional ones. Making debts involves the future (Will I get a raise next year? Will interest rates fall?), which often cannot be foretold and hence makes people anxious. The anxiety draws them to make decisions in irrational ways, ranging from inaction to procrastination. Sometimes emotions help rather than hinder decisions; for example, when we experience a sudden fright, that fear enables us to escape a danger, where stopping and thinking could have wasted valuable time. But whether emotions help or hinder, rarely do we find people who make the cold-blooded calculations neoclassicists assume.

Slowly a new conception of how people make choices emerges:

• *Most choices are not decisions at all.* A monumental study of millions of purchases over more than four decades shows that 70 percent of purchases are made out of habit: people buy the same thing they bought last time. The neoclassicist would argue that this shows people found that more comparative shopping did not improve their lot. Socio-economists respond that there is a lot of habit buying, regardless of whether it would pay to shop around.

• *Decisions are boxed in by emotion and values.* Far from examining all the alternatives that objective observers recognize deserve attention, most people do not examine many alternatives because their emotions and values tell them that these options are "unthinkable." Thus, very few high school or college graduates, in choosing a vocation, consider becoming a funeral parlor director. It is not a question of this being a poor career choice or a declining industry, the option is simply not considered. Similarly, when middle-class parents have a sudden cash shortfall, they do not consider sending their children to panhandle or to sell blood.

Those options people do consider, to reiterate—a small subset of those they "ought" to consider if they acted rationally—are heavily "loaded" by emotions and values. As a result, not only do facts and logic play a role in rendering decisions, but also various "irrelevant" factors. For example, for years after World War II, many Americans did not buy German or Japanese cars, regardless of whether they were a better buy than American cars.

Finally, there is a small subset of options (often no more than two) among which people choose on the basis of facts and logic. Here they run into their intellectual limitations, such as their inability to focus their attention for long, remember much, or calculate probabilities.

While emotional and value-based limitations and loading of decision making renders the process inefficient from the viewpoint of an objective observer, the decision-making process is often quite justified because people have other concerns that are affected, such as expressing their patriotism.

The "I&We"

The image neoclassical economists have of the decision maker is one of a homemaker going down the aisle in the supermarket, or an investor calling a broker: both are isolated individuals acting on their own. But most people are members of one or more social groups, groups that do not oppress them—as a ''They''—but of which the person feels very much a part—as a ''We.'' What seem to the untrained eye to be individual decisions in fact tend to reflect a mixture of what the We-groups favor, and what the individual members within these groups make out of what is urged upon them by their groups. Thus, foreign cars may be ''in'' these days in many yuppie suburbs, but not in upper-working-class neighborhoods in Detroit. In the Northeast, many people mix soda with Scotch; in the Midwest, the mixer tends to be ginger ale. Millions of people in each region have not decided individually what to drive or to drink and happened by chance to hit on the same item; shared social factors and subcultures make up a good part of their decision.

Although the label ''Socio-Economics'' is a new one, there are numerous scholars in many universities who are socio-economists. They are beginning to develop a shared conceptual framework and a network for exchange of information. In 1989 an international Society for the Advancement of Socio-Economics was formed at Harvard University. In 1990, 600 attended the Second International Conference in Washington, DC. There are many more who are severely critical of neoclassical economics and its products—from policy advice to MBAs. And quite a few members of the neoclassical ''orthodoxy'' are raising serious questions from within. Still, neoclassical economics is clearly the entrenched discipline; socio-economics is a rising challenger.

2

PAUL R. LAWRENCE

Socio-Economics

A Grounded Perspective

The emerging field of socio-economics has strengths and weaknesses that are in sharp contrast to those of neoclassical economics. Socio-economics is weak in terms of unified theory and strong in terms of grounded, empirical data. Neoclassical economics is strong in its tightly reasoned deductive theory but weak in terms of empirical evidence. Faced with this trade-off, academics often choose theory; managers in business and in government, however, usually prefer empirical accuracy.

Perhaps the best way I can clarify the nature of the new field of socio-economics is by using my own professional career and its institutional setting, the Harvard Business School, as an example. Since its earliest days, the Harvard Business School's primary reference group has been the business community—not traditional economists. The dean who had the strongest hand in shaping the school was a businessman who was actually quite suspicious of economists. It was no accident that theory took a distant backseat to field-based research. It was no accident that the primary teaching tool was the case study, a richly textured description of an actual business situation where someone was expected to act responsibly on behalf of a business institution. This approach emphasized developing such products as a useful conceptual scheme, a way of thinking geared for practitioners, and currently useful generalizations. Looking back on these endeavors, I and many of my colleagues at Harvard Business School now realize that we were practicing socio-economics all the time: not one or the other but a mix of both. For example, faculty in marketing have learned to analyze brand loyalty as well as supply and demand factors. Those in business strategy have learned to analyze the politics of competition as well as its economics. Those of us in organizational behavior have examined the cultural ties that can bind the action and commitment of employees around an institutional identity as well as the economics of labor markets. We have examined the leadership acts that can shape a winning team as well as those that calculate when to buy or sell divisions. This was all done in a straightforward effort to map the complex world of business. Only now do we discover that we were speaking socio-economics all the time. To me it seems fitting that the first meeting of the Society for the Advancement of Socio-Economics was held at the Harvard Business School in March 1989.

While reflecting on the intersection of socio-economics and the Harvard Business School is historically revealing, it does not speak to the future and the question of whether this new field deserves the attention it is, in fact, receiving from scholars from many countries and disciplines. I see many reasons why focused attention on socio-economics is especially needed in today's world. I will cite but four reasons that I find compelling.

First, I would cite the crisis in health care in the United States and worldwide. Our current models are clearly inadequate to explain the escalation of health care costs in combination with the shortage of care for certain people. Neither economic nor sociological models, by themselves, can fill the need for guiding national health policy. A more adequate model could come from a socio-economics approach.

Business in the United States is still struggling with the lack of competitiveness in global competition in industry after industry. Proposed remedies, based on the dominant theories in economics, are not helping. A richer theory, based on both social and economic perspectives, could have a stronger chance of providing an intellectual underpinning for national policy.

The challenge of environmental conservation will probably be the hottest political issue of the 1990s. It is an issue that is supersaturated with both moral and economic considerations. Wise policy must take both considerations into balanced account or it will fail.

Finally, consider the challenge to our knowledge posed by the opening up of Eastern Europe and the Soviet Union: It is in the best interest of the United States and other industrialized countries to help the reform movement in these countries succeed. Political democracy and economic success must go hand in hand. Do we know how to be truly helpful? Our well-intended advice can have a major impact for better or for worse. The magnitude of the opportunity creates an awesome responsibility.

I believe the sudden burst of interest in socio-economics is in response to real-world challenges of the types I have cited. Certainly these are the issues behind the papers that are being produced. The knowledge base of socio-economics is still too limited and fragmentary for comfort but, at least, the assumptions of more narrow disciplines are being relaxed, and fresh, creative inquiry is proceeding.

II

Socio-Economics— A General Approach

3

Richard M. Swedberg

"The Battle of the Methods"

Toward a Paradigm Shift?

In order to understand what socio-economics is—in the version of Amitai Etzioni as well as in its earlier, less well known Weberian version—one clearly has to look at the historical circumstances in which it has made its appearance. This is generally true for any complex of ideas, but in this case it is especially true. The reason for this is that socio-economics is basically a response against something else, namely, the narrow vision of mainstream economics. Socio-economics, in brief, is a reaction against today's neoclassical economics as well as an attempt to go beyond it. In his recent book on socio-economics, *The Moral Dimension: Toward a New Economics*, Etzioni (1988, p. ix) writes: "We are now in the middle of a paradigmatic struggle. Challenged is the entrenched utilitarian, rationalistic-individualistic, neoclassical paradigm which is applied not merely to the economy but also increasingly to the full array of social relations, from crime to the family."

What is at the center of this new "paradigmatic struggle" (which is roughly the current American term for what the Germans used to call "*Methodenstreit*") is in other words the relationship of economic analysis to other kinds of social analysis. The key issue is not necessarily so easily presented, since what is at stake is exactly what the term "economics" is to denote. Is there, for example, a nonsocial, purely "economic" area, that is surrounded by institutions? Or is it rather so that "the economy" consists exclusively of social institutions? Several other positions, as we soon shall see, are possible as well.

From a historical perspective, it is important to distinguish between several distinct phases in the way social dimensions have been included in the economic analysis. Before presenting these, a caveat, however, has to be inserted: being a sociologist, I will basically equate "social analysis" with "sociology" in this article. This is of course not entirely proper, since "social analysis" also includes history and political science, as well as social psychology and social philosophy. For a full view of what is currently going on in today's paradigmatic struggle, the relationship of each of these sciences to economics has to be investigated. This represents a fascinating task, where many pieces of information are still missing. Take, for example, political science: according to Albert O. Hirschman (1980, p. xv), Machiavelli chose deliberately to exclude economics from the analysis in *The Prince*, a choice that was to have a profound impact on political science. Or take philosophy: according to Amartya Sen (1987), the kind of ethical-philosophical concerns that one can find in early economics have been more or less eliminated from contemporary economics, with its exclusive emphasis on an "engineering approach." Also, psychology has lost contact with twentieth-century economics. This happened around the turn of the century, when the link of economics to utilitarian psychology was deliberately cut off by such people as Joseph Schumpeter, whose first major work, *Das Wesen und der Hauptinhalt der theoretischen Nationalökonomie* (1908), reads in this aspect like a veritable Monroe Doctrine for economics: there are to be no links between the new science of economics and the Old World of utilitarian psychology (Schumpeter 1908, pp. 541–47). Note also that this break with psychology took place *before* modern psychology had had its scientific breakthrough. Economics, in other words, never had to face theories, like those of Freud and Jung, where it is more or less taken for granted that human behavior is not always rational.

The phases that can be distinguished in the relationship between economics and social analysis are roughly the following:

1. *The Time of Political Economy (late eighteenth century to late nineteenth century).* During these years economists knew about many other aspects of society than economics, and there was an easy mingling in their books of institutional analysis, philosophical reflections, and straightforward economic analysis. According to John Stuart Mill, "A person is not likely to be a good economist who is nothing else. Social phenomena acting and reacting on one another, they cannot rightly be understood apart" (Mill as cited in Marshall 1891, p. 72).

2. *The* Methodenstreit, *or the First Paradigmatic Battle between Economics and the Other Social Sciences (1880s–1910s).* This is the period in modern economics when the transition from "political economy" to "economics" is made. This entails the radical separation of economics from history as well as from sociology, and it leads to the birth of economic history as a separate science. The motto of the winning side in the *Methodenstreit* now became the very opposite of what Mill had said: "A person is likely to be a good economist who is nothing else. Social phenomena acting and reacting on each other, economics can still be best understood apart."

3. *Mutual Ignorance and Distortion in the Social Sciences (1920s–1960s).* During these years modern economics comes into its own and is mathematized. The result is a series of successful analyses. The nonexisting relationship be-

tween economics and the other social sciences, which had been proclaimed in the *Methodenstreit*, is now routinized. Interdisciplinary interest among economists is replaced by ignorance in the other social sciences. The noneconomic social scientists, in their turn, stay away from economics. All of this has a distorting influence on the social disciplines.

4. *Economic Imperialism and the Challenge of Redrawing the Boundaries in the Social Sciences (1970s–).* Today we are witnessing two tendencies in the mainstream economic community vis-à-vis the other social sciences. On the one hand, economic analysis is turning even further inwards. But on the other hand, the economic approach is being used to analyze a host of topics that by tradition have been dealt with by only the other social sciences, such as the political system, the family, and law. This "economic imperialism," which represents a radical attempt to redraw the boundaries in the social sciences, is becoming increasingly accepted by mainstream economists, who were at first skeptical and hostile to it. It has also led to the emergence of alternative ways of redefining the boundaries between economics and the other social sciences.

Now, what Etzioni calls "socio-economics" belongs to the last of these periods and can be seen as both a response against the aggressive inroads of economic imperialism into the other social sciences, and as a reaction to the incapacity of economics to include any kind of genuine social dimension in its analyses of economic phenomena. In the rest of this article we shall devote much space to economic imperialism, since this movement represents something of a revolution in the history of economics, since it represents the first attempt since the turn of the century, insofar as economics is concerned, to redraw the map of the social sciences and end the isolation between economics and its scientific neighbors. Through the aggressive way in which it proposes to do this, it also threatens to unleash a new *Methodenstreit* or paradigmatic battle. *The three main theses of this paper are (1) that such a new battle of the methods is on the horizon; (2) that it can easily become as destructive for the social sciences as the original* Methodenstreit; *and (3) that socio-economics represents a creative and reasonable response to this threat.* In order to show this, we need first to take a brief look at the German *Methodenstreit.* An additional reason for going back to this famous incident, it can be added, is that it was during the original battle of the methods that the idea of a broad synthesis of the social sciences called "socio-economics" was formulated for the first time. As we shall see, it was Max Weber who invented "socio-economics" or "*Sozialökonomik,*" to use the original German term. Weber's thoughtful comments on the destructive potential of the *Methodenstreit* and the need for a new synthesis of neoclassical economics and the other social sciences, are part of the tradition of modern social science and should therefore be taken into account today when we are on the verge of a new *Methodenstreit.*

The First *Methodenstreit*—and the First Appearance of Socio-Economics

In hindsight, it has been agreed that the *Methodenstreit* should never have taken place. People like Knut Wicksell, Joseph Schumpeter, and others who have studied the battle of the methods all feel that what was to become the key issue—should one only use abstractions or rather rely on detailed historical facts when doing economics?—was really a pseudo-issue (see, e.g., Wicksell 1904; Schumpeter 1954, pp. 814–15; Hansen 1968; Bostaph 1976, 1978). Still, the fight between the neoclassical economists and the historically oriented economists *did* take place—and with quite disastrous consequences for economics and the social sciences in general.

The battle broke out in the early 1880s and the two main protagonists were Gustav von Schmoller (1838–1917) and Carl Menger (1840–1921). Schmoller was professor of economics in Berlin and a singularly powerful figure in German academics (e.g., Bostaph 1976; JITE 1988). He was the founder and leader of the Younger Historical School of Economics, which was an outgrowth of the work of an earlier generation of historically oriented economists. German economics had been historical in nature from the very beginning, drawing on and adding to the tremendous prestige that surrounded history as an academic field in the young German nation. Schmoller saw economics as an ethically oriented science that focused on the community as opposed to the individual. Economic activities were an organic part of the life of the nation and could therefore not be separated out. Schmoller disliked the abstract, theoretical style of British economics. He also detested laissez faire capitalism and was a strong advocate of state intervention in the economy. Economics, Schmoller felt, had to be treated as a historical science, where one patiently studies the myriads of historical facts. On the basis of studies of this sort, one could then in principle advance general laws. He also felt, however, that this was all in the future; as he used to complain, "You see, gentlemen, it is all so infinitely complicated!" ("Aber, meine Herren, es ist alles so unendlich compliziert"—Gay 1953, p. 411).

Carl Menger, Schmoller's great opponent, was professor in Vienna, the capital of the Austro-Hungarian Empire (e.g., Hayek 1934; Schumpeter 1951). The academic status of a chair in Vienna was high, but considerably lower than the status of one in Berlin, which was the center of German-speaking academia. In 1871 Menger published *Grundsätze der Volkswirtschaftslehre*, or *Principles of Economics*, and thereby became—together with Walras and Jevons—one of the originators of the marginal utility revolution. Menger's work was clearly in the tradition of British economics in the sense that he saw the formulation of general, abstract theorems as the main task of economics. He did not do any historical research himself, and he felt that historical economics represented an outmoded way of doing things.

Menger's epoch-making work from 1871 did not get a good reception in Germany, where it was either ignored or misunderstood. Schmoller, for example, did not review it in the journal he controlled, *Jahrbuch für Gesetzgebung, Verwaltung und Volkswirtschaft*. This angered Menger, who now sat down to write a justification of his method. This ended up as a general treatise on methodology in the social sciences with special reference to economics, *Untersuchungen über die Methode der Sozialwissenschaften und der Politischen Ökonomie insbesondere* (1883) *(Investigations into the Method of the Social Sciences with Special Reference to Economics)*. In this work, which was to become the opening shot in the *Methodenstreit*, Menger argued that the exclusive emphasis on history in German economics was blocking all progress in economics. A historical approach might be useful in economics, if one wants to understand the development of a specific economic institution or of a specific country, but there has to be room for a theoretical perspective in economics—"theoretical economics"—which looks at more general economic phenomena, such as exchange, price, demand, and supply. Economics should not be subordinate to history; it has to be its own science.

This time Schmoller responded with an angry review of Menger's work (Schmoller 1883) in which he vehemently denied that there was any validity whatsoever to Menger's approach. In economics, he said, one must begin by studying the individual details. On the basis of studies of this type, one can then proceed to more general statements in economics. This, however, was of little consequence in this case since Menger was not properly educated in history. Menger was nothing but "a poor imitator" ("eine Epigone") of British political economy, with its "abstract dogmatics" (Schmoller 1883, p. 251). Schmoller agreed with Menger that economics had a great future. But progress in economics, he said, "will happen only through the utilization of the whole body of historical, descriptive, and statistical material which is now being assembled—not through the continued distillation of abstract dogmas which have been distilled a hundred times before" (Schmoller 1883, p. 242).

Menger was infuriated by Schmoller's insulting review and quickly put together a small volume, *Die Irrthümer des Historismus* (1884) *(The Errors of Historicism)*, which contains a blistering attack on historical economics. Schmoller is here accused of being a particularly vulgar and superficial scientist; his work is nothing but "detail mongering" ("historich-statistische Kleinmalerie"), and so on (p. 37). The attack on history was also escalated in Menger's pamphlet, according to which "Historians have stepped onto the ground of our science as foreign invaders" (Menger 1884, p. vi). History has nothing to teach economics; it can only lead it astray:

> The erroneous assumption that political economy could be reformed simply by connecting it with historical knowledge—this is what the application of the false dogma of "Historismus" means in our field—was doomed to failure from the start. Any science can be reorganized only from the inside, from the center of its own sphere of ideas. Reforms must be the work of students who are immersed in the problem of their own discipline. Political economy will

> not be lifted from its present low state by historians, mathematicians, physiologists, or those who follow blindly the example of those disciplines. The transformation of political economy can only begin with ourselves, with the scholars dedicated to this particular science. [Menger 1884, pp. iv–v]

Schmoller was so angered by Menger's book that he returned his review copy to Menger together with an insulting letter in which he explained that he was sending the book back, since the only other alternative would have been to destroy it. The letter was printed in Schmoller's journal and became a *cause célèbre* (Schmoller 1884). Menger did not reply to this letter, which thus represents the last projectile in the battle between Schmoller and Menger. The *Methodenstreit* itself, however, continued for several decades in German-speaking academics and kept polarizing scholars into the two opposite camps. Schmoller also succeeded for a long time in blocking all appointments at German universities of scholars he suspected of being positive to economic theory. Not until the mid-1920s, when Schumpeter got the chair in public finance at the University of Bonn, was economic theory taught again in a German university.

The most important effect of the *Methodenstreit* was clearly that Schmoller's one-sided defense of the historical method in economics succeeded in discrediting it in a most fateful manner. Versions of the battle of the methods were soon reproduced in other countries, such as England and the United States; and everywhere historical economics, by squarely opposing recent developments in economic theory, helped to polarize economics (e.g., Swedberg 1987, pp. 14–24; Mongiovi 1988). As a result, history was now totally squeezed out of economics and ended up as its own academic discipline—economic history—which had little interest in economic theory. In addition, the hostility to history was extended to sociology, which meant that economists became suspicious of sociologists and vice versa. This, for example, was the case in England and the United States, where it was common that advocates of the historical approach saw their own approach as a form of sociology.[1]

In Germany, the role of sociology was to be somewhat different, at least insofar as Max Weber was concerned. Weber was horrified by the *Methodenstreit* and how it had created "*two* sciences of economics" (Weber 1949, p. 63). As a way of getting out of this deadlock, he suggested a synthesis of the neoclassical and the historical approach. This synthesis he tried to accomplish in various ways and the term he used for his project was "*Sozialökonomik,*" or "*socio-economics.*" The term itself had been introduced into German academic discourse in the 1890s, and Weber seized on it as a suitable replacement for the term "political economy," which was becoming outmoded in Germany (as in other countries) around the turn of the century.[2] It was also Weber who, more than any other scholar, tried to popularize the term "socio-economics" in Germany, as Schumpeter tells us (1954, pp. 21, 535).

To Weber, socio-economics had both an intellectual side and a practical side. The intellectual program of socio-economics is most clearly outlined in his essays on methodology, especially " 'Objectivity' in Social Science and Social Policy." Weber here argues that socio-economics is part of the cultural sciences (*Kulturwissenschaften*), and that it draws not only on "economic theory" but also on "economic sociology" and "economic history" (Weber 1949, pp. 45, 63–67; see also Wegener 1962, pp. 108–22). One of Weber's key ideas was centered around the proposition that real progress in economics could only be gained by drawing on both historical economics and theoretical economics *simultaneously*. In order to make an analysis, one can therefore not rely on theory *or* history—it has to be theory *and* history. In other words, a synthesis between the two approaches is needed. Weber's famous notion of "ideal types" exemplifies what he had in mind when he spoke about synthesis in this context: ideal types must be based on solid historical data, but they also imply an "analytical accentuation of certain elements of reality" (Weber 1949, pp. 80–81). Weber's effort to strike a balance between the historical and the theoretical approaches in economics can also be seen in his stance on the question of whether economic theory is applicable to all societies. According to Weber, economic theory, as outlined in marginal utility theory, was particularly applicable to capitalist reality, since "the historical peculiarity of the capitalist epoch [is that] the approximation of reality to the theoretical propositions of economic theory has been a *constantly increasing* one" (Weber 1975, p. 33). As his debate with Eduard Meyer makes clear, however, Weber rejected the idea that economic theory, which had been developed with one type of society in mind, could also be applied to all forms of society (e.g., Weber 1976). Weber finally felt that discussions of methodological problems were usually counterproductive; science in general, including socio-economics, develops "only by laying bare and solving *substantive problems*" (Weber 1949, p. 116).

Weber also tried to use socio-economics in a practical way to reconcile the two warring camps in the battle of the methods. He thus approached the Schmoller camp as well as the Menger camp in a very conciliatory fashion, sometimes praising the one, sometimes the other.[3] He tried to break down the personal animosities between the two camps in several different ways and used whatever institutional resources he had for this purpose. His major attempt in this direction was no doubt the giant handbook of economics, *Grundriss der Sozialökonomik*, which he had started to edit around the turn of the century. This is an extremely important and interesting work, which has unfortunately fallen into oblivion. In any case, Weber here got representatives from the two warring factions in the *Methodenstreit* to work together on a collective project. *Grundriss der Sozialökonomik* appeared during the years 1914–30, and is a testimony to Weber's statement in the preface to the first volume, where he writes that insofar as methodology is concerned, "*all roads come together in the end*" (Weber et al., 1914, p. viii; emphasis added).

Mutual Ignorance and Distortion in the Social Sciences (1920s–1960s)

Weber's project of a socioeconomic science could not stop the rapid polarization process that had been set off by the *Methodenstreit.* A few scholars kept trying to unite an economic and a social approach, but usually without too much success (e.g., Parsons 1935, forthcoming; Löwe 1935). Schumpeter was an exception, and the sharp separation between sociology and economics, which Pareto (1935) had just proclaimed, does not exist in his work.[4] Schumpeter was basically very sympathetic to the neoclassical approach—von Wieser and Böhm-Bawerk had after all been his teachers in Vienna—but he also held Schmoller and the Historical School in high regard (e.g., Schumpeter 1926). During the battle of the methods, Schumpeter took a position that was similar to that of Max Weber, with whom he also collaborated on *Grundriss der Sozialökonomik.* And throughout his life Schumpeter would advocate a vision of economics as a broad social science that incorporated much more than just theoretical economics. In the posthumously published *History of Economic Analysis*, we read, for example, that "[scientific] economics" or "Sozialökonomie" consists of four "fields": "*theory,*" "*economic history,*" "*statistics,*" and "*economic sociology*" (Schumpeter 1954, pp. 12–21). It is also in this manuscript that we find Schumpeter's well-known statement to the effect that if he could relive his life as an economist and had to choose between the various fields of economics, he would definitely pick economic history (Schumpeter 1954, pp. 12–13). This should not necessarily be read as a disapproval from Schumpeter's side of the neoclassical project. It was, rather, his way of restoring the balance: the neoclassical economists of the 1930s and 1940s were on the right track, but they had clearly overstated their case by eliminating practically all social and historical elements from their analyses.

Scholars like Schumpeter became exceedingly rare during the 1930s and 1940s. Instead there appeared a new breed of economists during these years. These were very theoretically minded and mathematically gifted. In quick pace they made a series of important discoveries, crowned by the general equilibrium theorem as classically stated by Debreu and Arrow in the 1950s. These economists had as a rule little or no professional knowledge of history and sociology. The reason for this is simple: to do neoclassical economics during these years, one basically did not need to know history and sociology. Indeed, a series of simplifying assumptions were built into the neoclassical paradigm, which enabled the economist to ignore large parts of social reality. The feeling that concrete reality basically has no place in economic theory came to a particularly famous and provocative expression during these years in Milton Friedman's essay on "the methodology of positive economics" (Friedman 1953).

During this "heroic period of neoclassical economics," as the Norwegian sociologist Gudmund Hernes (1978, pp. 202–3) has called it, the following simplifying assumptions were made:

1. The actors—firms, households, and so on—are unitary or ''black boxes'';
2. The actors are rational and have consistent preferences in the sense that the firms maximize profit and the households maximize utility;
3. The actors are fully informed about their surroundings and they also have perfect knowledge about all possible alternatives;
4. The actors have no costs of calculation; they instantaneously pick the best alternative or the best combination of alternatives;
5. The transactions between the actors are free;
6. The consumers decide over the producers, and any change in their needs or desires is automatically taken into account through the price mechanism;
7. Economics is about production and consumption—how scarce means with alternative uses are utilized to reach a social optimum;
8. Ideally, this optimum is described with the help of the notion of general equilibrium; and such an equilibrium is reached when all the direct and indirect effects of the myriads of mutual decisions by consumers and producers become stabilized or, so to speak, settle down.

A few more simplifying assumptions should be added to Hernes's list. The actors in neoclassical theory from this period are as a rule not connected to each other except through momentary exchange. This means that most social bonds and networks are ignored. The economy is also seen as basically independent of the rest of society. Or, alternatively, the major social institutions are so stable that they for all practical purposes can be taken for granted. This means, among other things, that most forms of power are ignored. And finally, the fact that the economist is part of the reality that he or she studies is of no particular consequence since positive knowledge is perfectly possible.

Since the author of this article is a sociologist, it would have been comforting at this point to be able to say that even if economics went wrong in some important aspects during this period, sociology did not. That, however, is not the case. In the sociology from these years one often finds the same ideas that Schmoller fought for in the battle of the methods, such as an unreflective empiricism and a dogmatic rejection of analytical abstractions. This is, for example, the case with the Chicago School from the 1920s and 1930s. Concepts such as rationality and methodological individualism are not at all discussed in the sociology from these years, even though Weber had made it perfectly clear that they were important to sociology. We therefore end up with a sociology and an economics during this period that are to some extent distorted images—mirror images—of each other (see Table 3.1).

During these years there was no development of the ''economic sociology,'' which Weber as well as Schumpeter had seen as an integral part of socio-economics. The sociologists stayed away from core economic questions such as price formation, investment decisions, and the like, and were much more interested in marginal economic issues that seemed ''sociological'' for some reason

Table 3.1

The Neoclassical Paradigm and the Sociological Paradigm as Mirror Images of Each Other (Mid-Twentieth Century)

	Homo economicus	Homo sociologicus
Actor	individual actor	collective actor
Principle of action	freedom of action	constraint of social structure
Motive of action	rational calculation	irrational feelings, tradition, and values
Arena of action	the market	all society but the market
Steering principle	multiple, decentralized decisions	decisions involving social and political power
Type of concepts used	analytical and abstract	empirical and descriptive
Goal of the analysis	prediction as explanation	description as explanation
Image in relation to the other science	self-sufficient	self-sufficient

Sources: Samuelson [1947] 1983; Schumpeter 1954; Parsons and Smelser 1956; Dahrendorf [1958] 1968; Wrong 1961; Granovetter 1985; Hirsch, Michaels, and Friedman 1987.

or another, such as attitude formation in work groups, why people would choose one consumer brand rather than another, and so on. As a result, the economic sociology for which Weber and Schumpeter had had such high hopes was fragmented into a series of new subdisciplines such as industrial sociology and consumer sociology.

Part of the problem was also the fact that there was practically no communication between economists and sociologists during these years. When Parsons and Smelser wrote *Economy and Society* in 1956, they complained that one could hardly find any economists and sociologists who were competent in both fields (p. xviii). A few years earlier, Schumpeter had made the same observation in *History of Economic Analysis*. He also noted that the lack of communication between economics and sociology had helped to produce considerable distortions *within* each science. Just because sociologists had no contact with economists and tried to avoid economic topics as much as possible, Schumpeter said, this did not mean that they in fact *could* bypass economic questions (and vice versa of course for the economists and social topics). "Economic and non-economic facts *are* related to each other," as he put it (Schumpeter 1954, p. 13). But what it did mean was that economists and sociologists had to do without professional knowledge about the other science and could only fall back on their own rather primitive ideas about the other field. Schumpeter (1954, pp. 26–27) phrased it like this: "both [economists and sociologists] have grown steadily apart until by now the modal economist and the modal sociologist know little and care less about what the other does, each preferring to use, respectively, a primitive sociology and a primitive economics of his own to accepting one another's professional results."

Economic Imperialism and the Threat of a New *Methodenstreit*

From 1930 to 1960 there existed a certain balance between economics and the other social sciences in the sense that the economists only dealt with economic topics and the other social scientists stayed away from economic subjects. Today, however, this is not the case. *Instead we are witnessing a major attempt to redraw the boundaries between economics and the other social sciences* (see, e.g., Swedberg 1990). This is, for example, true for sociology. Economists are thus increasingly taking on sociological topics, and sociologists have suddenly become interested in economic topics. What exactly has caused the attempt to change the traditional division of labor in social science is somewhat unclear. One can, for example, argue that the difficulties the world economy has gone through since the oil shocks must have something to do with the challenge to the old, artificial separation between neoclassical economics, on the one hand, and sociology, history, and political science, on the other. It is also reasonable to assume that some sociologists and political scientists got interested in economic questions as a result of the revival of Marxism in the 1970s (see, e.g., Swedberg 1987).

As far as economics is concerned, it is clear, however, that a major role in this process has been played by ideas developed inside the economics profession, more precisely by that strand of thought known today as "economic imperialism." The claim that is made here is exactly that the old division of labor between economics and the other social sciences is outmoded and should be replaced by a new division, where the economic approach is recognized as the master model for all the other social sciences. Economic imperialism is often advancing its ideas and claims to solve age-old problems in a provocative manner. It is thereby threatening to set off a new major battle about methodology in the social sciences, which may well end up being as destructive as the original *Methodenstreit*.

Given the key role that is attributed to economic imperialism in the argument in this article, it is important to pause here for a while to describe it in more detail: where it comes from, what it wants, and what it has accomplished thus far. The term "economic imperialism" seems actually to have made its first appearance in the 1930s, more precisely in a book by a young economist at Columbia University, Ralph William Souter.[5] The book in question had the somewhat awkward title *Prolegomena to Relativity Economics: An Elementary Study in the Mechanics and Organics of an Expanding Economic Universe.* The relevant part, for our purposes, is hinted at in the last few words of the subtitle: "*an expanding economic universe.*" In his book, Souter introduces the geopolitical imagery that has become so popular with today's economists. His main argument can be found in the following passage:

> The salvation of Economic Science in the twentieth century lies in an enlightened and democratic "economic imperialism," which invades the territories of its neighbors, not to enslave them or to swallow them up, but to aid and enrich them and promote their autonomous growth in the very process of aiding and enriching itself.
>
> Under such circumstances, occasional armed conflict among the sciences is inevitable. Such conflicts must be conducted according to the rules of civilized warfare; and it is the duty of each science to subordinate its strategy, as best it knows how, to the ultimate goal of the harmonious unification of knowledge. Mistakes and injustices are bound to occur from time to time; but the "science" which cannot maintain its integrity and vitality in such an environment deserves to perish. And, for *any* science, a cowardly isolationist pacifism which cries peace! peace! when there is no peace is the stigma of intellectual disintegration and decay. [Souter 1933, pp. 94–95]

Souter's book was published by a well-known press, Columbia University Press, but was not reviewed in any of the major economic journals. It still, however, left some traces behind. It was, for example, drawn into the debate around Lionel Robbins's book *On the Nature and Significance of Economic Science* (1932) by another young economist who was fascinated by questions of this type—Talcott Parsons. Parsons carefully went through Souter's argument about economic imperialism in an article in the *Quarterly Journal of Economics* from 1934 and concluded that "economic imperialism . . . results not only in enriching these neighbouring 'countries,' which of course it does, but in putting some of them into a strait jacket of 'economic' categories which is ill-suited to their own conditions" (Parsons 1934, p. 512). If pushed far enough, Parsons argued, economic imperialism will lead to the extinction of the other social sciences. It is a tendency, he stressed, "*against which the sociologist, as well as other scientists, must stand up and fight for his scientific life*" (p. 535; emphasis added).

Today, Souter's book is mainly interesting because it contains the first mention of the term "economic imperialism." The fact that it was published in the 1930s is also a reminder that economic imperialism has its intellectual roots in the economics of this period. It is, however, not until many years later—more precisely in the late 1950s—that we find the first attempts by economists actually to practice economic imperialism and take on topics from the other social sciences. Why this was happening just in the 1950s is not clear. George Stigler (1984, p. 312) has suggested that it is perhaps related to the fact that by about this time young American economists had for the first time been trained in seeing economics as "a general analytical machine": "The abstraction increased the distance between economic theory and empirical economic phenomena . . . and made the extensions to other bodies of phenomena easy and natural."

The pioneer works from the late 1950s include Gary Becker's doctoral dissertation, *The Economics of Discrimination* (1957), Anthony Downs's *Economic Theory of Democracy* (1957), and A.H. Conrad and J.R. Meyer's article, "The Economics of Slavery in the Antebellum South" (1958). These three works signaled the introduction in the 1950s of the economic model into three new disciplines: sociology, political science, and economic history. To this can be added a fourth: anthropology. The economic approach had actually been introduced several years earlier into anthropology, but it was not until now that its presence was really noticed. At this time anthropology actually became the center for a stormy debate between those who were for and those who were against the use of neoclassical theory, the so-called formalist-substantivist controversy.[6]

During the 1960s and 1970s there appeared an avalanche of works by economists in the four social sciences just mentioned—sociology, political science, anthropology, and economic history—as well as in some new ones, such as law (including criminology), demography, education, and organization theory (see, e.g., Becker [1960] 1976, 1964; Coase 1960; Calabresi 1961; Buchanan and Tullock 1962; Posner 1973; Ehrlich 1975; Williamson 1975). Several skirmishes also took place between the advocates of the new economic approach and those who defended the traditional ways of doing social science. In economic history, for example, the publication of *Time on the Cross* (1974) by Robert Fogel and S.L. Engerman caused an uproar of anger. Heated debates also took place in criminology and demography.

Still, it seems that by the early 1970s the proponents of the economic approach were not all that sure of themselves and their collective identity; they rather saw themselves as single individuals swimming against the stream than as part of a new intellectual movement. It was actually at this time that the term "economic imperialism" was used for the first time to identify all the works that advocate the introduction of the neoclassical analysis into the other social sciences. In 1972 Gordon Tullock published an article with just this title, in which he complained that the analyses by such people as Buchanan, Becker, and others have attracted "remarkably little attention" (Tullock 1972, p. 318).[7] Already a few years later, however, the first textbook in the field appeared, suitably entitled *The New World of Economics* (Tullock and McKenzie 1975). The movement also got its intellectual program in the mid-1970s from Gary Becker's article and book on "the economic approach to human behavior" (Becker 1976). Becker here makes a frontal attack on the old division of labor in the social sciences, according to which economics is the science of wealth and production, and where all noneconomic forms of human behavior are said to be irrational, traditional, and value-oriented, so that they can be handed over to the other social sciences without any bad feelings. The principal attributes of economic imperialism or "the economic approach," as Becker prefers to call it, are presented in the following way: "The combined assumptions of maximizing behavior, market equilibrium, and stable preferences, used relentlessly and unflinchingly, form the heart of the economic approach" (Becker 1976, p. 5). The definition itself is not particularly novel, but that the economic approach should be used "relentlessly and unflinchingly" gives a hint of the new tone of discourse. The same is true for Becker's remark that the economic approach is applicable to "all human behavior" (Becker 1976, p. 8).

In the mid-1970s, when Becker wrote his programmatic statement about the economic approach, economic imperialism was still a minority movement, even if it by now had an identity. Becker (1976, p. 12) thus complains that "many economists" are openly hostile to all but "traditional applications" of economics and keep insisting that there exists irrational behavior, ad hoc shifts in the values of people, and the like. This complaint is also echoed by Becker's colleague George Stigler in a well-known article from a few years later on economics as "an imperial science" (Stigler 1984). Stigler here says that many "senior members" of the American Economic Association are "not enthusiastic" about extending the economic approach to the other social sciences. He notes especially that no proponent of the economic approach—neither Buchanan nor Coase nor Becker—has been made president of the AEA, and adds that, in his opinion, "younger economists" are probably much more friendly to economic imperialism than the older generation.

During the few years that have elapsed since the publication of Stigler's article, economic imperialism has advanced very quickly. Buchanan has, for example, received the Nobel Prize and Becker has been president of the AEA. Maybe sensing the impending change of opinion in the economic profession toward the economic approach, Jack Hirshleifer published a particularly bombastic article on economic imperialism in 1985 in the *American Economic Review*, entitled "The Expanding Domain of Economics." Economics is here described as "the universal grammar of social science," and it is prophesied that the noneconomic social sciences will soon become "increasingly indistinguishable from economics" (Hirshleifer 1985, p. 53). From the way Hirshleifer talks about the works using the economic approach, it is clear that economic imperialism is now seen as a major movement of thought within contemporary economics. We are, for example, told that when economists invade a neighboring science, there is first "an initial phase of easy success"; then "a second phase, when doubts begin to emerge"; and so on (Hirshleifer 1985, p. 54).

Besides Hirshleifer's article, there are several other signs that the temperature is rising in and around economic imperialism. There has, for example, been a minor flood of books on the advantages of using the concept of rationality in social science in general (see, e.g., the works as cited in Elster 1986). These have generally been well received, but there are also exceptions (e.g., Etzioni 1987a, 1987b). The debate around public choice has also intensified, as empirical findings keep accumulating that contradict the theories of Downs et al. (see, e.g., the works as cited in Lewin 1988). A new conquest—Marxism—has also been made, which has angered the more traditional Marxists (e.g., Roemer 1982; Hindess 1984). A major confrontation with mainstream sociology is also about to take place. A concerted effort is presently being made at the University of Chicago to introduce the economic approach into sociology (see Swedberg 1990). The two leading figures here are James Coleman and Gary Becker. The latter has had a joint appointment at the departments of economics and sociology since 1983. Coleman and Becker have put together a graduate program in rational choice sociology; they have just started up a new sociological magazine called *Rationality and Society* (1989–), and they are also planning a book series on rational choice. In 1990, finally, a major theoretical treatise on rational choice sociology—*Foundations of Social Theory* by James Coleman—appeared.

The Need for a Socioeconomic Approach

Economic imperialism has had a positive impact on the social sciences in the sense that the borders between economics and its neighbors are now much more open. But even if we grant the economic imperialists the merit of having ended much of the artificial separation between economics and the other social sciences, which has characterized so much of the twentieth century, it is also clear that they have a very specific vision of what the relationship between economics and its neighbors should be like. And this vision amounts, for all practical purposes, to a closing of the borders again. There is no desire among the proponents of the economic approach to draw wisdom from the works of such superb scholars as, say, Otto Hinze, Max Weber, and Fernand Braudel. In their view, practically everything that has been produced until now by noneconomists in the social sciences can be dispensed with and replaced by the insights gained by using the economic approach.

What is needed instead of economic imperialism is therefore an approach that can steer the situation in the social sciences, as it exists today, into the kind of renaissance in the study of economics that many of us think is possible. Such an approach would as a minimum have to fulfill certain conditions. These would, in my mind, be the following: there should be multiple approaches to economic problems (*Condition 1*); the borders between economics and the other social sciences must be kept open (*Condition 2*); substantive issues are more important than methodological principles (*Condition 3*); and allowance must be made for the complexity of human behavior and culture (*Condition 4*).

What Weber at the turn of the century called socio-economics fits these four conditions very well. And so does socio-economics in its present-day version. This is clear from the programmatic statements on socio-economics that Etzioni has produced thus far: "Making Policy for Complex Systems" (1985), in which socio-economics is presented as a kind of policy science for economics; "Founding a New Socio-economics" (1986), in which the major research tasks of socio-economics are outlined; and *The Moral Dimension* (1988), which is a major social-philosophical treatise on socio-economics.

In all of these works it is emphasized that not only one but several approaches are needed to solve economic problems successfully (*Condition 1*). In socio-economics, as in medicine or in policy science, one needs to use "findings from a variety of basic sources" (Etzioni 1985, p. 385). This would include, for example, mainstream economics, political science, experimental psychology, and quantitative sociology. The reason for drawing on several sciences is simply that most economic problems are extremely complex, and there is no single science that can handle all of them on its own. One therefore has to be pragmatic, use second-best solutions, and rely on different sciences in each concrete case.

Implicit in the first condition—that multiple approaches are used in economics—is also the fact that the boundaries between economics and the other social sciences have to be kept open (*Condition 2*). People need to be able to communicate freely across the boundaries in order to have access to the findings in the various sciences. There is also the argument that the boundaries between the social sciences should be left a bit unclear since, if drawn too sharply, this tends to separate problems arbitrarily into the different sciences. There is finally the fact that many essential problems in the social sciences seem to be situated exactly at the boundaries of a science.

Socio-economics also stresses that solving substantial issues must have precedence over discussions of methodology (*Condition 3*). There are several reasons for this. Etzioni argues, for example, that mainstream economics cannot be challenged by mere critiques of existing solutions to economic problems; alternative solutions must be presented, and these have to be superior to the existing ones. In "Founding a New Socio-economics," Etzioni (1986) also outlines several of the areas where he considers it particularly important that research be done. The first of these are preferences, or more precisely the factors and processes that shape the preferences. Another key area of study is the market and its interactions with the rest of society. Markets are not self-regulating, and mainstream economics has failed to deal with the way power—economic power as well as political power—structures the interactions in the marketplace. More research, according to Etzioni's program, also needs to be done on the subject of rationality. A major task here would be properly to introduce emotions and values into a theory of rationality.

There is finally the need for complexity (*Condition 4*). Socio-economics, as Weber already pointed out, is a member of the family of *Kulturwissenschaften*, which means that the complexities of culture and history have to be taken into account. "Culture" should here be understood first of all in terms of intersubjective meanings—meanings constructed and communicated between people in and around economic interaction. Involved in this, as Etzioni makes clear in *The Moral Dimension* (1988), is also the question of human values: social action is always structured in various ways around values and ethical issues of different kinds. The demand for complexity emerges as a major dimension of socio-economics, if we contemplate that one of its major tasks is exactly to synthesize or reunite the social and economic analyses. These two types of analyses were artificially separated in the beginning of the twentieth century, and they now need to be reintegrated with one another along several dimensions. Which these dimensions are is clear from Table 3.1, to which the reader is referred again. The analysis of economic phenomena must be able to deal with the individual and with the group; with the market as a unit of its own as well as a subunit of society; with the impact of power as well as with decentralized decision making. All this demands complexity and subtlety in the analysis.

In conclusion it can be said that presently a redefinition of the division of labor in the social sciences is going on that focuses on economics. This process represents a unique opportunity to end the lack of communication between economics and the other social sciences that has characterized much of the twentieth century, but that was alien to the founders of economic theory such as Adam Smith and John Stuart Mill. Today there is a clear chance to steer things in a positive direction. Economic imperialism, however, does not represent a good alternative in this regard, since it is basically trying to impose a new single-minded vision on economics and its scientific neighbors, whereby it threatens to close the door to the new and promising developments of a multidisciplinary economics. Socio-economics, on the other hand, offers a possibility to keep the door open.

Notes

1. The similarity between the historical approach and the sociological approach was clear to many people. According to Durkheim, for example, Schmoller's *Grundriss der allgemeinen Volkswirtschaftslehre* "is clearly a kind of sociology, from the viewpoint of economics" (Durkheim and Fauconnet 1903, p. 496).

2. The term "Sozialökonomik" is associated in German economics with the name of Heinrich Dietzel (1857–1935), who was professor in economics at the University of Bonn (see Arndt 1935). Dietzel introduced the term first through an article in 1883 and then in *Theoretische Sozialökonomik* (1895), which was published as a volume in Wagner's handbook of political economy (Winkelmann 1986, p. 12; see Dietzel 1883, 1895). Dietzel (1895, p. 54) himself traces the term "Sozialökonomik" to some early Italian economists and especially to Jean-Baptiste Say, who used it in the early 1820s. Also, John Stuart Mill ([1838] 1844, pp. 136–37) incidentally traces the term "social economy" to Say. In Mill's opinion, Say uses "social economy" to mean "every part of man's nature, in so far as influencing the conduct or constitution of man in society." Dietzel himself, however, defined "Sozialökonomik" somewhat differently. He was first of all interested in finding a substitute for the terms "Nationalökonomik" and "politische Ökonomik," which he felt misrepresented economics by connecting it to "the nation" and to "politics." Dietzel himself defined "Sozialökonomik" in an organic and holistic manner:

"Sozialökonomik is an organism which comes into being as soon as a group of individual economic aggregates [Einzelwirtschaften] start interacting with each other in a regular manner" (Dietzel 1883, p. 3). Dietzel basically sided with Menger in the *Methodenstreit*, and saw more or less "theoretische Sozialökonomik" and "Wirtschaftsgeschichte" as each other's opposites (Dietzel 1895).

3. According to Weber (1975, p. 33), Menger had proposed "excellent views." On Schmoller's seventieth birthday, Weber wrote to him that "at a time of the most barren economic rationalism you have created a home for *historical* thought in our science" (Weber, as cited in Schön 1987, p. 59). A few years earlier Weber had recommended that Böhm-Bawerk be given an honorary doctorate at the University of Heidelberg with the motivation that "he would make a particularly happy complement to the strictly historically inductive work by Professor *Schmoller*, whose promotion has been recommended by the other side" (Weber, as cited in Schön 1987, p. 60).

4. I am grateful to Mark Granovetter for emphasizing this point to me.

5. The idea of economic imperialism (if not the term) should probably be credited to Alfred Marshall (see, e.g., Parsons 1934, pp. 522, 535).

6. The economic approach had been introduced into anthropology through three works, all of which appeared in 1939–40: Raymond Firth's *Primitive Polynesian Economy* (1939), D.M. Goodfellow's *Principles of Economic Sociology: The Economics of Primitive Life as Illustrated from the Bantu Peoples of South and East Africa* (1939), and Samuel Herskovitz's *The Economic Life of Primitive Peoples* (1940). It was not, however, till the 1950s that a debate about the use of economic models in anthropology took place. This debate was especially prompted by the appearance in 1957 of *Trade and Market in the Early Empires* by Karl Polanyi, Conrad Arensberg, and Harry Pearson.

7. The term "economic imperialism" was no doubt also popularized by the fact that Kenneth Boulding used it in his presidential address to the AEA in 1968. Boulding (1969, p. 8) here defined "economic imperialism" as "an attempt on the part of economics to take over all the other sciences."

References

Arndt, Paul. (1935) "Heinrich Dietzel (1857–1935)." *Economic Journal* 45:797–98.

Becker, Gary S. (1957) *The Economics of Discrimination.* Chicago: University of Chicago Press.

———. ([1960]1976) "An Economic Analysis of Fertility." In *The Economics of Discrimination*, pp. 171–94. Chicago: University of Chicago Press.

———. (1964) *Human Capital: A Theoretical and Empirical Approach.* New York: Columbia University Press.

———. (1976) *The Economic Approach to Human Behavior.* Chicago: University of Chicago Press.

Bostaph, Samuel Harvey. (1976) "Epistemological Foundations of Methodological Conflict in Economics: The Case of the Nineteenth-Century 'Methodenstreit.' " Ph.D. diss., Southern Illinois University.

———. (1978) "The Methodological Debate between Carl Menger and the German Historicists." *Atlantic Economic Journal* 3:3–16.

Boulding, Kenneth E. (1969) "Economics as a Moral Science." *American Economic Review* 59:1–12.

Buchanan, James M., and Gordon Tullock. (1962) *The Calculus of Consent.* Ann Arbor: University of Michigan Press.

Calabresi, Guido. (1961) "Some Thoughts on Risk Distribution and the Law of Torts." *Yale Law Journal* 70:499–553.

Coase, Ronald H. (1960) "The Problem of Social Cost." *Journal of Law and Economics* 3:1–44.

Coleman, James. (1990) *Foundations of Social Theory*. Cambridge, MA: Harvard University Press.

Conrad, A.H., and J.R. Meyer. (1958) "The Economics of Slavery in the Antebellum South." *Journal of Political Economy* 66:95–130.

Dahrendorf, Ralf. ([1958]1968) "Homo Sociologicus." In *Essays in the Theory of Society*, pp. 19–87. Stanford, CA: Stanford University Press.

Dietzel, Heinrich. (1883) "Der Ausgangspunkt der Sozialwirtschaftslehre und ihr Grundbegriff." *Zeitschrift für die gesamte Staatswissenschaft* 39:1–80.

———. (1895) *Theoretische Sozialökonomik*. Leipzig: C.F. Wintersche Verlagshandlung.

Downs, Anthony. (1957) *An Economic Theory of Democracy*. New York: Harper & Row.

Durkheim, Emile, and Paul Fauconnet. (1903) "Sociologie et Sciences Sociales." *Revue Philosophique* 55:465–97.

Ehrlich, I. (1975) "Capital Punishment: A Case of Life and Death." *American Economic Review* 65:397–417.

Elster, Jon, ed. (1986) *Rational Choice*. New York: New York University Press.

Etzioni, Amitai. (1985) "Making Policy for Complex Systems: A Medical Model for Economics." *Journal of Policy Analysis and Management* 4:383–95.

———. (1986) "Founding a New Socio-economics." *Challenge* 29(5):13–18.

———. (1987a) "How Rational Are We?" *Sociological Forum* 2:1–20.

———. (1987b) "On Thoughtless Rationality (Rules-of-Thumb)." *Kyklos* 40:496–514.

———. (1988) *The Moral Dimension: Toward a New Economics*. New York: The Free Press.

Firth, Raymond. (1939) *Primitive Polynesian Economy*. London: Routledge & Sons.

Fogel, Robert, and Stanley Engerman. (1974) *Time on the Cross: The Economics of American Slavery*. Boston: Little, Brown.

Friedman, Milton. (1953) *Essays in Positive Economics*. Chicago: University of Chicago Press.

Gay, Edwin F. (1953) "Introduction to Arthur Spiethoff." In F.C. Lane and J.C. Riemersma, eds., *Enterprise and Secular Change*, pp. 431–43. London: George Allen & Unwin.

Goodfellow, David Martin. (1939) *Principles of Economic Sociology: The Economics of Primitive Life as Illustrated from the Bantu Peoples of South and East Africa*. London: Routledge & Sons.

Granovetter, Mark. (1985) "Economic Action and Social Structure: The Problem of Embeddedness." *American Journal of Sociology* 91:481–510.

Hansen, Reginald. (1968) "Der Methodenstreit in den Sozialwissenschaften zwischen Gustav Schmoller und Karl Menger. Seine Wissenschaftshistorische und Wissenschaftstheoretische Bedeutung." In A. Diemer, ed., *Beiträge zuer Entwicklung der Wissenschaftstheorie im 19. Jahrhundert*, pp. 137–73. Meisenhweim am Glan: Verlag Anton Hain.

Hayek, Friedrich von. (1934) "Carl Menger." *Economica* 1:393–420.

Hernes, Gudmund. (1978) "Mot en institutionell oekonomi." In *Forhandlingsoekonomi og blandingsadministrasjon*, pp. 196–42. Bergen: Universitetsforlaget.

Herskovitz, Samuel. (1940) *The Economic Life of Primitive Peoples*. New York: A. A. Knopf.

Hindess, Barry. (1984) "Rational Choice Theory and the Analysis of Political Action." *Economy and Society* 13:255–77.

Hirsch, P., S. Michaels, and R. Friedman. (1987) " 'Dirty Hands' versus 'Clean Models': Is Sociology in Danger of Being Seduced by Economics?" *Theory and Society* 16:317–36.

Hirschman, Albert O. (1980) *National Power and the Structure of Foreign Trade*. Berkeley: University of California Press. Originally appeared in 1945.

Hirshleifer, Jack. (1985) "The Expanding Domain of Economics." *American Economic Review* 75(6):53–68.

JITE. (1988) "Views and Comments on Gustav Schmoller and the Methodenstreit." *Journal of Institutional and Theoretical Economics* 144:524–600.

Lewin, Leif. (1988) *Det gemensamma bästa: om egenintresset och allmänintresset i västerländsk politik* (The common good: on private interests and the common good in Western politics). Borås, Sweden: Carlssons.

Löwe, Adolph. (1935) *Economics and Sociology: A Plea for Co-operation in the Social Sciences*. London: George Allen & Unwin.

Marshall, Alfred. (1891) *Principles of Economics*. London: Macmillan.

Menger, Carl. (1871) *Grundsätze der Volkswirtschaftslehre*. Vienna: Braumüller.

———. (1883) *Untersuchungen über die Methode der Sozialwissenschaften und der Politischen Ökonomie insbesondere*. Leipzig: Duncker & Humblot. Translated into English in 1985 as *Investigations into the Method of the Social Sciences with Special Reference to Economics*. New York: New York University Press, 1985.

———. (1884) *Die Irrthümer des Historismus in der deutschen Nationalökonomie*. Vienna: Alfred Hölder. Most of this work can be found in an abbreviated form in Albion Small, *The Origins of Sociology*. Chicago: University of Chicago Press, 1924.

Mill, John Stuart. ([1838]1844) "On the Definition of Political Economy; and on the Method of Investigation Proper to It." In *Essays on Some Unsettled Questions of Political Economy*, pp. 120–64. London: John W. Parker.

Mongiovi, Gary. (1988) "The American Methodenstreit." *History of Economic Society Bulletin* 10(1):57–66.

Pareto, Vilfredo. (1935) *The Mind and Society (Trattato di Sociologia)*. New York: Harcourt, Brace, Jovanovich.

Parsons, Talcott. (1934) "Some Reflections on 'The Nature and Significance of Economics,' " *Quarterly Journal of Economics* 48:511–45.

———. (1935) "Sociological Elements in Economic Thought, I–II." *Quarterly Journal of Economics* 49:414–53, 645–67.

———. *The Integration of Economic and Sociological Theory* ("*The Marshall Lectures*"). Forthcoming in Sociological Inquiry.

Parsons, Talcott, and Neil J. Smelser. (1956) *Economy and Society: A Study in the Integration of Economic and Social Theory*. London: Routledge & Kegan Paul.

Polanyi, Karl, Conrad M. Arensberg, and Harry W. Pearson, eds. (1957) *Trade and Market in the Early Empires: Economies in History and Theory*. New York: The Free Press.

Posner, Richard. (1973) *Economic Analysis of Law*. Boston: Little Brown.

Radnitzky, Gerard, and Peter Bernholz, eds. (1987) *Economic Imperialism: The Economic Method Applied outside the Field of Economics*. New York: Paragon House.

Robbins, Lionel. (1982) *An Essay on the Nature and Significance of Economic Science*. London: Macmillan.

Roemer, John. (1982) *A General Theory of Exploitation and Class*. Cambridge, MA: Harvard University Press.

Samuelson, Paul. ([1947]1983) *Foundations of Economic Analysis*. Cambridge, MA: Harvard University Press.

Schmoller, Gustav von. (1883) "Review of Carl Menger, *Untersuchungen über die Methode der Sozialwissenschaften und der Politischen Ökonomie insbesondere*." *Schmollers Jahrbuch* 17:239–58.

———. (1884) "Letter on Carl Menger's book *Die Irrthümer des Historismus in der deutschen Nationalökonomie.*" *Schmollers Jahrbuch* 8:333.

Schön, Manfred. (1987) "Gustav Schmoller and Max Weber." In W. J. Mommsen and J. Osterhammel, eds., *Max Weber and His Contemporaries*, pp. 59–69. London: George Allen & Unwin.

Schumpeter, Joseph A. (1908) *Das Wesen und der Hauptinhalt der theoretischen Nationalökonomie.* Leipzig: Duncker & Humblot.

———. (1926) "Gustav von Schmoller und die Probleme von heute." *Jahrbuch für Gesetzgebung, Verwaltung und Volkswirtschaft* 50:337–88.

———. (1951) "Carl Menger (1840–1921)." In *Ten Great Economists*, pp. 80–90. London: Oxford University Press.

———. (1954) *History of Economic Analysis.* London: George Allen & Unwin.

Sen, Amartya. (1987) *On Ethics and Economics.* Oxford: Basil Blackwell.

Souter, Ralph William. (1933) *Prolegomena to Relativity Economics: An Elementary Study in the Mechanics and Organics of an Expanding Economic Universe.* New York: Columbia University Press.

Stigler, George J. (1984) "Economics—The Imperial Science?" *Scandinavian Journal of Economics* 86:301–13.

Swedberg, Richard. (1987) "Economic Sociology: Past and Present." *Current Sociology* 35(1):1–221.

———. (1990) *Economics and Sociology: On Redefining Their Boundaries. Conversations with Economists and Sociologists.* Princeton, NJ: Princeton University Press.

Tullock, Gordon. (1972) "Economic Imperialism." In J. M. Buchanan and R. D. Tollison, eds., *Theory of Political Choice*, pp. 317–29. Ann Arbor: University of Michigan Press.

Tullock, Gordon, and Richard B. McKenzie. ([1975]1985) *The New World of Economics: Explorations into the Human Experience.* 4th ed. Homewood, IL: Richard D. Irwin, Inc.

Weber, Max. (1949) *The Methodology of the Social Sciences.* New York: The Free Press.

———. (1975) "Marginal Utility Theory and the Fundamental Law of Psychophysics." *Social Science Quarterly* 56:21–36.

———. (1976) "Economic Theory and Ancient Society." In *The Agrarian Sociology of Ancient Civilizations*, pp. 39–79. London: Verso.

———. (1978) *Economy and Society: An Outline of Interpretative Sociology.* Berkeley: University of California Press.

Weber, Max et al. (1914) "Vorwort." In K. Bücher et al., *Grundriss der Sozialökonomik*, pp. vii–ix. Tübingen: J.C.B. Mohr.

Wegener, Walther. (1962) *Die Quellen der Wissenschaftsauffassung Max Webers und die Problematik der Werturteilsfreiheit der Nationalökonomie.* Berlin: Duncker & Humblot.

Wicksell, Knut. (1904) "Mål och medel i nationalekonomien" (Ends and means in economic theory). *Ekonomisk tidskrift* (Sweden) 6:457–74.

Williamson, Oliver E. (1975) *Markets and Hierarchies: Analysis and Antitrust Implications.* New York: The Free Press.

Winkelmann, Johannes. (1986) *Max Webers hinterlassenes Hauptwerk: Die Wirtschaft und die gesellschaftlichen Ordnungen und Mächte.* Tübingen: J.C.B. Mohr.

Wrong, Dennis H. (1961) "The Oversocialized Conception of Man in Modern Sociology." *American Sociological Review* 26:183–93.

4

RICHARD M. COUGHLIN

The Economic Person in Sociological Context

Case Studies in the Mediation of Self-Interest

If I am not for myself, who will be for me?
And if I am for mine own self, what am I?
—Hillel

The subject of this paper is an old question that has attracted renewed interest in recent years.[1] Broadly stated, the question is whether individual behavior is motivated by essentially egoistic criteria—if not selfish concerns, then at least paramountly self-centered ones—or by criteria defined and operating at the supraindividual level.

This paper explores tne general hypothesis that economic self-interest is mediated by social bonds and the normative influences such relationships exert on individuals. The first part of the paper is devoted to a brief critique of the behavioral models specified by neoclassical (rational choice) and major sociological theories. This theme is further developed in the second section of the paper using some recent survey data on attitudes toward government spending for a range of ''public goods'' to assess empirically the proposition that a hybrid model incorporating the mediation of self-interest by social relationships and normative factors can explain outcomes that cannot be readily accommodated by the neoclassical model of economic behavior.

Neoclassical and Sociological Approaches Compared

In their behavioral assumptions and models of action, sociology and neoclassical economics are opposite sides of a coin. Neoclassical economists have been preoccupied with rational choices made by individual actors; sociologists have tended to look beyond the individual to behavior at the level of the group or collectivity. While the charge that sociology has concerned itself with the irrational aspects of behavior is debatable, it is true that it has paid insufficient attention to the question of rationality at the individual level. Where neoclassical economists have encountered difficulty in making the Economic Person a social being, sociologists have had problems disentangling individuals from the web of social relations in which they are enmeshed.[2]

The intellectual distance separating neoclassical economics and sociology has fostered a little hostility, some suspicion, and a good deal of indifference (Hechter 1987). Like tribes living in neighboring valleys separated by high mountains, the two disciplines have developed their own languages, symbols, and customs to the point of near mutual incomprehensibility. One consequence of this isolation is the widespread belief that economics and sociology have little to offer one another. While there are crucial differences between the models of behavior employed by the two disciplines, some of these differences are complementary rather than contradictory, with each approach having something to offer the other. As Wrong (1961) has suggested, sociology's "oversocialized" conception of human behavior is the direct counterpart of the "undersocialized" conception of classical liberalism.

The Problem of Missing Variables

Both neoclassical economics and conventional sociological modes of explanation suffer from the problem of missing variables or, to be more precise, incompletely specified models. In sociological theories the question of individual motivation often has been left unattended (Turner 1987), leaving ambiguous the question of what, sociologically speaking, constitutes self-interest. Is the Sociological Person driven to attain social status, to dominate and control, to fill a need for ontological security, to conform or otherwise seek the validation of others? The answer is that there is not much agreement among sociologists on these matters. The fact that sociology has so many theories of deviant behavior and criminality, each with insufficient explanatory power, to account for departures from normative behavior testifies to the need to fill in the gaps in theory between micro- and macro-levels of analysis. In contrast, the neoclassical model of behavior lacks virtually all variables having to do with the collectivity. For purposes here, I will limit discussion to the most important omissions concerning the role of variables contributing to social solidarity.

Social Solidarity

It has been suggested that the problems encountered by rational choice theory in explaining collective action can be traced to the critical absence of social solidarity as part of its explanatory framework. For example, Fireman and Gamson (1979, p. 21), writing from the perspective of resource mobilization theory of social movements, state that "the utilitarian approach to collective action [exaggerates] the role of self-interest while obscuring the role of solidarity and principle." The authors go on to define solidarity as "the configuration of relationships linking members of a group to one another . . . in a number of ways that generate a sense of common identity, shared fate, and general commitment to defend the group." They further suggest a variety of conditions that contribute to group solidarity, including kinship, participation in organizations and voluntary associations, shared problem-solving techniques, similarities of subordinate and superordinate relations with outsiders, and the difficulty of exit from the group. The key insight here is that solidarity acts to inhibit the retreat to self-interest by "rational" actors, and so makes possible collective action without the selective incentives or sanctions deemed essential on strictly utilitarian grounds (cf. Olson 1965).

Other studies have identified group size, homogeneity, and moral density as determinants of solidarity. Others have singled out conflict along class, racial or ethnic, or national lines, as a catalyst for sharpening the delineation of boundaries between groups and thus contributing to the development of solidarity within groups (Coser 1956). Still others have cited major disasters, such as earthquakes and floods, as triggers for the spontaneous emergence of solidarity in the form of cooperative, helping behavior among strangers.

Although there are some variations on the surface, manifestations of social solidarity all appear to involve one or more of the following: (1) the coalescence of a group identity, which is often characterized by (2) a high degree of embeddedness of social relationships (cf. Granovetter 1985), and (3) a structurally defined common interest. While it is not possible here to explore fully the conditions under which solidarity occurs, it is clear that these elements are to some degree mutually reinforcing. A strong sense of group identity and frequent interaction make it easier to recognize commonalities of interest as such. The sacrifice or deferral of immediate self-interest, which is a requisite of collective action, is facilitated by densely formed networks of social interaction. It is entirely possible, of course, that in the long run collective action may be to the net benefit of the individual as well as the group; under such conditions solidaristic behavior becomes equivalent to so-called "enlightened self-interest." But since there is also a risk that the collective goal will never be achieved, the *sine qua non* of solidarity is a sufficiently strong social bond so that the individual chooses to cooperate rather than opting for a "free ride."

Normative Factors

In addition to the coalescence of group identities, solidarity has a second subjective dimension, consisting of normative values and beliefs. Normative factors are generally ignored in the neoclassical paradigm or are simply defined as individual preferences. For many economists, morality, like altruism, is just another taste. Sociological theories, in contrast, pay considerable attention to norms and values, but seem unable to reach accord on the relationship between these factors and elements of social structure. In large part, the disagreement centers on which way the causal arrows point: from social structure to norms; from norms to social structure; or in both directions at once. Such debates tend to be endless.

For purposes here, it is sufficient to recognize that both norms and social structural factors are potentially important in the creation and maintenance of solidarity. It is reasonable to posit a positive relationship between the two: that is, solidarity based on structural interests should reinforce the moral commitment of the individual to the group; in turn, moral commitment should promote the recognition among individuals that structural interests are group interests. Indeed, in the extreme case the two dimensions collapse into one and the same thing—moral commitment becomes a special case of group interest in which the welfare of the individual and the welfare of the collectivity become indistinguishable from one another. Such a description may, in fact, accurately depict the situation in tightly knit groups or small, simple societies.[3]

In large and complex societies the relationship is not so simple. Although structural bases of solidarity may coincide with shared normative values and beliefs, more frequently the two retain some independence. The tendency toward pluralism and rapid social change ensures that, outside of ethnic enclaves and closed religious communities, socialization to collective norms and values occurs at many levels and loci of society. Just as there are overlapping and cross-cutting group identities and structural interests in modern societies, the normative and moral foundations of behavior may be indistinct or even contradictory (Coughlin 1980). The multiple layers and heterogeneity of norms and values found in modern societies tend to inhibit the development of broad-based solidary group ties, but they do not preclude them.

Finally, it should be noted that the concept of social solidarity, particularly in regard to normative/moral commitment, can be used in place of—that is, it replaces—the concept of altruism as it is usually employed in neoclassical economic theories.[4] Functionally, altruism can be reduced to a sentiment or action based on the recognition of some commonality of interests, or an action undertaken on moral or ethical grounds, or some combination of the two. Even the slightly pejorative connotation of altruism—that is, an act performed merely to assuage individual feelings of guilt—can be accommodated here, since why would an individual feel guilty in the face of misery or suffering if not for some stirring of moral sensibility?[5]

Empirical Evidence

This section presents some empirical case studies that explore the hypothesis that social solidarity, and normative factors especially, play an important role in economic behavior, specifically, in shaping attitudes toward government spending programs. While this effort is exploratory, the results clearly point toward the significant advantages that an explicitly socioeconomic approach has over models based exclusively on neoclassical economic or traditional sociological assumptions.

This exercise draws mostly on data collected from 1973 to 1988 by the National Opinion Research Corporation (NORC) as part of the General Social Survey (GSS). In the main, the GSS data analyzed below concern public willingness to support spending for various governmental programs and activities—all of which are, in a broad sense, "public goods."[6] These items are supplemented in some places by other items from the GSS and data from other surveys.

Limits of Rational Choice Explanations

A basic version of the rational choice model holds that individuals always seek maximum rewards at minimum cost, and that in making these assessments individuals apply criteria that are logical-empirical in nature (Etzioni 1988). Under these assumptions, we would expect individuals to support only those expenditures for those public goods from which they might benefit and for which they would not expect to pay—or at least pay less than they expect to receive in return. Conversely, we would expect rational actors to oppose spending for public goods they perceive to be of little or no benefit to them, and for which they are likely to have to pay in the form of taxes or higher prices.

Actual results of the GSS items on attitudes toward spending for various public goods from 1973 to 1988 are summarized in Table 4.1.

In its basic form the rational choice model can account for some of the results shown in Table 4.1, such as the low levels of public support for foreign aid and welfare, but on the whole it fares quite poorly as an explanation for the observed results. We can improve the model's fit by interpreting as "self-interested" a variety of indirect benefits that individuals may perceive in some kinds of spending. Support for increased expenditures to combat crime can be interpreted in terms of "purchasing" some protection against harm from criminal acts. Similarly, the assumptions of rational choice can be stretched a bit to explain support for measures to combat drug addiction. Making this connection presupposes that nonaddicts are willing to help those who are addicted out of fear of the danger untreated addicts pose to nonaddicts or their families. Applying a similar logic, a (nearly) rational actor might also support increased efforts to improve race relations.

Other results, however, seem to defy interpretation in rational choice terms. Consider, for example, the extremely generous public attitudes toward Social Security and education. Such attitudes are difficult to reconcile with the alleged advantages of private alternatives so often cited by critics of government programs (see Coughlin 1986). Moreover, armed only with elements of rational choice theory, it is hard to see how we even begin to account for the extraordinarily high levels of support for aid to the poor over the years.

Table 4.1

Attitudes toward Government Spending, 1973–88

Category of expenditure	Mean percent responding current level of spending is "too little" (by year)	
	1973–83	1984–88
Halt the rising crime rate	70.4	69.0
Assistance to the poor	—	67.0
Deal with drug addiction	62.7	66.1
Improve nation's health	61.3	64.2
Improve nation's education system	54.6	64.2
Protect the environment	57.0	64.0
Protect Social Security	—	56.3
Solve problems of the big cities	50.7	49.2
Highways and bridges	—	39.7
Improve conditions of blacks	31.5	38.0
Improve mass transportation	—	33.3
Parks and recreation	—	32.1
Military, armaments, and defense	26.9	16.4
Welfare	19.5	23.4
Space exploration	11.3	14.1
Foreign aid	4.5	6.4

Source: NORC, General Social Surveys.

Many proponents of rational choice will undoubtedly object to this line of analysis. They might respond that survey responses cannot be taken at face value, and that apparent attitudes concerning government spending programs are influenced by the fact that individuals are not free to choose whether or not to contribute, since contributions in the form of taxation are exacted under threat of criminal prosecution, and so individuals' true preferences cannot be discovered. At one level this is a reasonable argument, although it becomes quite unrealistic when carried to its logical conclusion.[7] The argument can be countered, however, by asking the obvious question, why individuals presumed to be thusly coerced do not avail themselves of the opportunity offered by the survey interview to register blanket objection to government spending of all sorts? That so few people actually do object to spending for all or most public goods suggests that another dynamic is at work.

This brings up another criticism sometimes heard from the rational choice camp, to the effect that individuals do not object to spending for public goods because they are unaware of true costs. This criticism is the mirror image of the coercion argument. Without linking potential benefits to actual costs, the argument goes, individuals are prone to the "fiscal illusion" that benefits can be had at little or no cost (see Lewis 1982). The argument is that it "costs" virtually nothing to respond to a survey interviewer that more money should be spent on *X* (where *X* may be a ballistic missile, a freeway, or a day care center), but it is quite another thing to have to pay for it. Underlying this argument is the assumption that if respondents were aware of true costs, support for public goods would decrease or disappear.

While it is possible that respondents in surveys (and, by inference, the public at large) underestimate the actual costs of many or most public goods, they nonetheless appear quite able and willing to draw distinctions among different categories of such goods. If respondents actually priced all public goods equally at zero, would not the "rational choice" be to want "more" of everything? Except where the marginal value of the good is valued at zero or even negatively—that is, the "good" is seen as "bad"—the rational choice model's answer to the question would have to be yes. Yet in practice this result does not occur in any survey or any other context of which I am aware. Again, it seems clear that another type of explanation is needed.[8]

Toward a Socioeconomic Explanation

Let us begin to look for an alternative explanation by restating the problem in socioeconomic terms. First, note the extraordinary stability in the pattern of results reported in Table 4.1. Indeed, the results are more stable than they should be given changes in real and relative levels of program spending over time, the ebb and flow of the political debate over taxing and spending, the ups and downs of the economy, and other changes that took place from 1973 to 1988. Empirically, however, the public's assessment of how much money should be spent on public goods hardly seems to have budged. In virtually all spending categories, the mean deviation over the period is on the order of the variation expected due to sampling error.

How can we account for this remarkable stability? The answer does not lie in the conventional economic explanation. Judging by the end result, the process by which people determine how much money should be spent on a particular public good is not rational in the usual sense. Individuals do not, apparently, attempt to calculate the marginal utility of the *n*th increment of spending for each program or activity. If this were the case, attitudes would almost certainly be more responsive to actual spending patterns, both across programs and over time, than appears to be the case. Instead, these policy-related attitudes appear to be a function of rather general orientations, what Sears et al. (1980) call "stable affective preferences," that tend to be quite stable over time.[9] In other words, the results in Table 4.1 are more representative of a rough rank ordering of public priorities for government spending than they are detailed calculations of the expected value of marginal changes in spending for each program or activity. In a narrow sense, then, the critics of surveys are right when they say that the polls

Figure 4.1. **Typology of Support for "Public Goods"**

Logical/Empirical Valuation	Normative/Affective Valuation: Positive	Normative/Affective Valuation: Negative
Gain	High	Mixed
Loss	Mixed	Low

cannot be taken at face value. But it is a mistake to dismiss the results as meaningless. The challenge is to locate and correctly interpret their meaning.

The interpretation I shall argue for here is socioeconomic in nature: viz., that these general orientations toward public goods are the product of interaction along two dimensions of valuation. The first consists of individual perceptions of probable net gain or loss from spending changes in a public good—that is, considerations of conventional self-interest. The second dimension consists of reactions to the desirability or worthiness of the public good itself based on the normative or affective associations it possesses. Following Etzioni (1988), I refer to these as, respectively, the *logical-empirical* (L/E) and *normative-affective* (N/A) dimensions.

Figure 4.1 shows a simple typology based on the interaction between the L/E and N/A dimensions of valuation.[10] Where L/E and N/A valuations reinforce one another, the net effect is clear-cut. For example, where a positive N/A valuation is combined with a positive L/E perception, a high level of public support is virtually assured. Spending to protect Social Security and improve health care and education fall into this category. All are widely regarded as inherently desirable goods that individuals are likely to view as beneficial to themselves and their families or their communities. As discussed in more detail below, efforts to protect the environment have similarly come to be widely regarded as positive along both N/A and L/E dimensions.

Where negative N/A valuations coincide with negative perceived L/E effects, overall public support is likely to be low. Welfare and foreign aid are both goods that have tended to have negative N/A associations, and for a majority of Americans neither is perceived as contributing positively to self-interest.

Where L/E and N/A valuations cross-cut one another, public support is less predictable. The combination of positive N/A and negative L/E produces a mixed pattern of support. For example, "helping the poor" evokes an extraordinarily high level of public support, while "space exploration" falls near the bottom of the list. In the proposed typology both are assumed to have positive N/A loadings, in the sense of being viewed as desirable activities, but both are likely to be generally perceived as negative in terms of L/E effect. So why such different levels of support? The difference, it seems, lies in the strength of the N/A factors involved. In American society, "helping the poor" is not only normative behavior, it carries overtones of moral duty as well. Exploring space, on the other hand, may be thought of as worthwhile, but it may also be viewed as a luxury that the nation can ill afford—and it certainly does not suggest any moral imperative.

The combination of negative N/A and positive L/E also tends to produce a mixed pattern. On the GSS items concerning efforts to fight crime and drug addiction, negative N/A loadings manage to coexist with widespread willingness among the public to spend more money. A plausible explanation is that fear of crime and drugs (negative N/A) contributes to the perception that increased spending might lessen the danger to oneself and one's property (positive L/E). In the case of military spending, however, public support for spending was low for nearly the entire period between 1973 and 1988. The only exception occurred in the 1980 GSS, when the endorsement for increases in military and defense spending shot up to 60 percent. The fact that 1980 was a year marked by heightened tensions in the Middle East, focused around the highly emotional issue of American hostages held captive in Iran and the recent Soviet invasion of Afghanistan, is likely significant. It suggests that L/E perceptions of self-interest, in this case the threat to national security, and N/A associations (hating the Ayatollah and, perhaps, the Russians by loving the military) can change rapidly in the face of external events. But they can also change back again: in 1982 the proportion of the GSS national sample supporting increases in defense spending dropped back to 28 percent, about where it had stood in 1978 before the crises.

A few public goods do not appear to fit neatly into the typology. For example, public support for roads and bridges, and parks and recreation is lower than expected given the imputed positive N/A, positive L/E combination. This may be due to low intensity of the N/A loading or some ambiguity in the L/E valuation, neither of which is captured by the dichotomies of this simple typology.[11] In addition, as suggested by the volatility of attitudes toward military spending from 1978 to 1982, the location of items may change depending on circumstances or interpretation. Such illustrations underline the preliminary and exploratory nature of this effort. Nonetheless, the typology serves to demonstrate the advantages of incorporating both logical-empirical and normative-affective factors in the analysis of public goods.

To reject the narrow, self-interested model of rational choice is not, however, to embrace diametrically opposed assumptions that solidarity or moral commitment are exclusive determinants of behavior. A model in which individuals evaluate public goods solely in terms of perceived effect on the common good, giving no weight whatsoever to considerations of individual gain or loss fares little better than the unmodified rational choice model. As seen in the next section, a model of economic behavior codetermined by self-interest and normative factors not only accounts for much of the aggregate pattern of attitudes toward public goods, it also provides a good basis for explaining the distribution of attitudes within the population.

Case Studies in the Relative Impact of L/E and N/A Factors

The case studies included in this section explore in greater detail the interaction and relative impact of L/E and N/A valuations in shaping attitudes toward a range of public goods. The examples included in this section probe the effects of solidarity, normative values, and moral commitment as explanations of variations within the general orientations toward public goods discussed in the preceding section.

Support for Welfare among Blacks

For most Americans welfare carries strongly negative associations along both N/A and L/E dimensions. The low level of public support for more welfare spending (refer again to Table 4.1) is consistent with the negative esteem in which public assistance programs aimed at the nonelderly, nondisabled poor are held.[12] The only significant exception to the American public's unwillingness to spend more on welfare is found among blacks as a group, individuals in low-income families, and people who have been unemployed in the last five years. Since all of these conditions are associated with increased likelihood of actually receiving welfare benefits, and there is potentially considerable overlap among these conditions, the first task is to disentangle the relative effects of each.

Because of the small number of categories on the dependent variable, and other violations of assumptions of ordinary least squares regression, a series of logit regressions were run using dependent dummy variables representing, respectively, "too little" and "too much" spent on welfare (see Cleary and Angel 1984). The independent variables included were race (coded as a dummy variable including only blacks and whites, excluding a small number of respondents of "other" races), total family income, recent unemployment, subjective social class identification, political views (measured by the respondent's self-location on a scale running from extremely liberal to extremely conservative), and total years of education. The last three variables, for reasons explained below, are treated as controls. To achieve a large enough subsample of blacks, GSS samples for the years 1983 to 1988 were pooled prior to running the regressions.

The results, shown in Table 4.2, point toward a codetermination model to explain both support for and opposition to welfare spending. Income and unemployment both represent a component of self-interest. To the extent that individ-

Table 4.2

Attitudes toward Spending for Welfare, 1984–88

	Logit regression coefficient (standard error)	
Variables	Current spending is "too little"	Current spending is "too much"
Race	0.426**	–0.365**
	(0.087)	(0.094)
Political views	–0.118**	0.088**
	(0.025)	(0.022)
Income	–0.053**	0.060**
	(0.012)	(0.012)
Unemployed in the past 5 years	0.155*	0.067
	(0.070)	(0.062)
Social class identification	–0.064	–0.015
	(0.054)	(0.048)
Education	0.003	–0.021*
	(0.012)	(0.011)
Intercept	5.702**	4.106**
	(0.223)	(0.197)

Source: NORC, General Social Surveys.
Note: 5 added to intercept and logit divided by 2; $^{**}p < 0.001$; $^{*}p < 0.05$.

uals are low income and recently unemployed, they are more likely to perceive welfare as a program of potential benefit to them.[13] Conversely, those with high incomes and no unemployment experience will likely see little or no personal advantage in the welfare system. The magnitude and sign of the logit regression coefficients of income and unemployment in Table 4.2 bear out this interpretation

The influence of race on attitudes toward welfare spending, however, remains significant apart from any indirect effects attributable to income and unemployment. Variables measuring education, social class identification, and political views were included as controls, in the sense that the correlation of each variable with race raised the possibility of confounding the net effect of race. In the full model, race nonetheless retains significance as a determinant of both "too little" and "too much" responses.

I interpret this result as evidence of some degree of solidarity among blacks with respect to welfare, in the sense that black support for welfare contains a component that does not represent either individual economic self-interest, generalized liberal views, class consciousness per se, or cognitive differences associated with education. There is, of course, an inferential leap from the finding that race retains a strong independent statistical effect and the interpretation that the source of this effect is solidarity among blacks. The implicit link between the two is the assumption that blacks continue to support welfare even when they personally do not benefit from it because they perceive welfare to be a benefit to blacks as a group.

Some indirect evidence in support of the solidarity hypothesis comes from a question asked of black respondents only in the 1982 GSS about product boycotts. Asked whether they had ever stopped buying certain products because of the way a company or country has treated blacks, over a quarter (28 percent) of all blacks and nearly half (46 percent) of those with at least some college education responded yes. This figure seems surprisingly high, given the absence of any highly publicized product boycotts involving blacks. To be sure, various trade embargoes and institutional boycotts of South Africa have received widespread attention in recent years, but outside of shunning South African diamonds and gold coins, there would appear to be few opportunities for individual blacks to participate in these efforts.

Additional support for the solidarity hypothesis is found below in the analysis of support for income redistribution.

Support for Income Redistribution: Blacks versus Whites

In narrow economic terms, the issue of income redistribution is approximately the same as that of welfare spending, and so the perception of L/E interests should be substantially the same in both cases. In terms of N/A associations, however, income redistribution is mostly free from the negative moral overtones associated with welfare. The first question, then, is whether or not this difference makes a difference.

The results shown in Table 4.3 suggest fundamental differences in the respective patterns of response to income distribution and welfare spending—differences that cannot be explained solely by the slightly differing formats of the two items. Faced with the choice between government action to reduce income differences between the rich and poor and no such action, the 1978 GSS sample expressed a plurality preference in favor of redistribution.[14] Moreover, excluding neutral responses and don't-knows, the proportion of the entire sample supporting income redistribution was over 60 percent. Among black support, the corresponding figure was more than 80 percent.

Table 4.3 shows that attitudes toward income redistribution are strongly associated with income among whites but not among blacks. Among whites, nearly thirty percentage points divide support in the lowest income group from the highest income group (74.3 percent for those making less than $5,000 per year versus 44.9 percent for those making $20,000 or more, in 1978 dollars). In contrast, among blacks the differences in responses at extremes of income are negligible (80.3 versus 77.2 percent).

The interpretation of these findings is straightforward and strongly supportive of the solidarity hypothesis. American blacks support government efforts to nar-

Table 4.3

Support for Income Redistribution, ca. 1978

	Income[a]						
	(1)	(2)	(3)	(4)	(5)	Refused	Total
United States	74.3	71.0	64.5	58.5	44.9	54.5	60.4
(N =)	(167)	(217)	(217)	(176)	(323)	(33)	(1133)
Blacks[b]	80.3	81.6	91.0	82.3	77.2	88.9	81.9
(N =)	(147)	(136)	(89)	(62)	(149)	(18)	(601)
Sweden	91.5	88.8	84.6	84.4	73.0	83.9	83.3
(N =)	(213)	(295)	(280)	(250)	(389)	(174)	(1601)

Source: NORC, General Social Surveys (for United States); Verba et al. (1987), unpublished data (for Sweden).

[a] Total annual family income: (1) less than $5,000 or SEK 50,000; (2) $5,000–$9,999 or SEK 50,000–69,999; (3) $10,000–$14,999 or SEK 70,000–89,999; (4) $15,000–$19,999 or SEK 90,000–109,000; (5) $20,000 or more, or SEK 110,000 or more.

[b] Pooled black subsamples, 1978–86.

row income differences even at higher income levels where as individuals they will probably not benefit and may well be hurt by such action. White support for income redistribution, in contrast, decreases monotonically as a function of economic self-interest. In sum, for blacks the prominent explanation is solidarity (N/A), while for whites self-interest (L/E) plays a more important role.

But there is one more point that should not be overlooked: some 45 percent (excluding don't-know responses) of the highest-income whites in the 1978 GSS survey expressed some support for income redistribution. While low by comparison to less affluent whites and blacks of all income levels, this figure is high if judged solely in terms of economic self-interest. The conclusion that suggests itself is that income redistribution, like other public goods, has an N/A component that mediates the effect of L/E considerations and raises the baseline of public support above the level expected on the basis of simple rational choice.

Support for Income Redistribution: United States versus Sweden

The normative dimension of income redistribution, and by inference other public goods, can be further illustrated by comparing the GSS responses on income redistribution to data from a survey conducted in Sweden in 1978 by Verba et al. (1987).[15] As shown in Table 4.3, the U.S. and Swedish responses to very similar questions concerning income redistribution differed in two important ways. First, the overall level of support for redistributive policies is much higher among

Swedes than among Americans (83.3 percent versus 60.4 percent, respectively). Although some allowance needs to be made for minor methodological differences between the surveys, other studies have reached similar conclusions about the broad support for the welfare state in Sweden (e.g., Hadenius 1986; Svallfors 1989). Second, the relationship between income and attitudes toward redistribution is weaker among the Swedish sample than in the American sample. Although higher-income Swedes favor income redistribution less than those of lower income, the total spread across income categories is only about two-thirds of that found in the GSS sample (18.5 points for Sweden, 29.6 for the United States).

These patterns suggest that although attitudes in both nations appear to be codetermined by N/A and L/E factors, the N/A factors have a greater impact in Sweden than in the United States. Put another way, the "general orientation" toward income redistribution in Sweden tilts more in the direction of norms and values emphasizing economic and social equality, which serves to attenuate expressions of narrow economic self-interest. In the United States, the general orientation toward income redistribution is located more toward the ideological center, allowing more competition among conflicting norms and values concerning equality and collectivism, leaving self-interest more room to operate, as it were.

Qualitatively, the argument for Swedish solidarity is further supported by the efforts that Social Democratic governments have assiduously promoted for the nearly sixty years they have been in power (Heclo and Madsen 1987; Logue and Einhorn 1989). These efforts have succeeded in fostering a high degree of support for collectivist principles of the welfare state (Zetterberg 1979; Hadenius 1986; Milner 1989; Svallfors 1989). In addition, it has been suggested that Sweden's small size, high degree of ethnolinguistic homogeneity, and high degree of unionization have all conduced to the development of a higher degree of solidarity than is found in other industrialized nations (Stephens 1979).[16] For purposes of this analysis, it is sufficient to note the strong role that N/A factors play in constraining manifestations of narrow self-interest.

Attitudes toward Abortion for the Poor

Abortion is usually thought of as a political issue or a moral question, and it is not often discussed in economic terms. An economic dimension of abortion was tapped, however, in the GSS item probing attitudes toward legalized abortion under circumstances where the family "has a very low income and cannot afford to have more children." Whether or not the question on abortion and low income was intended to tap the question of economic costs, there are indications that this is how it was perceived by some respondents. Approval of abortion for the poor shows a moderate positive correlation with income ($r = 0.10$), with about a 15-point spread between the highest and lowest income categories. This relation-

Table 4.4

Approval of Legal Abortion for the Poor, 1984–88

Variables	Logit regression coefficient (standard error)
Frequency of church attendance	–0.109** (0.006
Education	0.067** (0.006)
Catholic	–0.437** (0.066)
Protestant	–0.393** (0.061)
Political views	–0.079** (0.012)
Sex	0.096* (0.032)
Income	0.017* (0.006)
Race	–0.041 (0.045)
Intercept	4.874** (0.122)

Source: NORC, General Social Surveys.
Note: 5 added to intercept and logit divided by 2; ** $p < 0.001$; * $p < 0.01$.

ship can readily be interpreted in terms of a simple (if somewhat cynical) economic self-interest argument: upper-income groups disproportionately approve abortion for the poor as a means of reducing the future number of children added to the public assistance rolls.

A series of logit regressions were conducted to test the multivariate effect of income and other determinants of abortion attitudes suggested by previous research.[17] In addition to income, variables representing education, sex, race, and religion were included in the model. Two different measures of religion were introduced: dummy variables representing respondent self-identification as a Catholic or Protestant, and a simple measure of the frequency of church attendance. Finally, as in the analysis of welfare attitudes, the measure of political views was introduced as a control variable.

The results of the regression analysis, shown in Table 4.4, indicate that even in the presence of powerful determinants, income retains statistically significant explanatory power on attitudes toward abortion for the poor. But income is by no means the most important variable in the model. Church attendance and education exert powerful, opposing influences on abortion attitudes, followed by religious affiliation (independent of church attendance), political views, and gender. Race adds nothing to the explanatory power of the model.

In one sense, these results are not surprising. That abortion is fundamentally a question of normative values and moral commitment has been driven home by more than a decade of intense debate and bitter conflict. Those most likely to oppose abortion for the poor—but not only for the poor—are members of religious congregations in which opposition to abortion is based on moral and theological grounds, who practice their religion by attending church often, and who define themselves as political conservatives. In contrast, those mostly likely to support the availability of abortion tend to be highly educated, female, and political liberals, for whom the right to choose may also be an important matter of principle.[18]

In the clash of these opposing positions, economic costs and benefits (L/E) are not likely to be accorded much importance. However, our results indicate that income (L/E) retains some explanatory power in the presence of powerful N/A variables. The lesson here seems to be that where moral commitment or deeply held normative values are at stake, as they are in the abortion question, the calculation of marginal economic costs and benefits plays only a minor role—but a role nonetheless.

Support for Environmental Protection

Since emerging as a political issue in the 1960s, environmentalism has gained prominence in the public debate in the United States and other industrialized nations. The new issue of protecting the natural environment has given rise to new expressions of common interest and normative value orientations organized around a consciousness of interdependence (Mitchell 1988)—the idea that the planet is a fragile ecosystem of which humanity is only a part and on which it is no less dependent for survival than are rain forests, humpback whales, or bald eagles. In socioeconomic terms, environmentalism may provide the basis for the definition of a new "We." Compare the subtle but crucial difference in the connotations of the following two statements:

"Protect *the* environment."
"Protect *our* environment."

One indicator of the growing importance of environmental issues is the high level of public support for increased spending found in the 1973–88 GSS (refer again to Table 4.1). As discussed above, a plausible explanation of the support environmentalism has enjoyed is the confluence of a strongly positive N/A loading with an emergent positive L/E perception of the issue. Protecting the environment has for some time been seen as an inherently good thing, but only recently has a widespread awareness developed that it may be to everyone's rational long-term interest to protect the planet's biosphere against destruction.

Table 4.5

Attitudes toward Spending to Protect the Environment, 1984–88

	Logit regression coefficient (standard error)	
Variables	Current spending is "too little"	Current spending is "too much"
Age	–0.011**	0.009**
	(0.001)	(0.003)
Political views	–0.110**	0.115**
	(0.016)	(0.034)
Size of community	0.0001**	–0.0001
	(0.00003)	(0.0001)
Education	–0.018*	–0.019
	(0.008)	(0.016)
Income	0.011	0.011
	(0.008)	(0.017)
Race	0.012	–0.237
	(0.064)	(0.159)
Intercept	5.894**	2.788**
	(0.151)	(0.324)

Source: NORC, General Social Surveys.
Note: 5 added to intercept and logit divided by 2; ** $p < 0.001$; * $p < 0.01$.

To explore the underpinnings of attitudes toward protecting the environment, a series of logit regressions were run using pooled data from the 1984–88 GSS. Two dummy variables were created as dependent variables, representing "too much" and "too little" responses to the question about spending "to protect the environment." Included as independent variables were income, education, age, size of community, race, and political views.[19]

The results of the logit regression analysis are shown in Table 4.5. In the case of both "too little" and "too much" responses, age and political views have the biggest impact. Size of place and education show up as significant for the "too little" response, but not for "too much." Income and race show no significant effects. These results are consistent with the image that is commonly attached to proponents of environmental issues: young, urban, and well educated; but not, according to these results, disproportionately high income or white.

What is the balance between narrow self-interest and a "consciousness" of environmental responsibility? The answer lies in how one chooses to interpret the empirical findings. It might be argued that the negative relationship between age and support for environmental protection is a result of rational calculation: older members of the population have, so to speak, discounted the future value of a clean environment. Similarly, the tendency of those who live in urban areas to support spending for the environment might be explained in terms of self-interest, on the grounds that pollution is arguably more serious a problem in big cities than in rural areas.

The other interpretation is that concern for the environment is an emerging issue, one that has been embraced first by the vanguard segments of the population—the young, urban, educated—and so represents the wave of the future. As discussed above, environmental protection is already one of the most widely supported public goods in the United States. Indications are that this trend will continue, if not accelerate, in the future, due to continued degradation of the natural environment (Mitchell 1980). If this occurs, it will be due in large part to a coalescence of a potent new normative orientation with a decidedly novel transnational expression of solidarity.

Conclusion

This paper has explored some of the contrasts and complementarities of neoclassical and sociological approaches to explaining economic behavior. I have argued that the variables omitted from neoclassical models, namely social solidarity and its normative concomitants, are essential to understanding attitudes toward public goods and, by inference, other types of economic behavior. Conversely, conventional sociological models have not dealt adequately with individual-level variables, including the pursuit of self-interest, that also play a role in explaining attitudes toward public goods.

To conclude the discussion, I will address some remarks to the implications for further development of an explicitly socioeconomic theory. The propositions offered below serve both to formalize somewhat the conclusions drawn from the main body of the paper and to suggest hypotheses for future research in socio-economics.

First, the analysis strongly supports the basic position of socio-economics, viz., that behavior is codetermined by individually centered and collectively centered concerns (cf. Etzioni 1988, p. 63ff.). In more formal terms, this proposition can be stated as follows:

> *Economic behavior and other types of behavior take place in a field defined by the interaction of (a) individual concerns ("self-interest"), and (b) collective concerns (i.e., affiliations, obligations, and/or commitments to the collectivity). These dimensions are represented, respectively, by L/E and N/A factors.*[20]

Each group identity and network of social relationships potentially defines a different set of common interests and normative value orientations. These elements vary in strength, content, and form. In modern societies they are manifold, overlapping, and often cross-cutting; there is little reason to expect that patterns in one field will necessarily extend to other fields (i.e., transitivity cannot be assumed). In other words,

Interaction between L/E and N/A factors is not uniform across all fields of economic behavior. Empirically, the following combinations are possible:

a) L/E is a first approximation to explain some behavior; introducing N/A variables adds little or nothing to the explanatory power of the model.
b) L/E is the first approximation; introducing N/A variables significantly improves the explanatory power of the model.
c) N/A is the first approximation; introducing L/E variables has little or no effect.
d) N/A is the first approximation; introducing L/E considerations significantly improves the model.

The balance between L/E and N/A factors is not predetermined, and may be subject both to cross-sectional and longitudinal variation. In the case studies of public goods conducted above, attitudes toward welfare and income distribution are consistent with *b)*, while attitudes toward abortion tend to fit *c)*. Attitudes toward environmental protection might be described by either *b)* or *d)*, depending on how one defines L/E factors in this instance. The absence of an empirical example in this paper reflecting *a)* is likely due to the sample of survey items available for analysis. Conceptually, *a)* represents the pure market relations approximated in many economic transactions.

Third, codetermination of behavior, in which both L/E and N/A factors exert some independent influence, is a common, perhaps modal, condition. All other things being equal, however, the two factors tend to be inversely related, so that:

L/E factors tend to gain explanatory power as N/A factors diminish within a particular field as a result of conditions that weaken the social bonds and normative values and moral commitment within a collectivity;

and,

L/E factors tend to recede and N/A factors gain explanatory power within a particular field as a result of conditions that strengthen the social bonds and/or normative values and moral commitment within a collectivity.

In simple terms, the hypothesis is that the more solidary the group (in terms of group identities, social networks, and normative integration), the less expressions of narrow self-interest will predominate. Conversely, the less solidary the group, the more self-interest will tend to take on importance. While both hypotheses receive some support from the empirical case studies in this paper, further research using other data and methodologies is clearly needed to develop this model more fully.

Finally, this analysis has implications for the attempt to extend the concept of rationality to include N/A and L/E factors on an equal basis. Such a socially constructed conception of rationality would allow for more than one possible "rational" response to a given situation based on the specific content and interaction of N/A and L/E factors.[21] Such a formulation might well serve as a bridge between neoclassical economics and sociology and other social sciences. It would certainly be applicable to the public goods problem addressed above, but its usefulness might well extend to other types of economic behavior that appear to defy neoclassical assumptions. Possible examples of socially rational (but economically "irrational") behavior include the curious wagering habits Geertz (1973) describes in Balinese cockfighting, or the apparently uneconomical purchasing habits of Japanese consumers (*The Economist* 1987). By expanding the concept of what behavior is deemed rational in any given social setting, socio-economics can begin to rehabilitate Sen's (1977) "rational fool," making the Economic Person less of a "social moron."

Notes

1. Earlier versions of this paper were presented at the Conference on Socio-Economics, Harvard Business School, March 31–April 2, 1989, and the Meetings of the Pacific Sociological Association, April 13–16, 1989, in Reno, Nevada. I would like to thank Paul DiMaggio, Robert Fiala, and Henry Milner for their comments and suggestions.

2. See Hechter's (1987) discussion of this issue.

3. Durkheim (1964) made much of the rigid moral uniformity of small homogeneous communities. The notion of perfect congruence between individual volition and collective need can also be found in Rousseau's concept of the General Will. On this point, Dahl states, "In a solidary community, egoism is indistinguishable from altruism. One's interests are those of the community; the interests of the community are one's own" (1980, p. 4).

4. In the neoclassical literature, altruism is typically invoked to account for behavior that departs from self-interest. While a few neoclassical theorists have steadfastly sought to reduce altruistic behavior to individual utility maximization (e.g., Hammond 1975; Kurz 1977), the majority seem willing to allow that under some circumstances individuals may act to forgo some utility for the benefit of others. In Becker (1981), for example, altruism amounts to solidarity: the family is a solidary unit.

5. Sen (1977, p. 326) argues that such altruism ("sympathy") is consistent with neoclassical assumptions, since "pleased at others' pleasure and pained at others' pain . . . one's own utility may thus be helped by sympathetic action." This may be true, but the question remains, what makes an individual "pleased" or "pained" by someone else's condition?

6. A "public good" is a good provided through collective action that has widely distributed benefits. A "pure public good" is one from which no individual can be excluded.

7. The prospect of a society without any coercion ignores a variety of benign social controls, such as traffic lights, without which social life would be chaotic.

8. I do not mean to imply that linking program benefits to costs (e.g., an increase in taxes) would not provide useful information. My point is that even in the absence of an explicit statement of costs, the relative ranking of programs is clear and remarkably stable.

9. See Green (1988) for a critical review of self-interest in political behavior.

10. This typology is similar to the one I proposed to explain levels of public support of social welfare programs in eight industrialized societies (Coughlin 1980, p. 122).

11. Nor does this simple typology make allowance for such potentially important variables as individual attentiveness to issues and access to accurate information (Green 1988).

12. The term "welfare" is most often associated with the Aid to Families with Dependent Children program, although at times it may also include food stamps and other public assistance programs. See Coughlin (1989) for a review of negative welfare myths and stereotypes.

13. In one survey the GSS asked respondents if they had actually received welfare in the past five years. This variable turned out to be very highly correlated with recent unemployment experience and behaved in essentially the same way in the regression analysis. The unemployment question, which was asked in every year of the GSS, was used in the final regressions because of the much larger number of cases it yielded.

14. The year 1978 was chosen to allow comparison with the corresponding data for Sweden.

15. Verba and his colleagues did not publish the mass sample survey data in their book. They have generously made the raw data available for secondary analysis.

16. Whether or not one accepts the solidarity argument in its fullest form, it is clear that the public debate in Sweden over income equality and related issues is strongly influenced by normative factors that act to buffer expressions of crude economic individualism. Related issues, such as public disenchantment with high taxes and excessive bureaucracy (see Hadenius 1986; Svallfors 1989) are important, but remain beyond the scope of this paper.

17. For a review of the determinants of attitudes toward abortion, see Rodman et al. (1987), and Hall and Marx Ferree (1986).

18. Some inherent tension between normative commitments and individual self-interest is not restricted to one side of the ideological spectrum. In the debate over legalized abortion, for example, pro-choice ideology derives its inspiration and internal logic from feminist theory, which links the individual woman's "right to choose" to the emancipation of women as a class—an essentially solidaristic ideology. The trend in American public opinion on abortion since *Roe* v. *Wade*, however, can be just as readily explained in terms of rational choice by women who seek to minimize the costs imposed by an unwanted pregnancy.

19. The choice of independent variables was suggested by various studies, including Dunlap (1985), Gillroy and Shapiro (1984), and Mohai and Twight (1987). Preliminary attempts to include a variable reflecting respondents' type of work were abandoned because of problems with the GSS industry codes.

20. See Etzioni (1988) for an in-depth discussion of L/E and N/A concerns. The concepts of individually centered and collectively centered factors are similar to Margolis's (1982) utility functions of *S* (utility from the point of view pure self-interest) and *G* (utility from the point of view of pure group-interest).

21. Cf. Taylor (1988) on the concept of "thin" and "thick" rationality.

References

Becker, Gary S. (1981) *A Treatise on the Family*. Cambridge, MA: Harvard University Press.

Cleary, Paul D., and Ronald Angel. (1984) "The Analysis of Relationships Involving Dichotomous Dependent Variables." *Journal of Health and Social Behavior* 25:334–48.

Coser, Lewis. (1956) *The Functions of Social Conflict*. New York: The Free Press.

Coughlin, Richard M. (1980) *Ideology, Public Opinion, and Welfare Policy*. Berkeley: Institute of International Studies.

———. (1986) "Understanding (and Misunderstanding) Social Security: A Behavioral Perspective on Public Policy." In Stanley Kaish and Benjamin Gilad, eds., *Handbook*

of Behavioral Economics, vol. B, pp. 133–58. Greenwich, CT: JAI Press.
———. (1989) "Welfare Myths and Stereotypes." In Richard M. Coughlin, ed., *Reforming Welfare: Limits, Lessons, and Choices*, pp. 79–106. Albuquerque: University of New Mexico Press.
Coughlin, Richard M., and Philip K. Armour. (1985) "Social Control and Social Security: Theory and Research on Capitalist and Communist Nations." *Social Science Quarterly* 66:770–88.
Dahl, Robert A. (1980) *Egoism, Altruism, and the Public Good.* Urbana-Champaign: Department of Political Science, University of Illinois.
Dunlap, Riley. (1985) "Public Opinion: Behind the Transformation." *EPA Journal* 11:15–17.
Durkheim, Emile. (1964) *The Division of Labor in Society*. New York: The Free Press.
The Economist. (1987) "A Critique of Pure Irrationality about Japan." December 12:39–43.
Etzioni, Amitai. (1988) *The Moral Dimension: Toward a New Economics*. New York: The Free Press.
Fireman, Bruce, and William A. Gamson. (1979) "Utilitarian Logic in the Resource Mobilization Perspective." In Mayer N. Zald and John D. McCarthy, eds., *The Dynamics of Social Movements*. Cambridge, MA: Winthrop Publishers.
Geertz, Clifford. (1973) *The Interpretation of Cultures*. New York: Basic Books.
Gillroy, John M., and Robert Y. Shapiro. (1984) "The Polls: Environmental Protection." *Public Opinion Quarterly* 50:270–79.
Granovetter, Mark. (1985) "Economic Action and Social Structure: The Problem of Embeddedness." *American Journal of Sociology* 91:481–510.
Green, Donald P. (1988) "Self-Interest, Public Opinion, and Mass Political Behavior." Ph.D. diss. University of California, Berkeley.
Hadenius, Axel. (1986) *A Crisis of the Welfare State?* Stockholm: Almqvist and Wiksell International.
Hall, Elaine J., and Myra Marx Ferree. (1986) "Race Differences in Abortion Attitudes." *Public Opinion Quarterly* 50:193–207.
Hammond, Peter. (1975) "Charity: Altruism or Cooperative Egoism?" In Edmund S. Phelps, ed., *Altruism, Morality, and Economic Theory*. New York: Russell Sage.
Hechter, Michael. (1987) *Principles of Group Solidarity*. Berkeley: University of California Press.
Heclo, Hugh, and Henrik Madsen. (1987) *Policy and Politics in Sweden*. Philadelphia: Temple University Press.
Kurz, Mordecai. (1977) "Altruistic Equilibrium." In Bela Belassa and Richard Nelson, eds., *Economic Progress: Private Values and Public Policy*. Amsterdam: North-Holland.
Lewis, Alan. (1982) *The Psychology of Taxation*. New York: St. Martin's Press.
Logue, John, and Eric Einhorn. (1989) *Modern Welfare States*. New York: Praeger.
Margolis, Howard. (1982) *Selfishness, Altruism, and Rationality*. Cambridge: Cambridge University Press.
Milner, Henry. (1989) *Sweden: Social Democracy in Practice*. Oxford: Oxford University Press.
Mitchell, Robert Cameron. (1980) "How 'Soft,' 'Deep,' or 'Left'?: Present Constituencies in the Environmental Movement for Certain World Views." *Natural Resources Journal* 20:345–58.
———. (1988) "Environmental Mobilization in the United States." Unpublished paper.
Mohai, Paul, and Ben W. Twight. (1987) "Age and Environmentalism: An Elaboration of the Buttel Model Using National Survey Evidence." *Social Science Quarterly* 68: 798–815.

Olson, Mancur, Jr. (1965) *The Logic of Collective Action.* Cambridge, MA: Harvard University Press.
Parsons, Talcott. ([1937] 1968) *The Structure of Social Action.* New York: The Free Press.
Rodman, Hyman, Betty Sarvis, and Joy Walker Bonar. (1987) *The Abortion Question.* New York: Columbia University Press.
Sears, David O., R.R. Lau, T.R. Tyler, and H.M. Allen, Jr. (1980) "Self-interest vs. Symbolic Politics in Policy Attitudes." *American Political Science Review* 74:1141–47.
Sen, Amartya K. (1977) "Rational Fools: A Critique of the Behavioral Foundations of Economic Theory." *Philosophy and Public Affairs* 6:317–44.
———. (1982) *Choice, Welfare and Measurement.* Cambridge, MA: MIT Press.
Stephens, John. D. (1979) *The Transition from Capitalism to Socialism.* Urbana: University of Illinois Press.
Svallfors, Stefan. (1989) *Vemälskar v älfardsstaten?* Lund: Arkiv Avhandlingsserie.
Taylor, Michael. (1988) "Rationality and Revolutionary Collective Action." In *Rationality and Revolution.* Cambridge: Cambridge University Press.
Turner, Jonathan H. (1987) "Toward a Sociological Theory of Motivation." *American Sociological Review* 52:15–27.
Verba, Sidney, Steven Kelman, Gary R. Orren, Ichiro Miyake, Joji Watanuki, Ikuo Kabashima, and G. Donald Ferree, Jr. (1987) *Elites and the Idea of Equality.* Cambridge, MA: Harvard University Press.
Wrong, Dennis H. (1961) "The Oversocialized Conception of Man in Modern Sociology." *American Sociological Review* 26:183–93.
Zetterberg, Hans. (1979) "Maturing of the Swedish Welfare State." *Public Opinion* (October/November): 42–47.

5

AMITAI ETZIONI

Contemporary Liberals, Communitarians, and Individual Choices

The recent flurry of exchanges between contemporary liberal philosophers and their communitarian critics points to a theoretical middle ground, directly relevant to economics. The link between economics and social philosophy is not surprising, given the latter's significant role in developing ideas and concepts that still reverberate throughout economic theory (the writings of Adam Smith, J. Bentham, and J.S. Mill, to mention but three). From the rich contemporary discourse, this article focuses on one major issue: a philosophic convergence developing between individualistic, atomistic positions and collectivistic positions. The age-old debate between proponents of liberalism (also referred to as laissez faire conservatives or individualists) and social conservatives (in some eras known simply as conservatives) may be moving toward a synthesis. This synthesis, the ''I&We'' paradigm, leads to rethinking three pivotal concepts of neoclassical economics: the concept of the acting self (the ''chooser''), the basis of choices (preferences), and the right to choose, or, individual liberty.

From the Individualist Camp

In *A Theory of Justice*, perhaps ''the major text of contemporary liberal philosophy,'' Rawls (1971) develops a conception of justice that considers every individual's chosen good (''way of life'') to be ultimately equal. Rawls does not choose any one substantive view of the good over another. He further presumes that each ''person possesses an inviolability founded on justice that even the welfare of society as a whole cannot override'' (p. 3). Rawls arrives at his notion of justice by considering what persons in a modern reformulation of the state of nature, the ''original position,'' would choose as principles of a just society. Individuals in the original position are rational agents stripped of all particular attributes as social beings; they debate behind a "veil of ignorance" that prevents them from knowing their future position in society. Because they are unsure of where they will "end up," they cannot but rationally choose a just (or "fair") order. For example, someone who argued in the original position for a system that favored men might end up as a woman. Rawls's basic philosophic construct thus emphasizes the primacy of the individual, and derives largely from individuals' rational choices, a position familiar to and essentially compatible with the core assumptions of neoclassical economics.[1]

Communitarians, led by Sandel (1982, 1984), Walzer (1983, 1987), and MacIntyre (1984), charge that contemporary liberal philosophers—Rawls, as well as Dworkin (1977) and Nozick (1974)—are preoccupied with individual rights, that they neglect the common good. Sandel (1984, p. 5) characterizes the basic communitarian position as "a view that gives fuller expression to the claims of citizenship and community than the liberal vision allows"—a philosophy to combat "the presence of moral chaos and the absence of common purposes" (Thigpen and Downing 1987, p. 638). Two of the most essential communitarian criticisms, directed toward the liberal conceptions of self and community, will now be examined more closely.

Communitarians argue that liberal philosophy embodies a misleading picture of the nature of persons because it uproots them from their social context. MacIntyre (1984, p. 221), for example, rejects the possibility of theorizing about justice with an abstract self as the subject: "particularity can never be simply left behind or obliterated. The notion of escaping from it into a realm of entirely universal maxims which belong to man as such . . . is an illusion." Sandel argues that Rawls's representative rational agent does not account for our nature as social beings. In Sandel's view, we are not—indeed, cannot be—entirely autonomous agents, "independent from our . . . attachments" (1982, p. 168): such hypothetical individuals are "wholly without character, without moral depth" (p. 172). Persons as we know them, Sandel maintains, are always "situated" or "embedded" in a social context, they are "encumbered" by ties of community: "we cannot conceive of our personhood without reference to our roles as citizens, and as participants in a common life" (1984, p. 5). For Sandel, self-knowledge is impossible outside of the social world: "where the self is unencumbered and essentially disposed [as in the Rawlsian original position], no person is left for *self*-reflection to reflect upon" (1982, p. 180; emphasis in original). The community is a part of us, tangible in "those more or less enduring attachments and commitments which taken together partly define the person I am" (p. 179).

Communitarians decry not only contemporary liberalism's vision of the abstract, isolated self, but also what they charge is a weak conception of community and common good. A "strong" liberal position (which, for example, Nozick espouses), holds that individuals' ends are either competing or independent, "but not in any case complementary . . . [no] one takes account of the good of others"

(Rawls 1971, p. 521). To these "strong" liberals (or libertarians), social arrangements are "a necessary burden," and "the good of community consists solely in the advantages individuals derive from cooperating in pursuit of their egoistic ends" (Sandel 1982, p. 148).

Not all liberals adhere to this strong position. For Rawls, the community is far more than a "necessary burden"; he must be distinguished from Nozick. As Wallach (1987, p. 607, n. 4) states, "[the] belief that Rawls'. . . theory implies an opposition between the preservation of rights and the promotion of the common good is incorrect and unfair, except in some Pickwickian sense. Surely, Rawls' principles of justice comprise his vision of the foundations for the common good." Indeed, Rawls (1971, p. 525) contends that a well-ordered society founded on the principles of justice as fairness possesses "shared final ends and common activities valued for themselves," the two features of "social union." This common end is realizing the principles of justice: "the successful carrying out of just institutions is the shared final end of all the members of society" (p. 527). The entire society finds "satisfaction" in this achievement. Rawls sees just institutions as "good in themselves" because they provide each individual's life with "a more ample and rich structure than it would otherwise have" (p. 528).

What allows Rawls to advance a conception of a common good is an important distinction between substance and procedure. Rawls's common good involves realizing the principles of justice—a *procedural* end. He does not make a substantive claim, does not establish a specific notion about qualities or characteristics that persons or society ought to possess. As Rawls writes:

> this larger plan [the realization of just institutions] *does not establish a dominant end*, such as that of religious unity or the greatest excellence of culture, much less national power and prestige, to which the aims of all individuals and associations are subordinate. The *regulative* public intention is rather that the constitutional order should realize the principles of justice. And this collective activity . . . must be experienced as a good. [1971, p. 528]

Moderate liberal theory thus allows for at least a partial vision of community. Selznick writes that

> [moderate] welfare liberalism strains toward a communitarian perspective. But it is held back by an irrepressible commitment to the idea that individuals must decide for themselves what it means to be free and what ends should be pursued. [1987, p. 447]

Yet this straining continues: both Rawls and Dworkin have modified their positions. According to Wallach (1987, p. 584), Rawls concedes that the representative moral agent's—now called the citizen's—"basic values and characteristics no longer are derived from our intuitions but from an 'overlapping consensus' that undergirds the modern democratic state." Rawls embeds his theory in a distinct kind of community by acknowledging that "social and historical" particulars (specifically, the democratic society reflected in contemporary, advanced, Western industrialized nations) "profoundly affect the requirements of a workable conception of political justice" (1985, p. 225). In kind, Dworkin now considers his fundamental liberal concept of "equal concern and respect" to be historically and politically, i.e., socially embedded (Wallach 1987, p. 608, n. 16). Both through its critics and its apologists, liberal theory has moved (somewhat) toward recognizing an important, fundamental sphere, beyond the individual.

From the Communitarian Camp

While liberalism maintains the primacy of the rights-bearing individual and his or her prerogative to choose the good, communitarians seek to establish a common good that is shared by and transcends each individual. The moral values and traditions[2] of the community, not rational, autonomous agents, provide for communitarians the basis of moral-philosophic discourse. Communitarians replace the autonomous self, independent of its personally chosen ends, with an "embedded" self, a "citizen" bound to a common good: "certain of our [social] roles are partly constitutive of the persons we are . . . [and we are] implicated in the purposes and ends characteristic of those communities" (Sandel 1984, p. 6). But in their attempt to establish common ends within a strong community, communitarians risk submerging what Nozick calls "the fact of our separate existences," and Rawls, "the distinction between persons." This is the communitarian trap: defending the moral standing of the community and the value of shared purposes, but in the process failing to provide any fundamental, principled basis for individual autonomy, and hence, no moral barrier to collectivism.

MacIntyre's work illustrates a strong communitarian position and its problems. In *After Virtue* (1984), MacIntyre argues that the moral foundations of modern society are incoherent, fragmented; he contends that "we have—very largely, if not entirely—lost our comprehension, both theoretical and practical, of morality" (p. 2). The standard of moral community against which he assesses our current condition (the "new dark ages") is the Aristotelian tradition of civic virtue. In the Aristotelian tradition, persons are understood to have "an [i.e., *one*] essential purpose" (p. 58)—a *telos*—that they attain by exercising "virtues" (particularly "acquired human qualities") to achieve the intrinsic goods of "socially established" human activities known as "practices" (pp. 187, 191). Practices include, for example, "arts, sciences, games, politics in the Aristotelian sense [and] the making and sustaining of family life" (p. 188).

Individuals in such a community do not (as liberals would have it) choose their own good; they find a common good as members of a distinct moral order. Each person seeks to acquire the socially prescribed virtues, to discover and achieve their *telos*; and each finds that "my good as a man [or woman] is one and the same as the good of those others with whom I am bound up in human community" (MacIntyre 1984, p. 229). And MacIntyre writes, "What is good for me *has to be* good for one who inhabits these roles'' (p. 220). In rejecting individualism, he goes so far as to state that ''[n]atural or human rights . . . are fictions'' (p. 70). MacIntyre seems bound to Rosenblum's (1984, p. 586) observation that in the communitarian vision, ''there is no conflict between obligation and personal inclination.''

Other communitarians are more moderate in their vision of community, but they, like MacIntyre, affirm its centrality. In *Spheres of Justice* (1983), Walzer advances a new vision of equality, ''complex equality,'' that both depends on and provides for community and shared values. Complex quality arises from ensuring the autonomy of the various spheres of social goods—for example, money should not influence politics; nor should political office bring entrepreneurial opportunities or better medical care. Walzer's notion depends on community, for he argues that a community's shared values about the meanings of goods determine the principles of distributive justice in that community: ''All distributions are just or unjust relative to the social meanings of the goods at stake'' (1983, p. 9). Complex equality provides for community because, Rosenblum argues, Walzer implies that the measure of a community's existence ''is the strength of its members feeling that they belong to a just order'' (1984, p. 586), and in a society of complex equality, ''feelings of relative deprivation are minimized'' (Walzer 1987, p. 169).

In their efforts to restore and nourish the shared values and purposes of the community, communitarians do not adequately provide for individual rights and may not distinguish individuals from their roles in the community. They are not, however, unaware of these problems. Indeed, their efforts to avoid collectivism suggest progress toward a synthesis recognizing both ''the distinction between persons'' and the moral standing of community. MacIntyre, for example, writes: ''The fact that the self has to find its moral identity in and through its membership in communities . . . does not entail that the self has to accept the moral *limitations* of the particularity of those forms of community'' (1984, p. 221). In response, Thigpen and Downing (1987, p. 643) observe that MacIntyre's work does not identify aspects of the self that transcend those limitations. They add:

> Without a source of moral authority outside role requirements, roles are simply *vehicles for the societal imposition of values*. . . . MacIntyre shrinks from this implication of his theory. However, MacIntyre fails to provide a theory of the self which can account for a critical stance against society. [pp. 642–43]

In fact, MacIntyre does provide a source of moral authority outside of roles. He offers that ''a morality of laws'' is a necessary supplement to the virtues. But laws for MacIntyre are important because they address types of behavior that ''injure *the community* to some degree and make its shared project less successful'' (1984, p. 152), not because they protect the individual.

Walzer is more attendant to individual rights and autonomy than is MacIntyre.

Like MacIntyre, he challenges the liberal notion of abstract persons and he declares community "conceivably the most important good" (1983, p. 29). Unlike MacIntyre, though, who favors a community with a single, overarching moral code, Walzer advocates multiple spheres of justice—each sphere relevant to the meanings of particular "social" goods (e.g., money, political power, prestige, education). The result is a pluralism of moral foundations. However, Walzer does not indicate whether the individual is free to choose among these foundations. Further, he does not provide in *Spheres of Justice* a plausible critical basis for individuals to stand apart from consensual social meanings, and hence, existing values, whatever they may be, saying only that "justice requires that society be faithful to disagreements" (1983, p. 313). As Fishkin (1984, p. 757) remarks, Walzer's "theory is threatened with silence in the face of serious moral controversy."

Walzer does allocate a measure of independence and critical latitude to philosophers—whose task he sees as unearthing the implicit unifying consensus lurking behind this plurality—and to social critics, who oppose the "apologetic" interpretations of a community's morality when "we do not live up to the standards that might justify us" (1987, p. 48). The philosopher's role in Walzer is thus akin to that of the proletariat or advanced consciousness in Marx—to ensure a progressive stance. But Walzer still leaves the "other" individuals, the non-philosophers, submerged in the community's norms. This threat of submergence is tempered by Walzer's acknowledgment of a "background" of rights (in fact, he implies that the rights to "life and liberty" [1983, p. xv] might be universal). But this view is, at best, in the background. Characterizing the moderate communitarian position, Selznick (1987, p. 459) concludes that:

> A communitarian morality is not rights-*centered* but it is not opposed to rights or indifferent to them or casual about them. From the perspective of community, however, rights are derivative and secondary.

Thus, for communitarians, the moral force of community is a central—perhaps *the* central—constituent of persons, but it does not comprise their entire being.

The Synthetic Position: "I&We"

The emerging synthesis, as I see it, assumes from the beginning that individual and community *both* command a fundamental moral standing. Rather than attempting to derive an entire philosophical position from one essential assumption—either the moral primacy of the individual or the moral primacy of the community—the synthetic position presupposes that neither individual nor community can be cast in a subordinate role. To stress the interlocking, mutually dependent relationship of individual and community, and to acknowledge my mentor, Martin Buber, I refer to this synthetic position as the "I&We" paradigm (the "We" signifies social, cultural, and political, hence historical and institutional, forces that shape the collective factor—the community; see Etzioni 1988).

Three considerations, empirical, moral-philosophical, and pragmatic, supply this approach. First, while it is possible to theorize about abstract individuals apart from a community, if individuals were actually without community, they would have very few of the attributes commonly associated with the notion of the autonomous person. As a starting point, the discussion has, until now, drawn on widely used concepts that imply that individual and community are two clearly distinct entities. This conceptual separation enables liberals to talk about groups of individuals deciding to form a polity, and to conceive of aggregates of individuals without community, a notion that underlies the utilitarian goal of "the greatest happiness of the greatest number." But a basic observation of sociology and psychology is that *the individual and the community "penetrate" one another and require each other*, and that individuals are not able to function effectively without deep links to others. House et al. (1988) conclude that a lack of social relationships heightens a person's susceptibility to illness. Berelson and Steiner (1964, p. 252), in their overview of more than 1,000 social science studies, remark: "Total isolation is virtually always an intolerable situation for the human adult—even when physical needs are provided for." The experiences of American POWs in isolation during the Korean War (Kinkead 1959) and of solitary explorers and voyagers (for example, Byrd 1938), and the results of numerous laboratory experiments (for example, Appley and Trumbull 1967) all point to the conclusion that to remain viable, psychologically "sound," the individual needs deep bonds with others.

A significant strand of the sociology literature has long contended that community has weakened within modern society, adversely affecting individuals. Fromm (1941) argues that individuals won excessive autonomy as industrialization, or more precisely, urbanization transformed society. He believes that this extreme autonomy was gained at the cost of weakened social bonds in both the family and the community. This excessive independence left the individual highly anxious, even hysterical, looking despairingly for synthetic affiliations to replace the lost bonds. Totalitarian political movements appeal to this malaise because they provide a proxy for such bonds. Similar to urbanization, the decline of religion and "traditional values" left people yearning for firm direction; and demagogues and dictators provided the strong leadership to fill this void. (Riesman [1950] also follows this line of reasoning, arguing that people have become other-directed, seek excessively to conform, and have lost inner orientation.)

Sociology's concept of the mass society also points to the significance of social bonds. This concept does not refer exclusively to great numbers of people, although mass relations are less likely to occur in small populations. Mass society describes the aggregate of individual people, each on his or her own—somewhat like the mass in a crowded railroad station—that has replaced the closely woven social fabric of numerous, small, direct, and stable social units (villages). Cities in a mass society are viewed as places where great numbers of individuals aggregate but tend not to favor solid social bonds. The high level of geographic mobility in the modern era, the constant reshuffling of individuals, is believed to further flatten ties. Religious and ethnic groups are also seen to be losing their influence, as people join large associations that may represent their interests (e.g., labor unions or political parties), but, at least in the United States, often provide little social cohesion. Early critics of mass society saw it as a dangerous result of the transition from a socially ordered world to one of masses open to charismatic demagogic appeal. De Tocqueville's work (1835) supports the argument that maintaining pluralism and the social fabric (conditions that he found in America) enables the preservation of democracy. (While he turned more pessimistic after the 1848 revolution in France, many adopted his earlier position.)

Not all sociologists agree on the adverse effects of modern society. The studies cited here have been challenged, as have most findings in social sciences. For example, Gans (1962), in *The Urban Villagers*, argues contrary to Fromm that there *is* village-like life in modern cities. But in fact, such works do not challenge the consensus of sociological and psychological research, that isolation erodes the mental stability necessary for individuals to form their own judgments and resist undue external pressure and influence. They merely suggest that isolation is not as prevalent in modern society as some sociologists have feared.

Second, the I&We position finds support in that, taken alone, its constituent elements—radical individualism or collectivism—lead to policy conclusions with which even their own advocates are often uncomfortable. As discussed above, those who recognize only the primacy of the community and consider individual rights either secondary and derivative or assert simply that "there are no such rights" (MacIntyre 1984, p. 69), open the door to the intolerance, or worse, the tyranny found not only in totalitarian ideologies but also in absolutist theology and authoritarian political philosophies. Equally unacceptable are positions that focus exclusively on individual rights, particularly the extreme libertarian stand; few endorse policy ideas such as those that allow an individual the right to choose whether or not he or she wishes to defend his or her country (Nozick 1974). This may leave few to defend a country, and such a policy is patently unfair if some opt out, because those who do not serve reap the benefits of protection provided by those who do. The problems of the libertarian position hold for other common goals we all value, from concern for future generations to the condition of the environment. In sum, while there are obviously significant differences in what people regard as the common good(s), few deny the significance of the category.

Finally, there are pragmatic considerations: will the I&We paradigm facilitate the development of both public policy and norms of behavior that members of relevant communities will consider compatible with their principles? For example, what insight might the I&We bring to the pornography debate? Elshtain (1984) explores the philosophical underpinnings of the opposing positions taken by feminists and civil libertarians (as well as neoconservatives) in the debate over the distribution and use of pornography. Feminists have chosen to fight pornography with the same conceptual tool that libertarians use to defend it—the language of individual rights. Feminists argue that pornography violates the civil rights of (individual) women; libertarians respond that limiting pornography violates the right to free speech. Elshtain (1984, p. 18) remarks that "the idea of [individual] 'rights' cannot bear all the weight being placed upon it. But without reference to rights, how can someone press the case for cultural change in a *liberal* society?" She approaches the problem partly from a communitarian perspective, suggesting that communities "should have the power to regulate and to curb open and visible assaults on human dignity" (1984, p. 20). Thus, she confers upon the community a prerogative to determine the boundaries of individual rights in the name of a particular *substantive* good—human dignity. Adding to her criterion of preserving "human dignity," she writes:

> To the extent that pornography is symptomatic of, and helps to further, social disintegration, in which the least powerful (especially children) suffer the most, it [pornography] becomes an appropriate target for action, regulation, and reproof. [1984, p. 20]

Elshtain limits this prerogative, however, by warning that communities "should not seek, as groups avowedly do, to eradicate or condemn either sexual fantasies or erotic representations as such." These individual prerogatives are to be preserved. Sandel buttresses Elshtain, remarking that communitarians might allow a town to bar pornographic bookstores "on the grounds that pornography offends its way of life and the values that sustain it" (1984, p. 6). A line must be drawn on individual expression, then, even though we maintain vigorous concern for individual rights. It remains for another occasion to show that other public policies based on the I&We position are both more plausible and acceptable than those derived from strictly individualistic or collectivist positions.

Further specification of the I&We raises a question that represents a significant restatement—a more productive one, I submit—of the fundamental liberal-communitarian debate: to what extent should the position draw on individual rights, to what degree should it be based on obligations to the community? Wherein lies the proper balance? While no simple guideline suggests itself, the social-historical context provides an important criterion: societies that lean heavily in one direction tend to "correct" in the other. Thus, communist societies have been moving recently to enhance individual liberties. At the same time, American society, believing itself to have tilted too far toward Me-ism and interest-group dominance, has been shifting toward a greater emphasis on national priorities and obligations to the community. Other such "balancing" criteria remain to be evolved.

Now that the basic I&We paradigm has been outlined, its significance for central concepts in neoclassical economics can be explored. We will examine the different views provided by neoclassical economics and the I&We on three fundamental issues: the concepts of self, preferences, and liberty (here conceived of as the freedom to choose).

The Divided Self

Neoclassical economists tend to assume a unitary self, an internally ordered and consistent bundle of urges. This view is essentially compatible with the strong liberal view, which considers the individual as the primary decision-making unit, apart and prior to society. (The "strong" communitarian position would posit an individual entirely constituted by community.)

In contrast, the I&We takes the position of many philosophers and social scientists who have argued (Elster 1985) that it is more reasonable and productive to assume an internally divided self, for example, a self that has preferences and meta-preferences (a position developed by Frankfurt 1985; Hirschman 1984; and McPherson 1984b). The main source of meta-preferences is moral values, which tend to conflict with consumption values, resulting in economic behavior that is inconsistent, guilt-ridden, often cooperative rather than competitive, and otherwise "nonrational" (Etzioni 1988).

These moral values are *in part* supported by social forces (the *We*) and *in part* developed and advanced by individuals. The economic activity of saving typifies the interaction between self-interest and the moral values that deeply affect meta-preferences. The extent to which a person saves reflects in part interest rates, tax levels, and his or her age, but also *values*, such as how deeply the person believes it is unethical to be in debt. Maital (1982, pp. 142–43) points out that the success of credit cards and bank-check credit is attributable to the fact that they allow people to be in debt without experiencing the dissonance between their feeling that "debt is wrong" and their desire to use credit. And personal values, in turn, partly reflect the community. For example, the taboo of debt, an integral component of the American creed before World War II, was deliberately modified by the business community (supported by government) after 1945, to preclude the expected massive unemployment (buying on credit was legitimized).

Neoclassicists do not necessarily deny the existence of community or of value systems. However, they tend to treat these agents as external, "environmental" factors, or as "constraints" on the self. Thus, individuals deal with values as they do with other "cost" factors, and rationally calculate whether or not they wish to "conform" to such values. In contrast, the I&We paradigm assumes that *some* social/moral values are *internalized*, become constitutive elements of the self. Individuals experience these value commitments as *their own*, and these commitments help *shape their preferences*, not merely the constraints under which they operate. That individuals do sometimes calculate whether or not to conform should not be construed as evidence that there is no significant internalization, for persons often engage in both modes of behavior. For example, many feel compelled to (feel that they "must") contribute to charity, but calculate how much to give. Society, then, is not a neoclassical "constraint" but an entity within each person—an integral part of the self.

Preferences: An Unnecessary Blind

As the I&We sees the self partly constituted by community, so it sees the preferences of the self as malleable and affected by that community. This position replaces the neoclassical claim that preferences are constant and given. Take, for example, the observation that Americans have consumed less alcohol during the 1980s than in the preceding decades. Economists, who take preferences as given and unchanging, will look to increased prices, higher drinking ages, and other such factors to explain this change in behavior. However, the price of alcohol has risen less than other prices, and drinking seems to be lower even in states that have not raised their drinking ages. The I&We suggests that the main factors at work are two social movements: one that emphasizes health and fitness (resulting, among other things, in much lower consumption of beef and especially pork, and much higher consumption of seafood), and one that is strongly opposed to drunk driving. The result has been a change in social values and moral climate, and hence in preferences (or "tastes"). For example, in many circles now, it is no longer considered appropriate to be intoxicated.

Several neoclassical economists have objected to such thinking, providing various methodological reasons for arguing that preferences ought to be treated as given and stable, that one ought to assume that only constraints change, at least for the purposes of analysis. One reason neoclassicists offer is that factors that shape preferences are "irrational" and therefore not subject to positive study (Stigler and Becker 1977). It is difficult for a sociologist to understand why economists keep repeating this argument after three generations of sociological studies have indicated that what is irrational from the viewpoint of the actor is not necessarily so from the viewpoint of the observer: *irrational behavior is not random and can be studied.*

Becker and Stigler espouse a particularly extreme version of the position that preferences are to be treated as given: "Preferences are assumed not to change substantially over time, not to be very different between wealthy and poor persons, or even between persons in different societies and cultures" (Becker 1976, p. 5; see also Stigler and Becker 1977, p. 76). Asked to clarify the somewhat ambiguous term "not . . . very different," Becker responded that he means "quite similar" (private communication). In an often-cited article, Stigler and Becker (1977) assert that those who see in addictions a change of taste (people consume some of a good and subsequently increase their taste for it) resort to an "unilluminating 'explanation' " (1977, p. 78), and state that instead, all such changes can be explained by searching for differences in price and income, assuming constant tastes. They then make several assumptions that seem quite farfetched (e.g., people have no time preference) to depict apparently simple instances of acquiring a taste for, say, music, as if tastes represented an investment of time and human capital that "produces" music appreciation. This strained attempt to keep the "lid" on preferences requires rather intricate theorizing and the introduction of numerous ad hoc assumptions, compared to the simple assumption that both tastes and constraints change (Blaug 1984, especially p. 240ff.). Ironically enough, economists prefer simple models, and often reject the scholarship of other social sciences as overly complex.

Liberty: The Freedom to Choose

Whether or not one considers preferences malleable has deep implications for the question of *who* makes the choices, that is, the extent to which individuals are free to follow their own chosen course. At the core of the neoclassical paradigm is the assumption that autonomous individuals are the decision-making unit, the actors. This is far more than a working hypothesis; it is an article of faith grounded in a deep commitment to the value of liberty. The neoclassical assumption of fixed preferences (see Tisdell 1983; Thurow 1983; and McPherson 1984a, pp. 237–38) supports the normative contention that individuals are the best judges of their interest and are able to render decisions that shape both aggregate and collective behavior. Neoclassicists maintain that if one assumes that individuals' preferences can be manipulated or changed by social forces, one undermines the foundations of liberty—the notion that persons are able to render decisions on their own. They thus argue that individuals can and ought to direct the polity (via voting) and shape the allocation of resources within the economy to maximize welfare (via their purchases).

Rothenberg (1966, p. 240) expresses this argument as follows: any particular individual "sometimes" may project only "imperfectly" what is good for him. However, it would require a psychiatrist or spouse to add in the "missing touch"; no outsider possibly could. Rothenberg then argues that such idiosyncrasies disappear in the aggregate, although he does not explain why. But this convenient disappearance is to be expected only if individual idiosyncrasies are random and cancel each other out in the aggregate; in fact, the existence of social groups, social structure, and values indicates there is little reason to assume that preference distribution is random and considerable reason to assume that it is somewhat systematic. Rothenberg concludes that:

> on the level of the population as a whole, no concentrated group of outside evaluators can be found which come anywhere near as close to expressing what is good for them as the individual members of the population themselves. Thus, the set of individual preferences becomes accepted as the arbiter of their own welfare . . . [and] "descriptive individualism in positive economics becomes transformed into normative individualism in welfare economics." [pp. 240–41]

That is, the assumptions of individualistic, fixed preferences employed for the sake of theoretical convenience are used to justify laissez faire positions as if economics had scientifically demonstrated that preferences are indeed individually set and fixed in the real world.

In contrast to neoclassicism, the I&We paradigm's "opening of the preferences," the assumption that they are mutable and malleable, acknowledges the possibility that group processes, societal values, and power relations shape individual preferences significantly, that is, that individual "tastes" largely reflect factors beyond those controlled individually. From this observation, it also follows that individual preferences may be manipulated (say, via persuasive advertising). Hence, people may not act in their own interest or according to their genuine desires. West and McKee (1983, p. 1110) argue that the " 'tastes are different' school presents the greater potential for social manipulation." However, this claim confuses the normative implications of an approach with its descriptive intentions. The I&We does not open individuals to greater manipulation, it merely recognizes that they are in fact susceptible to it.

These observations have several normative implications. First, people are often *not* in full, or even extensive charge of their actions. Therefore, to blame them for the consequences of poor choices because presumably *they* made them, may be seen partly as blaming the victims of manipulation and coercion for choices they did not make. Second, not all of these extraindividual forces are necessarily harmful; hence, criteria must be developed to be able to discriminate between benign and destructive extraindividual influences. For example, few would object to education that stresses the value of liberty.

Last, but not least, the recognition that extraindividual factors affect choices is not a prescription for intervention, for substituting another's judgment (or that of the government's) for that of individuals. It points, for those concerned about the individual's capacity to choose, to the need to establish which factors protect and develop a person's ability to form his or her own decisions, rather than assuming a priori that all individuals have an innate ability to develop and act on their preferences. Only when these major forces are acknowledged by a paradigm, can we begin the systematic search for the conditions that reinforce liberty.

We have already cited findings in sociology and psychology indicating that isolated individuals—the actors of the neoclassical world—are unable to act "freely," while individuals bonded through comprehensive, stable relationships and cohesive groups and communities are much more able to make sensible choices, render judgment—in essence, *are* free. Indeed, from a sociological perspective, the greatest danger to liberty arises when the social moorings of individuals are cut. The atomization of society, the reduction of communities into aggregates of isolated individuals, results in the loss of individuals' competence, capacity to reason, and self-identity; this atomization preceded the rise of twentieth-century totalitarian states. As de Tocqueville so keenly observed, the best protection against such totalitarianism is a pluralistic society enriched by local communities and voluntary associations. The I&We paradigm is as much concerned with individual liberties as is the neoclassical paradigm. However, the I&We assumes that liberty requires a viable—but not overbearing—community, and the paradigm therefore calls for identifying the conditions under which such a community evolves and is sustained.

Notes

The author has drawn, for this chapter, on a previous publication, "Liberals and Communitarians," *Partisan Review*, Spring 1990. He is indebted to Brandt Goldstein for research assistance, and to Kyle Hoffman and John DuVivier for comments on a previous draft.
Note: All emphasis has been added to quotes unless otherwise indicated.

1. *A Theory of Justice* has been interpreted by some as somewhat more communitarian than portrayed here. We maintain, however, that Rawls's view is essentially individualistic, although he has become more concerned with community in recent articles.
2. Commutarians use a variety of terms to describe moral values and other conceptions common among members of a community, including the terms "shared understandings," "practices," and so on.

References

Appley, Mortimer H., and Richard Trumbull, eds. (1967) *Psychological Stress: Issues in Research.* New York: Appleton-Century-Crofts.

Becker, Gary S. (1976) *The Economic Approach to Human Behavior.* Chicago: University of Chicago Press.

Berelson, Bernard, and Gary A. Steiner. (1964) *Human Behavior: An Inventory of Scientific Findings.* New York: Harcourt, Brace and World.

Blaug, Mark. (1984, 1985) *The Methodology of Economics: or How Economists Explain.* 5th & 6th eds. New York: Cambridge University Press.

Byrd, Richard E. (1938) *Alone.* New York: G.B. Putnam's Sons.

Dworkin, Ronald. (1977) *Taking Rights Seriously.* Cambridge, MA: Harvard University Press.

Elshtain, Jean Bethke. (1984) "The New Porn Wars: The Indecent Choice between Censorship and Civil Libertarianism." *New Republic* 190:15–20.

Elster, Jon. (1985) *The Multiple Self.* Cambridge: Cambridge University Press.

Etzioni, Amitai. (1988) *The Moral Dimension: Toward a New Economics.* New York: The Free Press.

Fishkin, James S. (1984) "Defending Equality: The View from the Cave." *Michigan Law Review* 82:755–60.

Frankfurt, Harry G. (1971) "Freedom of the Will and the Concept of the Person." *Journal of Philosophy* 68:5–20.

Fromm, Erich. (1941) *Escape from Freedom.* New York: Farrar and Rinehart.

Gans, Herbert J. (1962) *The Urban Villagers.* New York: The Free Press.

Hirschman, Albert O. (1984) "Against Parsimony: Three Easy Ways of Complicating Some Categories of Economic Discourse." *Bulletin of the American Academy of Arts and Sciences* 37:11–28.

House, James S., Karl R. Landis, and Debra Umberson. (1988) "Social Relationship and Health." *Science* 241:540–45.

Kinkead, Eugene. (1959) *In Every War But One*. New York: Norton.
MacIntyre, Alasdair. (1984) *After Virtue*. 2d ed. Notre Dame, IN: University of Notre Dame Press.
McPherson, Michael S. (1984a) "Limits on Self-Seeking: The Role of Morality in Economic Life." In David C. Colander, ed., *Neoclassical Political Economy*. Cambridge, MA: Harvard University Press.
———. (1984b) "On Schelling, Hirschman and Sen: Revising the Conception of the Self." *Partisan Review* 51 (2): 236–47.
Maital, Shlomo. (1982) *Minds, Markets, and Money*. New York: Basic Books.
Nozick, Robert. (1974) *Anarchy, State and Utopia*. New York: Basic Books.
Rawls, John. (1971) *A Theory of Justice*. Cambridge, MA: The Belknap Press of Harvard University Press.
———. (1985) "Justice as Fairness: Political Not Metaphysical." *Philosophy and Public Affairs* 14:223–51.
Riesman, David. (1950) *The Lonely Crowd*. New Haven, CT: Yale University Press.
Rosenblum, Nancy L. (1984) "Moral Membership in a Postliberal State." *World Politics* 36:581–96.
Rothenberg, Jerome. (1966) *The Economic Evaluation of Urban Renewal*. Washington, DC: Brookings Institution.
Samuelson, Paul A. (1955) *Foundations of Economic Analysis*. Enlarged ed. Cambridge, MA: Harvard University Press.
Sandel, Michael J. (1982) *Liberalism and the Limits of Justice*. Cambridge: Cambridge University Press.
———, ed. (1984) *Liberalism and Its Critics*. New York: New York University Press.
Selznick, Philip. (1987) "The Idea of a Communitarian Morality." *California Law Review* 75:445–63.
Stigler, George J., and Gary S. Becker. (1977) "De Gustibus Non Est Disputandum." *American Economic Review* 67:76–90.
Thigpen, Robert B., and Lyle A. Downing. (1987) "Liberalism and the Communitarian Critique." *American Journal of Political Science* 31:637–55.
Thurow, Lester C. (1983) *Dangerous Currents*. New York: Random House.
Tisdell, C.S. (1983) "Dissent from Value, Preference and Choice Theory in Economics." *International Journal of Social Economy* 10:32–43.
Tocqueville, Alexis de. ([1835–40] 1945) *Democracy in America*. 2 vols. New York: Random House (Vintage Books).
Wallach, John R. (1987) "Liberals, Communitarians, and the Tasks of Political Theory." *Political Theory* 15:581–611.
Walzer, Michael. (1983) *Spheres of Justice*. New York: Basic Books.
———. (1987) *Interpretation and Social Criticism*. Cambridge, MA: Harvard University Press.
West, Edwin G., and Michael McKee. (1983) "De Gustibus Est Disputandum: The Phenomenon of 'Merit Wants' Revisited." *American Economic Review* 73:1110–21.

6

Mark Granovetter

The Social Construction of Economic Institutions

The discipline of economics has seen two strong and, at first glance, mutually inconsistent trends over the past twenty years: a return to dominance by the pure neoclassical tradition, after a period of contention with competing paradigms, and an attempt by economists to greatly broaden their subject matter. This odd, simultaneous narrowing and broadening of perspective has resulted from the virtual demise of institutional economics in its mid-century form.

Earlier contention had resulted from the inability of the neoclassical synthesis to explain the broad institutional framework within which economic transactions took place. The resulting theoretical vacuum was filled by "institutionalist" economists, whose explanations drew on historical, political, sociological, and legal factors, with minimal use of formal economic reasoning. Such widely followed figures as Thorstein Veblen, John Commons, Wesley Clair Mitchell, and John Dunlop often seemed as closely allied to other disciplines as they were to economics.

A broad counterattack began in the 1960s, spearheaded by Gary Becker, who was later joined by many of the best and brightest mathematical economists. They inventively applied rigorous neoclassical arguments to problems previously abandoned to the institutionalists. The expansion of educational institutions, long considered a cultural phenomenon, was declared the outcome of rational individuals investing in their own capacities. Rigid wages and long tenures in internal labor markets were attributed not to social pressures or a "new industrial feudalism" (a metaphor common in 1950s labor economics), but to "implicit contracts" optimally structured by rational employers and employees faced with otherwise difficult problems of shirking and bad faith. Huge wage discrepancies between categories of workers resulted not from restrictions on entry based on differences in group power, but from optimal arrangements for distributing talent in society. Vertical integration occurred not because of the suppliers' "conspiracy against the public" denounced by Adam Smith, but as an arrangement to reduce transaction costs in markets where business had become too complex to conduct between independent units.

This "New Institutional Economics"—distinguished from the old by its reliance on arguments for the economic efficiency of observed institutions—was closely allied to the "New Economic History," which made similar claims for historical settings. Property rights, enclosures, and all manner of political and legal institutions came to be interpreted as the outcome of rational individuals pursuing their self-interest. And these new interpretations were applied even to spheres far from economists' traditional domain, such as the family, crime, altruism, and animal behavior. Representative of the claims of this optimistic new school is Jack Hirshleifer's comment that "economics really does constitute the universal grammar of social science" (1985, p. 53).

One unifying theme of my own book-in-progress, *Society and Economy: The Social Construction of Economic Institutions* (Granovetter, forthcoming), from which this paper draws, is that the new economic imperialism attempts to build an enormous superstructure on a narrow and fragile base. My critique builds on three assumptions, each deriving from the classic sociological tradition: (1) the pursuit of economic goals is accompanied by that of such noneconomic ones as sociability, approval, status, and power; (2) economic action (like all action) is socially situated, and cannot be explained by individual motives alone; it is embedded in ongoing networks of personal relations rather than carried out by atomized actors; and (3) economic institutions (like all institutions) do not arise automatically in some form made inevitable by external circumstances, but are "socially constructed."

The extreme version of methodological individualism that dominates much of modern economics makes it difficult to recognize how economic action is constrained and shaped by the structures of social relations in which all real economic actors are embedded. Economists who want to reform the discipline typically attack its psychology—proposing a more realistic model of decision making. While the psychology in neoclassical models may well be naive, I claim that the main difficulty lies elsewhere: in the neglect of social structure. Psychological revisionism has a following in part because it does not require economists to give up the assumption of atomized actors making decisions in isolation from broader social influences.

My book's title thus intentionally inverts another—*Economy and Society*—already used three times by sociologists: Max Weber (1921), Wilbert Moore (1955), and Talcott Parsons and Neil Smelser (1956). The inversion reflects a different assessment of causal priority, and a more aggressive stance than that of mid-century economic sociology, which operated at the fringes of economic activity, ceding the central topics of production, distribution, and consumption to economists. The more recent generation of economic sociologists, who make up what I call the "New Economic Sociology," have looked much more closely at core economic institutions, and are closer to such intellectual forebears as Emile Durkheim and Max Weber—who regarded economic action as a subordinate and special case of social action—than to the accommodationist stance of mid-century sociologists. In this spirit, the book will focus almost entirely on demonstrating the value of a sociological approach to the central topics of economics.

An important part of this focus is a sociological theory of the construction of economic institutions. Such a theory must make dynamics central, in contrast to most neoclassical economic work on institutions that (like many branches of economics) emphasizes the comparative statics of equilibrium states. Without explicit dynamic argument, we have the irony that economics, despite its devotion to methodological individualism, finds itself with no ready way to explain institutions as the outgrowth of individual action, and so falls back to accounts based on gross features of the environment. There are two such main accounts: culturalism and functionalism.

The former explains economic institutions as arising from cultural beliefs that predispose a group to the observed behavior, as in the claim that the stress in Japanese culture on "organic" unity and hierarchical loyalty produces trouble-free industrial organization. Functionalist accounts argue backwards from the characteristics of institutions to the reason why they must be present. Andrew Schotter (1981) states this principle in unusually candid form—that to understand any social institution requires us to "infer the evolutionary problem that must have existed for the institution as we see it to have developed. Every evolutionary economic problem requires a social institution to solve it" (p. 2). This implicitly assumes a system in equilibrium, since a still-evolving institution might not reveal by inspection what problem it had evolved to solve. These highly elliptical and often tautological culturalist and functionalist accounts become superfluous once the social construction of institutions is properly understood.

It is not enough merely to chip away at the insufficiencies of neoclassical economics. A theoretically persuasive economic sociology must also provide an attractive alternative that improves upon the explanatory power and predictive ability of existing accounts. Though I argue repeatedly against the reductionist methodological individualism of modern economics, I have no taste for the historicist views of some of its other opponents, who suppose that every case is unique and that anything can happen. I stress the contingencies associated with historical background, social structure, and collective action, and the constraints imposed by already existing institutions; but my aim is still the positivist one of finding general principles, correct for all times and places. This requires that the contingencies themselves be systematically explored and incorporated into the theoretical structure. It also requires us to understand under what circumstances economic institutions are malleable by the forces of social structure and collective action, or "locked in" in such a way that these forces are mainly irrelevant. Finally, and closely related to this last issue, a sophisticated economic sociology will not throw the valuable corpus of economic reasoning out the window, but will rather seek to understand how it can be integrated with a social constructionist account of economic institutions, and what the division of labor must therefore be between sociology and economics.

It may be useful here to illustrate the idea of "social construction" in an extremely condensed way, drawing on other discussions (Granovetter, forthcoming) of why and how economic action comes to be the activity of coordinated groups, rather than of isolated individuals. Among the cases I subsume to this theme are how firms and multifirm, multiindustry investment groups emerge in developing countries, and why particular industries take the form they do.

We call those who coordinate the economic activity of otherwise separate individuals "entrepreneurs." But the neoclassical theory of the firm ignores the entrepreneur because, as William Baumol (1968) points out, its model "is essentially an instrument of optimality analysis of well-defined problems, and it is precisely such . . . problems which need no entrepreneur for their solution" (p. 67). It is remarkable that in the recently burgeoning economic literature on why firms exist, exemplified by Oliver Williamson's (1975, 1985) work on "transaction cost economics," entrepreneurs still make no appearance and how firms come to exist receives no attention. Instead, it is assumed that firms emerge when needed to reduce transaction costs. In the functionalist style of the New Institutional Economics, this emergence is taken to be automatic.

But economic institutions do not emerge automatically in response to economic needs. Rather, they are constructed by individuals whose action is both facilitated and constrained by the structure and resources available in the social networks in which they are embedded. We can see this in many accounts from developing countries where firms would greatly reduce transaction costs but cannot be constructed. There are two main difficulties. One is lack of the interpersonal trust required to delegate authority or resources to others. But if such problems of trust are overcome, the fledgling firm is often swamped by the claims of friends and relatives for favors and support. Certain groups, however, such as the overseas Chinese in Southeast Asia, consistently overcome both problems. Trust is available because the community is so close-knit that malfeasance is not only difficult to conceal or execute, but often even hard to imagine. But because membership in social groups rarely overlaps—people belong to small and clear-cut kinship categories and other groups based on home area in China—the number of those whose claims may drain a firm is minimal. In other ethnic groups, by contrast, kinship and other group affiliations are so diffuse that the number with such claims is open-ended; the core group of any firm is then connected to members of too many other groups to put limits on these claims.

When connections of family and friendship are central in firms, the consequent importance of trust strongly limits their expansion. In many countries, this limitation is overcome by alliances of families into what are called in Latin America *grupos económicos*, economic "groups" that operate through one or more firms, in a variety of industries, coordinating their investment and production decisions, often through a bank formed through and closely identified with the group. Such groups have a strong and sometimes dominating role in the economies of these countries,[1] and have typically originated in relations of interpersonal trust based on similar personal or ethnic background. In some cases, the network of personal relations that initially builds the group becomes formalized into institutional patterns such as holding companies. And then the shape of these institutions results more from the original structure of personal relations than from the exigencies of the market: they are, in effect, congealed social networks. Economists have argued that such groups are responses to market imperfections in less developed countries, and will fade out as more "sophisticated" and impersonal arrangements are developed. But this neglects the fact that these groups typically operate in the most advanced industrial sectors of such countries and that many patterns of activity in advanced industrial societies look remarkably similar.[2]

Just as for firms and economic groups, how industries are organized is a social construction that often might have been otherwise. A case in point is the electrical utility industry in the United States from its inception in the 1880s to about 1930.[3] In 1885, certain alternatives to the current, investor-owned form of the industry appeared quite feasible: e.g., public ownership of all electrical utilities, or private generation of electric power by each large industrial company, which would have consigned utility companies to a minor role. Why did these not occur?

In the earliest stage, when there was no standard way to meet the demand for electricity, the personal networks of a few major individuals were crucial. Samuel Insull arrived in Chicago in 1894 to take over a small, new company, Chicago Edison, and brought with him a unique set of personal ties: to financiers in both Chicago and London, to local political leaders, to inventors in both the United States and Great Britain. Many of these ties had been forged as the result of his thirteen-year association with Thomas Edison. His combination of financial and technical expertise and political connections allowed him to assemble capital, political favors, and ways of operating that other utility companies had found impossible to implement, even though some were well aware of their potential.

Later, Insull and others encouraged regulation by states and developed the holding company form. Soon, the resulting network of firms, holding companies, and regulators congealed. Personal networks still mattered, but only those of people central in the holding companies. By the 1920s the institutional forms were in place, and the outcome that we now see in the industry was already recognizable.

Here, as for firms and *grupos económicos*, stable economic institutions begin as accretions of activity patterns around personal networks. Their structure reflects that of the networks, and even when those are no longer in place, the institutions take on a life of their own that limits the forms that future ones can take; they become "locked in."[4] Thus, economic problems and technology do not call forth organizational outcomes in some automatic and unconditional way. Instead, these economic conditions restrict the possibilities. Then, individual and collective action, channeled through existing personal networks, determine which possibility actually occurs. So even in identical economic and technical conditions, outcomes may differ dramatically if social structures are different. Where firms are in some sense "called for" by market conditions, they still may not arise if no group's social structure can sustain them; interindustry "groups" may or may not arise in favorable economic conditions, depending on the structure of connections among important families; and industries may be configured in quite different ways, depending on the shapes of the interpersonal networks of leading actors.

But this is far from saying that anything can happen; in all the cases, there are only a few major possibilities. In the language of economic dynamics, these situations have multiple stable equilibria, and so are economically underdetermined. Outcomes can only be understood when initial and boundary conditions are considered—namely, the social structure in which economic action is embedded. But this indicates one occasion for interdisciplinary cooperation. Without economic arguments on how markets and incentives were structured, it would be hard to understand how the set of alternative outcomes was determined. This, as well as social structure, is an important part of the picture, and it is only by taking both into account that we can understand the outcomes we see.

Notes

1. These groups have been studied most closely in Argentina, Mexico, (pre-Sandinista) Nicaragua, Chile, Pakistan, India, and Greece.

2. Some examples are the *zaibatsu* of prewar Japan, the *chaebol* of South Korea, and the economic groups in the very economically successful German state of Baden-Wurttemburg.

3. For this example, I rely heavily on the work of sociologist Patrick McGuire. In addition to the account that will appear in Granovetter (forthcoming), I am collaborating with McGuire and sociologist Michael Schwartz on a more detailed treatment of the social construction of this industry.

4. The idea that institutions may become "locked in" despite the possible greater efficiency of other conceivable forms is a generalization of the argument for lock-in of inefficient technologies by economic historians Paul David (1986) and Brian Arthur (1989). Their line of argument parallels that in industrial organization on "first-mover" advantage.

References

Arthur, Brian. (1989) "Competing Technologies, Increasing Returns, and Lock-in by Historical Events." *Economic Journal* 99, no. 394 (March): 116–31.

Baumol, William. (1968) "Entrepreneurship and Economic Theory." *American Economic Review* 58 (May): 64–71.

David, Paul. (1986) "Understanding the Necessity of QWERTY." In William Parker, ed., *Economic History and the Modern Economist*, pp. 30–49. London: Blackwell.

Granovetter, Mark. (Forthcoming) *Society and Economy: The Social Construction of Economic Institutions*. Cambridge, MA: Harvard University Press.

Hirshleifer, Jack. (1985) "The Expanding Domain of Economics." *American Economic Review* 75(6):53–68.

Moore, Wilbert. (1955) *Economy and Society*. New York: Doubleday.

Parsons, Talcott, and Neil J. Smelser. (1956) *Economy and Society: A Study in the Integration of Economic and Social Theory*. London: Routledge & Kegan Paul.

Schotter, Andrew. (1981) *Economic Theory of Social Institutions*. Cambridge: Cambridge University Press.

Weber, Max. (1921) *Economy and Society*. Edited and translated by Guenther Roth and Claus Wittich (1968). New York: Bedminster Press.

Williamson, Oliver. (1975) *Markets and Hierarchies*. New York: The Free Press.

———. (1985) *The Economic Institutions of Capitalism*. New York: The Free Press.

III

Utility, Goals, and Values

7

F. THOMAS JUSTER

Rethinking Utility Theory

A Summary Statement

Economists have had a longstanding concern with understanding and modeling the behavior of consumers, both in the narrow sense of their behavior as buyers of goods and services in product markets and as suppliers of services in labor markets, and in the broader sense of their collective purchases of public goods—schools and roads, air and water quality, national security, etc. Analysis of these issues has been cast as a constrained optimization problem: consumers are perceived as choosing a particular bundle of goods and services, or a combination of work and leisure hours, or a set of taxes and public goods, that represents the optimum mix subject to the constraints of income and prices.

This paper provides a brief history of the development of utility theory, and suggests a reconceptualization of the basic sources of utility. The new formulation extends the range of interesting and important phenomena encompassed by the theory, reexamines the role of goods and services in producing utility, and simplifies the conceptual structure—at the cost of complicating the measurement problem as well as the analytic properties of the system. Some recent data reflecting the new conceptual structure are examined, and we note some implications of the theory and data for both scientific and policy issues.

Goods

The original concept of utility, developed principally by the moral philosopher Jeremy Bentham in the late eighteenth century and formally integrated into the analysis of economic problems by Jevons, Menger, and Walras in the 1870s, was that it represented a cardinally measurable psychological flow of satisfactions attached to goods and services purchased in the market: consuming a mutton chop yields x utils of satisfaction or pleasure.[1] The utility function for the consumption of good x was presumed to be independent of the function for good *y*, and consumers were visualized as equating the utility of the last unit of each good purchased (the marginal utility) with its price.

The idea of cardinally measurable utility, independence of the utility functions for different goods, and declining marginal utility gradually eroded as economists began to recognize that not only was there little scientific underpinning to the notion that consumers could make precise assessments of the psychological satisfactions associated with utility (or that psychologists had satisfactory theories that could explain utility), but more importantly, that the assumption of cardinally measurable utility was not essential to an explanation of economic behavior. Thus, utility as a quantitative measure of psychological satisfaction began to be replaced by the simpler notion that consumers (for whatever reason) had preferences for one combination of goods over another, and that these preferences (or preference orderings) could be revealed by observing the choices that consumers made in the marketplace.

The idea that utility was constrained by total money income, and that the utility maximization problem consisted of deciding which commodities to consume, given their prices and the household's income, was significantly broadened when it became recognized that money income itself was a choice variable, and that consumers were really maximizing the utility derived jointly from a combination of goods and leisure (Robbins 1930; Hicks 1963). In effect, in earlier discussions, money income had been implicitly treated as an exogenous variable, essentially given to the consumer unit.[2] In later discussion, wage *rates* were the exogenous variable and money income was endogenously determined by the combination of the wage rate and the choice variable of work hours.[3] Thus, the utility function had consumers first choosing how much income to earn and how much leisure to consume, then deciding on the combination of goods and services to purchase with their money income. The constraints were that total money income fixed the total value of consumption (including future consumption or saving), and that total available time fixed the sum of labor market hours and leisure hours—with leisure defined to include all activities except work for pay in the market. It is worth noting that in these simple models, the utility function contains one item that reflects market choices (the consumption of goods and services) and a second that reflects nonmarket activities (the consumption of leisure). Thus, the model has consumers supplying labor to the market up to the point where the income produced by the last unit of labor produces just enough utility to overcome the distaste for work. In effect, the model treats income as producing positive utility, leisure activities as producing positive utility, but work activity as producing negative utility, at least at the margin of choice.[4]

Another interesting feature of these utility maximization models is that the earlier switch from cardinally measurable utility to ordinally measured preferences, while perhaps reflecting a more realistic assessment of the way consumers actually made choices,[5] also significantly modified the way in which economists thought about intertemporal (i.e., multiperiod) utility maximization. In the early (Bentham, etc.) theoretical structure, intertemporal utility maximization was accomplished by including in the current period utility function a particular representation of future utility—the current pleasure obtained by contemplating (savoring) future consumption (Loewenstein 1985). In that model, consumers could make choices about giving up current consumption to get consumption in the future, but all utility maximization took place during the current period: future consumption yielded utility only in terms of the current satisfaction obtained from anticipation of a future event.

When preference ordering replaced marginal utility, intertemporal utility maximization took the form of consumers optimizing over time by equating (at the margin) the flow of satisfaction yielded by current consumption with the future flow of satisfaction yielded by future consumption, not by equating the satisfaction from present consumption with the current satisfaction from savoring the prospect of future consumption. Thus, economists thought of future consumption as yielding utility only when it actually took place, and since future satisfactions were generally thought to be worth less than current ones, they had to be discounted to reflect their futurity.[6]

"Commodities" and Leisure

The notion that goods purchased in the market and leisure were the right way to think about utility functions was significantly modified by the household production framework introduced by Becker in the middle 1960s (Becker 1965; Mincer 1963; Michael and Becker 1973; Nerlove 1974).[7] Becker extended the notion of productive activity to include the proposition that households used elements of their own time as inputs to the production process, along with goods purchased in the market, to produce outputs ("commodities") that were the ultimate objects of utility. Thus, time could be allocated directly to the market, where it yielded income and thus command over goods and services, it could be used within the household to produce commodities, or it could be used as leisure (treated as a commodity in the Becker framework). The ultimate sources of utility, in this model, were commodities produced within the household—meals, children of certain quantity and quality, going to plays, etc., which typically involved the joint inputs of market-purchased goods and services plus the household's own time.

These "commodities" could be thought of as having shadow prices—the cost of the market-produced input plus the value (wage rate) of the time of household members. Thus, certain types of commodities were expensive to produce for certain types of households—child quantity and quality, for example, would be an expensive commodity to produce for households with highly educated mothers, since the opportunity cost of their market time would be relatively high. And given family income, adults with high (actual or potential) wage rates would tend to stay away from time-intensive activities in favor of goods-intensive ones (e.g., they would play squash rather than golf), while adults with low wage rates would favor time-intensive over goods-intensive activities (e.g., they would serve as community volunteers).

In this model, it is still true that household well-being is a joint function of consumption and leisure. However, instead of the relevant goods being only those produced in the market and reflected in, say, the Gross National Product, consumption was broadened to include a range of outputs that reflected nonmarket production as well as market production. Thus, a wider range of goods and services was included in the notion of commodities.

A major difficulty with this model was pointed out by Pollak and Wachter in 1975. They argued that the shadow prices in the household production model were indeterminate except under special conditions that were unlikely to hold. The household production function in which the time of household members is used to produce "commodities" specifies the wage rate as the cost of nonmarket production time. That specification assumes that consumers do not have any preference for the way in which their time is spent, quite apart from any preferences they may have for the output resulting from those inputs of time. Since the outputs and time use preferences are joint products of activity, Pollak and Wachter concluded that the system could not be uniquely solved for shadow prices, absent information about the intrinsic preferences of household members for time spent in various household production tasks.

Where Do We Go from Here?

These developments can be thought of as reflecting a broadening of utility theory in terms of the potential sources of human satisfaction. The focus on goods found in the eighteenth- and nineteenth-century writers came to include goods and leisure in the early twentieth century, and to include nonmarket "commodities" and leisure during the last few decades.[8] At the same time, there was a gradual but eventually complete stripping away of any notion that the theory had (or needed) any cardinally measurable utility content—it required only preference orderings that could be inferred from observed choices.

While the ordinalist view of utility is clearly the dominant strain of thinking among economists, the idea of direct measurement of utility, which implies cardinality, has always lurked uneasily in the background—even when the more vocal (rigorous?) proponents of ordinality thought that it had been stamped out as unnecessary (on the Occam's Razor principle) for models of consumer behavior. Even Hicks, who along with Allen "slit the throat of diminishing marginal utility" (1934, p. 4), came to think that (cardinally measurable) marginal utility was a better description of what consumers actually did than the idea of their equating marginal rates of substitution with price ratios (1976). Stigler and Becker, hardly cardinalist heretics, revived the notion of households as minifactories producing a stream of utility (1977)—just like real factories producing a stream of (cardinally measurable?) profits. And Pollak and Wachter (1975) suggested that the shadow prices for "commodities" in the household production framework could not be determined because these commodity prices were not exogenous to any household that had (cardinally measurable?) preferences over their use of time in household production.

This paper argues for the importance of direct (cardinal) measurement of utility, and outlines a conceptual framework in which such measurements play a central role. First, it is argued that a properly conceptualized utility theory implies measurements that cannot be inferred from behavior but must be obtained directly from consumers, and that this conceptualization can help to predict behavior that is not otherwise understandable. Second, the measurements suggested by this conceptualization relate directly to consumer well-being. Understanding what determines well-being, and how it is distributed among the population, is important in its own right independently of any behavioral implications.

Utility, Activities, and Goods

A little reflection (introspection, actually) on the nature of production and consumption, and on the characteristics of various sources of utility or satisfaction, provides some helpful clues about how the utility maximization problem might best be reformulated. Consumers do not generally get utility directly from any of the goods and services purchased in the market and presumed to enter the utility function. The purchase of food, clothing, housing, automobiles, or theater tickets does not do much for one's utility, nor does cooking food, cleaning and straightening the house, using an automobile to get from home to the theater, or disciplining a child. But utility is obtained directly from activities like eating meals (where the level of utility depends partly on the quality of the food), seeing a play (where the level of utility depends partly on the quality of the acting), entertaining friends in one's home (where the level of utility depends partly on the quality of the home and its furnishings), taking one's child on an outing, etc.

These illustrative comments suggest some general principles about the relation between goods, activities, and utility:

1. Utility flows are always derived from activities (eating, socializing, playing tennis, seeing a play, etc.).
2. The amount of utility derived from an activity depends partly on the amount of goods associated with it (quality and variety of food, clothing, housing, sporting equipment, etc.).
3. Some of the goods that influence the utility from activities are flows consumed during the activity (food, theater tickets), but many are capital stocks that yield service flows (housing, clothes, cars, television sets).

Are there aspects of utility that are not associated with activities of one kind or another? The answer seems to be yes. I do not necessarily have to be driving a

Porsche, and thus obtaining satisfaction from the process, in order to derive utility from owning one. I do not necessarily have to engage in conversation or interaction with my wife or children to derive satisfaction from the existence of a strong family relationship. I am likely to be more pleased about life generally if I think that the society I live in is characterized by equity in the tax laws, in the administration of justice, in the distribution of income, and by equality of opportunity. And so on.

Can we systematize these illustrative notions about utility, how it is produced, and how it might be assessed? Perhaps. A system with these general characteristics has been outlined, at least in embryonic form, in Juster, Courant, and Dow (1981a, 1981b, 1985), where the basic idea spelled out is that society can be thought of as having only two fundamental resources—the stock of wealth inherited from past productive activity and not consumed, and the available time of all members of society. Wealth is used here in a substantially broader sense than the tangible capital stock used in the production of goods and services in the market. While such wealth is clearly part of the total, a broader notion of wealth incorporates human capital assets (skills, health status), stocks of organizational capital (networks of associations within business organizations, within families, within neighborhoods, etc.), stocks of sociopolitical assets (the judicial system, the representational system, etc.), stocks of environmental assets (natural resource endowments, air and water quality), and stocks of abstract knowledge not embodied in existing capital equipment. Thus, the set of stocks relevant to the generation of utility includes any asset that conditions either the efficiency of, or the satisfactions associated with, various time uses.

In this model, time can be used as in the household production literature—for the production of nonmarket goods and services, for personal maintenance activities, or for leisure activities. The general idea is that the production of goods and services in the market is determined by capital stocks and labor market time, that market goods, nonmarket time, and stocks of capital affect the efficiency with which households can produce nonmarket commodities, and that flows of market goods and services and of household-produced commodities, along with capital stocks, condition the satisfactions (let us call them process benefits) associated with activities.

One of the interesting features of this way of thinking about the utility function is that all of the tangible and intangible outputs of various production processes, whether they take place in the market or within households, represent inputs into the intrinsic satisfactions (process benefits) associated with one or another activity, or else they represent goods and services that add to the stock of wealth available for the production of future satisfactions. But what is not so obvious is that the flows of all tangible or intangible products, which represent the extrinsic outputs from productive activity, disappear from the utility function, either because they are fully represented by the process benefits obtained from one or another activity or because they add to capital stocks.

An illustration may make the point clearer. Labor market time and capital stocks go into the production of food available in grocery stores, the time of household members in conjunction with market-produced food goes into the production of meals, and meals go into the production of two further types of output—the process benefits from eating and any change in health status associated with nourishment. Should we count the process benefits from eating along with the nonmarket time and household stocks that transform raw food into meals, or the labor market time and business capital stocks that go into the production of raw food? The answer seems to be no, anymore than we would include in GNP the automobile that was eventually purchased by consumers, the component parts like fenders and wheels, the steel that went into the fenders and the rubber that went into the tires, and the iron ore that went into the steel. That would clearly be double counting—once we count the car, we ought not to count the components as well. The solution, standard in National Income accounting, is to exclude from net output any purchased product that represents a production input, and to count only the value added at each stage of production.

But that is no more double counting than adding up the process benefits from eating along with the time and resources that go into the transformation of food into meals or the time and resources that go into the production of food. If we have properly measured the process benefits associated with eating meals, we have also measured the contribution to utility of the intermediate tangible outcomes (meals and raw food) as well. But what we have *not* measured are any process benefits associated with the various production processes, along with the fact that eating meals is not only a source of current utility but may also be a source of future utility because it has a possible impact on health status. In short, the flow of process benefit is the value-added equivalent of the household production function.

Generalizing this proposition across all production activities leads to the conclusion that accurate measurement of the process benefits associated with all activities fully comprehends the sources of current utility from goods and commodities, and adding to that any current or future satisfaction associated with the various capital stocks in the system fully comprehends all potential sources of utility.

Not only is it true that all of the tangible product flows of society enter the utility function by conditioning the process benefits from some activity, but it is also true than every activity contains an element of process benefits. Economists have typically thought of process benefits as largely associated with leisure—after all, the conventional wisdom is that consumers work in order to earn income so that they can enjoy leisure. But production activity, both within the market and the home, also produces a flow of process benefits (which may be negative, if one thinks of utility as having a true zero point). The only difference between production activities and consumption activities is that production activities have both a flow of extrinsic products as well as a flow of process benefits, while many leisure activities can be thought of as having only the latter.[9]

Assume for the moment that it is logically consistent to think about utility and well-being as fully represented by the flow of process benefits associated with a comprehensive set of activities, in addition to the current and future satisfactions represented by various kinds of capital stock. Does that framework tell us anything useful? More importantly, is there any way in which one could imagine implementing the idea empirically?

Direct Measurements of Utility

The division of utility into a component associated with time uses and another component associated with capital stocks of one kind or another is a useful starting point. We can clearly measure time uses, at least in principle. Whether we can measure the utility associated with time uses is another question. In principle, one could imagine measurements taking the form of attaching a perfectly calibrated "utility meter" to the appropriate part of a consumer's brain, and monitoring the level of utility associated with activity as consumers proceed to do various things throughout the day and the year. That procedure depends, of course, on the existence of a utility meter that uniquely maps actual utility; otherwise, it would be open to the objection that some characteristic of brain cell activity was being monitored, without it necessarily having anything to do with utility.[10]

Assume that problem away for the moment. It is obviously possible to measure utility in the population at large either by continuous monitoring of the utility flows associated with activities, or by sampling utility at randomly selected intervals of time throughout the day or the year. That procedure would not get around any of the problems associated with interpersonal utility comparisons, unless one is willing to assume that the brain monitor utilized an exactly equivalent utility metrics across all individuals. But the answer seems to be that, provided one can measure activities and measure the utilities associated with activities, the part of utility associated with activities could in principle be analyzed.

The part of utility associated with capital stocks is equally problematic. It is clear enough that this is a potentially important component of utility, and it may be that the utility involved in the existence or ownership of capital stocks is harder to capture because it has the character of a pervasive sense of satisfaction arising from some state of the world rather than being associated with some process or activity. But one could easily imagine a survey that asked consumers about the state of their marriage, the state of their durable goods, their perception of the state of the world, their satisfaction with the income distribution, etc.

In fact, both types of measurement actually exist. As a by-product of a national survey of time use among American households, motivated principally by a desire to understand the character of nonmarket activities in households, we obtained not only measurements of actual time uses among a probability sample of U.S. consumers, but also a measure of the process benefits associated with a subset of activities. The data do not come very close to representing a "utility meter" reading of the sort described above, and they do not represent the instantaneous satisfaction obtained from momentary activities. Rather, they represent statements about the average amount of satisfaction from activities with descriptive labels like watching television, going to the movies, playing sports or games, cleaning the house, working at a job, taking care of children, etc. Thus, they are not quite mapped into instantaneous utilities associated with current activities.

As to the capital stocks, sociologists and social psychologists (and even a few economists) have in recent decades developed a keen interest in what are called "quality of life" measurements. On inspection, these turn out to be largely measures of satisfaction with various kinds of "capital stocks," defined broadly as above, although some of them are closer to satisfaction with activities than with capital stocks. But reported satisfaction with marriage, friendships, financial security, durable good stocks, etc., has been examined in a series of studies (Campbell, Converse, and Rogers 1976; Bradburn 1965; Cantril and Roll 1971; Andrews and Withey 1976; Juster, Courant, and Dow 1981a).[11]

Whether this way of thinking about well-being is useful or not has to be determined in the usual way—those who think it is useful produce analyses based on it, and those analyses either influence the way other economists think about related problems or they do not. But some interesting insights can be obtained from the existing measurement. We focus on the activity measurements, and on the intrinsic satisfactions associated with them. Measurement of the capital stock utility flows is a different story, and is ignored in this paper.

As indicated, relatively crude data of this sort were obtained in the mid-1970s and the early 1980s, as part of national studies of time allocation among American households. Twenty-four-hour time diary data were obtained from a random sample of American adults. Respondents were also asked to rate a comprehensive list of activities on a ten to zero scale, with ten characterizing an activity from which the respondent derived a great deal of satisfaction (enjoyment was the actual term), zero an activity associated with a good deal of distaste ("dislike" was the actual term), and five an activity to which respondents were indifferent—"don't care about it one way or the other" was the description. On a cardinal utility scale, five can be thought of as equivalent to a zero point, with higher numbers being positive and lower numbers negative.

The basic data are displayed in Table 7.1, ordered by the mean population values of the process benefit scores in the mid-1970s survey. We show activity categories, mean process benefits in 1975 and 1982, the "reliability" proportion (described below), and the mean amount of time spent on the activity, measured in hours per day. Not all activities are included (e.g., sleep and personal care are

Table 7.1

Basic Process Benefit Data Reported by Respondents

Activity	N	Mean process benefit score 1975	Mean process benefit score 1982	"Reliability" proportion	Time spent in 1975 (hours/day)
Talking with children	312	9.16	8.98	0.80	0.07
Care of children	312	8.87	8.74	0.82	0.50
Trips with children	311	8.87	8.72	0.74	0.03
Games with children	308	8.62	8.24	0.74	0.05
Talking with friends	678	8.38	8.27	0.66	0.28
Going on trips, outings	657	8.24	8.17	0.67	0.75
Job	397	8.02	7.79	0.72	5.03
Home entertainment	662	7.76	7.54	0.62	0.79
Reading books, magazines	668	7.60	7.49	0.67	0.31
Going to church	631	7.23	7.28	0.66	0.17
Reading newspapers	675	7.17	7.10	0.63	0.24
Making things for house	635	6.78	6.47	0.57	0.17
Playing sports	606	6.76	6.23	0.56	0.12
Going to movies, plays	629	6.65	6.38	0.52	0.10
Gardening	642	6.55	6.27	0.60	0.15
Cooking	668	6.17	6.13	0.60	0.70
Television	677	5.93	6.00	0.62	2.01
Other shopping	673	5.69	5.30	0.57	0.02
Housing repairs and alt.	635	5.11	4.94	0.57	0.19
Work, school orgs.	587	5.00	5.13	0.50	0.27
Grocery shopping	673	4.57	4.55	0.56	0.34
Cleaning house	672	4.22	4.18	0.57	1.13

Source: Basic data from Juster, "Preferences for Work and Leisure," in Juster and Stafford (1985).
Note: The "reliability" proportion is the fraction of the sample giving the same response to the process benefits question, plus or minus one scale point, from different surveys taken six months apart in 1982.

excluded), hence the total time is less than twenty-four hours. These data provide a number of points of interest.

1. The rank ordering and the quantitative differences among activities indicate considerable stability in the process benefits from activities. There is hardly any change in rank ordering between two periods seven years apart, and the mean values across the population are very similar.
2. The reliability of the data at the level of the individual is quite high—the proportion who gave the same scale response plus or minus one, separated by a six-month span in the 1982 study, ranges from half the sample to over 80 percent.

3. Activities that are interactive—i.e., that involve other people—tend to dominate the top half of the rankings, while activities that are not interactive or less interactive tend to dominate the bottom half of the rankings.
4. The process benefits associated with paid employment outrank all but a few leisure activities, and clearly have a mean value that is above the mean for all leisure activities, the latter weighted by actual time spent in the activity.
5. The process benefits associated with work in the home, with the exception of childcare, tend to rank at the bottom of the list, and clearly have a mean value well below that of paid employment.

The chief surprise in these data is the next-to-last finding—that average process benefits from work outrank average process benefits from leisure. After all, standard utility theory has always argued that it is the combination of income from work (the extrinsic rewards) plus the intrinsic rewards from leisure that go into the utility function, and that the intrinsic rewards from work are negative—people need to be induced to work by the payment of wages, and the function of wages is to overcome the distaste for work.[12] But these data present quite a different picture. They suggest that the intrinsic rewards from work are, on average, at least as high as the intrinsic rewards from leisure. If that result is taken at face value, it suggests that economists need to do a major rethinking of the elements that go into individual utility functions.[13]

Since that result is counterintuitive, we designed some methodological tests of the intrinsic satisfaction data in the study conducted in the early 1980s. Basically, we took two activities—work for pay in the market, and cleaning the house—and tried to determine whether the responses we were getting could be explained by the respondent's inability to distinguish extrinsic from intrinsic rewards. That is, were the relatively high rankings of work for pay on the process benefits scale a simple consequence of the fact that our respondents were reporting that they liked their jobs because they were well paid? The test was to ask respondents, after they had provided scale values for paid work and cleaning the house, why they had made the judgments they had just given us? Specifically, we asked: What is it about your job, or about cleaning the house, that makes you rate it a _____? Responses were then coded into various categories, some clearly reflecting extrinsic rather than intrinsic rewards, some equally clearly reflecting intrinsic rewards only.

Statistical tests on the data showed unambiguously that the intrinsic satisfactions reported by respondents as associated with paid employment were not contaminated because respondents mixed up some of the extrinsic rewards with the intrinsic ones. People who gave relatively high scores to paid employment reported that they were thinking about the nonmonetary aspects of the work environment—the people they worked with, the challenge or learning opportunities involved, the amount of supervision and responsibility, whether the job was boring or repetitious, etc. Reference to the financial characteristics of the job did not distinguish respondents who provided relatively high scores from those who provided relatively low scores (Juster 1985).

Interestingly enough, while contamination of the intrinsic satisfaction data with extrinsic reward considerations did not appear to be a factor in interpreting the paid employment responses, it was clearly a major factor in explaining responses to the "cleaning the house" data. When asked why they had provided the ranking they did, the single most important factor for those who provided relatively high rankings was that they "felt good about having a clean house." That is clearly an extrinsic reward, not a process benefit. Adjusting the data for respondents who thus misinterpreted the question dropped the overall population mean score by a full scale point, thus making the gap between the process benefits from paid employment with those from work in the home even larger than shown by the data in the table.

Some Implications

Is there any independent evidence suggesting that these results reflect a real phenomenon rather than some kind of socially determined intrinsic satisfaction story derived from a self-report scale? To begin with, we have already noted that these results do not necessarily negate the proposition that people are willing to trade work for leisure at the margin. The data clearly relate to average process benefits from particular activities, and do not represent marginal process benefits—the satisfaction obtained from the last minute or hour of a particular activity. Thus, process benefits from work could be very high on average, but could be very low at the margin—that would be true if the function dropped off very sharply as work hours increased. Thus, the data can be interpreted as saying that many individuals prefer an activity pattern that includes an element of work for pay, not that individuals generally prefer to work longer hours than they now do. The data are thus not inconsistent with the observed long-term decline in work hours and the associated growth in leisure hours.[14]

Moreover, the notion that intrinsic rewards from work are relatively high helps to explain a number of anomalies that represent puzzles for the conventional analysis of utility maximizing behavior:

- A number of studies have looked at what happens to people who win major prizes in lotteries. The typical result is that most people continue to work, often at jobs that contribute only marginally to their total income, taking account of the value of the lottery prize.
- Of the individuals and families eligible for various forms of welfare assistance, a substantial fraction choose not to avail themselves of welfare payments and opt instead to work at jobs that yield total income no better than that obtainable through welfare. Such observations have often been explained on the grounds that people are ill informed, or that they want to avoid the social stigma

attached to welfare, or that they are investing in future income by building up labor market experience. But a simpler explanation is that people have a strong preference for work as an activity.

• Over the last sixty or so years, there has been a strong and consistent growth in women's participation in the labor force, usually explained in economic models as the consequence of the relative growth in market wage rates compared to the value of nonmarket activities. That story has always been unsatisfactory. Labor force participation growth rates have been just as strong in periods when wage rates have been rising slowly or not at all as when wage rates have been rising rapidly, and there has never been any evidence that the gap between productivity in the market and productivity in the home has been increasing. A simpler explanation is that work in the market is associated with significant intrinsic rewards, and quite possibly that these rewards have been shifting upward over time as working wives have become a more socially acceptable phenomenon.

The general proposition advanced here—that the intrinsic rewards from activities are an essential ingredient in individual and household utility functions—has other potentially far-reaching implications for a variety of economic and social phenomena. For example, it is widely argued that many work environments could be more efficiently organized on a cottage industry basis—electronic communications devices make it unnecessary for people to travel to a common work location, and both communication and decision-making processes can conserve on time by creating technically efficient work environments in people's homes. The evidence that interactive activities are more strongly preferred than noninteractive ones makes this vision of the future a dubious one, except for special occasions and special circumstances. Generally speaking, most members of the work force are unlikely to find that type of work environment very satisfactory, since it precludes the kind of interaction that appears to underlie the preference data. A good many commercial enterprises have adopted the view that serving consumers with technology is a more efficient way to provide a variety of services—banking, shopping, etc. To the extent that preferences for interactive activities are an important phenomenon in the market, those technically more efficient arrangements will not be adopted by a good many consumers if they are only slightly less costly.

While the data suggest that a set of activities that includes work for pay in the market will often be preferred to a set that does not, they certainly do not suggest that people have preferences for an activity package that includes a standard (forty-hour) work week. In fact, the long historic trend of decreasing work hours suggests precisely the opposite, and has usually been interpreted to mean that people prefer leisure to work at the margin of choice. An interpretation consistent with the historical trend, and also with the data and theory discussed above, is that a great many people prefer an activity package that includes some modest amount of paid work, but not necessarily full-time paid work. But the labor market is such that part-time jobs are typically hard to find and often regarded by employers as a more costly way to organize work activities. If these preference data are an accurate reflection of true preferences, an employer able to reconfigure work flows to capitalize on the demand for part-time work would be able to attract a productive labor force at relatively modest wage rates, and make a profit by so doing.

Summary

This reformulation of utility theory in terms of satisfactions derived from activities and those derived from wealth is an insight of considerable potential usefulness. It is simpler and more general than the present formulation, it provides useful insights into behaviors that are difficult to explain with present theory, and it predicts future behaviors that existing theory does not. Its weakness, from the viewpoint of traditional theory, is that it relies directly on subjective phenomena that cannot be directly observed, that cannot be traded between participants in a market (except indirectly), and whose implications cannot easily be contradicted by observed behavior. But some of those problems exist also for the current theory of consumer choice, which also cannot easily be contradicted by observed behavior.

Perhaps the best way to assess this theoretical structure is that it provides an accounting framework for describing and measuring well-being, both among individuals and societies, that in principle has great generality and power. The framework involves the measurement of subjective variables, which have never been a great favorite of economists. While variables of this sort contain measurement errors and interpretive ambiguities that are not present in objective variables, that might be better seen as an opportunity and a challenge rather than as a proscription.

Notes

The research underlying this paper has been supported in part by the National Science Foundation, Grant #SES–8219275. Helpful comments on the paper were received from Charles Brown, Greg Dow, Roberta Miller, Albert Rees, and Hal Varian.

1. The introductory material in the paper leans heavily on the excellent summaries of the historical development of utility theory provided by Stigler (1950a, 1950b) and Meeks (1985), especially the former. A recent doctoral dissertation by Loewenstein (1985) provides some interesting insights into the intertemporal optimization aspects of utility theory.

The literature on utility theory has been enormous over the years, and includes many of the profession's heavyweights. Nobel Prize winners, for example, are prominent among major contributors (Hicks, Arrow, Samuelson, Stigler, Friedman), and if Nobel Prizes had been around earlier, Menger, Marshall, Jevons, Pareto, Walras, Slutsky, and Edgeworth would surely have been recipients.

2. A plausible reason is that economists tended to think of the labor force as being determined by population characteristics, and work hours as being determined by employers.

3. Of course, wage rates also came to be perceived as a choice variable: one could invest in productivity-related skills by deciding to spend time in school, or by accepting a job with a large training component (Mincer 1974).

4. The literature does contain some suggestion that work activity per se does not necessarily produce negative utility. That is certainly true of the very early discussion in Jevons (1911), and can be found in more recent discussions of labor supply (Rees 1973). In addition, there is a substantial literature on compensating wage differentials, which implies that the direct utility from work varies according to job characteristics (e.g., Brown 1980; Smith 1979; Duncan and Holmlund 1983).

5. J.R. Hicks, who was an early enthusiast for preference ordering, thought otherwise in his later writing, seeing marginal utility calculations as closer to what consumers actually do than marginal rate of substitution calculations (Hicks 1976).

6. This change is usually interpreted (Loewenstein 1985; Meeks 1985) as reflecting a desire to de-psychologize utility theory on the grounds that the fewer the assumptions, the better the theory. Loewenstein interprets it as reflecting increased uneasiness on the part of many economists with the shaky psychological foundations of cardinally measurable utility. Stigler (1950b) notes that many of the big guns in the early development of utility theory (e.g., Pareto, Slutsky) viewed the detaching of the theory from psychological underpinnings as an important simplification.

7. A different departure from the goods-leisure model was introduced by Lancaster, who argued that characteristics of products rather than products were what produced utility. Thus, consumers were paying for the functions performed by goods, not for the goods themselves (Lancaster 1966).

8. This is obviously a gross oversimplification of the development of utility theory. For example, it entirely omits the spirited discussion in the literature about whether individual utility functions could be compared or aggregated (Marshall 1920; Pigou 1932; Jevons 1911); whether aggregation of utility functions necessarily yielded consistency in social choices (Arrow 1965; Bergson 1938); whether any social policy change could be shown to be an improvement in utility terms (Hicks 1946; Arrow 1950, 1963; Samuelson 1948; Robbins 1930); and the relation between National Income aggregates and societal well-being (Kuznets 1941; Scitovsky 1976; Nordhaus and Tobin 1972; Juster 1973; Eisner et al. 1982). In addition, there is the extensive literature concerned with whether consumers maximize expected utility in situations involving risky outcomes. The von Neumann–Morgenstern axioms (1947) are the standard view, recently challenged by the prospect theory axioms (consumers are risk-averse when it comes to prospective gains, risk-loving when it comes to prospective losses) of Kahneman and Tversky (1979). Friedman and Savage (1948) and Arrow (1965) are important contributors to this topic.

9. It would be well not to push the latter point too hard—that leisure activities contain only process benefits, and have no extrinsic outcome of value. Many—perhaps most—leisure activities are quite likely to yield some enhancement of a capital stock of one kind or other—health status, the stock of relationships represented by marriage, friendships, etc.

The notion that activities are the basic source of utility turns out to have clearly identifiable historical roots. As Loewenstein (1985) notes in his literature survey, Edgeworth in *Mathematical Psychics* conceived of the individual as an enormously complex machine whose purpose was to convert inputs such as time and food and consumption goods into pleasure. The same theme was echoed several decades later by Irving Fisher, who wrote:

These and other illustrations will show that, if we include the body as a transforming instrument, while we must credit with their respective service all these outside agencies, such as food, clothing, dwelling, furniture, ornaments, and other articles, which, as it were, bombard a man's sensory system, we must also at the same time debit the body with these same items. In this case, the only surviving credit items after these equal debits and credits are cancelled are the resulting satisfactions in the human mind. In other words; in order that the external world should become effective to man, the human body must be considered as the last transforming instrument. *Just as there is a gradual transformation of services through the farm, flour mill, and bakery, so there is a gradual transformation within the human body itself.* It is a sort of factory, the products of which are the only uncancelled income of the consumer. [Fisher 1965, p. 167]

10. That argument can be found repeatedly in the earlier literature concerned with methods of measuring cardinal utility, e.g., Robbins (1935).

11. A consistent finding from the quality-of-life studies is that the most important dimensions of satisfaction with one's life as a whole turn out to be noneconomic factors—relationships with family and friends—rather than economic or financial ones.

12. The argument has always been carefully put in marginal terms—the wage rate is needed to overcome the distaste for the *last hour* of work—and goes back at least to Stanley Jevons.

13. Although the result described here is technically consistent with the traditional theory, it seems unlikely to me that the relevant functions have the necessary shapes. Traditional theory equates the marginal utility of consumption, U_c', with the marginal utility of leisure, U_l'. The marginal utility of consumption is equal to the marginal utility of income, U_y', plus the marginal utility of work, U_w', presumed to be negative in equilibrium. Thus, at the point of choice, $U_l' = U_c' = U_y' + U_w'$, where all the terms except U_w' are presumed to be positive. The data indicate that the *average* utility of U_w' is *higher* than the *average* utility of U_l'. Since the maximum utility yielded by the first minute (or hour) for all possible activities is unlikely to be associated with work (there are hundreds of leisure activities, and at least one should represent the maximum), and since leisure activities can be easily substituted for each other as their marginal utility declines, it takes a very peculiar shape for the U_w function to get the result that we observe and still maintain the marginal equality conditions shown above. A more plausible interpretation is that disequilibrium often exists, probably because of labor market rigidities on the demand side—e.g., the absence of a rich and continuous set of market opportunities to work 5, 7.5, 10 . . . hours per week at a wage consistent with one's productivity.

14. For an expansion of this point, see Juster and Stafford (1990).

References

Andrews, F.M., and S.G. Withey. (1976) *Social Indicators of Well-Being in America.* New York: Plenum.

Arrow, K.J. (1950) "A Difficulty in the Concept of Social Welfare." *Journal of Political Economy* 58(4):328–46.

———. (1963) *Social Choice and Individual Values.* 2d ed. New Haven, CT: Yale University Press, 1963.

———. (1965) *Aspects in the Theory of Risk-Bearing.* Helsinki. Reissued as *Essays in the Theory of Risk-Bearing.* Chicago: Markham, 1971.

Becker, G.S. (1965) "A Theory of the Allocation of Time." *Economic Journal* 75:493–517.

Bentham, J. (1970) *An Introduction to the Principles of Morals and Legislation.* London: Athlone Press. (Originally published in 1789.)

Bergson, A. (1938) "A Reformulation of Certain Aspects of Welfare Economics." *Quarterly Journal of Economics* 52:310–34.
Bradburn, N.M. (1965) *The Structure of Psychological Well-Being*. Chicago: Aldine.
Brown, C. (1980) "Equalizing Differences in the Labor Market." *Quarterly Journal of Economics* 94:113–34.
Campbell, A., P. Converse, and W. Rodgers. (1976) *The Quality of American Life*. New York: Russell Sage.
Cantril, A.H., and C.W. Roll, Jr. (1971) *Hopes and Fears of the American People*. New York: Universe.
Dow, G.K., and F.T. Juster. (1985) "Goods, Time, and Well-Being: The Joint Dependence Problem." In F.T. Juster and F.P. Stafford, eds., *Time, Goods, and Well-Being*. Ann Arbor: Institute for Social Research, University of Michigan.
Duesenberry, J. (1952) *Income, Savings and the Theory of Consumer Behavior*. Cambridge, MA: Harvard University Press.
Duncan, G.J., and B. Holmlund. (1983) "Was Adam Smith Right after All? Another Test of the Theory of Compensating Wage Differentials." *Journal of Labor Economics* 1(4):366–79.
Edgeworth, F.Y. (1967) *Mathematical Psychics: An Essay on the Application of Mathematics to the Moral Sciences*. New York: Augustus M. Kelley. (Originally published in 1881.)
Eisner, R., E.R. Simons, P.J. Pieper, and S. Bender. (1982) "Total Incomes in the United States, 1946–1976: A Summary Report." *Review of Income and Wealth*, Series 28(2):133–74.
Fisher, I. (1930) *The Theory of Interest*. New York: Macmillan.
———. (1965) *The Nature of Capital and Income*. New York: A.M. Kelley, Reprints of Economic Classics. (Originally published 1906.)
Friedman, M., and L. Savage. (1948) "The Utility Analysis of Choices Involving Risk." *Journal of Political Economy* 56:279–304.
Griliches, Z., ed. (1971) *Price Indexes and Quality Change* (Price Statistics Committee, Federal Reserve Board). Cambridge, MA: Harvard University Press.
Hicks, J.R., (1940) "The Valuation of the Social Income." *Economica* 7:105–24.
———. (1963) *The Theory of Wages*. 2d ed. New York: St. Martin's Press.
———. (1976) "Some Questions of Time in Economics." In A.M. Tang, F.M. Westfield, and J.S. Worley, eds., *Evolution, Welfare and Time in Economics: Essays in Honor of Georgescu Roegen*. Lexington, MA: Lexington Books.
Hicks, J.R., and R.G.D. Allen. (1934) "A Reconsideration of the Theory of Value, Part 1 and Part 2." *Economica* 1 (New Series):52–76, 196–219.
Hill, M.S., and F.T. Juster. (1985) "Constraints and Complementarities in Time Use." In F.T. Juster and F.P. Stafford, eds., *Time, Goods, and Well-Being*. Ann Arbor: Institute for Social Research, University of Michigan.
Jevons, W.S. (1911) *The Theory of Political Economy*. 4th ed. London: Macmillan.
Juster, F.T. (1973) "A Framework for the Measurement of Economic and Social Performance." In M. Moss, ed., *The Measurement of Economic and Social Performance*. New York: National Bureau of Economic Research.
———. (1985a) "The Distribution of Well-Being among Households." *Bulletin of the International Statistical Institute* 51(1):1.1–1.15.
———. (1985b) "Preferences for Work and Leisure." In F.T. Juster and F.P. Stafford, eds., *Time, Goods, and Well-Being*. Ann Arbor: Institute for Social Research, University of Michigan.
Juster, F.T., P.N. Courant, and G.K. Dow. (1981a) "A Theoretical Framework for the Measurement of Well-Being." *Review of Income and Wealth*, Series 27(1):1–31.

———. (1981b) "The Theory and Measurement of Well-Being: A Suggested Framework for Accounting and Analysis." In F.T. Juster and K.C. Land, eds., *Social Accounting Systems: Essays on the State of the Art*. New York: Academic Press.

———. (1985) "A Conceptual Framework for the Analysis of Time Allocation Data." In F.T. Juster and F.P. Stafford, eds., *Time, Goods, and Well-Being*. Ann Arbor: Institute for Social Research, University of Michigan.

Juster, F.T., and F.P. Stafford. (1990) *The Allocation of Time: Empirical Findings, Behavioral Models, and Problems of Measurement*. Working Paper no. 8038. Ann Arbor: Institute for Social Research, University of Michigan.

———, eds. (1985) *Time, Goods, and Well-Being*. Ann Arbor: Institute for Social Research, University of Michigan.

Kahneman, D., and A. Tversky. (1979) "Prospect Theory: An Analysis of Decision under Risk." *Econometrica* 47:263–91.

Kaldor, N. (1939) "Welfare Propositions of Economics and Interpersonal Comparisons of Utility." *Economic Journal* 49:549–52.

Kaplan, R. (1985) "Lottery Winners and Work Commitment." *Journal of the Institute for Socioeconomic Studies* 10(2):82–94.

Kendrick, J.W. (1979) "Expanding Imputed Values in the National Income and Product Accounts." *Review of Income and Wealth*, Series 25(4):349–63.

Kuznets, S. (1941) *National Income and Its Composition, 1919–1938*. New York: National Bureau of Economic Research.

Lancaster, K. (1966) "A New Approach to Consumer Theory." *Journal of Political Economy* 74:132–57.

Little, I.M.D. (1957) *A Critique of Welfare Economics*. 2d ed. Oxford: Oxford University Press.

Loewenstein, G.F. (1985) "Expectations and Intertemporal Choice." Ph.D. diss. Yale University.

Marshall, A. (1920) *Principles of Economics*. 8th ed. London: Macmillan.

Meeks, J.G.T. (1985) "Utility in Economics: A Survey of the Literature." In C.F. Turner and E. Martin, eds., *Surveying Subjective Phenomena*, vol. 2. New York: Russell Sage.

Michael, R.T., and G.S. Becker. (1973) "On the New Theory of Consumer Behavior." *Swedish Journal of Economics* 75:378–96.

Mill, J.S. (1968) *Utilitarianism*. New York: Dutton, Everyman's Library. (Originally published in 1863.)

Mincer, J. (1963) "Market Prices, Opportunity Costs and Income Effects." In C.F. Christ et al., *Measurement in Economics: Studies in Mathematical Economics and Econometrics in Memory of Yehuda Grunfeld*. Stanford, CA: Stanford University Press.

———. (1974) *Schooling, Experience, and Earnings*. New York: Columbia University Press for the National Bureau of Economic Research.

Mishan, E.J. (1967) *The Costs of Economic Growth*. New York: Praeger.

Nerlove, M. (1974) "Household and Economy: Toward a New Theory of Population and Economic Growth." *Journal of Political Economy* 82(2):S200–21.

Nordhaus, W., and J. Tobin. (1972) "Is Growth Obsolete?" In *Economic Growth*. 50th Anniversary Colloquium V. New York: National Bureau of Economic Research.

Pareto, V. (1897) *Cours d'Economie Politique*. Lausanne: Rouge.

———. (1927) *Manuel d'Economie Politique*. 2d ed. Paris: Gerard.

Pigou, A.C. (1932) *The Economics of Welfare*. 4th ed. London: Macmillan.

Pollak, R.A., and M.L. Wachter. (1975) "The Relevance of the Household Production Function and Its Implications for the Allocation of Time." *Journal of Political Economy* 83:255–77.

Rees, A. (1973) *The Economics of Work and Pay*. New York: Harper & Row.
Robbins, L. (1930) "On the Elasticity of Demand for Income in Terms of Effort." *Economica* 29(June):123–29.
———. (1935) *An Essay on the Nature and Significance of Economic Science*. 2d ed. New York: Macmillan.
Robertson, D.H. (1952) *Utility and All That*. London: George Allen & Unwin.
Ruggles, R. (1978) *The Measurement of Economic and Social Performance* (Report on National Science Foundation Project SOC 74–21391). New Haven, CT: Yale University.
Samuelson, P.A. (1948) *Foundations of Economic Analysis*. Cambridge, MA: Harvard University Press.
Scitovsky, T. (1976) *The Joyless Economy: An Inquiry into Human Satisfaction and Consumer Dissatisfation*. New York: Oxford University Press.
Slutsky, E.E. (1915) "Sulla Teoria del Bilancio del Consumatore." *Giornale Degli Economisti*, Series 3(51):1–26.
Smith, R.S. (1979) "Compensating Wage Differentials and Public Policy: A Review." *Industrial and Labor Relations Review* 32:339–52.
Stigler, G.J., (1950a) "The Development of Utility Theory I." *Journal of Political Economy* 58(4):307–27.
———. (1950b) "The Development of Utility Theory II." *Journal of Political Economy* 58(5):373–96.
Stigler, G.J., and G.S. Becker. (1977) "De Gustibus Non Est Disputandum." *American Economic Review* 67:76–90.
von Neumann, J., and O. Morgenstern. (1947) *Theory of Games and Economic Behavior*. 2d ed. Princeton, NJ: Princeton University Press.

8

ROBERT S. GOLDFARB AND
WILLIAM B. GRIFFITH

The "Theory as Map" Analogy and Changes in Assumption Sets in Economics

> [E]conomists are frequently consulted.... What is surprising is that those who seek this advice would, like most reasonable people, reject out of hand the behavioral principles on which these consultants rely.... [I]f economists stressed these as vigorously as they do the conclusions based on them, the profession would be classified as a form of medieval scholasticism instead of a modern social science.
>
> —J. Cross

Economists have tended over the decades to rely on various versions of a set of fundamental "behavioral principles" for microeconomic theorizing. For example, they have frequently assumed that economic agents singlemindedly aimed at maximizing utility or wealth or profits, were possessed of perfect information and perfect foresight, and so forth. Cross's complaint in the quote above is symptomatic of the fact that these principles have been both controversial within economics and subject to scathing criticism from outsiders virtually continuously since their formulation by Nassau Senior, J.S. Mill, and others early in the nineteenth century. It is striking that in defending against these criticisms, economists often tried to show that economics fit the current philosophical conception of what natural science *should be*, rather than attempting to work out a conception of economics as a discipline *sui generis*.

Thus, in the nineteenth century, when natural science was thought to assert general but abstract truths about the world, economics was defended as having the same character, although admitting to more difficulty in ascertaining precise situations where its basic assumptions held (Blaug 1980, chap. 3). Subsequently, responding to criticisms drawn from the logical positivist and especially "falsificationist" conceptions of natural science, defenders of economics fell back on an "instrumentalist" conception of science. On this view, the lack of "realism" of economic assumptions was not a proper concern; just as there existed nonobservable theoretical entities in physics, constructs in economics such as the "typical profit maximizing firm" and the "typical perfectly informed consumer" should be treated as theoretical entities whose "true existence" was not appropriately subject to empirical test because true existence was not relevant to the adequacy of the theory.[1] According to Milton Friedman's methodology essay (1953), which has been called "the most influential work on economic methodology in this century" (Hausman 1984, p. 41), the sole relevant question was whether the theory's predictions were "sufficiently good approximations." Since "sufficiently good" was defined in part by considering how well alternative hypotheses predicted, one result appeared to be the preservation of the standard set of basic assumptions. So long as "mainstream" economics maintained "professional unity" around this standard set of neoclassical assumptions, all alternative hypotheses would be generated within the same basic framework of assumptions; successful hypotheses based on alternative basic assumptions had little chance of appearing.

The instrumentalist view associated with Friedman and others suggests that basic assumptions might be surrendered in the face of conflicting empirical evidence; indeed, instrumentalism seems to imply that confrontation of predictions with conflicting evidence would be the driving force for improvement of the theory. This view that economists are vigorously searching for conflicting evidence and would willingly have revised their basic assumptions had such evidence been found, has been much criticized as a seriously inaccurate portrayal of normal practice in economics (see the summary of criticisms in Blaug 1980, chap. 15; Reder's elegant 1982 discussion of Chicago economics contains a remarkable testimonial to the incompatibility of this "conflicting evidence" view with actual Chicago practice).[2]

These claims of inconsistency between instrumentalism and actual procedures in economics have led students of methodology to consider whether other methodological conceptions might not provide better lines of defense for economics as scientific, despite the apparent lack of rigorous testing of its theories. The appearance of the so-called "growth of knowledge" perspective among methodologists influenced by Thomas Kuhn's (1970) celebrated historiography of development in the natural sciences generated interesting alternative models of scientific practice. Of particular interest to economists has been Imre Lakatos's (1978) "methodology of scientific research programmes" (MSRP), an amalgam of Karl Popper's falsificationist views and Kuhn's competing theory. Lakatos's model clearly recognized that under normal conditions scientists in a particular research program treated some assumptions as part of a "hard core," not to be subject to attempts at refutation; confrontation with evidence and resulting adjustments were permitted within a "protective belt" of "auxiliary hypotheses," all of this under firm guidance from the research program's "positive heuristic" about permissible ways to develop new hypotheses. On the Lakatosian view, the research program as a whole (rather than particular assumptions or hypotheses in isolation) is to be appraised by confrontation with experience; the program will be maintained so long as it is theoretically and empirically progressive enough to continue to attract new researchers.

This framework has obvious attractions for methodologists and philosophers of economics, and has led to some interestingly different "rational reconstructions" (as Lakatos called them) of key developments in economics (see the initial papers in Latsis 1976, and the influential work of Weintraub 1985 for examples). However, this framework has itself come under severe criticism from some philosophers for lack of clarity in key concepts (see Cohen, Feyerabend, and Wartofsky 1976; and Radnitzky and Andersson 1978), and from some economists as needing modification before being applicable to economics (see Leijonhufvud 1976; Weintraub 1985; and the survey of other work in Hands 1985).

In the face of these difficulties in fitting practices in economics into frameworks from the philosophy of science, a number of recent commentators have suggested abandoning this as a goal. They argue that it is unnecessary to assume that the practices of economists are only justifiable if they can be shown to satisfy some model of scientific practice drawn from the natural sciences. They argue in addition that one should not automatically assume that the methodology economists say they follow coincides with their actual practice.[3] Along these lines, Brennan (1984) asks, "Is economics methodologically special?" and Hamminga (1983) and McCloskey (1983, 1985) both urge a close skeptical examination of the ways in which economists tend to justify their practices and procedures. Moreover, Hausman (1984), Rosenberg (1986), and McCloskey (1983, 1985) all strongly suggest that we shift our focus away from a priori schemes derived from the natural sciences and instead study the actual practices economists do adopt.

In this paper we take these suggestions that we examine actual practice seriously. In particular, we want to focus on the practice of assumption choice. Moreover, we join forces with others such as Sen (1977), Hirschman (1985), Etzioni (1986), and Nooteboom (1986) in refusing to accept the defensive posture of shielding basic assumptions in economics from direct evaluation, criticism, and potential revision; rather than attempting to rationalize this shielding via Lakatos's MSRP or in other ways, we focus on situations where assumption sets in economics have in fact been subject to criticism and change. Several recent developments lend support to our predilection for evaluation and possible changes in assumptions over shielding. First, there is the increasing importance of economics as a policy tool. This has meant that assumptions that are justifiable in positive economics applications also come to be used in normative evaluations of alternative policies, although their justifiability in normative settings is far more questionable and typically unexamined. A second development is the infiltration of economic assumptions into other social sciences, sometimes suggestively referred to as "economic imperialism." Third, there is the proliferation of competing paradigms in macroeconomics, paradigms whose relative merits seemingly cannot be conclusively determined solely on the basis of empirical performance. However, while we believe that assumption choice in economics needs careful examination, we also believe that criticism of assumptions from outside economics often fails to come to grips with real issues of theory choice and design as economists see them.

Our approach to examining the actual practice of assumption choice in economics will proceed as follows: first, in accordance with the intuitively plausible thesis put forth by McCloskey (1985, p. 61) that the informal arguments and rhetorical devices used by economists—e.g., in initiating unbelieving students—may yield more insight as to what economists really find persuasive than their formal methodological statements, we take up for close analysis a particular analogy often found in textbook defenses of the abstract assumptions used in economics: the likening of economic theory to maps.

Second, accepting the need identified by Hausman, McCloskey, Rosenberg, and others for more direct study of actual practice in economics, we develop two provocative case studies of actual assumption changes. Both cases involve an initial failure to revise intuitively criticizable assumptions, followed by eventual acceptance of modifications, without much apparent effort within the discipline to articulate why change suddenly became acceptable.

Finally, in a concluding section, we reverse what seems to be a standard direction of inquiry in economic methodology: starting with a particular favorite philosophy of science methodology, and seeing if economics "measures up" to its requirements. Since, as Laudan (1987) recently pointed out, there are a number of rival methodological conceptions available, "not all of which can be right" (p. 19), we ask whether our case studies shed any light on the descriptive accuracy for economics of any of several rival models of scientific practice.

The Map Analogy and Its Implications for Investigating Assumption Choices in Economics

The map analogy provides a useful starting point for investigating how assumption choices are made in economics because it illustrates a way in which some economists think about theory construction, and because its weaknesses as an analogy suggest crucial aspects of actual assumption choices in economics.

What Is the Map Analogy?

While we are unsure of the map analogy's origins, we have encountered it several times in recent years in conversations with economists of diverse backgrounds. It has appeared in at least two leading introductory textbooks (Baumol and Blinder 1985, pp. 9–12; Wonnacott and Wonnacott 1982, pp.

28–29, 1985, pp. 36–37), and Leijonhufvud (1976, p. 304) asserts its widespread textbook use in "standardized sermons on the theme 'all useful theory is abstract.' "[4]

To examine this analogy, we look first at those similarities between maps and theories stressed in textbook presentations of this rhetorical device. Consider how Baumol and Blinder introduce the comparison:

> Some students find economics unduly abstract and "unrealistic." Economists do make unrealistic assumptions. . . . But this propensity to abstract from reality results from the incredible complexity of the real world. . . . If economists tried to keep track of every aspect of human behavior, they could surely never hope to understand the nature of the economy. [pp. 9–10]

To drive this point home, the text asks students to compare the usefulness of three different road maps in light of a specific goal: finding a convenient route between two particular Los Angeles locations a considerable distance apart. The three maps offered are: an interstate highway map including all of Los Angeles and the surrounding region; a map showing only the major connecting streets in Los Angeles; and a detailed, presumably complete representation of all Los Angeles streets. The text suggests (p. 11) that the most useful map for the stated purpose is the one that shows only the major connecting streets in the city. It further argues that a similar point holds for theory choice: whether a theory abstracts too much from detail (like the interstate map) or too little (like the complete representation map) depends on the use to which the theory is to be put. Moreover, the appropriateness of a theory's level of detail cannot be determined in the abstract and need not be absolutely fixed. The same theory may have too much detail for one use, adequate detail for a second use, and too little for a third.

This use of the analogy suggests that economists in supplying theories are like mapmakers offering a variety of maps of different levels of abstraction. These different levels of maps (economic theories) are designed to be suitable to the different purposes users of the maps (users of theories) might have in mind. We will evaluate this view later.

A related presentation of the analogy with a somewhat different emphasis is in Wonnacott and Wonnacott:

> In a sense, theory is like a map. A road map is necessarily incomplete. . . . If a road map were more realistic, it would be less useful for its intended purpose; if it tried to show every house and every tree, it would be an incomprehensible jumble of detail. A road map is useful precisely because it is a simplification that shows in stark outline the various roads which may be travelled. [1985, p. 37]

On this view, simplification by elimination of detail is essential to the usefulness of all maps and theories. Thus, general criticism of theoretical assumptions as "unrealistic" because they omit details of relationships that indisputably exist in reality would appear to be beside the point. By implication, criticism of any specific assumption would presumably need to be grounded in some showing that the lack of "realistic" detail interfered with the theory's intended use.

Wonnacott and Wonnacott extend the analogy a bit further, noting that a road map will typically be "in many ways . . . downright wrong. Towns and villages are not round circles. Roads of various qualities do not really come in different colors" (1985, p. 37). A striking inference can be drawn from Wonnacott and Wonnacott's observation about "wrong" features on road maps. It seems to follow that misrepresentation or "false features" can actually increase the usefulness of maps. Portraying different-quality roads by a variety of different colors that never grace actual roads conveys, by appeal to a convenient convention, more (and more useful) information than would be provided by literal faithfulness to "true road color fact."[5] The analogy to theories is to suggest that literal falsity of economic assumptions not only may not hinder but may actually help to enhance a theory's usefulness. This argument has remarkable similarities to Friedman's controversial claims about the positive value of "wildly inaccurate" assumptions (1953, p. 14).

Exploring the Implications of the Analogy

These particular appeals to the map analogy have a somewhat narrow pedagogical purpose; some economists might therefore argue against taking them too seriously. We think, however, that they are worth exploring for what they may reveal about the intuitive conceptualization of the discipline (particularly about the nature of assumption choices) that economists fall back on when pressed.

To investigate how much the map theory comparison really tells us about assumption choice in economics, we need to evaluate carefully the aptness of the analogy. Every analogy has its limits; deeper understanding of an analogy's usefulness requires careful probing of these limits through systematic elaboration of the comparison. Such probing may reveal distinctive and important differences between the phenomena being compared; failure to investigate these limits may lead to use of the analogy in inappropriate or positively misleading ways.[6] It is possible, for example, that economists' informal use of the map analogy might contain untested propositions about features of economic theory, propositions that, on careful examination, are not viable.

A useful way to derive insights from the map analogy about assumption choice in economics is to pursue the analogy's claims about the merits of economic modeling methods. The map analogy as used in textbooks purports in part to justify the lack of "realism" in the assumptions of economic theory by pointing out that maps are not completely realistic either, and this lack of complete realism actually contributes to their usefulness. But for this justificatory explanation to be completely convincing, the underlying determinants of descriptive incompleteness in maps should bear a close resemblance to the underlying determinants of descriptive incompleteness (embodied in "unrealistic" assumptions) in economic theory. Closer examination of the map theory comparison, however, suggests potentially important differences between the underlying determinants in the two cases.

A major distinction results from differences in the market characteristics of the situations in which each activity takes place. Maps are explicit commodities sold in explicit markets. Thus, the choice and degree of omitted detail has to meet a direct market test; if a mapmaker continually fails to make decisions about inclusion of details that are acceptable to users, he is unlikely to remain in business. That map users do not take umbrage at cities being circles and roads being red is no surprise; this merely reflects the fact that the mapmakers have correctly anticipated that these "wrong" features do not critically inhibit actual uses. In contrast, economic theories are not explicit products sold in explicit markets; the acceptability tests they must meet are not obviously comparable, so that the decisions about "omitted detail" are not obviously validated in the same "direct market test" way.[7]

A related distinction involves the division between producers and users. In the map case, a generally valid description is that "cartographers supply and noncartographers demand"; that is, suppliers and demanders are largely separate groups. Thus, in the map market, suppliers are responding to a demand generated by a group of users other than the suppliers themselves. In economics, this distinction between the group supplying theories (and supplying the assumption sets accompanying these theories) and those demanding theories is nowhere near as clear. Ghiselin (1987, p. 274), for example, suggests that economists as theorists are "both users and producers" of the product. More broadly, when economists specify their theories, they are writing largely for an audience of other economists. If cartographers drew maps only to please other cartographers, would we still expect the preponderance of decisions about omission of detail to enhance the usefulness of maps for people taking trips? We might well expect instead that the criteria for inclusion and omission would reflect aesthetic and other professional standards for what is "good," "elegant," "rigorous," etc.

All of which brings us back to the issue of "use-value." A principal feature of the analogy is the suggested assessment in terms of use-value when judging whether a map or theory is "sufficiently realistic." The analogy seems to suggest that judging the usefulness of an economic theory is pretty much the same as judging whether or not a map is useful. For this to be true, it would seem that we would need to identify usage goals that were sufficiently comparable in the two cases. In the map case, a variety of reasonably clear goals can be specified: to locate something in relation to other things, to find the shortest route, to compare relative features. But what are the typical goals of the users of economic theory? More specifically, if economists are (as the last paragraph suggested) the direct users, can their usage goals be specified in a way sufficiently comparable to the goals of map users? If there are also indirect users (business managers, labor negotiators, private investors, government policy makers, moral philosophers, and philosophers of science), how could we specify their usage goals? Moreover, given the absence of an explicit market like the one for maps, by what indirect mechanisms could they make their demands effective?

The celebrated methodological position of Milton Friedman (1953) does of course suggest a usage goal for economic theory: its ability to predict. Friedman's methodology has been characterized as "instrumentalist" (see, for example, Boland 1979), a characterization with which Friedman himself apparently concurs (see Caldwell 1980, p. 367). To slightly restate Friedman's view in the language of our discussion, an economic theory's assumptions are not to be appraised in terms of their realism, but only judged by the theory's success in achieving its goals. Friedman then identifies these goals as relative success in prediction. So long as the given theory predicts better than competitors, challenges based on realism of assumptions can be justifiably ignored. But this specification of usage goals ought to leave us quite uneasy. First, there is considerable reason to be skeptical that this view of methodology focusing on prediction captures actual practice (and therefore actual goals) in economics. To repeat a point made earlier, the view that economists are vigorously searching for conflicting evidence and would willingly revise their basic assumptions based on such evidence has been much criticized as a seriously inaccurate portrayal of actual practice. Second, even if the Friedman view were an accurate description of the usage goals of economists, we still have to worry about the usage goals of the indirect (noneconomist) users. Are the goals of these other groups primarily predictive? To the extent that they are, will they necessarily be for the same variables the economists focus on? In any case, to what degree, if at all, will these indirect demands make themselves effective?

We have tried to document a number of important ways in which the map analogy fails to be ironclad. But it is still possible that the Friedmanesque instrumentalist view it suggests about assumption choice in economics is in part or largely applicable. How can we shed further light on the actual aptness of the analogy, and much more fundamentally, on the actual practice of assumption choice in economics?

To further investigate these questions, we take up two case studies of actual changes in assumption sets. Looking at actual cases where assumption sets have changed allows us to try to identify factors that induced or promoted these changes. For example, did predictive failures lead to assumption changes, or did other nonpredictionist criteria internal to economics contribute?

Changes in Assumption Sets in Economic Theory: Two Examples

Assumption Changes to Incorporate Employee Turnover

Our first example of changes in assumption sets involves the modeling of labor demand in the presence of employer concerns about employee turnover. The simplest standard model of the firm's demand curve for labor indicates that labor demand is inversely related to the wage rate. Typically, this result is derived from a first-order condition equating marginal revenue product (that is, marginal physical product times marginal revenue) to the wage for all categories of firms facing horizontal labor supply curves.

One striking feature of this simple characterization of labor demand is that it implies that the firm in question is indifferent to employee turnover. To see this, suppose the firm's labor demand curve stays stable over many periods, and the wage it faces does not change. Under these conditions, the theory indicates that the firm in question would want to hire the same number of units of labor each period. The theory does not suggest that the firm cares whether the units of labor are the same or different individuals from period to period. All that concerns the firm is the volume of labor, not its "continuity."

Anyone familiar with the concerns of personnel officers at large corporations, or even with the inconvenience and disruption caused by turnover in clerical staff of the economics or philosophy department office, will realize that turnover of employees is often a matter of importance to employers. Yet this concern is not reflected in the simple marginal productivity theory of factor demand. Since this concern with turnover reflects the costs imposed by turnover, it is likely to lead to adoption of personnel policies, possibly including wage policies and hiring criteria, to lessen these costs. The failure of the simple theory to "expect" that turnover matters to employers means that the theory may fail to incorporate these turnover adaptations when modeling the firm's wage and hiring decisions.

What changes in the assumption set emerged to make labor demand theory consistent with employer concern about turnover, and what factors led to these changes? One simple alteration to the assumption set of labor demand theory creates a theory that is consistent with employer concern about turnover. All that is needed is to recognize that labor costs include fixed as well as variable elements. In the simple theory, the wage is the only cost of labor, and it is a totally variable cost. Changing the assumption set to recognize some fixed costs of employment arising from firm expenditures on hiring and training makes the theory "recognize" the payoff to labor continuity. The presence of such costs associated with replacing current employees makes turnover costly; every time a worker leaves and must be replaced, a new hiring and training cost is imposed that would be avoided if the worker stayed.

How did this particular alteration in the assumption set enter the literature? Walter Oi (1962, pp. 538–65) stressed the importance of fixed costs due to hiring and training activities. His work, along with Becker's analysis of human capital (1962, 1964), led to a growing appreciation by labor economists of the importance of these costs. A recent survey article by Sherwin Rosen indicates the link between Oi and Becker's work and explanations of employment continuity:

> The rationale for observed employment continuity ultimately rests on Gary Becker's (1964) concept of firm-specific human capital, which formed the basis of the earlier quasi-fixed cost theory of employment fluctuations originated by Walter Oi (1962). [Rosen 1985, p. 1147][8]

It is quite striking that the two originators of the crucial assumption change were not primarily concerned with the theory's failure to focus on employer interest in turnover. Becker's initial interest was in rates of return to education. Oi's concerns did touch on turnover, but largely in the context of cyclical changes in employment.

Rosen's survey indicates one important reason why a theory incorporating turnover is of considerably more interest to researchers today than it would have been in the early 1960s, when Oi and Becker were writing. Rosen observes that "recent empirical observations" of labor market institutions have reinforced the view that:

> Many features of labor markets bear little resemblance to impersonal Walrasian auction markets. Chief among them is the remarkable degree of observed worker-firm attachment. [Rosen 1985, p. 1147]

Rosen implies that it is this finding of worker continuity at the firm that needs to be explained by the theoretical framework. Since the empirical studies cited by Rosen establishing this continuity date only from the 1970s, it is not surprising that this issue was not a primary motivation for Oi or Becker in the 1960s. One can almost say that an important alteration in the assumption set had been introduced considerably before one of the strongest logical and empirical reasons for needing it became obvious to most labor economists!

So far, the story seems to be that a useful change in the assumption set fortuitously anticipated one of the strongest reasons for needing that change. The example itself seems to raise all kinds of questions about what causes a theory to progress or fail to progress, how labor economists could apparently be relatively satisfied with a theoretical framework that failed to recognize (and therefore could not explain the comparative statics of) turnover, a phenomenon of great importance to employers and the labor market, and so forth. However, our object here is the narrower one of exploring how assumption sets change. For that purpose, a quite striking implication emerges.

The example shows that a very serious issue about economic theory is embodied in the following far-from-trivial question: "How do we know when a theory is omitting something important from its set of results, thereby calling into question some of the results it does obtain?" For a long time, analysts oriented toward the use of microeconomic theory for analyzing labor markets apparently did not focus on the fact that received marginal productivity theory failed to account for a labor market phenomenon—i.e., turnover—that was central to the employer's staffing problem.[9] Yet, realization of this fact casts doubt on the usefulness of the theory for explaining other labor market phenomena that it purports to analyze. If it does not recognize employer concern with turnover, are we sure that its view of firm wage setting is correct, when many employers may in fact set wages with the goal of managing turnover?[10] The reader may feel that we have overstated the "threat" that the existence of turnover poses to the simple marginal productivity theory of factor demand.[11] But even if the reader feels that way, an important underlying implication for sources of change in the assumption sets of theories is still present, since the question about crucial omissions posed above is a real and significant one. Interestingly enough, the issue does not seem to arise in the same way for modern road maps. For today's road maps, there simply is no issue about "not knowing" we are omitting something important. Today's mapmaker knows the universe of features it is helpful to include on a road map; space constraints or lack of knowledge that a particular road was very recently extended may cause omission of some of them, but "ignorance of what's important" is not an issue. In the theory case, on the other hand, omission clearly could be (and in the case of turnover, apparently was) at least in part due to incomplete appreciation of what labor market features it might be important to model or explain. Since our knowledge is never complete or definitive, omissions from the assumption set based on incomplete appreciation of what it is important to explain is always a danger. Apparently, this same difficulty arises in the natural sciences: Toulmin (1960, pp. 117–19) points out that fundamental differences in perceptions about what needs to be explained have been the source of important disputes in physics.

What does the turnover example suggest about the degree to which assumption set change is driven by predictive failure? A Friedmanesque instrumentalist view would seem to imply the importance of predictive failure as a force leading to assumption change. Suppose we ignore the somewhat inconvenient fact that the change in the assumption set needed to incorporate concern about turnover into the theory predates the widespread recognition of the need to incorporate turnover. Then the turnover case does seem to fit the predictive failure view. An implication of the turnover example seems to be that the economist's use of descriptive incompleteness (his choice of assumption sets) does in fact exhibit a mechanism for adjusting to revelations that his theories embody important omissions. In this case, an important omission—failure of the theory to incorporate turnover—was recognized. This omission also embodied a predictive failure, since it prevented the derivation of predictions associated with turnover phenomena. Recognition of the omission contributed to the widespread adoption of a modification of the theory's standard assumptions to incorporate turnover phenomena. "Fixed costs of employment" are now part of the standard analytical baggage of the vast majority of neoclassical labor economists.

On Resistance to Changing Assumptions When "Perturbations Far beyond Sequencing" Are Involved: The Case of Imperfect Information

The turnover example appears to suggest that economists will in fact modify their standard assumptions when such a modification seems empirically beneficial (in the sense of allowing the theory to deal with empirical phenomena it previously could not handle) and *does not fundamentally conflict with the existing assumption set*. In the turnover case, adding or modifying an assumption produced a closer approximation to complex reality, involving an assumption change that did not disturb the underlying principles on which the whole sequence of theories was based. An assumption change that adds richer detail, such as recognition of turnover, is not likely to be one that involves jettisoning the existing fundamental bases for the entire sequence of theories; it does not require abandoning the underlying paradigm.

However, one line of serious criticism of economics seems to call for much more fundamental changes in assumptions, changes that might require jettisoning the underlying paradigm. These critics, sensing that economics is not giving a satisfactory picture of what is going on in some important sphere of behavior, believe that what is needed is not some additional micro-detail, but a basic change in the fundamental assumptions. There is a strong impression that economists will not readily give up crucial underlying assumptions, and that an important reason for this is that these basic, allegedly grossly oversimplified postulates ("agents always and invariably maximize utility," "firms always and invariably profit maximize," "all agents have perfect foresight and perfect information," "preferences are stable and well-ordered," etc.) are seen to be linked together in ways that cause the whole modeling paradigm to crash if one principle is given up (Hutchison 1978, p. 201; Morgenstern 1935, pp. 171, 183).

A very interesting case study of a much more basic change in assumptions involves allowing agents to have less than perfect knowledge. In that case, the long-maintained fundamental assumption that agents had perfect information did yield over a relatively short time period to less restrictive characterizations. How and why did this happen?

The view that information is imperfect seems to accord far better with most observers' intuitive sense of the human situation than does assuming perfect information. Yet perfect information was maintained as a basic postulate of much of microeconomic theory until very recently, despite strong (but minority) pleas even within the profession that it was fundamentally unacceptable.[12] What was the process by which imperfect information, after being denied admission for so long, began to make significant inroads into the main body of microeconomic theory?

That perfect information was accepted over a long period of time as a fundamental basis for much economic theorizing is hardly in dispute, and can readily be documented. Morgenstern, writing in 1935, views the perfect information assumption as an "often-professed and an often-unchallenged premise of every theory" (p. 169). Hutchison, writing in 1978, finds it "remarkable how far economists have managed to avert their gaze from the extreme unrealities of the abstractions involved in the adequate knowledge assumption. Until very recently, those who have paid significant attention to this decisive assumption have been few and far between" (p. 203).

Of those who did explicitly consider the perfect information assumption, not every analyst accepted the desirability of incorporating imperfect information into the theory. An articulate advocate of the view that inclusion of less restrictive knowledge assumptions is not necessarily crucial is Machlup, who argues that inclusion of imperfect information in the theory of the firm is not necessary when comparative static propositions about industry prices and quantities are being developed:

> The firm as a theoretical construct has exactly the kind of information the theorist chooses to endow it with in order to design a good, useful theory . . . for purposes of competitive price and allocation theory, it does not make much difference whether the information which we assume the firm to have concerning . . . supply, production or demand . . . is correct or incorrect, as long as we may safely assume that any change in these conditions is registered correctly. [Machlup 1967, p. 24]

Reacting to a literature stressing the imperfections of information flows within hierarchies, Machlup asks:

> But what can be "imperfect" about information on, say, a tax increase? Why should it take special theories of bureaucracy to explain how the news of a wage increase "flows" through various hierarchical levels . . . ? Yet this, and this alone, is the information that is essentially involved in the theory of prices and allocation, since it is the adjustment to such changes in conditions for which the postulate of maximizing behavior is employed. [Machlup 1967, p. 25]

Machlup's overall claim is that introducing imperfect information produces no benefits when the aim is to derive comparative static propositions at the industry level.[13] A model incorporating incomplete information might seem more "realistically descriptive of the human condition" to critics of economics, just as a map with every house on it would seem more completely descriptive of a geographical area, but neither the theory nor the map would therefore be any more useful.

Along similar lines, Rothschild's (1973) survey of the imperfect information literature contains a particularly striking testimonial to these differences of opinion about the importance of including imperfect knowledge. Rothschild points out that market situations in which "participants act on the basis of sketchy and incomplete information . . . are common." Indeed, "anyone can establish" this "by recalling virtually any transaction he has ever participated in":

> But whether they are important is a harder question. I have a colleague whose position on this matter runs roughly as follows: "The friction caused by disequilibrium and lack of information accounts for variations in the numbers we observe at the fifth or sixth decimal place. Your stories are interesting but have no conceivable bearing on any question of practical economic interest." [Rothschild 1973, p. 1283]

Rothschild strongly disagrees with his colleague's assessment about the importance of including imperfect information in the assumption set of economic theories. The central point for us, however, is that such a fundamental disagreement about the yield of including imperfect information in the assumption set could exist.[14]

All of this suggests that, in considering whether to incorporate additional or alternative features into the assumption set, an implicit cost-benefit calculation is likely to be made by the researcher. Both Rothschild's anonymous colleague and Machlup argue that the gross benefits of incorporating imperfect information may be close to nil. Suppose, however, that a good part of the profession has for some time disagreed with this view about gross benefits. It does not immediately follow that the profession would therefore quickly move to incorporate imperfect information into the theory. An important stumbling block might be the costs of such an attempt. Even with high gross benefits, very large costs can reduce net benefits to less than zero. Indeed, how to incorporate imperfect information usefully, including the "tractability" of doing so, has over the years been a major obstacle to more thorough treatment of the topic. At the most primitive level, if incorporating imperfect information seemed to analysts to incur the extremely high costs of having to abandon available modeling principles of maximizing behavior or of equilibrium, it would hardly be surprising if there was no mass movement to model imperfect information. In the extreme case, analysts simply would not know how to proceed to analyze situations productively without these modeling principles.

The benefit-cost framework suggests that explaining the infusion of the imperfect knowledge assumption into economic theory will require investigating how the costs of including this assumption fell. We pursue this issue by discussing a major obstacle to the lowering of costs, and then describing two kinds of analytical insights that seemed to have lowered the barriers to, and therefore the costs of, analytically incorporating imperfect information.

For several decades the most important analytical framework for attempting to deal with uncertainty was the expected utility analysis associated with von Neumann and Morgenstern. Yet the framework contained what seemed to be a major flaw—its apparent inability to deal in a simple but successful way with individuals who both gamble and buy insurance. The inability over a long period of years to produce a succinct explanation of this seemingly widespread behavior surely must have given pause to many of those who considered using a von Neumann–Morgenstern framework to incorporate uncertainty into their analyses.[15]

Even in the face of this major conceptual difficulty, there has still been a tremendous increase in the volume of studies incorporating analysis of knowledge imperfections. This increase has been due at least in part to several analytical insights or innovations that have made modeling imperfect information situations tractable, thereby lowering the costs of performing such analyses.

One major innovation was George Stigler's seminal work (1961, 1962) which investigated how imperfectly informed consumers (workers) facing a distribution of prices (wages) might cope with the existence of this distribution. These articles are largely responsible for generating the large literature on "search theory," including but not limited to the search-theoretic analyses of Phillips curves. Rothschild refers to Stigler's 1961 paper as a "fundamental article" that "directly or indirectly inspired most of the work" (1973, p. 1287). Stigler's way of posing and analyzing one aspect of the imperfect knowledge problem—the existence of a distribution of prices or wages—provided other researchers with a viable way of incorporating one feature of imperfect information into their analyses. Thanks to Stigler, researchers saw that they could include imperfect information in a nontrivial way by recognizing the existence of a distribution of wages or prices facing the individual worker or consumer, and modeling how this individual might react to that distribution.

Work by Akerlof (1970) provides a second example of a new and fruitful way of looking at how imperfect information might enter the analysis. Akerlof's insight was to stress the importance of information asymmetries, situations in which sellers (for example) are privy to information that is not available to buyers. The presence of asymmetries—that is, systematically unequal access to information—leads to some quite striking departures from standard results obtained in the certainty case. This notion of asymmetry has now found its way into a good deal of the literature incorporating imperfect information.

What is notable for the issues we are considering is that insights such as Akerlof's and Stigler's are needed to provide analysts with fruitful ways of actually incorporating imperfect information in the analysis. It is not enough to recognize that "uncertainty is all around us"; researchers also need methods for allowing its incorporation in their analyses. In terms of our net benefit approach, such new insights not only lower the costs (increase the tractability) of incorporating imperfect information, but they may also heighten our perceptions of the (gross) benefits of its incorporation. Akerlof's analysis, for example, suggested new sources of market failure.

Both the Stigler and Akerlof contributions increased tractability by giving other researchers a particular insight or method for putting imperfect information into the analysis. But something a bit more specific can be said about the way in which this heightened tractability is obtained. Rather than proceeding by asserting "imperfect knowledge is important, so let's find a very general way to incorporate it in all analyses," each contribution instead defines, carves off, and analyzes a much narrower problem. That is, neither innovation provides a general analysis of imperfect information. Stigler, for example, picks out one very particular feature that can result from imperfect information and proceeds to analyze only that specific feature (a distribution of wages or prices that in a perfect-information world would usually collapse to one price or wage). It is by focusing only on this particular isolated phenomenon that Stigler is able to make so much headway and provoke so much additional research by others. Similarly, Akerlof's success seems to stem from his isolating one particular feature (asymmetric information) that may, but need not always, arise in imperfect knowledge settings. Thus, progress in introducing imperfect information seems to have depended on carving off digestible bits and pieces of the broader phenomenon for analysis. These examples make it seem as though "divide to conquer" is the key to tractability innovations.

We have already seen that if we ignore an awkward fact about the timing of assumption changes, a Friedmanesque instrumentalist view is roughly compatible with the pattern of assumption changes that emerged to deal with turnover. How well does the Friedmanesque view versus a Lakatosian view fit the imperfect information case? Lakatos, like Popper and Kuhn, focused on the process by which theories succeeded other theories. His view of the process of scientific change incorporated the notion that it did not make sense to (and, as a historical matter, scientists would not) abandon an existing analytical structure until an alternative analytical structure was available that was at least as attractive. He used as his unit of analytical structure the concept of a "scientific research program." A scientific research program is a series or progression of scientific theories "characterized by a certain continuity which connects their members. . . . The programme consists of methodological rules: some tell us what paths of research to avoid (negative heuristic), and others what paths to pursue (positive heuristic)" (Lakatos 1978, p. 47). Our imperfect information example seems quite consistent with a Lakatosian description of how science actually proceeds in several ways. First, in a Lakatosian framework it is hardly surprising that neoclassical analysis was not abandoned because of criticisms about unrealistic "perfect information" assumptions; there was simply no obviously superior paradigm or research program available to fall back on. Second, the fact that it required "tractability innovations" to get imperfect information incorporated into the assumption set is, in Lakatos's language, a recognition that improvements in the theory generated within a research program can only be made in a way *consistent with the positive heuristic.* Tractability innovations, as the term is used in this paper, are innovations that show how to incorporate a new assumption without destroying the core analytical devices of a particular methodological approach or "research program." That is, they are "paradigm-enhancing" innovations allowing enrichment of the theory in a way that is consistent with the positive heuristic of the research program.[16]

While our version of Friedmanesque instrumentalism fits the turnover case in a rough sort of way, it seems clear that it does not fit the imperfect information case anywhere near as well as the Lakatosian framework does. The incorporation of imperfect information into the assumption set was not provoked in any simple way by some overwhelming sense among the innovators of a predictive failure in microeconomic theory; Stigler's work, for example, does not display or express such a view. Instead, the episode looks more like an alteration of basic assumptions *in response to a long tradition of criticism of those assumptions*. That is, direct unease with assumptions rather than unease with predictive results created the conditions for assumption change. The episode better fits a Lakatosian scientific research program setting, in which analytical modifications of the program's structure of theories (not necessarily generated by any particular empirical shortcoming) are seen to be an important part of the way in which research programs progress.

Conclusion

The approach in this paper starts from the supposition that economists' choices of assumptions deserve considerable scrutiny; careful descriptive attention to the way in which economists actually go about choosing and modifying assumptions may lead to a deepening of our understanding of the state of the discipline. To begin investigating this topic, we pursued an analogy between detail simplification in maps and simplifying assumptions in economics. The analogy led us to an issue that is important to understanding how economists typically proceed: how is the particular mix of descriptive incompleteness found in economic theory arrived at? In order to shed light on this issue, we examined two examples of historical changes in actual assumption sets. One conclusion was that perceptions as to what economic phenomena need to be explained change over time in economics, just as they do in the natural sciences. Such changes in perceptions can be a source of changes in assumption sets, since new assumptions may be needed to incorporate explanations of new phenomena. A second conclusion was that a Friedmanesque instrumentalist view, stressing the prime importance of predictive failure in provoking assumption changes, is unlikely to provide as satisfactory an explanation of certain assumption shifts as would a Lakatosian view. Our imperfect information example did not fit the Friedmanesque predictive failure view at all, while our labor turnover example only fit in a very inexact way. In that example, the assumption change seemed to predate general recognition of the predictive failure, although this later recognition may have helped assure the widespread acceptance and popularity of the assumption change.

Two telling results emerged from examining our concrete cases from the Lakatosian viewpoint: first, criticisms of economic theory that focus on the unreasonableness of assumptions or results are not likely to provoke revisions of the assumption set unless and until the tractability problem involved in such revisions is successfully addressed. Assumption changes responsive to such criticisms are unlikely to be adopted unless they allow important elements of the received analytical structure to be maintained, as in the labor turnover case. Thus, criticisms like "imperfect information is important; ignore it at your peril" can be repeated over and over again for extended periods with little effect on the assumption set. Such criticisms only lead to changes when someone shows how to incorporate imperfect information into the existing analytical framework in a manner such that existing (suitably modified) analytical methods can continue to be used. Interestingly enough, Stigler's own explanation of why his work on imperfect information was so influential stresses its consistency with received techniques of economic analysis.[17] This result also seems to us to support the proposition that analyzing the researcher's situation using a simple (and, in our example, quite primitive) benefit-cost framework can be useful.

A second result is that "suitable" or "paradigm-enhancing" modifications were produced in the imperfect information case by breaking a large analytic issue into smaller pieces that could be handled more easily. This suggests that important assumption modifications may largely take place by slicing off and attacking "smaller" analytical problems at the margin of the paradigm.

Notes

Unbeknownst to either of the authors, Garth Mangum and Isabelle Sawhill are jointly responsible for provoking this paper. Amitai Etzioni also bears a bit of the blame, for reasons we are sure he will understand. Discussions with Allen Lerman and Harry Watson provided crucial insights at critical junctures in this paper's development. Comments on earlier drafts by Steve Baldwin, Bryan Boulier, Michael Bradley, Timothy Brennan, Joseph Cordes, C.Y. Hsieh, Andrew Kohen, John Kwoka, David Lindauer, William Long, John Lowe, Stephen Mangum, Elijah Millgram, Len Nichols, and Charles Stewart sharpened our thinking, as did comments by seminar participants at the University of Maryland, Baltimore County (Department of Economics), and at a Political Economy workshop in Cambridge, MA.

1. A particularly explicit advocate of this view is Machlup (1967). See the discussion in note 13 below. Nooteboom (1986) testifies to the existence of this view in order to attack it.

2. Reder indicates that the "paradigmatic nature" of the Chicago approach "gives its adherents a particular perspective on empirical evidence. . . . Because in 'normal science' it is presumed that the currently accepted theory is valid, new findings are accepted far more readily if they are consistent with the theory's implications" (1982, p. 21). Reder indicates that, in the face of anomalous empirical findings inconsistent with the received theory, the Chicago approach involves "shunning" the "alteration of the theory to ac-

commodate behavior inconsistent with the postulates of rationality (constrained maximization)" (p. 13). A case can be made for this approach to evidence and assumption change, but that case would not be a Friedmanesque instrumentalist one.

3. As Laudan (1987, p. 19) notes, many leading philosophers of science now reject the notion that methodologies of science have, or ought to have, prescriptive force for theory choice. As for the descriptive role of methodologies, Hilary Putnam (1987) has recently argued that there is no one approach to the philosophy of science that even manages to fit all the natural sciences adequately.

4. Stephen Toulmin (1960) contains a chapter entitled "Theories and Maps," but its focus is quite different from that involved in the economic theory-map analogy.

5. Another interesting and unavoidable source of "misrepresentation" is highlighted in a leading cartography text: Robinson, Sale, Morrison, and Muerke (1984). One of the text's focuses is on constraints on information content imposed by the size limitations of maps. Considerable attention is paid to the fact that "on all but the largest-scale maps, most features must be exaggerated to make them reasonably visible. . . . It is important to keep in mind that the reduction of available space takes place as the square of the difference in linear scales. For example a region mapped at 1:25,000 will only occupy one-sixteenth as much space when mapped at 1:100,000. It is quite obvious that the compression that results from scale reduction often allows only limited portrayal" (p. 126). Thus, decisions must be made about what geographical features to retain, and the degree to which "distinctive characteristics should be portrayed . . . even if that requires exaggeration" (p. 129). That is, once map scale is reduced, making certain features acceptably visible requires that their dimension be exaggerated. In our language, the cartographer is confronted with a choice among descriptive incompleteness (leaving out the feature), descriptive "misrepresentation" or "falseness" (exaggerating the scale of the feature to make it acceptably visible), or useless descriptive accuracy (including the feature to correct scale, so that it is not acceptably visible). We are indebted to Professor of Geography John Lowe for this reference and for helpful discussions about cartography.

6. Cf. Leatherdale (1974) and Hesse (1966).

7. Discussions with Timothy Brennan led us to focus on the importance of the explicit market in determining criteria for detail omission in maps. There are other suggestive breakdowns in the analogy in addition to those discussed in the text. A particularly interesting one has to do with the observation that the appropriate level and mix of detail depends on the use to which the map is to be put. In fact, one important characteristic of maps appears to be that they are often most useful when utilized in sets, different maps in the set having different coverage and levels of detail. A typical traveler driving from the U.S. East Coast to the West Coast wants long-distance maps with little local detail for getting through the interior of the country, but local maps to find his exact destination in San Francisco. That is, the availability of a sequence of presentations with a very systematic and particular variation in level of detail increases the usefulness of maps. Yet the way in which economic theory has developed does not always seem to provide a series of "maps" that allow increased detail—closer and closer approximation to "full reality"—depending on the needs of the user. Instead, the user must make do with isolated available choices about the level of detail. This (at least partial) unavailability of a sequence of presentations makes it harder to appreciate what is given up versus what is gained by using the particular level of detail available.

A sequencing concept actually does arise in a particular way in discussions of macroeconomics that illustrates the failure to achieve successful sequencing. The movement to develop the micro-foundations of macroeconomics can be thought of as an attempt to provide the beginnings of a sequence of analytical "maps," while the development of large-scale (multiequation, multisector) macroeconometric models can be thought of as an attempt to provide a sequence of empirical "maps." That these movements exist indicates that there is a belief in the usefulness of sequences of presentations. However, with respect to micro-foundations, Leijonhufvud (1976) questions whether neo-Walrasian microeconomics is the appropriate micro-foundation for Keynesian macroeconomics, suggesting that a Marshallian approach might work better. He also asserts that neo-Walrasian micro should have a non-Keynesian macro associated with it. Solow (1986) provides a similar discussion. The existence of such fundamental issues about proper approaches to sequencing indicates how far away economics is from a situation where complete sequences are readily available. Further testimonial to this point is the general disrepute into which large-scale macroeconometric models have fallen, and the longstanding recognition of the fundamental difficulties in aggregating both quantities (for example, "capital") and microeconomic relationships (for example, "production functions"). Analogous aggregation problems do not seem to exist for maps. (It should be noted that sequences do exist in some areas of economics: one goes from the consumer to market demand, from the firm to market supply, etc.)

8. The Rosen quote cites Becker's 1964 book, *Human Capital,* but a Becker article setting forth the relevant concepts appears in 1962, and Oi (1962, p. 588) acknowledges Becker's influence (through Oi's reading of Becker's unpublished work) in a footnote.

9. A number of distinguished labor market analysts steeped in a more institutionalist tradition carried out studies of specific city labor markets in the 1940s and 1950s (see, for example, Reynolds 1951). These analysts clearly recognized the importance of turnover considerations for the employer. This recognition was not picked up by mainline neoclassical labor market theorists at the time, however.

10. Two knee jerk reactions dismissing this issue are: (1) "All firms are perfect competitors in the labor market, therefore they are wage takers, with no wage-setting decision to make"; and (2) "The question is methodologically incorrect. We can test the earlier 'no turnover' version of the theory by its comparative statics. We only need reject it if these comparative static predictions do not hold up." In answer to (1), it is easily shown that, in a world with fixed costs of employment, a firm may wish to pay wages above the "wage taker" wage it needs to pay to get enough applicants. It pays this higher wage to obtain lower turnover (quits), thereby reducing its overall labor costs. A large literature now embodies this idea (see Salop 1973; Pencavel 1972; and even Hamermesh and Goldfarb 1970 for early examples). Even if such models are not to one's taste, there is extensive empirical evidence in the Bureau of Labor Statistics Area Wage Surveys of immense wage diversity by narrowly defined occupation within particular standard metropolitan statistical areas (SMSAs). Moreover, the whole labor market search theory literature is based on the proposition that searchers face a nontrivial distribution of wage offers. Given the popularity of search theory, some sizable percentage of the profession must sympathize with this proposition. In answer to (2), we would point out that the earlier no-turnover version of the theory, even if its comparative statics with respect to wage changes turned out to be largely correct, would still be deficient by failing to produce any comparative static predictions about changes in turnover. Moreover, we challenge the reader to find a sizable number of studies aimed at providing compelling empirical tests of the marginal productivity theory of factor demand.

11. The reader might, for example, argue that even if an extended theory is developed that also recognizes and makes predictions about turnover, it is still likely to generate a negative relation between the wage and the employer's desired employment level, other things being equal. We would point out in response that the addition of fixed costs of employment allows development of propositions about the effects of wage changes on the employer's choice between "more hours or more employees," propositions that do not emerge out of simple marginal productivity theory in the absence of fixed costs. See texts

by Hamermesh and Rees (1984) and Ehrenberg and Smith (1985) for useful discussions of the effects of fixed costs on the hours-versus-workers choice.

12. For particularly striking examples, see Terence Hutchison, *The Significance and Basic Postulates of Economic Theory* (1960, first published 1938), chap. 4, and Oskar Morgenstern (1935). In commenting on Hutchison's stress on expectations, Caldwell (1984, p. 4) notes that "a number of economists grappled with the problem of knowledge and its acquisition in the 1930's . . . interest in the topic dwindled as the Keynesian Revolution gathered momentum." Morgenstern indicates that "the assumption of perfect foresight is to be cut out from economic theory" (1935, p. 182); "The problem could be put in the following manner: exactly which division of different degrees of expectation and foresight corresponds to the conditions of equilibrium described by the Walrasian equations? It is a long road until a satisfactory answer may be obtained. . . . Who knows whether the idea of equilibrium can be retained at all?" (p. 183).

13. These claims are meant to apply largely to industries with "more than a few firms and with free entry" (Machlup 1967, p. 14). Machlup views the theory's aim to be comparative statics at the industry level. Indeed, the firm in the relevant theory is a "theoretical construct," not to be confused with "the firm as an empirical concept" (p. 9). The theory is not designed, Machlup argues, to produce propositions at the firm level, and interpreting firms in the theory as real firms is committing the fallacy of misplaced concreteness (p. 9).

14. While it is not central to the concerns of this paper, one cannot help but wonder how Rothschild's colleague deals with insurance and gambling markets. These commodities exist only because particular outcomes are not known with perfect certainty in advance of the event.

15. That the Friedman and Savage (1958) attempt to resolve this problem has remained unconvincing is indicated by Dowell and McLaren (1986), who say that the purpose of their paper "is to provide a relatively more convincing rationale for the Friedman-Savage function than is contained in the current literature" (p. 669). For a review of major empirical studies bearing on the expected utility (or EU) model, see Shoemaker (1982), who concludes that "at the individual level, EU maximization is more the exception than the rule" (p. 552).

16. Our analysis of the imperfect information example also fits neatly into a framework proposed by the philosopher Larry Laudan in his 1977 book, *Progress and Its Problems.* Building on the work of Kuhn and Lakatos, Laudan generates an analysis of "research traditions" that manages to avoid some of the conceptual difficulties in the Kuhn and Lakatos approaches. It could be argued in a Lakatosian vein that perfect information was for decades a crucial element of the "hard core" of a neoclassical or neo-Walrasian (to use Weintraub's term) research program. If this view is adopted, then a change in a hard-core assumption seems to require a change in the research program. But our discussion suggests that the incorporation of imperfect information was a natural development in the ongoing research program. This view exactly fits Laudan's framework, where the neoclassical approach would be treated as a research tradition. Within such traditions, Laudan writes, changes in some once-crucial components are to be expected. "As new arguments emerge which buttress, or cast doubt upon, different elements of the research tradition, the relative degree of entrenchment of the different components will shift . . . when it can be shown that certain elements, previously regarded as essential to the whole enterprise, can be jettisoned without compromising the problem-solving success of the tradition itself, these elements cease to be part of the 'unrejectable core' of the research tradition"(1977, p. 100).

The text discussion concerns positive rather than normative features of Lakatos's view of scientific change, since our focus in this paper is on positive modeling of how economists choose assumptions. However, there is one further connection between our imperfect information example and Lakatos's view of scientific progress that has implications for the normative features of his analysis. Lakatos contrasts his views about progress in science to those of Thomas Kuhn as follows: Lakatos sees the replacement over time of one scientific research program by another as a rational process, based on accumulating evidence that the new program is scientifically superior to the one it is superseding, whereas "in Kuhn's view scientific revolution is irrational, a matter for mob psychology" (Lakatos 1978, p. 91). Put somewhat less flamboyantly, in Lakatos's view, Kuhn provides no reasons other than psychological ones why there arise "crises" that lead to the overthrow of the prevailing scientific paradigm. It seems to us that our (suitably elaborated) benefit-cost framework applied to the scientific researcher would provide a way of thinking about the decision of the individual researcher as to which paradigm he would choose to work in, and under what conditions he might decide to switch. Thus, it seems to provide a more concrete basis for beginning to build up a positive theory of what researchers choose to work on, which in turn would allow us to think more systematically about Lakatosian grand scientific rationality versus Kuhnian crises as models of how paradigm switches take place.

It is important to stress three things about the suggested approach: first, we are proposing to substitute an economic model of paradigm switches (in Kuhn's vocabulary) for Kuhn's sociological model. Second, our economic model includes private benefits and costs to the researcher, which need not be (indeed are unlikely to be) identical to "scientific" or "social" or "pure knowledge" benefits and costs. Examples of private benefits that are not necessarily social benefits include building the individual researcher's reputation, his obtaining of grants, and so forth. In recent work arguing for and focusing on an economic approach to modeling the researcher's choice of research program, both Ghiselin (1987) and Radnitzky (1987) stress that researchers are subject to private incentives, which may or may not work to maximize scientific discovery. To cite one especially cogent line, Ghiselin notes that "the question is not, whether we act out of self-interest, but how we act out of self-interest. In some cases self-interest leads to lapses of scholarly objectivity, in other cases it has the opposite effect" (1987, p. 280). We adopted a cost-benefit approach before becoming aware of Ghiselin's and Radnitzky's work, and neither of them focuses on the use of a cost-benefit type of model to reinterpret the Lakatos criticism of Kuhn. A much briefer reference to a cost-benefit view of the researcher's choices of assumptions is in Nooteboom (1986, pp. 208–9). Although Laudan (1977) does not adopt an explicit cost-benefit framework, he has a very interesting discussion (1987, pp. 109–14) of what he calls "the context of pursuit," the researcher's choice of which theory or research tradition to pursue. He focuses in particular on situations in which the researcher might reasonably decide to work in a newer tradition even though it was as yet far less successful than the dominant tradition. Third, once the point about private versus social benefits is recognized, it becomes clear that the Lakatos argument that the process by which scientific research programs are displaced is "rational" could be right in the small but wrong in the large. It could be right in the small in that individuals are acting rationally given their private goals in aligning themselves with particular research programs. These researchers are rational calculators, not victims of scientific "mob psychology." However, this "rationality of the individual researcher's choice" does not insure that the process is "rational" (the economist's term is "optimal") in the large, from a normative social efficiency point of view. The issue of social optimality is far more complex, and depends crucially on how well the private incentives facing the individual researcher approximate social incentives. Is the "invisible hand" behind the private incentives pushing as effectively as possible in the right direction? Only with a good deal more modeling of the research process can this issue be better understood.

17. Stigler's own view (1983, p. 539) is that his imperfect information analysis was so influential and widely accepted "without even a respectable minimum of controversy" because "no established scientific theory was being challenged," and his work showed how "the economics of information was susceptible to study by quite standard techniques of economic analysis."

References

Akerlof, George. (1970) "The Market for 'Lemons': Quality Uncertainty and the Market Mechanism." *Quarterly Journal of Economics* 84:488–500.

Baumol, William, and Alan Blinder. (1985) *Economics: Principles and Policy*. New York: Harcourt Brace Jovanovich.

Becker, Gary. (1962) "Investment in Human Capital: A Theoretical Analysis." *Journal of Political Economy* 70:9–49.

———. (1964) *Human Capital*. New York: Columbia University Press.

Blaug, Mark. (1980) *The Methodology of Economics*. Cambridge: Cambridge University Press.

Boland, Lawrence. (1979) "A Critique of Friedman's Critics." *Journal of Economic Literature* 17:503–22.

Brennan, Timothy J. (1984) "Is Economics Methodologically Special?" *Research in the History of Economic Thought and Methodology* 2:127–40.

Caldwell, Bruce. (1980) "A Critique of Friedman's Methodological Instrumentalism." *Southern Economic Journal* 47:366–74.

———, ed. (1984) *Appraisal and Criticism in Economics*. Boston: Allen & Unwin.

Cohen, R., P. Feyerabend, and M. Wartofsky. (1976) *Essays in Memory of Imre Lakatos*. Dordrecht: D. Reidel.

Cross, John. (1983) *A Theory of Adaptive Economic Behavior*. Cambridge: Cambridge University Press.

Cross, Rod. (1982) "The Duhem-Quine Thesis, Lakatos and the Appraisal of Theories in Macroeconomics." *Economic Journal* 92:320–40.

Dowell, Richard, and K. McLaren. (1986) "An Intertemporal Analysis of the Interdependence between Risk Preference, Retirement, and Work Rate Decisions." *Journal of Political Economy* 94:667–82.

Ehrenberg, Ronald, and Robert Smith. (1985) *Modern Labor Economics*. New York: Scott Foresman.

Etzioni, Amitai. (1986) "The Case for a Multiple-Utility Conception." *Economics and Philosophy* 2:159–83.

Friedman, Milton. (1953) "The Methodology of Positive Economics." In *Essays in Positive Economics*. Chicago: University of Chicago Press.

Friedman, Milton, and Leonard Savage. (1958) "The Utility Analysis of Choices Involving Risk." *Journal of Political Economy* 56:279–304.

Ghiselin, Michael. (1987) "The Economics Of Scientific Discovery." In Gerard Radnitzky and Peter Bernholz, eds., *Economic Imperialism*. New York: Paragon House.

Hamermesh, Daniel, and Robert Goldfarb. (1970) "Manpower Programs in a Local Labor Market: A Theoretical Note." *American Economic Review* 60:706–9.

Hamermesh, Daniel, and Albert Rees. (1984) *The Economics of Work and Pay*. 3d ed. New York: Harper & Row.

Hamminga, Bert. (1983) *Neo-classical Theory Structure and Theory Development*. Berlin: Springer-Verlag.

Hands, Wade. (1985) "Second Thoughts on Lakatos." *History of Political Economy* 17:1–16.

Hausman, Daniel, ed. (1984) *The Philosophy of Economics*. Cambridge: Cambridge University Press.
Hesse, Mary. (1966) *Models and Analogies in Science*. South Bend, IN: University of Notre Dame Press.
Hirschman, Albert. (1970) *Exit, Voice and Loyalty*. Cambridge, MA: Harvard University Press.
———. (1985) "Against Parsimony." *Economics and Philosophy* 1:7–21.
Hirshleifer, Jack. (1985) "The Expanding Domain of Economics." *American Economic Review* 75:53–68.
Hutchison, Terence. (1960) *The Significance and Basic Postulates of Economic Theory*. New York: Kelley. (Originally published in 1938.)
———. (1978) *On Revolutions and Progress in Economic Knowledge*. Cambridge: Cambridge University Press.
Kuhn, Thomas. (1970) *The Structure of Scientific Revolutions*. 2d ed. Chicago: University of Chicago Press.
Lakatos, Imre. (1970) *Proofs and Refutations*. Cambridge: Cambridge University Press.
———. (1978) *The Methodology of Scientific Research Programmes*. Cambridge: Cambridge University Press.
Latsis, Spiro. (1976) "A Research Programme in Economics." In *Method and Appraisal in Economics*, pp. 1–42. Cambridge: Cambridge University Press.
Laudan, Larry. (1977) *Progress and Its Problems*. Berkeley: University of California Press.
———. (1987) "Progress or Rationality? The Prospects for Normative Naturalism." *American Philosophical Quarterly* 24:19–31.
Leatherdale, W.H. (1974) *The Role of Analogy, Model and Metaphor in Science*. Amsterdam: American Elsevier.
Leijonhufvud, Axel. (1976) "Schools, 'Revolutions,' and Research Programmes in Economic Theory." In Spiro Latsis, ed., *Method and Appraisal in Economics*, pp. 65–108. Cambridge: Cambridge University Press.
McCloskey, Donald. (1983) "The Rhetoric of Economics." *Journal of Economic Literature* 21:481–517.
———. (1985) *The Rhetoric of Economics*. Madison, WI: University of Wisconsin Press.
Machlup, Fritz. (1967) "Theories of the Firm: Marginalist, Behavioral, Managerial." *American Economic Review* 57:1–33.
Morgenstern, Oskar. (1935) "Perfect Foresight and Economic Equilibrium." *Zeitschrift fur Nationalokonomie* 6, part 3. (Reprinted in A. Schotter, ed., *Selected Writings of Oskar Morgenstern*, pp. 169–83. New York: New York University Press.)
Nooteboom, Bart. (1986) "Plausibility in Economics." *Economics and Philosophy* 2:197–224.
Oi, Walter. (1962) "Labor as a Quasi-Fixed Factor of Production." *Journal of Political Economy* 70:538–55.
Pencavel, John. (1972) "Wages, Specific Training and Labor Turnover in U.S. Manufacturing Industries." *International Economic Review* 13:53–64.
Popper, Karl. (1959) *The Logic of Scientific Discovery*. London: Hutchinson.
Putnam, Hilary. (1987) "The Diversity of the Sciences: Global versus Local Methodological Approaches." In Philip Pettit, Richard Sylvan, and Jean Norman, eds., *Metaphysics and Morality*, pp. 137–53. Oxford: Basil Blackwell.
Radnitzky, Gerard. (1987) "Cost-Benefit Thinking in the Methodology of Research: The Economic Approach Applied to Key Problems of the Philosophy of Science." In Gerard Radnitzky and Peter Bernholz, eds., *Economic Imperialism*. New York: Paragon House.

Radnitzky, Gerard, and Gunnar Andersson. (1978) *Progress and Rationality in Science.* Dordrecht: D. Reidel.
Reder, Melvin. (1982) "Chicago Economics: Permanence and Change." *Journal of Economic Literature* 20:1–38.
Reynolds, Lloyd. (1951) *The Structure of Labor Markets.* New York: Harper.
Robinson, Arthur, Randolph Sale, Joel Morrison, and Phillip Muerke. (1984) *Elements of Cartography.* 5th ed. New York: John Wiley.
Rosen, Sherwin. (1985) "Implicit Contracts." *Journal of Economic Literature* 23:1144–75.
Rosenberg, Alexander. (1983) "If Economics Isn't a Science, What Is It?" *Philosophical Forum* 14:296–314.
———. (1986) "Lakatosian Consolations for Economics." *Economics and Philosophy* 2:127–39.
Rothschild, Michael. (1973) "Models of Market Organization with Imperfect Information: A Survey." *Journal of Political Economy* 81:1283–1308.
Salop, Steve. (1973) "Wage Differentials in a Dynamic Theory of the Firm." *Journal of Economic Theory* 5:321–44.
Samuelson, Paul. (1963) "Discussion." *American Economic Association Papers and Proceedings* 53:231–36.
Sen, Amartya. (1977) "Rational Fools: A Critique of the Behavioral Foundations of Economic Theory." *Philosophy and Public Affairs* 6:317–44.
Shoemaker, Paul. (1982) "The Expected Utility Model: Its Variants, Purposes, Evidence, and Limitations." *Journal of Economic Literature* 20:529–63.
Solow, Robert. (1986) "What Is a Nice Girl Like You Doing in a Place Like This?—Macroeconomics after Fifty Years." *Eastern Economic Journal* 13:191–98.
Stigler, George. (1961) "The Economics of Information." *Journal of Political Economy* 69:213–35.
———. (1962) "Information in the Labor Market." *Journal of Political Economy* 70:94–105.
———. (1983) "Nobel Lecture: The Process and Progress of Economics." *Journal of Political Economy* 91:529–45.
Toulmin, Stephen. (1960) *The Philosophy of Science.* New York: Harper & Row.
Weintraub, E. Roy. (1985) "Appraising General Equilibrium Analysis." *Economics and Philosophy* 1:23–37.
Wonnacott, Paul, and Ronald Wonnacott. (1982) *Economics.* 2d ed. New York: McGraw-Hill.
———. (1985) *Economics.* 3d ed. New York: McGraw-Hill.

9

DRAZEN PRELEC

Values and Principles

Some Limitations on Traditional Economic Analysis

Introduction

Economic theory is often criticized on the grounds that it ignores the role of values in human action. Subsumed under this criticism are two distinct complaints: One, that economics has a narrow view of human motives, which typically excludes social and moral concerns; two, that the rational choice model presents an inadequate picture of the choice processes associated with value-governed action.

In this paper, I draw a structural distinction between values as social sentiments, which can be assimilated to the economic notion of tastes, and values as crystallized rules or principles, which resist such assimilation. This distinction operates independently of content (i.e., independently of whether the values are in the service of personal or social goals), so that, for example, the belief that one should vote, and that one should stay fit, would both count as instances of the second category. Rule-governed action is a specific decision-making style, whose main characteristics form a contrast to the rational model.

Decision analysis, which codifies the rational model, views choice as a fundamentally technical problem of choosing the course of action that maximizes a unidimensional criterion, such as value or utility. The primary mental activity involved in decision analysis is the reduction of multiple attributes or dimensions to a single one, through a specification of value trade-offs, and the assessment of subjective probabilities for uncertain events. For rule-governed action, the fundamental decision problem is the quasi-legal one of constructing a satisfying interpretation of the choice situation. The primary mental activity involved in this process is the exploration of analogies and distinctions between the current situation, and other "canonical" choice situations in which a single rule or principle unambiguously applies.

The Problem of "Tastes"

"Profound moral conviction was the basis of Mr. Gladstone's political influence," remarked Bertrand Russell, explaining: "Invariably he earnestly consulted his conscience, and invariably his conscience earnestly gave him the convenient answer." From the perspective of a rational agent, Russell's witticism ought to be cryptic, but, of course, it is not, especially to those whose conscience is not as obliging and versatile. At the level of common sense, we all recognize that actions are shaped by such things as values, rules, principles, that are in part our own creation but that can also appear to us as an external constraint, over which we have little control.

In this paper, I would like to suggest the importance of having a theory of human nature and action within which the paradox inherent in Gladstone's supposed decision-making style would find some natural explanation. I do not have such a theory, and I do not think a fully satisfactory one is available, hence the paper will have the more modest aim of showing the need for a missing psychology of legal reasoning and interpretation whose purpose would be to describe how people use principles in decision making, as well as how principles are integrated with rational cost-benefit calculations.

First, some background on the problem. Lately, there has been much debate over the proper role of values and moral considerations in economic theory.[1] A central issue in this debate is whether social and moral motives for action can be assimilated to the economist's notion of *tastes* or *preferences.* The prevailing view, even among critics of traditional economic theory, seems to be that such assimilation is possible, but yields little insight into economic phenomena. Thus, for example, Etzioni follows his Proposition 7.1 (1988, p. 254):

> All items have at least two valuations: their ability to generate pleasure and their moral standing

with the acknowledgment that (Proposition 7.3),

> It is technically possible but unproductive to reduce the two kinds of valuations to one.[2]

An economist would view this as an important admission, since his estimate of the potential benefits of translating all valuation into the uniform language of preference will naturally be much more optimistic. But is this concession really necessary? To examine this question, I think it is helpful first to blur one key distinction, but sharpen a secondary one (see Table 9.1). The distinction that needs blurring, for the time being, is that between selfish and altruistic motives for action. Although important, this contrast has the unfortunate effect of framing the issue in a way that makes the case for taste assimilation most plausible. As Howard Margolis put it, why must we "distinguish between the bread Smith buys to give to the poor and that which he buys for his own consumption."[3]

Table 9.1

Preferences and Principles Are Relevant for Decisions Having Personal or Public Significance

	Matters of preference	Matters of principle
Individual level	Innocuous consumption decisions, concerning food, clothes, entertainment, etc.	Decisions about health, fitness, debt, alcohol consumption, etc.
Social level	Decisions affected by social and moral sentiments, such as compassion, envy, gratitude, etc.	Decisions governed by social and moral obligations, by standards of honesty, loyalty, duty, etc.

Altruistic values, of some kind at least, can be cleanly assimilated to "tastes," with nothing left over. Such values may be termed moral or social "sentiments," in that it is almost as if the inner states of other persons become the direct object of our own utility. A fan at a boxing match, to pursue another illustration, possibly feels pain with each blow that his boxer absorbs. It seems idle to debate whether the feeling falls in the category of selfish or altruistic sentiments.

The distinction that needs sharpening, however, is between action governed by cost-benefit calculation—however broadly the relevant costs and benefits are understood—and action governed by a binding rule or principle.[4] Now, a curious and psychologically most significant aspect of rules or principles is that they can be found to cover not only social actions, having impact on the well-being of others, but also actions that affect no one besides the decision maker. Examples of such would include prohibitions against borrowing, gambling, uncleanliness, certain types of food, drink, entertainment (all of which have been described with great insight in the work of George Ainslie). Ordinary language indeed bears further witness to the notion that moral and prudential principles tap a common psychological mechanism: one speaks of feeling guilt or remorse for having overspent, or broken a diet.

Although such rules of self-management may appear less important than explicit moral principles, the fact that they do exist indicates that the tendency to form and follow rules requires some explanation at the level of individual psychology.

In brief outline, the next section of this paper defines rules or principles, and explores their possible function. The third section then discusses why rule-governed behavior resists assimilation to the rational model. This same issue is taken up again in the fourth section, but now with respect to so-called "multiple-self'' models, which view the individual agent as a collection of noncooperating but individually rational subunits. The paper concludes with a short summary of the basic differences between rational and rule-governed action.

Three Systematic Biases in Cost-Benefit Calculation

Essential to the application of a principle is the belief that a principle does not *supplement* ordinary cost-benefit analysis, but rather *replaces* it (Etzioni 1988). In other words, by invoking a principle, one does not add another consideration onto what Janis and Mann (1977) call the ''decisional balance-sheet,'' but instead discards the balance-sheet altogether.

By a rule or principle, then, I refer to any behavioral policy that overrides cost-benefit calculations, even—or especially—when the calculations can be made without any difficulty. The purpose of rules must therefore be derived from some weakness of our natural cost-benefit accounting system, and one might expect to find rules proliferating in exactly those choice domains where a natural utilitarianism does not produce satisfactory results.

There seem to be at least three different factors that create trouble for ordinary cost-benefit analysis, and they are each describable in the form of a biasing asymmetry or ''mismatch'' in the disposition of the costs relative to the benefits that flow from an action:

1. *Temporal mismatch*, in which the cost and benefit are separated by a substantial time interval.
2. *Saliency mismatch*, in which one element of the pair is vivid and easy to imagine, while the other is not.
3. *Scale mismatch*, in which one element of the cost-benefit pair is perceived to have impact only in an aggregate sense, that is, only if the same action is repeated many times, or on a larger scale.

We will refer to these as asymmetries of time, saliency, and scale, respectively. In all three cases, the cost-benefit fails because it assigns insufficient weight to one element of the pair. The excessive discounting of future consequences is amply demonstrated by both casual observation and experimental research (Ainslie 1975). The importance of vividness has been demonstrated in the domain of probability judgments by Tversky and Kahneman (1981), and there does not seem to be any reason why a comparable bias should not afflict judgments about utility and value.

The third mismatch, which could also be described as the ''drop in the bucket'' phenomenon, has been analyzed by Herrnstein and Prelec (1988), as an example of *distributed choice*. This label denotes the class of situations in which the economically significant variables are aggregates of many temporally distinct choices, each of which, individually, has little impact (rates of cigarette consumption, frequency of exercise, or social interaction, etc.). To the extent that this impact is ignored by decision makers, their choices will in the long run be predictably suboptimal.[5]

The first, and most critical function of a rule, according to this line of thought, is to *disengage* the cost-benefit calculus. If this is true, then we should be able to trace specific rules to specific (possibly multiple) mismatches in the cost-benefit accounting. Here are some examples.

Rules Pertaining to Health and Personal Safety

Decisions that affect health are clear examples of distributed choice (or scale mismatch), because the cost of engaging in some unhealthy or risky action is negligible unless the action becomes a permanent pattern or lifestyle. Try, for example, to evaluate the cost of

(i) one cigarette;
(ii) one chocolate cake;
(iii) one trip without a seat belt;
(iv) one missed visit to the health club;
(v) one more day at the beach.

In some of these examples, a temporal mismatch is also present (e.g., the health risks from smoking), but it is conceptually a distinct problem, and one that may not be of primary importance. Consider the seat belt case: the cost, if it appears, is instantaneous; it is also quite vivid (mismatch no. 2 does not apply). Furthermore, if you survive the trip, there are no insidious after-effects—the balance sheet is cleared. Hence the problem is primarily one of scale.

Let us pursue this a bit further. In the seat belt case, it seems that the cost-benefit problem could be tackled either "in the small," for the one-shot decision, or "in the large," for the decision whether to buckle up always or never. Neither format is convenient for a cost-benefit analysis, because of the mismatch in scale: in the large problem, the substantial probability of harm that follows from a no-buckle-up policy can perhaps be appreciated, but how does one perform the aggregation of modest comfort increases across thousands of driving episodes? In the small problem, the comfort can be appreciated, but the tiny probability of harm has little subjective meaning.

For some of us it may be difficult to find a problem here, accustomed as we are to thinking in terms of rules. Even though the stakes "in the small" are difficult to grasp, nothing prevents one from solving the large problem and deciding to use seat belts always. But although on a subjective level we may feel that we have decided "once and for all," objectively we are not given the opportunity to make such a choice. It is critical to bear in mind that the objective situation only presents us with choices "in the small," each covering one trip only; if it were possible to buy a car that did not start with seat belts unbuckled, then we could choose a policy. As it is, we may *decide* on a policy, but that is no guarantee that we will indeed follow it, when making the objective sequence of choices.

Rules that Build Up and Maintain Character, or "Personal Identity"

It is commonplace that people derive satisfaction from their internal moral standing, or, more generally, from the subjective correspondence between their self-image and some ideal. But maintaining such an image is very much a problem of distributed choice. A character, for example, is the product of a lifetime of decisions, any given one of which could have been reversed without major impact. It is probably true that a person can consider himself honest, generous, brave, in spite of a few deceptions, or occasional acts of cheapness or cowardice. (However, is this a truth for a moralist to advertise?)

Rules for Spending or Saving Decisions

Certain types of overspending may be due to a pure saliency mismatch. In "home shopping clubs," for example, we are shown products that can be ordered by phone. Now, it is clear to anyone that purchasing the product (for, say, $19.95) means that there will be $19.95 less to spend on something else—there is a loss of $19.95 in general purchasing power. But where, specifically, will the sacrifice be felt? Most people do not know. This creates an initial bias for overspending—the benefit is concrete and visible, while the cost is a sort of abstract corollary. The bit of consumption that got canceled by the purchase is not present to the mind to make its case felt.[6]

Notice that the element of time (which is usually invoked to explain overspending) does not seem to be a prerequisite for "impulsive" behavior. In the case of purchases through television orders, the product will take time to arrive. One also cannot say that it is the immediate expectation of using the product that drives the decision to buy, because the loss in expectation from not using the money on something else is also realized immediately.

Undersaving, in general, may reflect the simultaneous operation of all three mismatches. First, the benefits of savings are delayed; second, the benefits of savings may be imagined at the level of aggregate future income, which is not appreciably affected by single acts of current consumption; third, the benefits are less concrete, given the uncertainty surrounding one's future circumstances.

Prohibition against Crime and Self-abuse

Pure examples of a temporal mismatch are somewhat hard to find; they would be cases in which the delayed consequence was clear, and hinged on a single action. Some criminal acts probably fall in this category (Wilson and Herrnstein 1985), especially "crimes of passion" committed in the face of certain punishment.

Other examples might include drug, alcohol, or sexual "binges," in which the negative "hangover" phase is fully expected, but discounted.

When Opportunities and Information Have Negative Value

The tentative hypothesis is that rules or principles take over in situations where the cost-benefit analysis fails in a systematic and predictable way. This still leaves open the question whether the use of rules can itself be rationalized by some higher-order conception of individual rationality. Without going into technical detail, the modern conception of rational action derives from three fundamental psychological assumptions:

1. A person's preferences over end-states are independent of how choice among end-states is constrained.
2. All aspects of individual psychology can be resolved into matters of taste (preferences) or knowledge (information).
3. A person chooses the most preferred end-state, given the information at his or her disposal.

From these three postulates flow two elementary theorems about how changes in opportunities, information, and preferences should affect the utility or welfare derived from a choice situation:

1. Expanding opportunities can only increase personal welfare.
2. Having more information can only increase personal welfare.

It is important to recognize the utter generality of these deductions. They are valid independently of a person's tastes, or of the extent to which he understands the choice situation; hence, they constitute the empirical rock bottom of the rational model. In view of this, it is significant that decisions involving principle will often produce violations of these two theorems, even in cases where the principle turns out not to be the decisive factor.

Costly Opportunities

Suppose that you are given an opportunity to do something, which, upon consideration, you refuse. If the rational model is correct, this should leave your welfare unchanged—you are exactly where you were prior to the offer. And indeed, where pure *tastes* are concerned, the prediction holds: you are about to order steak from the restaurant menu when the waiter informs you of a special unlisted dish; you reject this new possibility, without impairing your enjoyment of the steak.

But now suppose, instead, that you are an unemployed football player, invited to join one of the "replacement" teams during the 1987 football strike. If you reject the offer, the regret over lost income may make you suffer, or perhaps you might enjoy the newly discovered self-esteem; in either case, it is most unlikely that your subjective welfare will be unaffected by the decision. These phenomena are indeed recorded in speech, when we say things like, "It was a tempting opportunity, but I regret I cannot accept it." If the opportunity failed to pass a comprehensive cost-benefit evaluation, if it is truly inferior to the status quo, then what is the reason for regret?

The job offer is a form of temptation, and temptations—invitations to break a principle—cannot be refused without cost. For this reason, it is considered unfair to offer cigarettes to a recently converted nonsmoker, or cakes to someone on a diet, or a drink to a recovering alcoholic. Numerous customs and regulations, such as minimum wage laws, prohibitions on the sale of sexual activities, blood, and the like, have the effect of shielding people from temptations.

Notice, also, that the best possible solution, in a sense, would be to be compeled to accept the temptation, so that you can enjoy its benefits but are absolved from the responsibility. When external constraints are potentially welfare-improving, there will exist pressure to manufacture subjective constraints even though none "really" exists. If you can find an alternative dominating principle that will accommodate the desired action, then you are in the best of all possible worlds, for you can really have your cake and eat it too.

Presenting someone with an opportunity to *affirm* a principle can also have costs. Consider the following two hypothetical situations:

Scenario 1: You buy a rather expensive bottle of wine that turns out to be quite mediocre; you drink it, making note not to buy it again.

Scenario 2: You order a comparable bottle in a restaurant (for the same price); after a great deal of thought, you decide not to send it back; however, your dinner has been spoiled.

The opportunity set in Scenario 2 is strictly larger, because it contains the action of returning the wine (not available in Scenario 1). How can this produce a lower "utility" level? By not sending the wine back, you have sacrificed a principle (something like, "Get the fair value for purchases") for pragmatic reasons (i.e., avoiding a scene, embarrassment if the establishment refuses to take the wine back, perhaps you know the owner personally, etc.). The violation of principle exacts an additional cost, which is absent from Scenario 1.

One could say, generally, that in circumstances when the rule is not followed (for pragmatic, cost-benefit reasons), the subjective utility level will be *inversely* related to perceived freedom of action, that is, the smaller the opportunity set, the lower will be the cost of rule violation.

Costly Knowledge

A famous experiment of Stanley Milgram illustrates how information may hurt, in contradiction to the second theorem. In Milgram's experiment, many subjects discovered that they were willing to cause great apparent harm to another person, if pressed sufficiently hard by the experimenter.[7] For many subjects, participation in the experiment was not a utility-enhancing event. While some of the cost can be attributed to the stress of the actual experiment, it seems that the more significant source of suffering was the knowledge that one has failed a unique but critical test, which will not be offered a second time.

This reaction is so understandable, that it takes some thought to see how puzzling it must appear on strictly rational grounds. There is a difficulty, first of all, with the implied lack of self-knowledge, prior to the experiment, but let us pass over that. The second difficulty is that if we construe the results as providing fresh information about one's own internal state—something like a medical test—then the psychological reaction should be one of relief—relief, that is, that the important information has been obtained in time to take morally corrective measures.

Valuable Misinformation

A less grim example can be constructed from a hypothetical problem of Kahneman, Knetch, and Thaler (1986). In the problem, you imagine yourself lying on the beach, on a hot day, thinking about how nice it would be to have a cold beer. A friend offers to get one, from a place nearby, which is described as either a "fancy resort" or a "run-down grocery store," in the two versions of the story. Not knowing the price of the beer, the friend requests instructions about the maximum amount that she should pay.

Thaler reports that the subjects' median reservation price was $1.50 for the grocery store, and $2.65 for the resort, the lower grocery store price reflecting presumably a matter of principle. Suppose, now, that the friend goes to the grocery store and finds out that the price is $1.75. What should she do? Purchase the beer, and explain, upon returning, that the grocery store was unfortunately closed, but that just down the road there was a fancy resort, offering a surprisingly reasonable price?

Multiple Selves and Ainslie's Theory of Rule Formation

That there do exist situations where both opportunities and information have negative value for the decision maker has been recognized for some time by a small (but growing) group of economic theorists. Aside from the work of Kahneman, Knetch, and Thaler (1986), which is concerned with the specific issue of perceptions of fairness, these researchers have typically maintained the analytical techniques of the rational model, but view the single person as being composed of several "sub agents," each of which may have distinct preferences, as well as access to private information (Ainslie 1986; Elster 1986; Schelling 1980; Thaler and Shefrin 1981; Winston 1980).

Observed from the outside, a single person would exhibit the behavior of a collective of rational agents, which, as formal game theory indicates, will not be consistent with the two theorems mentioned earlier. There are many games (the Prisoners' Dilemma being only the most famous example) in which rational play produces poor results, and in which the elimination of some strategies would improve the payoffs of everyone. The promise of the new "mathematical Freudianism," then, is to understand the perceived suboptimalities in individual choice, by game-theoretic analogy, as the result of harmful strategic interactions between individually rational subsections of the self.

These attempts also fall short, however, for lack of a key analytical instrument—something that would provide an analytics of *legal rationality.* To develop this argument, I turn first to the work of George Ainslie, which, although less formal, contains a most clearly articulated account of how rules and principles emerge from a strategic struggle for mastery within a single individual.

The theory that Ainslie proposes is extraordinarily simple, in terms of its underlying assumptions. Because of a peculiarity of our time-perception—documented experimentally (Ainslie 1975)—people are prone to a systematic ambivalence about actions that create an initial benefit (or cost) followed, after some delay, by a larger cost (or benefit). When the moment of choice is relatively far away, we intend to give proper weight to the later consequence; however, when the moment of choice arrives, the smaller but earlier consequence overshadows the later one, causing an "impulsive" reversal of the original preference.

This intertemporal ambivalence sets the stage for an internal struggle between the individual's long- and short-term interests. Since the short-term interest is most often the "executive" (i.e., the one that actually makes the choice), it is naturally positioned to sabotage the intentions and plans of the long-term interest, unless the latter can alter the structure of rewards and punishments that are effective at the moment of choice. Ainslie has proposed a number of devices by which the long-term interest can prevail, but the most interesting, for our purposes, is the stratagem of *private rules*, or *side-bets.*

The key step in the private rule strategy is to convince the short-term interest that the current decision will constitute a binding precedent for a long series of future choices. A current decision to, say, indulge some temptation, becomes a sign that the temptation will be indulged on *all* such occasions. A single bite of the forbidden desert, for instance, destroys the expectation that the diet will be followed in the future. The short-term interest is thus kept in line, as it were, by the threat of a severe and *immediate* loss in expectations.

Linking this account with our earlier discussion, we could say that a principle is a mechanism that the long-term interest sets up, for the purpose of correcting the three types of cost-benefit mismatches that were discussed above. It amplifies the scale of the decision, transforms unclear consequences into vivid ones, and, through the device of staking expectations, brings the future to bear on the present.

A Calculus for Principles

But this argument now brings us to a central difficulty. Suppose that at the time of decision, we find that the short-term interest is inclined to choose one way, but is reined in by the presence of some overarching rule. What is to prevent the short-term interest from interpreting the rule so that it does not apply to *this* particular case, which, after all, must differ in some respects from previous occasions when the rule was invoked, or, if that option is too farfetched, from invoking another, stronger principle that overrides the original one? At the moment of choice, the short-term interest is both the judge and the jury for any disputes over interpretation, which makes mysterious its presumed fidelity to the interpretations as they were originally laid down.

The missing element of the story, then, is some account of the psychological constraints that limit the extent to which a rule can be stretched, or defeated by another dominating rule. We can focus the discussion by means of the following, somewhat trivial example. Suppose that one particular Friday evening, I have to choose between going to an entertainment movie, or a documentary about famine in Africa (the proceeds of which will be donated to charity). It is the last showing for both movies. I choose the entertainment film.

Now, to change the problem slightly, suppose that Friday after lunch, I have the opportunity to take off early and see one of the two films (again, the last opportunity to see either one). I will refuse the entertainment film, but I might in fact go see the documentary. Am I being irrational? On narrow revealed preference grounds, yes, because whatever the objective cost of taking the afternoon off, it is not affected by the movie that I see—the benefits of either movie, hedonic, moral, or educational, are no doubt technically separable in preference from the benefits that are derived from several hours' work.

It is not hard to reconstruct an internal argument that leads to the preference reversal. I have rules against taking off early—especially for play. The documentary, however, is a hard case: in a sense it might be "work," especially if the film is not *too* enjoyable. There is also a secondary principle at stake, namely, contributing to charitable causes. Such ambiguities form the raw material for a decision to leave work, but they need to be shaped into a principle that has sufficient power to sanction the original desire to leave.

It is doubtful that rational calculation can shed much light on this process. Careful decision analysis may help decide whether in a particular instance it might be better to go against principle (one would rationally assess the costs of sacrificing the principle—a hard but not impossible task), but it does not help in deciding whether the principle actually applies to the issue at hand.

Decision analysis, which codifies the model of rational behavior, operates by resolving each problem into either a matter of preference or a matter of information. Let us start with the most obvious question: does the documentary constitute work or play? This does not seem to be a matter of information, in the sense

Table 9.2

Two Normative Methods of Decision Making: Decision Analysis and Rule Selection

	Action by decision analysis	Action by rule or principles
Goal	Maximize a given criterion	Discovery of appropriate criterion
Method	Logical/empirical	Legal
Internal structure	Compensatory dimensions or attributes	Hierarchy of principles
Main cognitive activity	Assessment of multiattribute value functions; Probability estimation	Interpretation; Judgments of grouping and similarity

of uncertainty about some objective "state of the world." For example, if you think that it is work, and I think that it is play, then our disagreement is not of the type that can be resolved by a scientific debate. There is no critical *fact* that establishes the correct labeling.

There is a temptation then to shift the question into the domain of tastes, which so often serves as the catchall category for any nonobjective matter. Although the labeling is indeed subjective, the thought processes that one would go through in trying to classify the film do not seem to correspond to an interrogation of subjective *preference*. Quite possibly, I have a good idea of how much I would enjoy the film; what I am in doubt about is whether to allow myself this enjoyment.

In the example, we see a rather complete (and characteristic) fusion of tastes and beliefs. If I believe that the film is work, then I can see (and enjoy) it; if I believe that it is entertainment, then my enjoyment will be corrupted by the knowledge that I have violated a personal rule.

We also see that the arena in which principles compete is somewhat autonomous. If someone were trying to convince me to see the film, he or she would not appeal to preferences, but would rather try to present me with an alternative interpretation or principle. This is the method of seduction through rhetoric: to provide arguments that sanction one's inclinations.

The divided-self models capture something important in describing moral ambivalence as a struggle—a game—between different, temporally segregated aspects of the individual, but fall short in not having much to say about the rules by which this game is conducted. This particular ingredient is absent because the psychological processes that make the game possible are not well captured by variations on preferences and information (the twin building blocks of rational modeling).

I have tried to show here that action by rules or principles involves a distinct mode of decision making, irrespective of whether the rules pertain to moral or prudential concerns, or whether the decisions to which they apply are profound or trivial. Table 9.2 lists the main contrasts between this legal mode, and the familiar procedures of decision analysis. Instead of evaluating trade-offs among the competing arguments of the utility function (such as risk versus expected return), the process revolves around a search for a unique principle that covers the decision at hand, and that is not itself dominated by another more powerful principle.

This second mode of decision making has not yet benefited from the sustained psychological research and attention that has been bestowed on the rational agent model, perhaps because there is no normative theory to set the agenda. Once a model of rule-governed action is developed, however, it will have no shortage of applications in economics and the other social sciences.

Notes

This paper was originally presented at the session ''Socioeconomics: The Roles of Power and Values,'' at the 1989 Annual Meeting of the American Association for the Advancement of Science, San Francisco, January 14–19, 1989. I wish to thank Pankaj Ghemawat, Richard Herrnstein, and George Loewenstein for their valuable discussion and comments on the ideas presented here. The research support of the Russell Sage Foundation and the Research Division of the Harvard Business School is also gratefully acknowledged.

1. For a comprehensive, and penetrating analysis of the issues in this debate, see *The Moral Dimension*, by Amitai Etzioni (1988).

2. A similar sentiment is expressed by Richard Zeckhauser, in an otherwise sympathetic ''axiomatic'' commentary on behavioral (i.e., nonrational) theorizing (1986, p. 438):

> AXIOM 2: For any ''violation'' of rational behavior discovered in the real world market (e.g., the fact that hardware stores do not raise snow shovel prices shortly after a storm), the rationalists (e.g., Gary Becker) will be sufficiently creative to reconstruct a rational explanation.

3. Margolis (1982, p. 11), cited by Etzioni (1988, p. 26).

4. Perhaps a clarification of the word ''rule'' might be useful. There is a tradition of ''bounded rationality'' theorizing in economics that has viewed decision-making rules, for individuals as well as for economic organizations, as a necessary response to the daunting complexity of the typical decision problem that these economic agents face. The tradition probably can be traced to Herbert Simon (1957), and shows its influence today in the work of Heiner (1983), and Nelson and Winter (1982), among many others. Simplifying somewhat, we could say that a rule, in this view, is a behavioral policy or routine that produces satisfactory results in the long run, without burdening the decision maker with case by case cost-benefit calculations. This is not

my usage of "rule." See Etzioni (1988, chap. 10) on "rules of thumb," or Nelson and Winter (1982) on "routines."

5. For a further discussion of the theory and relevant experimental evidence, see Herrnstein and Vaughan (1980) or Prelec (1982).

6. There is a parallel here with the so-called invisible lives problem in public project risk management. It is notorious that life-saving funds are much more easily appropriated if they will benefit a highly visible group than if they benefit an anonymous sample from the population (for this reason, expenditures for traffic safety are typically lower than would be justified by a "lives-saved" analysis).

7. Specifically, subjects were instructed to give a progressively more and more severe series of electrical shocks to another "subject" (an actor, in fact) who was seated in another room, but whose screams and pleading could be clearly heard.

References

Ainslie, G. (1975) "Specious Reward: A Behavioral Theory of Impulsiveness and Impulse Control." *Psychological Bulletin* 82:463–509.

———. (1982) "A Behavioral Economic Approach to the Defense Mechanisms: Freud's Energy Theory Revisited." *Social Science Information* 21:735–79.

———. (1986) "Beyond Microeconomics: Conflict among Interests in a Multiple Self as a Determinant of Value." In J. Elster, ed., *The Multiple Self.* Cambridge: Cambridge University Press.

Becker, G.S., and K.M. Murphy. (1986) "A Theory of Rational Addiction." Working paper no. 41, Center for the Study of the Economy and the State, University of Chicago.

Elster, Jon, ed. (1986) *The Multiple Self.* Cambridge: Cambridge University Press.

Etzioni, Amitai. (1988) *The Moral Dimension: Toward a New Economics.* New York: The Free Press.

Heiner, Ronald A. (1983) "The Origin of Predictable Behavior." *American Economic Review* 73:560–95.

Herrnstein, R.J., and D. Prelec. (Forthcoming) "Melioration: A Theory of Distributed Choice." *Journal of Economic Perspectives.*

Herrnstein, R.J., and W. Vaughan, Jr. (1980) "Melioration and Behavioral Allocation." In J.E.R. Staddon, ed., *Limits to Action: The Allocation of Individual Behavior*, pp. 143–76. New York: Academic Press.

Hirschman, Albert O. (1984) "Against Parsimony: Three Easy Ways of Complicating Some Categories of Economic Discourse." *Bulletin: The American Academy of Arts and Sciences* 37, no. 8:11–28.

Janis, Irving, and Leon Mann. (1977) *Decision Making: A Psychological Analysis of Conflict, Choice, and Commitment.* New York: The Free Press.

Kahneman, D., J.K. Knetch, and R. Thaler. (1986) "Fairness as a Constraint on Profit Seeking: Entitlements in the Market." *American Economic Review* 76:728–41.

Margolis, Howard. (1982) *Selfishness, Altruism and Rationality: A Theory of Social Choice.* Cambridge: Cambridge University Press.

Milgram, S. (1974) *Obedience to Authority.* New York: Harper & Row.

Nelson, R.R., and S.G. Winter. (1982) *An Evolutionary Theory of Economic Change.* Cambridge, MA: Belknap Press of Harvard University Press.

Prelec, D. (1982) "Matching, Maximizing, and the Hyperbolic Reinforcement Feedback Function." *Psychological Review* 89:189–230.

Schelling, T.C. (1980) "The Intimate Contest for Self-command." *Public Interest* 60:94–118.

Simon, H.A. (1957) *Models of Man: Social and Rational. Mathematical Essays on Rational Human Behavior*. New York: Wiley.
Stigler, G., and G. Becker. (1977) "De Gustibus Non Est Disputandum." *American Economic Review* 67:76–90.
Thaler, R. (1980) "Toward a Positive Theory of Consumer Choice." *Journal of Economic Behavior and Organization* 1:39–60.
Thaler, R., and H.M. Shefrin. (1981) "An Economic Theory of Self-control." *Journal of Political Economy* 89:392–410.
Tversky, A., and D. Kahneman. (1981) "The Framing of Decisions and the Psychology of Choice." *Science* 211:453–58.
Vaughan, W., Jr., and R.J. Herrnstein. (1987) "Stability, Melioration, and Natural Selection." In L. Green and J.H. Kagel, eds., *Advances in Behavioral Economics*, vol. 1, pp. 185–215. Norwood, NJ: Ablex.
Wilson, James Q., and R.J. Herrnstein. (1985) *Crime and Human Nature*. New York: Simon and Schuster.
Winston, G.C. (1980) "Addiction and Backsliding." *Journal of Economic Behavior and Organization* 1:295–324.
Zeckhauser, Richard. (1986) "Comments: Behavioral versus Rational Economics: What You See Is What You Conquer." *Journal of Business* 59:S435–31.

IV

Socioeconomic Perspective on Executive Leadership and Entrepreneurship

10

Lee E. Preston, Harry J. Sapienza,
and Robert D. Miller

Stakeholders, Shareholders, Managers

Who Gains What from Corporate Performance?

The wave of corporate mergers, takeover attempts, and buyouts during the 1980s focused new attention on an old issue: for what purposes, and for whose benefit, is the modern corporation operated? Or, as Dodd put it in the title of his 1932 classic: "For Whom Are Corporate Managers Trustees?" By the end of the decade, thirty-nine states had passed laws impeding management-opposed takeovers, and twelve had amended their statutes to permit (and in three cases *require*) board consideration of the interests of multiple stakeholders—employees, customers, communities, etc.—when important corporate decisions are being made. A 1988 Business Roundtable study of 100 major companies found "widespread recognition that corporate obligations extend to a variety of constituencies or stakeholders." Leading corporate-image advertisers (e.g., Mobil, NCR, IBM) have featured the stakeholder concept in their ads; and the notion that successful management requires effective performance with respect to multiple objectives is now a staple of the academic literature (see Andrews 1987, chap. 5; Steiner, Miner, and Gray 1986; Wheelen and Hunger 1986; Hatten and Hatten 1987, chap. 9; Macmillan and Jones 1985, chap. 4; Frederick, Davis, and Post 1988, chap. 4; Buchholz 1989, chap. 10 and pp. 457–60; Steiner and Steiner 1988, pp. 14–16, 251–52; stakeholder management is the main subject of Freeman 1984; O'Toole 1985; and Alkhafaji 1989). Little is known, however, about the extent to which major U.S. corporations are in fact managed to achieve multiple stakeholder objectives, or about the ways in which performance with respect to various stakeholder interests is interrelated. This paper discusses some critical aspects of the stakeholder concept that appear to be neglected in the literature, and reports the results of an empirical study designed to provide some evidence about the extent and implications of stakeholder management in a sample of large U.S. corporations.

The stakeholder model is a significant example of the "I&We paradigm" developed by Etzioni (1988). Both concepts rest on a common idea: that "utility" (i.e., the benefit gained by purposive activity), whether for individuals or organizations, is multidimensional, and in particular, that social and moral considerations must be added to individual objectives in order to account for any substantial portion of actual behavior and experience. The analogies between (a) individual "utility" maximization and shareholder wealth maximization, on the one hand, and (b) the social "We" and the interests of multiple stakeholders, on the other, seem almost perfect. It is also true that both the I&We paradigm and the stakeholder model are offered as alternatives to conventional thinking, but as alternatives that *embrace* rather than *replace* prior concepts. In particular, the stakeholder model is an alternative to the idea that shareholder wealth is (or should be) the exclusive aim of corporate activity, but shareholders nevertheless are recognized as prominent stakeholders. The stakeholder model can thus be regarded as an example of socioeconomic thinking in an organizational setting. And both the criticisms and problems of the stakeholder model and the evidence of its relevance and implications are germane to the broader question of the validity of socio-economics as an approach to social analysis.

Critique of the Stakeholder Concept

In spite of its apparent widespread acceptance, the stakeholder concept and the related notion that corporate management involves the balancing of multiple (and at least partially conflicting) stakeholder interests has not been without its critics. Rare surviving disciples of Milton Friedman continue to defend the proposition that corporations should (and/or do) exist entirely for the benefit of their investor shareholders. Jensen (1989) has recently argued that the large public corporation has outlived its usefulness, principally because of the inevitable conflict of interest between shareholders and managers. He argues that the current wave of takeovers and buyouts should be encouraged, rather than discouraged, because they "both create new value and unlock value destroyed by management through misguided policies" (p. 61). The notion that managerial concern with multiple interests is "misguided" implies, of course, complete rejection of the stakeholder perspective.

Even persons sympathetic with the goals of stakeholder management, however, should recognize some fundamental problems, both in conception and in implementation. One of these is the difficulty of identifying specific stakeholder groups and the sense in which any kind of "balance" among their diverse and potentially competing interests can or should be attained. A second problem arises from the fact that managers are stakeholders themselves, as well as architects of "balance" among the interests of others. And finally, the stakeholder role of institutional and fiduciary investors—who own potentially dominant portions of the shares of most large publicly held companies—raises some special and difficult issues for the implementation of "stakeholder management" principles.

Applying the Model

As to the first of these issues, the difficulties involved in identifying actual stakeholders (as opposed to listing general categories such as "customers" or "employees") and the sense in which stakeholder management can be said to involve a "balance" among diverse interests are intimately linked, since the number and diversity of stakeholder interests have an important impact on the concepts and mechanisms of "balance" that may be appropriate. Unionized labor, for example, is effectively self-identified as a stakeholder group; relevant "stakes" may be pursued through collective bargaining, and "balance" may be defined as whatever conditions are agreed to by appropriately constituted bargaining parties. Similar formal stakeholder relationships are also established under European systems of "codetermination" and other legal arrangements. However, overt mechanisms that simultaneously (a) identify stakeholders, (b) define a workable concept of "balance" among their interests, and (c) establish a mechanism for achieving the desired "balance" are not observed. Moreover, within broad stakeholder categories—e.g., employees, customers, to say nothing of shareholders—there may be multiple subgroups with goal conflicts as great as (and perhaps more conspicuous than) those between distinct stakeholder categories.

A number of legal developments over the past decade have referenced some version of the stakeholder concept, particularly in connection with corporate takeovers. In a widely cited Delaware case, the court included among the "concerns" that may appropriately be taken into account by directors in such circumstances "the impact on 'constituencies' other than shareholders (i.e., creditors, customers, employees, and perhaps even the community generally)."[1] Delaware subsequently (January 1988) passed legislation requiring a three-year waiting period for hostile takeovers, and in the more recent Time-Warner merger case,[2] the Delaware court ruled that directors can ignore shareholder interests when following a "strategic plan" aimed at preserving the independence and integrity of the enterprise. Legal developments in Delaware are, of course, of particular importance since its liberal corporation laws have made it the legal home of approximately half of all companies listed in the New York Stock Exchange, and more than half of the Fortune 500.

Twelve other states have amended their corporation laws to legitimate the consideration of multiple stakeholder interests in corporate decision making. The language in most of these statutes (Illinois, Indiana, Louisiana, Maine, Minnesota, Missouri, Nebraska, Pennsylvania, and Wisconsin) is permissive; that is, "directors *may* consider. . . ." However, in three instances (Connecticut, New Mexico, and Ohio), an explicit duty to recognize multiple interests is required; i.e., *may* is replaced by *shall.* The lists of potential stakeholders included in these statutes are conventional—i.e., employees, customers, suppliers—and most include some reference to "communities" as well.

These legal developments might suggest, in Evan and Freeman's (1987) phrase, the creation of a kind of "Kantian capitalism" in which managers and directors are charged to pursue the interests of all parties whose interests are intimately tied to the viability and success of the enterprise. A similar idea is formally advocated by Lorsch and MacIver (1989) on the basis of their recent survey of directors in 400 large corporations. However, most legal experts apparently believe that these statutory amendments represent little more than clarifications of the traditional "business judgment" rule, and are not necessarily relevant to situations other than takeovers. In any event, neither the management literature nor the statutes contain adequate guidelines for identifying stakeholders and determining whether or not their interests have been appropriately "balanced" in specific managerial decisions.

Managers as Stakeholders

The second critical problem with the concept of "stakeholder management" is the inherent tension between its multidimensional objectives and the status of managers as stakeholders. If—as is almost universally the case in large corporations—professional managers actually control the company, largely determining the constituency and policies of the board and interacting with a remote, numerous, and ever-changing population of shareholders only through stock prices and dividend checks, then the most likely beneficiaries of "stakeholder management" are surely the managers themselves. Oliver Williamson (1985) is almost alone among academic analysts in acknowledging the difficulties that arise when "management" is recognized as one of the major "constituencies" of the firm; and his perception, based on several decades of research, is that the likelihood of "opportunistic" (i.e., self-aggrandizing) behavior among managers is quite high. This view is strongly supported by the more direct observations of Harold Geneen (1984, chap. 12) and the colorful comments of T. Boone Pickens (1987, esp. pp. 132, 280). The definitive critique is Edward Jay Epstein's Twentieth Century Fund Study, *Who Owns the Corporation?* (1986).

The belief that corporate managers are primarily pursuing their own objectives, often at the direct expense of the shareholders, is supported by several recent statistical analyses. Generalizing from a study of share price movements in connection with recent mergers, Weidenbaum and Vogt (1987) conclude (a) that rising share prices for *acquired* firms may indicate lax incumbent management; and (b) that lack of evidence of long-term benefits for shareholders of *acquiring* firms indicates that managerial goals (e.g., growth in total corporate size), rather than shareholder welfare, have been the primary merger motivators. When Posner and Schmidt (1984) asked 889 "executive managers" to rate the importance of sixteen different stakeholders in management decision making, the overall results showed "myself" as second only to "customers" (the scores were 6.28 and 6.40, respectively, out of a possible 7). Employee groups appeared high on the list, but—confirming the worst fears of the critics—"stockholders" were far down, roughly tied with "the general public" (4.52 and 4.51) for managerial attention. Alkhafaji's subsequent survey of 171 corporate managers found that fewer than 10 percent believed that even large (over 5 percent) shareholders *should* have proportional influence on corporate policies. In fact, these managers rejected increased corporate governance roles for *all* other stakeholders, but overwhelmingly supported the proposition that wider *management* participation in decision making would improve results (Alkhafaji 1989). Evidence from recent leveraged buy out attempts suggests that top managers, in a Hegelian reversal of the Berle and Means thesis, have simply tried to convert their actual positions of control over corporate decision making into a more legitimate form, i.e., ownership. Jensen's "Eclipse of the Public Corporation" (1989) argument is that these generally criticized changes in ownership-control arrangements are, in fact, desirable.

Third-Party Fiduciaries

A third fundamental problem with the stakeholder management concept arises from the fact that very large (potentially controlling) interests in many corporations are held by third-party institutions and fiduciaries that are themselves agents for numerous and diverse individual principals. Traditional third-party investment management emphasizes security and stability, following the so-called Wall Street Rule (i.e., if you disapprove of management, you sell your shares). However, many third-party investors are now adopting other tactics. The open criticism of specific corporate decisions by Harrison Goldin, comptroller of New York City and trustee of $35 billion in pension fund assets, produced direct responses from such firms as Chemical Bank and Exxon (*Economist*, April 29, 1989, p. 75). More recently, California and New York pension funds have sought to exert some influence on the top management succession at General Motors (*Wall Street Journal*, January 9, 1990, p. A4). In addition, trustees representing public pension funds, the largest third-party investors, have become increasingly concerned with economic conditions within the jurisdictions (i.e., states, cities) in which their contributors are employed, and have attempted to use their influence to preserve jobs and ameliorate conditions in local economies. As a result of all these developments, the objectives of third-party investors, their managers, and their own ultimate stakeholders have become increasingly central to the entire process of corporate governance and decision making. Integration of these considerations into the "stakeholder management" of ongoing business corporations has not, to our knowledge, been seriously addressed in the literature.

Stakeholder Management: Empirical Evidence

In spite of its long period of prominence, and the several interesting theoretical and empirical issues it appears to raise, the stakeholder model has not been subjected to any substantial amount of empirical research. Few investigators have systematically asked whether (or how) corporate managers believed themselves to be pursuing multiple stakeholder objectives; and no one to our knowledge has tried to discover the extent to which multiple stakeholder objectives are actually achieved in any significant sample of firms, or how (if at all) achievement of particular stakeholder objectives is associated with other aspects of corporate performance. (The numerous studies relating various measures of corporate "social" performance to financial data might be considered an exception to this statement; but as Ullmann [1985] has emphasized, most of this work can be described as "data in search of a theory.") For the past several years we have been developing a collection of data in which some interesting questions about the incidence and impact of stakeholder management can be examined, at least in an exploratory fashion, in a sample of large and important U.S. corporations. The remainder of this paper presents a progress report on this research.

The Data

Since 1982, *Fortune* magazine has annually asked a large sample of informed observers (executives, directors, and outside analysts) to rate the performance of leading American corporations along a number of dimensions. Companies selected for coverage are those classified as among the ten largest (or fewer if there are not ten large companies) in a number of narrowly defined industries. The number of industries and firms included in the survey has varied over time, and the total number of persons surveyed has varied as well; the average number of respondents rating each company in any year is approximately 100. Through the courtesy of *Fortune* and its professional survey organization (Erdos and Morgan), we have obtained the original data collected in these surveys, combined them with other data, and subjected them to statistical analysis. The results reported here focus on data for 107 companies for which all desired data items are available for each of the seven years 1982–88, and for which company size is measured in sales. (The general problems involved in the analysis of these data are discussed in a number of previous studies; see McGuire, Sundgren, and Schneeweis 1988; Chakravarthy 1986; and Wokutch and Spencer 1987. So far as we can discover, all analysts who have examined the *Fortune* data carefully have concluded that it is sufficiently valid to merit serious study, and this view is supported by comparisons with other data sources as well.)[3]

The *Fortune* surveys list eight dimensions of corporate performance, from which we have generated indicators relevant to the interests of four stakeholder groups: shareholders, employees, customers, and communities. We relate the *Fortune* survey data to the four stakeholder performance categories as follows:

Shareholder performance (FINPER)—measured by the average value, per firm per year, of three *Fortune* survey dimensions ("financial soundness," "long-term investment value," and "use of corporate assets").

Customer performance—measured by the survey ratings for "product and service quality" (PSQUAL).

Employee performance—measured by the survey ratings for "ability to attract, develop and keep talented people" (PEOPL).

Community performance—measured by the survey ratings for "community and environmental responsibility" (CERESP).

We begin by comparing the 107 seven-year companies with all companies included in the data set for each individual year in order to place the focal data set within its larger context. We then examine the associations among the four stakeholder performance indicators, first on a contemporaneous basis, and second in search of possible lead-lag relationships.

The number and relative size of companies covered by the *Fortune* surveys and included in our entire data set for each year, 1982–88, are shown in Table 10.1. The size distribution of firms is, of course, highly skewed, with the largest firms in the economy (e.g., Exxon, General Motors) typically twenty to thirty times as large as the smallest firms included in these data. Since data for most of the largest firms are available for every year, it is no surprise that the 107 seven-year companies appear to be on average substantially larger than the remaining companies. In fact, many of the firms in both parts of the data set have $1–10 billion in annual sales, so that typical firm sizes are not as different as simple comparison of the two means might suggest.

The data in Table 10.1 also show that the seven-year companies have, on average, slightly higher ratings than the other companies for every stakeholder performance dimension under study and for every year. The dispersion of the reputation ratings, however, is such that none of these differences is statistically significant; hence, the 107 seven-year companies can be taken as representative of all large companies with respect to these characteristics. Previous studies have generally found statistically significant, but relatively weak ($r = 0.25$), associations between most of these stakeholder performance ratings and both company size and rate of growth (Preston and Sapienza 1990).[4]

Stakeholder Performance: Trade-offs or Synergies?

The annual journalistic reports of the *Fortune* studies (Smith 1990 is the most recent) suggest that survey ratings in the various dimensions tend to be closely

Table 10.1

Comparison of Seven-Year Companies with Other Surveyed Companies, 1982–88

	Number of companies*			Average sales ($ billions)			FINPER			PSQUAL			PEOPL			CERESP		
Year	7-year	Other	Total	7-year	Other	Total	7-year	Other	Total	7-year	Other	Total	7-year	Other	Total	7-year	Other	Total
1982	107	84	191	14.7	11.8	13.42	6.26	5.70	6.01	7.06	6.63	6.87	6.25	5.89	6.09	6.32	5.82	6.10
1983	107	129	236	15.5	9.2	12.10	6.41	6.06	6.22	7.10	6.89	6.99	6.36	5.98	6.15	6.41	6.00	6.19
1984	107	129	236	16.9	9.4	12.80	6.41	6.12	6.25	7.09	6.93	7.00	6.40	6.03	6.20	6.42	6.10	6.25
1985	107	157	264	18.9	8.6	12.77	6.23	6.01	6.10	6.96	6.81	6.87	6.24	5.91	6.04	6.34	6.08	6.19
1986	107	154	261	18.6	9.5	13.23	6.25	6.12	6.17	6.98	6.84	6.90	6.18	6.01	6.08	6.32	6.05	6.16
1987	107	137	244	16.4	8.8	12.13	6.25	6.24	6.24	6.93	6.86	6.89	6.15	6.11	6.13	6.29	6.06	6.16
1988	107	114	221	21.5	10.3	15.72	6.30	6.32	6.31	6.98	6.95	6.96	6.24	6.21	6.22	6.35	6.15	6.25
Mean	107	129	236	17.5	9.7	13.17	6.30	6.08	6.19	7.01	6.84	6.93	6.26	6.02	6.13	6.35	6.04	6.18

*Companies included in the *Fortune* surveys and for which all relevant data are available for analysis.

Table 10.2

Average Values of Annual Correlation Coefficients among Stakeholder Performance Variables, 107 Corporations, 1982–88

	PSQUAL	PEOPL	CERESP
FINPER	0.77	0.92	0.64
PSQUAL		0.86	0.69
PEOPL			0.69

Note: All individual annual results significant at 0.01 level or better.

associated, and this impression is confirmed by correlation analysis. Correlation matrices for the four stakeholder performance measures have been computed for each year, and all results are strongly positive and statistically significant at the 0.01 level or better. Table 10.2 shows the average values for the correlation coefficients over the seven-year period. All of these average values can fairly be described as "high," but the associations between community performance (CERESP) and other indicators are clearly lower than those among the other three stakeholder performance indicators.

These results confirm the contentions of the strongest "stakeholder management" advocates that simultaneous achievement of multiple stakeholder performance objectives is feasible, and indeed likely. As early as 1950, General Robert E. Wood, then CEO of Sears, listed the "four parties to any business" as "customers, employees, community and stockholders" and declared that "if the other three parties are properly taken care of, the stockholder will benefit in the long pull" (quoted in Worthy 1984, p. 64). These results suggest that General Wood's prediction is strongly confirmed among this large sample of leading U.S. corporations during the 1980s.

Correlation, of course, does not reveal causation, and a number of authors have suggested that cause-effect relationships among corporate performance dimensions might be examined through lead-lag analysis. The recent study of McGuire, Sundgren, and Schneeweis (1989) is of particular importance in this connection. Combining data from the annual *Fortune* magazine corporate reputation surveys with a variety of financial and stock market data from COMPUSTAT, and using samples of 98 and 131 firms over different time periods within the 1983–85 time frame, McGuire and colleagues found strong positive correlations (0.41–0.52) between *Fortune* "community-environmental responsibility" ratings (i.e., CERESP) and some financial variables in *both* contemporaneous and lead-lag formulations. Given the small number of years covered by their data, they were not able to discriminate clearly between the relative strength of contemporaneous and lead-lag relationships, and they suggested that others pursue this issue.

McGuire and colleagues focused primarily on the hypothesis that financial performance would lead social performance; i.e., financially successful firms would be able to satisfy employees, communities, etc., whereas less successful firms would be unable to do so. They noted, however, the opposite possibility, that favorable financial results might *flow from*, rather than *follow*, superior performance with respect to customers, employees, etc. They cited specifically the contention of Cornell and Shapiro (1987) that fulfillment of the "implicit claims" of noninvestor stakeholders may have important implications for the financial *policies*, and thus for the financial *performance*, of the firm. Cornell and Shapiro contend that superior performance with respect to customers and employees may well facilitate the kinds of financial policies that lead to superior results. In this case, of course, we would expect other stakeholder performance indicators to *lead*, rather than lag, financial performance indicators. To discriminate between these two hypotheses, our analysis therefore examines the possibility of lead-lag relationships among financial and other performance variables in both directions.

Annual *Fortune* survey ratings in each dimension exhibit strong serial correlation; hence, high contemporaneous correlations among the stakeholder performance indicators (as shown in Table 10.2) necessarily imply strong lead-lag relationships (in both directions) among each pair of indicators. These statistics have been computed but yield no further information and are not displayed here. In order to introduce a more volatile variable, which might make discrimination between the two different lead-lag hypotheses more feasible, we introduce one-year and ten-year "Total Rate of Return" figures from the annual *Fortune* directories as objective measures of financial performance. Annual contemporaneous correlations between the four stakeholder performance indicators and these two financial performance measures are shown in Table 10.3. Evidently, although there are statistically significant associations between these objective financial data and all of the reputation-based performance indicators, these are weaker and more diverse than those among the stakeholder performance measures themselves.

The results shown in Table 10.3 form a "baseline" for the study of lead-lag relationships. By relating stakeholder performance indicators for year T to financial data for $T + 1$ and $T + 2$, $T - 1$ and $T - 2$, we seek to determine: (a) whether lead-lag effects are present in the data, and (b) if present, whether they are *stronger* than the contemporaneous associations shown in Table 10.3.

The Cornell-Shapiro hypothesis that stakeholder performance should lead financial data is tested with the data in Table 10.4.[5] All the correlation coefficients tabulated are for one-year lags; additional evidence of two-year or longer lags is indicated by an asterisk. A majority of the results are insignificant, and in only one instance (1988 one-year ROR) are the lead-lag correlations significantly stronger than the contemporaneous values. Hence, we conclude that these data provide no support for the hypothesis that high levels of stakeholder performance in one period would lead to financial success in the next.

Table 10.3

Contemporaneous Correlations between Stakeholder Performance Indicators and Financial Measures, 107 Companies, 1982–88

	One-year return				Ten-year return			
Year	FINPER	PSQUAL	PEOPL	CERESP	FINPER	PSQUAL	PEOPL	CERESP
1982	N.S.	N.S.	N.S.	N.S.	N.S.	N.S.	N.S.	N.S.
1983	–0.30[a]	0.24[a]	–0.27[a]	–0.26[a]	N.S.	N.S.	N.S.	N.S.
1984	0.29[a]	N.S.	0.22[b]	N.S.	0.20[b]	N.S.	N.S.	N.S.
1985	0.33[a]	N.S.	0.21[b]	N.S.	0.30[a]	N.S.	0.21[b]	N.S.
1986	0.33[a]	0.20[b]	0.25[a]	0.22[b]	0.50[a]	0.27[a]	0.41[a]	N.S.
1987	N.S.	N.S.	N.S.	N.S.	0.59[a]	0.43[a]	0.53[a]	0.29[a]
1988	–0.31[a]	–0.24[a]	–0.29[a]	–0.28[a]	0.32[a]	0.25[a]	0.28[a]	N.S.

[a]Significant at 0.01 or better.
[b]Significant at 0.05 or better.
N.S. = not significant at 0.05 level.

Table 10.4

Lead-Lag Correlations between Stakeholder Performance Indicators (Year *T*) and Financial (Year *T* + 1) Measures

	One-Year ROR			Ten-Year ROR		
Year	PSQUAL	PEOPL	CERESP	PSQUAL	PEOPL	CERESP
1983	–0.33[a]	–0.41[a]	–0.32[a]	N.S.	N.S.	–0.25[a]
1984	N.S.	N.S.	N.S.	N.S.	N.S.	N.S.
1985	N.S.	N.S.	N.S.	N.S.	N.S.	N.S.
1986	N.S.	N.S.	0.21[b]*	0.20[b]	0.36[a]*	N.S.
1987	N.S.	N.S.	N.S.	0.43[a]*	0.50[a]*	N.S.
1988	0.30[a]	0.35[a]*	0.22[b]	0.26[a]*	0.33[a]*	N.S.

[a]Significant at 0.01 or better.
[b]Significant at 0.05 or better.
N.S. = not significant at 0.05 level.
*Additional lags significant.

Turning the analysis around to address the McGuire hypothesis that financial performance leads social performance yields somewhat stronger results (see Table 10.4). More than half of the lead-lag correlations between financial statistics and FINPER are statistically significant, and some are larger than the corresponding contemporaneous values; this gives some indication of the intertemporal connection between reputation indicators and objective evidence. Among the nonfinancial stakeholder performance indicators, statistically significant positive associations with lagged one-year rates of return are found in eight instances, and seven of these coefficients are stronger than the corresponding contemporaneous values shown in Table 10.3. Lead-lag coefficients are not typically stronger for ten-year rates of return, but this result is not surprising since the rate of return data themselves are retrospective. Combining the results shown in Table 10.3 for ten-year returns and Table 10.5 for one-year lagged returns, we conclude that there is some support for the McGuire hypothesis—objective financial performance lead, reputational stakeholder performance lag—in the more recent years of data covered by this study.

In summary, the results of our empirical work to date reveal significant evidence that high and low levels of corporate performance relative to the interests of employees, customers, shareholders, and communities are closely correlated, and some evidence that actual financial results in one time period are associated

Table 10.5

Lead-Lag Correlations between Financial Measures (Year *T*) and Stakeholder Performance Indicators (Year *T* + 1)

	One-year ROR				Ten-year ROR			
Year	FINPER	PSQUAL	PEOPL	CERESP	FINPER	PSQUAL	PEOPL	CERESP
1983	N.S.	N.S.	N.S.	N.S.	N.S.	N.S.	N.S.	N.S.
1984	N.S.*	N.S.	–0.20[b]	–0.22[b]	N.S.	N.S.	N.S.	–0.22[b]
1985	0.45[a]	N.S.	0.37[a]	N.S.	0.20[b]	N.S.	N.S.	N.S.
1986	0.44[a]*	0.26[a]	0.32[a]*	0.20[b]	0.32[b]	N.S.	0.25[a]	N.S.
1987	0.41[a]*	0.32[a]*	0.37[a]*	0.34[a]*	0.39[a]	0.21[b]	0.36[a]	0.21[b]
1988	N.S.*	0.24[b]*	N.S.*	N.S.*	0.44[a]	0.34[a]	0.42[a]	N.S.

[a]Significant at 0.01 or better.
[b]Significant at 0.05 or better.
N.S. = not significant at 0.05 level.
*Additional lags significant.

with indicators of multiple stakeholder performance (as revealed by reputation surveys) in the next. These results by themselves do not tell us anything about the special position of managers within the stakeholder model. In other analyses, not reported here for reasons of space (see Preston and Sapienza 1990), we have found significant correlations between corporate growth rates and indicators of shareholder, employee, and customer performance (i.e., FINPER, PEOPL, and PSQUAL—but not with CERESP). If we adopt the hypothesis of Marris (1964) and many others that organizational growth is the ultimate objective of corporate managers, then these preliminary results suggest that the objectives of managers may not be as inconsistent with those of other corporate stakeholders—particularly shareholders—as some analysts may have believed.

Conclusion

Our results are, of course, limited by our data and methodology, and are certainly stronger in some respects than in others. However, if we tie our empirical results back to the more general discussion preceding them, it seems reasonable to conclude as follows:

1. "Stakeholder management"—i.e., achieving satisfactory levels of performance for all major groups of stakeholders—appears to be fairly common among major U.S. corporations. The broad pattern of stakeholder performance ratings is roughly consistent with the lip service paid to the stakeholder concept in the management literature.
2. "Stakeholder management" may be somewhat easier than might have been imagined, in the sense that major stakeholder groups apparently gain or lose from the same broad patterns of organizational success or difficulty, rather than confront management and each other with large and difficult trade-offs.
3. Managers typically do not sacrifice major stakeholder objectives in pursuit of conventional growth and profit goals; in fact, these two types of performance indicators appear to be closely linked.
4. Finally, if we take the incidence and impact of "stakeholder management" as revealed by these data to be a test of the relevance of the I&We paradigm in an organizational context, we may conclude that the paradigm itself is somewhat validated—or, at least, not rejected—on the basis of this analysis. That is, our analysis clearly reveals that multiple objectives, including both economic and social considerations, can be and in fact *are* simultaneously and successfully pursued within large and complex organizations that collectively account for a major part of all economic activity within our society.

It should also be noted that a major finding of our research is that the strength and character of all of the empirical relationships among the various I&We participants in corporate activity vary considerably from year to year. Even the serial correlation within each of the stakeholder performance indicator series does not eliminate year-to-year variations in the statistical results, and more variability is introduced when more volatile series are brought into the analysis. The mixed results yielded by previous studies of social-financial performance relationships have often been attributed to differences and deficiencies in the data selected for analysis. It now appears that the variety of results obtained may be equally due to differences in the time periods covered. Our comprehensive analysis of this large data collection over a seven-year period reveals negative associations in some cases, positive in others, and null results in still others. By appropriate choice of variables and time periods, one might produce almost any statistical result desired. It seems clear, therefore, that serious investigations of socioeconomic relationships within the corporation should focus on long-term and/or time-lagged relationships, rather than on short-term variables and snapshot results.

Notes

This paper presents results from an ongoing empirical study of indicators of corporate performance in a sample of major U.S. corporations, based upon data originally collected by *Fortune* magazine. We are indebted to the editors of *Fortune* for access to these data and to numerous student assistants—most recently Douglas Heck—for statistical and bibliographical work. Earlier results from this study, using a more limited set of data, are reported in Preston and Sapienza (1990).

1. *Unocal Corp.* v. *Mesa Petroleum Co.*, Del. Supr., 493 A.zd 946, 1985.
2. Time Inc. Shareholder Litigation, Del. Ch. LEXIS 77, July 17, 1989.
3. Limited available evidence indicates some rough consistency between the *Fortune* reputation ratings and other indicators of company performance in various areas. In appropriate samples of data for different time periods, we have found the following associations between the *Fortune* ratings under analysis in this study and other data:

(a) Significantly higher community-environment responsibility (CERESP) ratings for companies *not* involved in criminal convictions over the prior decade, as compared to those that *were* so involved (data from Ryan, Swanson, and Buchholz 1987).

(b) Significantly higher employee performance (PEOPL) ratings for companies listed among the "100 best companies to work for," as compared to unlisted companies (data from Levering, Moskowitz, and Katz 1984).

(c) Relatively high ratings on all three social performance dimensions under analysis here for the consumer goods companies (relatively few in our sample) listed as "Authors' Company of Choice" by Council on Economic Priorities researchers, as compared to other consumer goods companies and/or all companies (data from Lydenberg, Marlin, and Strub 1986).

Although the latter two observations may be contaminated by "halo" effects, the general consistency of these findings is reassuring. The correlation between financial reputation ratings and objective evidence of financial performance is discussed later in the paper.

4. *Fortune* ratings for product-service quality and for "innovativeness" (the latter not included in this study) are not, however, typically associated with size, and CERESP is not associated with growth rate.
5. Shareholder performance (FINPER) is excluded from this analysis since the idea that financial reputation should precede performance is not a logical possibility.

References

Alkhafaji, Abbass F. (1989) *A Stakeholder Approach to Corporate Governance*. New York: Quorum.

Andrews, Kenneth R. (1987) *The Concept of Corporate Strategy*. Homewood, IL: Irwin.

Buchholz, Rogene A. (1989) *Business Environment and Public Policy*. Englewood Cliffs, NJ: Prentice-Hall.

Chakravarthy, B.S. (1986) "Measuring Strategic Performance." *Strategic Management Journal* 7:437–58.

Cornell, B., and A.C. Shapiro. (1987) "Corporate Stakeholders and Corporate Finance." *Financial Management* 16:5–14.

Dodd, E. Merrick, Jr. (1932) "For Whom Are Corporate Managers Trustees?" *Harvard Law Review* 45:1145–63.

Epstein, Edward Jay. (1986) *Who Owns the Corporation?* New York: Twentieth Century Fund.

Etzioni, Amitai. (1988) *The Moral Dimension: Toward a New Economics*. New York: The Free Press.

Evan, William M., and R.E. Freeman. (1987) "A Stakeholder Theory of the Modern Corporation: Kantian Capitalism." In Tom L. Beauchamp and Norman R. Bowie, eds., *Ethical Theory and Business*. 3d ed. Englewood Cliffs, NJ: Prentice-Hall.

Frederick, William C., Keith Davis, and James E. Post. (1988) *Business and Society*. New York: McGraw-Hill.

Freeman, R. Edward. (1984) *Strategic Management—A Stakeholder Approach*. Marshfield, MA: Pitman.

Geneen, Harold, with Alvin Moscow. (1984) *Managing*. Garden City, NY: Doubleday.

Hatten, Kenneth J., and Mary Louise Hatten. (1987) *Strategic Management: Analysis and Action*. Englewood Cliffs, NJ: Prentice-Hall.

Jensen, Michael C. (1989) "Eclipse of the Public Corporation." *Harvard Business Review* (September–October), pp. 61–74.

Levering, R., M. Moskowitz, and M. Katz. (1984) *The 100 Best Companies to Work for in America*. Reading, MA: Addison-Wesley.

Lorsch, Jay, and Elizabeth MacIver. (1989) *Pawns or Potentates: The Reality of America's Corporate Boards*. Cambridge, MA: Harvard Business School.

Lydenberg, S.D., A.T. Marlin, and S.O. Strub. (1986) *Rating America's Corporate Conscience*. Reading, MA: Addison-Wesley.

McGuire, J.B., A. Sundgren, and T. Schneeweis. (1988) "Corporate Social Responsibility and Firm Financial Performance." *Academy of Management Journal* 31, 4:354–72.

Macmillan, Ian C., and Patricia E. Jones. (1985) *Strategy Formulation: Power and Politics*. St. Paul, MN: West.

Marris, Robin. (1964) *The Economic Theory of "Managerial" Capitalism*. New York: Basic Books.

O'Toole, James. (1985) *Vanguard Management*. Garden City, NY: Doubleday.

Pickens, T. Boone. (1987) *Boone*. Boston: Houghton Mifflin.

Posner, Barry Z., and Warren H. Schmidt. (1984) "Values and the American Manager." *California Management Review* 26, 3:202–16.

Preston, Lee E., and Harry J. Sapienza. (1990) *Journal of Behavioral Economics* (forthcoming).

Ryan, M.H., C.L. Swanson, and R.A. Buchholz. (1987) *Corporate Strategy, Public Policy and the Fortune 500*. New York: Blackwell.

Smith, Sarah. (1990) "America's Most Admired Corporations." *Fortune*, January 29, p. 58 ff.

Steiner, George A., John B. Miner, and Edmund R. Gray. (1986) *Management Strategy and Policy.* New York: Macmillan.

Steiner, George A., and John F. Steiner. (1988) *Business, Government and Society.* New York: Random House.

Ullmann, Arieh A. (1985) "Data in Search of a Theory: A Critical Examination of the Relationships among Social Performance, Social Disclosure, and Economic Performance of U.S. Firms." *Academy of Management Review* 10, 3:540–57.

Weidenbaum, Murray, and Stephen Vogt. (1987) "Takeovers and Stockholders: Winners and Losers." *California Management Review* 4:157–68.

Wheelen, Thomas L., and J. David Hunger. (1986) *Strategic Management.* Reading, MA: Addison-Wesley.

Williamson, Oliver E. (1985) *The Economic Institutions of Capitalism.* New York: The Free Press.

Wokutch, R.E., and B.A. Spencer. (1987) "Corporate Saints and Sinners: The Effects of Philanthropic and Illegal Activity on Organizational Performance." *California Management Review* 29, 2:62–77.

Worthy, James C. (1984) *Shaping an American Institution: Robert E. Wood and Sears, Roebuck.* Urbana: University of Illinois.

11

JENNIFER A. STARR AND
IAN C. MACMILLAN

Entrepreneurship, Resource Cooptation, and Social Contracting

A recent *Business Week* poll asserts that "entrepreneurs" are "out" and "dealmakers" are "in" (*Business Week* 1989). If the business press is to be believed, the innovative, altruistic, Economic Developer and Changemaster has been replaced by an expedient, self-interested Speculator and Snake Oil Salesman. This contradiction in terms appears frequently in the entrepreneurship literature, a love-hate relationship best summarized by Schumpeter's oft-quoted description of the entrepreneur as the harbinger of "creative destruction" (Schumpeter 1950). This simple example from the popular press captures the dual image of the entrepreneur in social theory—as Economic Savior and Social Deviant (Parsons and Smelser 1956; Casson 1982; Brenner 1987).

Rather than forcing a choice between the entrepreneur as innovator or dealmaker, a socioeconomic perspective of entrepreneurship acknowledges the essential conflict between the social and instrumental orientations inherent in new venture creation and management (Etzioni 1988). By incorporating moral commitments, principles, emotions, and values into the decision-making process, we expand the set of explanatory variables to be factored into the entrepreneur's success equation. While entrepreneurs may be motivated by personal ambition and profit-making potential, their innovations and business success depend upon their ability to deftly manage the junction of the entrepreneurial firm and multiple marketplaces (Vesper 1980; Etzioni 1986; Van de Ven 1986). In the product markets, the entrepreneur must garner customer approval for his innovations. In the financial markets, he must persuade investors to bet their risk capital on the future success of his firm. In the human capital markets, he must convince employees to contribute long hours to his novel experiment. And, in the social capital markets, he must invest *and* cash in social relationships to rally support for his new venture. These are not atomistic, perfectly competitive, anonymous neoclassical markets, but marketplaces "embedded in concrete, ongoing systems of social relations" (Polanyi 1957; Granovetter 1985; Swedberg 1987).

The unique problems of the entrepreneurial start-up require innovative solutions to traditional management problems. In the formative stage, a new venture is no more than a commercial experiment: a set of hypotheses or assumptions about market needs, product specifications, financing availability, and production and organizational capabilities that needs to be tested by practice (Block and MacMillan 1985). Given the uncertainty, resource constraints, and survival challenges inherent in most aspects of new ventures, successful entrepreneurs must seek "asset parsimony," deploying the minimum assets needed to achieve the desired business results and securing the resources to do this at minimum cost (Hambrick and MacMillan 1984). New venture managers must maintain the flexibility required to test, learn, and readjust their plans by making sequential, "small chunk," short-term investments (Hambrick and MacMillan 1984; Block and MacMillan 1985; Stevenson and Gumpert 1985). With a frugal investment strategy, the entrepreneur can pursue opportunities, and if necessary, abandon them, with limited exposure (Stevenson and Gumpert 1985).

Furthermore, the entrepreneurial firm faces major internal and external challenges to its survival (Stinchcombe 1965; Aldrich and Auster 1986). The fledgling firm must initiate new roles, governance structures, and systems, often among strangers with no previous history of relationships (Stinchcombe 1965). The firm also faces socioeconomic entry barriers and must establish its credibility with stakeholders who may be threatened by the new firm's capabilities or be resistant to innovation and change (MacMillan 1983; Etzioni 1986). As a result, entrepreneurs compensate for these "liabilities of newness" by building ventures that use intensely cooperative strategies (Barnard 1938; Starr and MacMillan 1990).

For entrepreneurs, the problems of scarcity loom the largest, for they have limited resources to invest. Thus, in order to obtain the goods and services they need for their start-up businesses, they must creatively exchange those resources that they have at their disposal: favors, information, friendship, gumption, enthusiasm, obligations, solutions for problems, their own time, and imagination. In socioeconomic marketplaces, entrepreneurs accumulate social assets and spend social resources, using social contracting skills to secure the goods and services they need. In these transactions, emotions and values, rather than logic and rational calculations, often play a primary role.

Thus, if ever there is a situation where a socioeconomic approach is important, it is in the case of the entrepreneurial start-up. For the new business has a particular problem: it needs resources under terms that the strictly rational owner would not consider. For who would provide resources at a higher risk for a lower price? Thus, the new venture is an intensely social endeavor, as well as being an economic one. The neoclassical economic exchange perspective alone cannot explain the interactions among entrepreneurs and their supporters. This paper will draw upon examples from entrepreneurial ventures to illustrate how entrepreneurs acquire resources for their new businesses using socioeconomic procurement strategies. From these vignettes we will provide some initial thoughts on a framework that applies a socioeconomic perspective to the acquisition of resources for entrepreneurial start-ups.

Resource Cooptation Strategies

Cooptation is one of the most flexible and easiest mechanisms for gaining access to resources, exchanging information, exercising influence, developing interfirm commitments, avoiding conflicts, and establishing legitimacy (Selznick 1948, 1949; Thompson 1967; Pfeffer and Salancik 1978; Burt 1980, 1983). Two cases will illustrate socioeconomic principles at work. Both of these cases will be discussed in depth, since they will be used to characterize a number of points throughout the remainder of the paper.

> A Cuban-American entrepreneur, starting a men's clothing import business from Brazil, needed a Fifth Avenue address to establish credibility with his Manhattan buyers. He identified a friend from business school who had just expanded and moved into new offices on Fifth Avenue. They had leased extra office space in anticipation of growth. He persuaded his friend to rent him a piece of the office at far lower than the market-rate rental prices. In addition, he persuaded the company to give him a telephone line that was answered by their receptionist. He used their secretary, their delivery van, Xerox machine, and computer equipment. He agreed to pay pro rata for all the office equipment and personnel that he used. He received permission to use their conference room. Every time buyers came around, he rushed his samples from the basement downstairs and assembled the display in the conference room so that it looked as if it were an ongoing operation. Once the buyers left, he dismantled his displays and returned the conference room to its original condition. This went on for about six months. Although he had originally agreed to pay pro rata for all the resources that were used each week, whenever he offered to settle up his account, his friend told him to forget about it. This arrangement not only enabled the entrepreneur to save thousands of dollars of fixed expenses, but gave him access to resources that he could never have afforded as a start-up company.
>
> This same entrepreneur found other ways to save money by creating transient social relationships. Instead of paying for overnight delivery rates for the samples and designs he was sending to manufacturers in Brazil, he would take the subway down to Kennedy Airport express for $3.50 and find people who were leaving on Varig airlines to Rio de Janeiro or Sao Paulo. He would start a discussion with them and persuade them to take his packages on the airplane. He would open the package to show it was inoffensive, and was always able to find someone to take the package. He would call his partner to tell him who was delivering the package. It saved him thousands of dollars in overnight freight costs. It also allowed him to respond very quickly to customer de-

mands. Here is a case where the entrepreneur used the fact that he could speak Portuguese as a way to create a social relationship, however transient, and create his own virtually costless delivery system.

Such imaginative resource acquisition strategies are not the sole realm of the independent entrepreneur.

A European entrepreneur has consciously considered what he has learned from being an entrepreneur and has institutionalized some of the instinctive processes that first-time entrepreneurs experience when they start a business. He has consciously formalized the importance of social contracts and influence networks and systematically builds and operates a network of consultants and a network of university professors, and consciously uses them to start his businesses. Using these networks, he and his two brothers have started thirty businesses in ten years.

Here is an example of how they consciously utilize their networks: the entrepreneur learned from one of his consultant colleagues that in the Swedish foundry industry there were serious problems with labor and automation. No sane Swede wanted to work in a foundry because of the poor operating conditions there—dust, grit, heat, humidity. The problem could not be exported, because foundry goods are so heavy that the transportation costs/price ratio is not economical. Conventional automated equipment would not work under these operating conditions either, and none of the manufacturers was prepared to create a special line just for the foundries. The entrepreneur took this strategic problem into his network and asked his consultants to find out if this was a problem in the rest of Europe. The consultants in his network started to ask others in their networks to find the answer and provide the market information. The word came back through the network that "Yes, a lot of foundries in Europe are having this problem." He then went into his second network of engineering professors and found that there was a technology that could solve this problem. It was not very difficult, but they needed $250,000 to develop a prototype. So he returned to his consultant network and accompanied each of the consultants on a visit to their foundry clients. To each client he said, "I want to develop a piece of equipment for you. Here is my track record of what I have done in the past. Here is *your* consultant, who will vouch for my credibility and reputation. I need $10,000, which is less than you will pay for annual coffee consumption or for a secretary in this company. I need to collect $10,000 from a number of foundries in Europe to develop this prototype." He soon raised the funds needed to develop the prototype. By using social networks, he was able to fund the venture and uniquely position the product without spending any of his own money. The foundries did *not* get a piece of the business. In exchange for their $10,000, all they received was his commitment to develop a prototype. But, since they had a real problem that sorely needed to be solved, from their perspective, $10,000 was inexpensive. More importantly, he differentiated himself and his product from the other equipment manufacturers. If he had developed the prototype independently, with his own money, he would have been just one of the many salesmen selling equipment that the foundry managers

> "knew" was not going to work. Instead, the foundry managers felt he was working on "their" product—they had a vested interest and a psychological commitment to the development and the success of the product.

The stories of these two entrepreneurs illustrate the unorthodox approaches entrepreneurs use to mobilize resources. Using socioeconomic rather than economic strategies, entrepreneurs involve outsiders in their organizations without formal employment contracts, negotiated fee structures, or capital investment. A college chum provides prestigious office space and necessary equipment and absorbs the administrative overhead, for free. A Brazilian tourist temporarily joins the importer's distribution system. A network of consultants and professors function as the marketing and research and development departments. Using cooptation strategies, entrepreneurs gain the cooperation of outsiders, absorbing them into the production and administrative structures of their firms.

In these vignettes we have seen evidence of the old adage, "Necessity is the Mother of Invention." Entrepreneurs use their ingenuity and resourcefulness to coopt sources of supply and distribution channels, marshaling virtually costless and readily available resources, such as public goods, information, imagination, friendship, time, solutions for problems, gumption, obligations, and enthusiasm. By spending cash substitutes to secure the goods or services needed for their ventures, entrepreneurs create new organizational forms, distribution channels, and sources of supply. In many instances, entrepreneurs utilize their creative abilities to "make a market" where there is no existing market, in the neoclassical sense of the word (Casson 1982). Transactions may be fleeting, instantaneous incorporations, such as the Brazilian tourist operating as an airline delivery system. Coopted goods such as endorsements, political backing, and moral support may not even be for sale in the marketplace. In contrast to neoclassical markets, where goods and services are exchanged for a price set in a perfectly informed and perfectly competitive marketplace of buyers and sellers, entrepreneurs secure and expand these resources in marketplaces that appear to operate according to a different set of rules.

Entrepreneurs also use social contracts to differentiate their firm and balance the power asymmetries they face in relation to influential established suppliers or large competitors who also sell to their distribution channel. While the neoclassical economic approach assumes atomistic competition among comparable competitors subject to random competitive forces, in reality, the new venture is the most susceptible to the vagaries of the marketplace. In situations where a supplier must ration output, a distributor must ration shelf space, or a customer decides not to pay, it is the small start-up company that is the most likely victim, for it does not have access to the formal sources of power, authority, and influence. However, if the entrepreneur has built psychological and social bonds, he can avoid the destructive potential of these rationing decisions. The European entrepreneur distinguished his product from other equipment manufacturers by gaining the foundry managers' financial *and* emotional support for the development of the prototype. The prototype became *their* product, and their feelings of ownership and vested interest caused them to help him aggressively through the typical difficulties encountered in prototype development. In socioeconomic marketplaces, entrepreneurs can create social contracts that reduce the uncertainty and constraints of the precarious markets in which they operate.

Our analysis of a large number of cases, such as those above, suggests a framework for viewing the techniques and strategies that entrepreneurs may use to acquire the resources they need that differs markedly from the conventional concepts of economic transactions. Two types of resource cooptation strategies seem to be critical to new ventures: coopting public goods and coopting underutilized goods.

Coopting Public Goods

One subset of strategies involves the cooptation and exploitation of public goods. The entrepreneur who is seeking ways of exploiting a public good to his advantage can do so in at least two ways—by capturing legitimacy or by exploiting publicly available information.

Coopting Legitimacy

Legitimacy, the institutional support of powerful external actors, is a critical ingredient for new venture success (Stinchcombe 1965). There are two generic ways in which legitimacy can be coopted to aid the new business—by association and by endorsement. By capitalizing on his college friendship, the importer-entrepreneur obtained a Fifth Avenue address, a public good, which, by association, conveyed the image of a fashionable, sophisticated, reputable clothing business. This communicated a message to his customers that was critical to the credibility of his business. Similarly:

> A travel charter company's business was threatened by a press story that predicted a shake-out of companies in the charter flight industry. In response, customers started canceling their reservations nationwide. Struggling to find a way to convince customers that he was not going out of business, one resourceful entrepreneur made an offer to purchase a well-known hotel that was known to be in serious trouble. It was also known that a large hotel chain had made an undisclosed offer on this hotel. The entrepreneur estimated that the offer was at least three million dollars, so he went to the owners and made them a secret offer of 2.8 million. The press "miraculously" found out about this offer and the next day it made the headlines of the financial pages. That information sent a message to customers that this firm had sufficient funding to buy the hotel, so it must be solvent. The business was saved as a result of that action.

In this case, the newspaper was coopted as a public communication channel that the desperate, but creative, entrepreneur was able to access for the benefit of his firm.

The reputation of celebrities or other credible persons can be tapped as a resource when they, wittingly or unwittingly, endorse the entrepreneur or his product. The European entrepreneur was able to gain credibility with the foundry managers based on the reputation of the consultants. Without this endorsement, no funding manager would have given up $10,000 for a "paper" prototype. Analogously:

> When Rachel's Brownies was first getting started, Rachel had her brownies delivered to Ronald Reagan when he came to Philadelphia because she had heard he liked brownies. As a result, Rachel's Brownies gained significant public recognition and free advertising through that association and endorsement. The cost to the company was a certain amount of Rachel's ingenuity and gumption.

Prestigious addresses, newspapers, television stations, and celebrities like Ronald Reagan are all public goods that entrepreneurs can, and do, harness to economize on start-up expenditures. Resources obtained through coopted associations and endorsements may be critical to the new business, and may be unaffordable or unobtainable in traditional markets.

Coopting Information

Another type of public good that the entrepreneur can exploit is information that is freely available and can be combined or packaged in novel ways that make it more attractive. Information is a valuable resource because it has infinite uses, but it cannot be consumed (Itami 1987). The entrepreneur can focus those resources that are freely available to him, namely time and imagination, to search out and coopt information to be used in a variety of ways. Coopted information can either be applied for direct use or for building a social asset inventory composed of friendship, liking, trust, gratitude, and obligation.

At the extreme, many a firm has been started by an entrepreneur who has made direct use of freely available information. These data-mining engineers simply reassemble and sell information that is otherwise freely available from official or other easily obtainable sources.

Instead of using information directly or immediately, information can also be coopted to create a social asset inventory. By repackaging and sharing the information, the entrepreneur may be able to build up an inventory of social obligations or social affinities that can be "spent" at a future date. For example:

> An entrepreneur starting a pump business was at a distinct disadvantage competing with several established manufacturers for a fairly large contract from a refinery. The entrepreneur discovered that the refinery manager was

> having a problem with a newly installed cooling tower system. Rather than give the standard pitch to sell his pumps, the entrepreneur asked the plant manager about his problem. The entrepreneur suggested that the plant manager call one of his other customers who had solved a similar problem the week before. The plant manager called the customer and got a solution in minutes. As a result, he was quite willing to give the contract to the entrepreneur. By exploiting his network and providing sorely needed information, the entrepreneur created an opportunity to differentiate himself. He solved a serious problem, thus creating feelings of gratitude that clinched the sale.

(We will explore the use of gratitude and other social assets in contracting resources in further detail in the section below.)

In our discussion of strategies for coopting public goods, we make no assertion that we have identified all public goods or techniques for harnessing them for the benefit of the new venture. Further observation of entrepreneurial activity will surely unearth additional public goods, such as public spaces (airports and shopping malls), transportation systems, or government services, and strategies for using them.

Coopting Underutilized Goods

Entrepreneurs are famous for their ability to identify new uses for goods and services that are being underutilized by others (Schumpeter 1934; Kirzner 1979). The Cuban entrepreneur identified and gained access to a number of underutilized resources—extra office space, a temporarily empty conference room, and an idle van. In another example:

> An entrepreneur needed catalogs of buyers for her mail order business. While these are commercially available, they are very expensive. Using her natural charm and ability to make friends, this entrepreneur convinced one of the big firms that repurchase these catalogs annually to give her their old catalogs. Since only 10 percent of the addresses change every year, she recycled the old catalogs with only 10 percent error and saved herself precious dollars that others might have spent to start a similar business.

In both instances, the entrepreneurs were able to find new uses for old or underutilized resources.

Examining our observations of the resource cooptation process, there appear to be four major classes of cooptation strategies for taking advantage of underutilized resources:

1. *Borrowing:* The entrepreneur temporarily (or periodically) secures the use of the good or service and eventually returns it. The Cuban entrepreneur's use of the van illustrates this approach.

2. *Begging:* The entrepreneur acquires the use of the good or service by appealing to the charity, honor, or goodwill of the owner of the resources, gaining access to the resources without needing to return them. The Cuban entrepre-

neur obtained the use of the typist's time, computer equipment, and telephone lines using this method.

3. *Scavenging:* The entrepreneur identifies and exploits assets about to be discarded, extracting usage that others eschew or do not intend to use, as in the case of the discarded catalogs.

4. *Amplifying:* The entrepreneur leverages the asset far beyond the perception and usage by the original owners. The Cuban entrepreneur converted the conference room into a showroom.

Once again, we do not claim that we have identified the full array of characteristics and mechanisms of coopting underutilized goods. But, we have seen that the entrepreneurial rule of thumb—"Don't own what you can lease, don't lease what you can otherwise liberate . . . Beg, borrow, scrounge"—is a heuristic for appropriating underutilized resources.

An issue that arises is why should any owner of an underutilized good be a party to the cooptation? A cynical view of these vignettes sees only the Snake Oil Salesman image of the entrepreneur. The entrepreneur is a "con artist" who manipulates and exploits personal relationships to serve his own purposes, or at best, syndicates the risk of the start-up to other people, using their money and their efforts. But in these examples a transaction process is actually underway. Even if, on occasion, entrepreneurs appear to receive something for nothing, there is a complex, poorly defined but very real process of social contracting that takes place—favors are extracted, but obligations are also built (Homans 1958; Blau 1964). The entrepreneur operates in a shifting web of social contracts in which the needed goods and services are implicitly traded for social "commodities." Although no formal contracting takes place, the entrepreneur begs, borrows, or scavenges with an implicit agreement that a social contract is being executed.

Imprecise and fuzzy mental accounts are recorded by the transacting parties. While the exact records may be ambiguous, each party knows that at some time in the future, on a completely different and totally unspecified transaction, the initial provider of the resource may ask a favor, recalling his "loan" or "cashing in" the obligation. In this system, there is the danger that differential record keeping and mental balances could give rise to grave problems of false expectations, increasing indebtedness, high uncertainty of future "payments," or possibilities of opportunistic behavior. In the beginning, the entrepreneur may have little choice *but* to use social contracting mechanisms. But, it is not surprising that as the business becomes more established, he will increasingly resort to more traditional economic transactions to avoid some of these difficulties.

Entrepreneurs often develop strategies that reduce their reliance on social contracts. One method that is often effective is to create business relationships that are mutually beneficial for all participants (Jarillo 1988). In the foundry industry example, everyone benefited from the arrangement: the foundry managers located new equipment custom designed to address their particular technical problem; the engineering professors earned research funds and had an opportunity to use their expertise to develop the prototype; the consultants enhanced their reputation by providing a service to their foundry clients; and the European entrepreneur began a new business. In another example:

> Four entrepreneurs, college classmates in different businesses, have recently joined forces in a kibbutz-like ownership structure. They have traded equity shares in exchange for each others' various services and expertise, thus bringing down the costs of each of the four enterprises. In addition, there are times when some are sharing revenue streams with others who are incurring cost streams.

Using such approaches, entrepreneurs coopt valuable goods and services, rather than risk capital, by inviting in-kind investors to join efforts, share resources, and contribute their time, energy, and skills to the start-up in such a way that there is the potential for future mutual gain. No matter how ingenious, it is not always possible to conceptualize mutually beneficial strategies. In these situations, entrepreneurs are then forced to call upon their inventory of social assets.

Social Contracting Strategies

We have suggested that resource cooptation is often accompanied by entry into an implicit contract between two transacting parties. Social capital—a set of obligations, expectations, information channels, norms, and effective sanctions—is built into the structure of these social relationships (Lin 1982; Coleman 1988). The social and mental accounts of both parties are adjusted up or down as a result of each transaction. By transforming social connections into instrumental relationships, entrepreneurs "cash in" on the governance structures and patterns of interaction built into these relationships (Zucker 1983; Johannisson 1987b; Starr and MacMillan 1990). Tapping these social assets, the entrepreneur may gain certain efficiencies unavailable to others. By weaving together an organization built on social contracts, entrepreneurs can capitalize on their investments in social assets. In our analysis of the exchanges among entrepreneurs and owners of the needed resources, we observe a range of social assets and social contracting strategies.

From our vignettes and a review of the literature, the social assets used by entrepreneurs to develop and maintain social contracts may be broadly classified into five categories: friendship, liking, gratitude, trust, and obligation. These categories vary along several dimensions, which we only briefly discuss here. At one end of the spectrum is *friendship*, a social asset that can be used over and over again without exhausting the account (Ben-Porath 1980). The act of helping a friend in need may even reinforce the friendship itself, so the asset could be used many times in different ways. Friends will gladly give and actually derive pleasure from doing so. Allowing a friend to provide assistance may even deepen the friendship. But friendship is rare, and to develop close friendships takes much nurturing and maintenance, so there are limited opportunities to construct these social assets deliberately (Gabarro 1987).

Liking is less intense than friendship, but some of the same characteristics apply. However, there is less spontaneity of giving and more need for an accounting of the levels of favors and obligations owed or discharged with each transaction. The important thing about liking and friendship is that within reason, they are both repeatedly deployable, and may even increase with usage as opposed to being discharged.

Gratitude is a case where there is some unspoken recognition that a favor may be repaid in the future. The debt will be discharged by the return of the favor if an occasion arises. Not only is it much easier to generate gratitude than to generate liking or friendship, but this social asset does not require much maintenance.

Trust is a neutral point, where favors are granted but the social transactions are more formally recognized as favors that must be returned eventually. The role of trust in these transactions is to reduce the uncertainty that an appropriate repayment will take place in the future (Granovetter 1985; Zucker 1986; Etzioni 1988).

Obligation is at the other extreme. Here there is a mutually perceived understanding that a debt is being incurred, and there are clear expectations that a return of the favor is required (Homans 1958). Obligation is earned and discharged like a commodity and is the closest to the tangible assets of the economic transaction.

Entrepreneurs accumulate a social asset inventory and deploy these assets through social contracts to secure resources for their new ventures. We next discuss the strategies they use to build social assets.

Building an Inventory of Social Assets

The development of social assets is not unique to the study of entrepreneurship (Walton and McKersie 1969; Kotter 1985). In their classic chapter on attitude restructuring, Walton and McKersie document dozens of strategies for building social assets. Rather than reiterating their comprehensive work here, we will summarize the essence of their suggestions, which can be used by entrepreneurs to build social assets. There appear to be at least four major types of strategies to build social assets.

1. *Sharing information:* A person who is a valued source of information, tips, or news can build a significant inventory of obligations, at a minimum, by sharing information that is of benefit to others. The experience of the pump

entrepreneur demonstrates the effectiveness of this approach. In order to develop this social asset, entrepreneurs must develop a broad information database, take the time to listen to other people's problems, and spend the imagination to solve those problems. By addressing people's problems, the entrepreneur can create a host of opportunities to help others and build a social capital asset inventory.

2. *Solving and receiving help with problems:* Solving problems for someone is an obvious way of developing certain social assets. Having your problems solved by another is a less obvious but equally successful strategy. People often develop an intense affinity or a high sense of responsibility for the people whom they assist. Entrepreneurs who seek and follow advice are often able to engage other types of support as well. Individuals who have given advice may also offer endorsements, recommendations, or funding. To draw upon this social asset, entrepreneurs must take the time and spend the imagination to identify individuals who can help them. Even more importantly, they must be willing to be vulnerable and ask for advice and assistance.

3. *Giving and receiving endorsements and favors:* This strategy operates similarly to solving and getting help with problems, described above.

4. *Creating opportunities for people to demonstrate their skills and competence:* Creating or seeking opportunities that enable individuals to display their abilities and to appear competent in front of others can engender considerable social goodwill. The European entrepreneur consistently provided this service to his consultant network, and as a result reaped the benefits from his investment in this network.

By investing time, imagination, and attention to the above strategies, there is ample opportunity to build a social asset base that becomes the gateway for using the resource cooptation strategies discussed previously. The ability to recognize ways to build social capital draws on a certain skill—and perhaps even thrill—in the process of scavenging, searching, and contracting. What is often most important is the ability to see beyond the immediate transaction, to consider alternative uses of the relationship. By thinking creatively and bringing forth unrelated or secondhand skills or information, the entrepreneur can meet the needs of the current social contract.

But building and managing these resources effectively requires a certain amount of skill and sensitivity to the emotional and value-laden attributes of these resources (Etzioni 1988). Feelings of empathy, charity, guilt, and enthusiasm can strike a sympathetic chord, arouse a personal interest, and gain the cooperation and commitment of business allies. Friendship and family ties built on sentiments of concern, sincerity, obligation, and altruism can be converted into business associations that willingly contribute necessary resources to the new venture (Ben-Porath 1980). Social contracts are bound by expectations, norms, and mutual understanding, and draw on feelings of respect, consideration, and fairness, obviating the need for legal intervention and concomitant transaction costs (Macaulay 1963; MacNeil 1974). By encouraging feelings of participation, obligation, and ownership, entrepreneurs can differentiate the entrepreneurial firm from its competitors, and perhaps even increase the cooperation and commitment of some supporters. In socioeconomic marketplaces, the challenge and the main objective is to create social contracts that cause people to respond with their hearts instead of with their heads.

Building and Utilizing Networks

The process of building this inventory of social assets inevitably leads to the development of a network of social connections that enables the entrepreneur to further leverage social asset investments. The network analysis literature has contributed much to our understanding of the structure of social networks generally, and specifically suggests how social networks might operate in the unique case of the entrepreneur (Granovetter 1973, 1985; Tichy, Tushman, and Fombrun 1979; Burt 1980; Aldrich and Zimmer 1986; Johannisson 1987b; Jarillo 1988). Entrepreneurs cultivate and utilize social networks to create additional opportunities, expanding their social capital asset base by building on the capital of others, "the strength of weak ties" (Granovetter 1973). The European entrepreneur converted his consultants' networks into a resource by using their many contacts to establish the scope of a new market.

Entrepreneurs use two broad strategies to acquire resources through social networks—gatekeeping and linking (Aldrich 1988). Using a *gatekeeping* strategy, entrepreneurs will tap their networks to gather resources that can be valuable to someone else. Providing access without revealing the network to the beneficiary preserves the value of the entrepreneur as a gatekeeper for the beneficiary. With a *linking* strategy, the entrepreneur exposes his network by putting the beneficiary directly in touch with the appropriate part of his network. For instance, the pump entrepreneur linked the refinery manager to the customer with a solution to the manager's problems. The problem with the linking process is that it may result in a reduction of the entrepreneur's perceived value since beneficiaries and network members can now bypass the entrepreneur.

Some Caveats

Although we have extolled the virtues of this approach, a few caveats have become apparent from our discussion, and there certainly may be other drawbacks that we have not yet uncovered. As firms grow, the original, simple structure and ad hoc relationships often must be replaced by more systematic, routine management and economic-oriented transactions (Kimberly 1979; Churchill and Lewis 1983). A business built on "nonmarket" social contracts that originally enabled the entrepreneur to avoid extensive resource commitments may backfire. "Social" switching costs may make the transaction more costly in the long run, due to potential conflicts with "rational" profit-maximizing or growth goals (Zeitz 1980). Alternatively, the addition of a new dimension, a business relationship, to an old social association may lead to unanticipated difficulties and the eventual loss of friendship if the business dealings sour (Gabarro 1987). And the classic concern with cooptation strategies applies: if key outsiders are invited to participate in the new venture, they may be placed in positions where they might raise questions or otherwise exert unwanted influence on the firm (Selznick 1948, 1949; Zeitz 1980). On the other hand, such strategies are often the only way that the business will be started. Since these resources are secured with vague, diffuse, implicit agreements with indefinite payback schedules, the future value of the current transaction is fuzzy, imprecise, and accountable only in the minds of the participants. As a result, the terms of the "debt" are usually flexible and postponable and entrepreneurs seem quite content to live with the potential negative aspects in exchange for the benefits—an opportunity to create a new firm.

In summary, the process of building an inventory of social assets with the associated social contracts and accumulated social networks is a crucial ingredient to the cooptation process. Owners of these resources simply would not knowingly release them to the entrepreneur if they did not feel that there was, in return, a net declining social asset exchange—either a decrease in their existing obligations or an increase in the obligation of the entrepreneur. And by using alternative media of exchange, entrepreneurs not only conserve their limited resources, but build flexible relationships that are critical for their new ventures.

Conclusion

The social scientist's study of *homo economicus* is evolving. In the beginning, there was Economic Man, an atomistic, fully informed rational actor who produced goods and services in a perfectly competitive market. He was succeeded by Administrative Man, a more limited species who was unable to optimize his wants and desires because of limited information-processing capabilities. As a result, he created organizations through which he satisfied rather than optimized, and struggled to manage conflicting goals and preferences (Simon 1947; Cyert and March 1963). A more recent mutation, Contractual Man, was versed in contract law, and negotiated agreements accordingly, eradicating opportunism through the selection of the appropriate, efficient governance structures (Williamson 1985). The most recent creature supported in this paper, Socioeconomic Man, is a character whose choices are influenced by collective norms, network structures, emotions, and values, as well as by logic and rational action. His foibles appear more human, and the range of his behavior is broader and more complex.

In a similar fashion, our appreciation of the Entrepreneur has matured. Generations of scholars have admired and applauded his individual talents, motives, and achievements—his extraordinary decision-making powers under conditions of uncertainty (Knight 1921); his remarkable alertness and intuition for identifying profitable business opportunities (Kirzner 1979); his ceaseless striving for achievement and autonomy (Schumpeter 1934; McClelland 1961); and his ingenuity in marshaling and coordinating resources to reach his objectives (Schumpeter 1934; Casson 1982). Traditionally, entrepreneurship research has focused on the unique or even deviant aspects of the entrepreneur's personality and behavior and the ventures he has created. We are only beginning to dispel the myth of the profit-seeking entrepreneur who singlehandedly builds his empire of innovations. Political perspectives on entrepreneurship acknowledge the critical role of stakeholders in sanctioning the new venture and shaping its development (Kanter 1983; MacMillan 1983; Etzioni 1986; Van de Ven 1986). And network theories of entrepreneurship recognize the importance of the structure and content of the entrepreneur's social relationships (Birley 1985; Aldrich and Zimmer 1986; Johannison 1987a, 1987b; Aldrich 1988; Jarillo 1988).

In our eagerness to find the keys to successful venturing and our desire to infuse the entrepreneurial spirit into business enterprise, perhaps we have been too quick to jump on the bandwagon of our discipline-based colleagues, looking for simple clues and solutions. Their theoretical approaches, research methods, and empirical instruments may be too limited to capture the essence of many entrepreneurial activities or to detect critical behaviors or key events that drive much of entrepreneurship (MacMillan 1988; Stevenson and Harmeling 1990). Theories that assume economic rationality may be more parsimonious and better predictors of a limited set of outcomes, but they underestimate the stretch of human imagination and the depth of human relationship. In order to grasp the full impact of entrepreneurship, we too must be entrepreneurs, bringing "new combinations" and innovations to our respective disciplines. This is the tradition that was established by the early scholars of the entrepreneurial phenomenon (Schumpeter 1934; Parsons and Smelser 1956; Chandler 1962; McClelland 1961; Aitken 1965; Cole 1965; Hirschman 1967; Leibenstein 1968).

In marketplaces built on social relationships, entrepreneurs can use the media of exchange and trade that are most freely and readily available, such as public goods, information, imagination, friendship, gumption, enthusiasm, obligations, solutions for problems, and time. With the exception of time, these resources are abundantly available, have infinite uses, are extremely flexible, and are difficult to consume. Because of their unique attributes, these resources are particularly suited to new ventures, where resource scarcity, short-term time horizons, and temporary commitments are the primary mode of operations. The challenge to students of entrepreneurship is to use a wide-angle lens to envision new ventures within a web of interorganizational relationships, social networks, and resource interdependencies, and to use a telephoto lens to examine closely the characteristics and subtleties of these exchange behaviors and interpersonal relationships.

Note

Excerpts from this paper will appear in J. Starr and I. MacMillan, "Resource Cooptation via Social Contracting: Resource Acquisition Strategies for New Ventures," *Strategic Management Journal*, Special Issue on Corporate Entrepreneurship, 11:79–92, 1990.

References

Aitken, H. (1965) "Entrepreneurial Research: The History of an Intellectual Innovation." In H. Aitken, ed., *Explorations in Enterprise*. Cambridge, MA: Harvard University Press.

Aldrich, H., and E. Auster. (1986) "Even Dwarfs Started Small: Liabilities of Age and Size and Their Strategic Implications." *Research in Organizational Behavior* 8:165–98.

Aldrich, H., and C. Zimmer. (1986) "Entrepreneurship through Social Networks." In D. Sexton and R. Smilor, eds., *The Art and Science of Entrepreneurship*, pp. 3–24. Cambridge, MA: Ballinger.

Barnard, C. (1938) *Functions of the Executive*. Cambridge, MA: Harvard University Press.

Ben-Porath, Y. (1980) "The F-Connection: Families, Friends and Firms and the Organization of Exchange." *Population and Development Review* 6:1–30.

Birley, S. (1985) "The Role of Networks in the Entrepreneurial Process." *Journal of Business Venturing* 1:107–17.

Blau, P. (1964) *Exchange and Power in Social Life*. New York: John Wiley.

Block, Z., and I.C. MacMillan. (1985) "Milestones for Successful Venture Planning." *Harvard Business Review* 85:184–97.

Brenner, R. (1987) *Rivalry in Business, Science and among Nations*. Cambridge: Cambridge University Press.

Burt, R. (1980) *Toward a Structural Theory of Action: Network Models of Social Structure, Perception and Action*. New York: Academic Press.

———. (1983) *Corporate Profits and Cooptation*. New York: Academic Press.

"*Business Week*'s 1989 Hip Parade." (1989) *Business Week*, January 16, p. 37.

Casson, M. (1982) *The Entrepreneur*. Totowa, NJ: Barnes & Noble Books.

Chandler, A. (1962) *Strategy and Structure: Chapters in the History of the American Industrial Enterprise*. Cambridge, MA: MIT Press.

Churchill, N., and V. Lewis. (1983) "The Five Stages of Small Business Growth." *Harvard Business Review* 83:3–12.

Cole, A. (1965) "An Approach to the Study of Entrepreneurship." In H. Aitken, ed., *Explorations in Enterprise*. Cambridge, MA: Harvard University Press.

Coleman, J. (1988) "Social Capital in the Creation of Human Capital." *American Journal of Sociology* 94(Supplement): S95–120.

Cyert, R., and J. March. (1963) *A Behavioral Theory of the Firm*. Englewood Cliffs, NJ: Prentice-Hall.

Etzioni, A. (1986) "Entrepreneurship, Adaptation and Legitimation." *Journal of Economic Behavior and Organization* 8:175–89.

———. (1988) *The Moral Dimension: Toward a New Economics*. New York: The Free Press.

Gabarro, J. (1987) "The Development of Working Relationships." In J. Lorsch, ed., *Handbook of Organizational Behavior*. Englewood Cliffs, NJ: Prentice-Hall.

Granovetter, M. (1973) "The Strength of Weak Ties." *American Journal of Sociology* 78:1360–80.

———. (1985) "Economic Action and Social Structure: The Problem of Embeddedness." *American Journal of Sociology* 91(3):481–510.

Hambrick, D., and I. MacMillan. (1984) "Asset Parsimony—Managing Assets to Manage Profits," *Sloan Management Review* 25:67–74.

Hirschman, A. (1967) *Development Projects Observed.* Washington, DC: Brookings Institution.

Homans, G. (1958) "Social Behavior as Exchange." *American Journal of Sociology* 62:606–27.

Itami, H. (1987) *Mobilizing Invisible Assets.* Cambridge, MA: Harvard University Press.

Jarillo, J.C. (1988) "On Strategic Networks." *Strategic Management Journal* 9:31–41.

Johannisson, B. (1987a) "Beyond Process and Structure: Social Exchange Networks." *International Studies of Management and Organization* 17:3–23.

———. (1987b) "Anarchists and Organizers: Entrepreneurs in a Network Perspective." *International Studies of Management and Organization* 17:49–63.

Kanter, R.M. (1983) *The Change Masters: Innovation and Entrepreneurship in the American Corporation.* New York: Simon & Schuster.

Kimberly, J. (1979) "Issues in the Creation of Organizations: Initiation, Innovation, and Institutionalization." *Academy of Management Journal* 22(3):437–57.

Kirzner, I. (1973) *Competition and Entrepreneurship.* Chicago: University of Chicago Press.

———. (1979) *Perception, Opportunity and Entrepreneurship.* Chicago: University of Chicago Press.

Knight, F. (1921) *Risk, Uncertainty and Profit.* Chicago: University of Chicago Press.

Kotter, J. (1985) *Power and Influence: Beyond Formal Authority.* New York: The Free Press.

Leibenstein, H. (1968) "Entrepreneurship and Development." *American Economic Review* 58:72–83.

Lin, N. (1982) "Social Resources and Instrumental Action." In P. Marsden and N. Lin, eds., *Social and Network Analysis.* Beverly Hills, CA: Sage Publications.

Macaulay, S. (1963) "Non-Contractual Relations in Business." *American Sociological Review* 28:55–70.

McClelland, D. (1961) *The Achieving Society.* New York: The Free Press.

Machlup, F. (1967) "Theories of the Firm: Marginalist, Behavioral and Managerial." *American Economic Review* 57(1):1–33.

MacMillan, I. (1983) "The Politics of New Venture Management." *Harvard Business Review* 61 (November–December): 4–8.

———. (1988) "Sampling." Academy of Management Paper, Anaheim, CA.

MacNeil, I. (1974) "The Many Futures of Contracts." *Southern California Law Review* 47 (5): 691–816.

Parsons, T., and N. Smelser. (1956) *Economy and Society.* New York: The Free Press.

Pfeffer, J., and G. Salancik. (1978) *The External Control of Organizations: A Resource Dependence Perspective.* New York: Harper & Row.

Polanyi, K. (1957) "The Economy as Instituted Process." In K. Polanyi, C. Arensberg, and H. Pearson, eds., *Trade and Market in the Early Empires.* Glencoe, IL: The Free Press.

Schumpeter, J. (1934) *The Theory of Economic Development.* Cambridge, MA: Harvard University Press.

———. (1950) *Capitalism, Socialism and Democracy.* New York: Harper & Row.

Selznick, P. (1948) "Foundations of the Theory of Organizations." *American Sociological Review* 13:25–35.

———. (1949) *TVA and the Grass Roots.* Berkeley: University of California Press.

Simon, H. (1945) *Administrative Behavior*. New York: The Free Press.

Starr, J., and I. MacMillan. (1990) "Resource Cooptation via Social Contracting: Resource Acquisition Strategies for New Ventures." *Strategic Management Journal* 11:79–92.

Stevenson, H., and D. Gumpert. (1985) "The Heart of Entrepreneurship." *Harvard Business Review* 85(March–April):85–94.

Stevenson, H., and S. Harmeling. (1990) "Entrepreneurial Management's Need for a More 'Chaotic' Theory." *Journal of Business Venturing* 5:1–14.

Stinchcombe, A. (1965) "Social Structure and Organizations." In J. March, ed., *Handbook of Organizations*. Chicago: Rand McNally.

Swedberg, R. (1987) "Economic Sociology: Past and Present." *Current Sociology* 35(1):1–221.

Thompson, J. (1967) *Organizations in Action*. New York: McGraw-Hill.

Tichy, N., M. Tushman, and C. Fombrun. (1979) "Social Network Analysis for Organizations." *Academy of Management Review* 4:507–19.

Van de Ven, A. (1986) "Central Problems in the Management of Innovation." *Management Science* 32(5):590–607.

Vesper, K. (1980) *New Venture Strategies*. Englewood Cliffs, NJ: Prentice-Hall.

Walton, R., and R. McKersie. (1969) *A Behavioral Theory of Labor Negotiations*. New York: McGraw-Hill.

Williamson, O. (1985) *The Economic Institutions of Capitalism*. New York: The Free Press.

Zeitz, G. (1980) "Interorganizational Dialectics." *Administrative Science Quarterly* 25:72–88.

Zucker, L. (1983) "Organizations as Institutions." *Research in the Sociology of Organizations* 2:1–47.

———. (1986) "The Production of Trust: Institutional Sources of Economic Structure, 1840–1920." *Research in Organizational Behavior* 8:53–111.

12

HOWARD H. STEVENSON AND
JOSE CARLOS JARILLO

A New Entrepreneurial Paradigm

Research on entrepreneurship is itself a typical "rags to riches" story. Although it has become almost customary to begin a study on entrepreneurship by complaining about how little attention the topic has been paid (see Cole 1968; Drucker 1985; and Kirzner 1973, for three very different works that insist on the same point), the truth is that, as Vesper (1988) points out, it has become a "successful field":

- The Academy of Management has set up its own "Entrepreneurship Division."
- Research conferences on entrepreneurship are being organized at leading business schools: 37 papers were presented at the 1983 Babson Conference on Entrepreneurship Research; in 1988, this figure had grown to 106.
- Scholarly books on the subject are being published frequently with contributions featuring interdisciplinary approaches (see, for instance, Backman 1983; Kent, Sexton, and Vesper 1982).
- New high-quality academic journals, such as the *Journal of Business Venturing*, specifically devoted to the field of entrepreneurship, are appearing. Other journals have changed focus from small business to entrepreneurship. At the same time, mainstream journals carry more and more articles on related issues (Churchill and Lewis 1985). The growth in nonacademic publications has been even faster (see McClung and Constantin 1982).
- As of today, most business schools in the United States have at least one course on entrepreneurship and studies of business education argue for more (Porter and McKibben 1988).

Many are the reasons behind that surge in interest, but two are, probably, the most powerful: first, the economic upheavals of the last fifteen years have led some scholars to reevaluate the role of small business and new ventures in job creation (Birch 1979, 1987): it is an oft-repeated fact that the 1,000 largest U.S.

corporations have lost over two million jobs in the last ten years, and the slack has been picked up by smaller, entrepreneurial firms. At the same time, large companies were told that entrepreneurship need not be totally alien to them: in fact, their only hope was to foster innovation and "intrapreneurship" (Pinchot 1985), to act "entrepreneurially." The well-publicized successes of the late 1970s and early 1980s, from Silicon Valley to Federal Express, did nothing but reinforce the appeal of the topic for business and economics scholars (Sahlman 1988).

This strong interest, however, has not brought clarity to the issue. There is no clear scheme as to where to fit all the studies that are produced, so as to obtain cumulative knowledge. The fact that so many of the recently endowed chairs on entrepreneurship remain vacant reflects both the rapid growth in their number and the difficulty young scholars have had in developing an "academically respected" track record in the field. There are few successful role models.

This paper reviews much of the scholarly literature on entrepreneurship, grouping most of the previous studies into a few underlying themes. It then proposes what is considered a wide—yet rigorous—enough framework to define entrepreneurship and entrepreneurial research in a way that, taking advantage of findings along all streams of research, produces operational results for the improvement of managerial practice. Such a framework can be defined as follows:

> *Entrepreneurship is the process by which individuals—either on their own or inside organizations—pursue opportunities without regard to the resources they currently control.* (Stevenson and Jarillo 1990)

This view avoids the limiting aspects of other definitions of entrepreneurship and at the same time captures many of the essential characteristics that have been identified in previous work. The traditional definitions of the entrepreneur such as "enterprise founder," "risk taker," and "innovator," fail to distinguish between small business and entrepreneurship and fail to examine the many complex dilemmas an entrepreneur faces. As will be shown, this paper takes the point of view of "entrepreneurial management": how research and teaching can be directed to improve entrepreneurial practice. It is from this perspective that the proposed framework is developed.

Three Main Streams of Research

The above-mentioned diversity of approaches has often led to an unfortunate occurrence: researchers ignore each other. This mistake has to be avoided, for most of these divergent perspectives make an important contribution to our understanding of the topic. But order has to be achieved for cumulative knowledge to develop. It is therefore necessary to integrate those studies in a fruitful way.

The plethora of studies on entrepreneurship can be divided into three main categories: *what* happens when entrepreneurs act; *why* they act; and *how* they act. In the first, the researcher is concerned with the *results* of the actions of the entrepreneur, not with the entrepreneur or even with his or her actions per se. This is generally the point of view taken by economists, such as Schumpeter, Kirzner, or Casson. The second current may be termed the "psychological/sociological approach," founded by McClelland (1961) and Collins and Moore (1964) in the early 1960s. Their work provides a useful emphasis on the entrepreneur as an individual, the idea that individual human beings, with their unique background and environment, their goals, their values, and their motivations, are the real objects of analysis. In these studies, the *causes* of individual entrepreneurial action constitute the primary interest of the researcher. Both the individual entrepreneur and the environment as it relates to the motives of individual entrepreneurial behavior are considered. It is the *why* of the entrepreneur's actions that becomes the center of attention. Finally, *how* entrepreneurs act is the third focus. In this case, researchers analyze the characteristics of entrepreneurial management, how entrepreneurs are able to achieve their aims, independent of their personal reasons for pursuing those aims and of the environmental inducements and effects of such actions.

The Results of Entrepreneurship

This area of the literature is dominated by economists. What matters here is the *net effect upon the general economic system* of the actions of the entrepreneur, and the role he or she plays in the development of the market system. It is true that for the most part, microeconomics has neglected the study of the entrepreneurial function, simply by assuming that markets would eventually reach equilibrium. Even Industrial Organization, the area of microeconomics that is closer to actual management practice (Porter 1981), by concentrating on the paradigm that the structure of a given industry drives the conduct of the firms in it, maintains this emphasis on suprafirm variables.

The early interest in entrepreneurship, however, was started by economists, who focused upon the economic role of the entrepreneur, rather than the individual who performs such a role. Ricard Cantillon, who coined the word "entrepreneur," said that entrepreneurship entails bearing the risk of buying at certain prices and selling at uncertain prices. Jean Baptiste Say broadened the definition to include the concept of bringing together the factors of production. Thus, the entrepreneur is the protagonist of economic activity in general.

Schumpeter (1934) takes a more specific view. He considers entrepreneurship to be the process by which the economy as a whole goes forward. It is something disruptive of the market equilibrium, or "circular flow." Its essence is "innovation": "The carrying out of new combinations is called 'enterprise'; the individuals whose function it is to carry them out are called 'entrepreneurs' " (p. 74). He thus distinguishes different roles:

> We call entrepreneurs not only those "independent" businessmen in an exchange economy who are usually so designated, but all who actually fulfill the function by which we define the concept, even if they are, as is becoming the rule, "dependent" employees of a company, like managers, members of boards of directors, and so forth, or even if their actual power to perform the entrepreneurial function has any other foundations, such as the control of a majority of shares. As it is the carrying out of new combinations that constitutes the entrepreneur, it is not necessary that he should be permanently connected with an individual firm; many "financiers," "promoters," and so forth are not, and still they may be entrepreneurs in our sense. On the other hand, our concept is narrower than the traditional one in that it does not include all heads of firms or managers or industrialists who merely may operate an established business, but only those who actually perform that function. [p. 74]

A few pages earlier (p. 66) he had spelled out in detail what he defined as the "new combinations" of interest:

> (1) The introduction of a new good—that is one with which consumers are not yet familiar—or of a new quality of a good. (2) The introduction of a new method of production, that is one not yet tested by experience in the branch of manufacture concerned, which need by no means be founded upon a discovery scientifically new, and can also exist in a new way of handling a commodity commercially. (3) The opening of a new market, that is a market into which the particular branch of manufacture of the country in question has not previously entered, whether or not this market has existed before. (4) The conquest of a new source of supply of raw materials or half-manufactured goods, again irrespective of whether this source already exists or whether it has first to be created. (5) The carrying out of the new organization of any industry, like the creation of a monopoly position (for example, through trustification) or the breaking up of a monopoly position.

After Schumpeter's work, most economists (and many noneconomists as well) have accepted his identification of *entrepreneurship* with *innovation.* This represents a change from the previous tradition, where the term "entrepreneur" meant basically "businessman," as we saw. (See Kilby 1971, for a summary of the term "entrepreneur" in classical economics.)

Some economists interpret the results of entrepreneurship in a different way: instead of disrupting the market equilibrium, thus advancing the economy to qualitatively higher levels, the entrepreneur works toward the accomplishment in real life of the (theoretical) equilibrium (Kirzner 1979). The first tradition, followed by Cole (1968) at the Harvard Research Center in Entrepreneurial History, has stressed the aspect of innovation in the entrepreneurial function (see Scherer 1984, significantly titled *Innovation and Growth: Schumpeterian Perspectives*). The second, represented by Kirzner, has stressed the informational aspects of the entrepreneurial function: the entrepreneur has a superior knowledge of market imperfections that he uses to his advantage. Leibenstein (1968), also based at Harvard, takes this approach beyond merely allocative efficiency: he makes the entrepreneur's basic function the destruction of pockets of inefficiency in the system.

The importance of the "entrepreneurial function" to the actual development of the economy of a given country, following more or less Schumpeterian lines, has been studied extensively, starting with Hirschman: "development depends not so much on finding optimal combinations for given resources and factors of production as on calling forth and enlisting for development purposes resources and abilities that are hidden, scattered or badly utilized" (1958, p. 5). These points of view open the way for an empirical study of the effects of entrepreneurship in the real economy. Birch (1979, 1987) has analyzed carefully the impact of entrepreneurial activity in the overall economy through the actual creation of jobs.

Thus, the study of the *effects* of entrepreneurship has the following characteristics: (1) it abstracts from the individual entrepreneur and his or her actions to focus on the process by which those actions affect the economic environment; (2) it recognizes the entrepreneurial function as responsible for economic improvement in our society, due to its "innovations," thus providing a theoretical base for the "advocacy studies" we shall discuss below; and finally (3) it makes possible the distinction between the roles of the "investor," the "manager," and the "entrepreneur." Entrepreneurship would then go well beyond the mere creation of small businesses (Scherer and Ravenscraft 1984). We shall come back to this point.

The Causes of Entrepreneurship

It is not surprising that entrepreneurs themselves have been a subject of interest. If entrepreneurship is at the root of economic improvement, then the implication follows that "we need more of it." Researchers must, therefore, understand those who provide it. This is consistent with a cultural emphasis upon the individual actor ("the cult of the individual"). It also fits with a need to understand why some depart from the norms of average behavior: the dramatic accomplishments of some entrepreneurs might lead one to think that the individuals behind those accomplishments must be of particular interest.

A first level of inquiry into the "causes" of observed entrepreneurial behavior conceptualizes entrepreneurship as "a psychological characteristic of individuals, which can be described in terms such as *creativity, daring, aggressiveness*, and the like" (Wilken 1979, p. 58). It was probably started by *The Enterprising Man*, by Collins and Moore (1964), who put at the core of entrepreneurship the "desire for independence," and who identified as the causal variable certain oedipal conflicts and neuroses of the entrepreneur. This early work has had much following, particularly among social scientists with a background in psychology. Thus, Brockhaus studied the locus of control belief of entrepreneurs (1975), and their risk tendency (1980); Marcin and Cockrum (1984) studied the psychological characteristics of entrepreneurs across different countries; Hochner and Granrose (1985) analyzed the characteristics of entrepreneurs, compared to their nonentrepreneurial fellow coworkers; a similar psychological study was performed on female entrepreneurs by Rowen and Hisrich (1986). Cooper and Dunkelberg (1986) compared the path to entrepreneurship (inheritance, purchase, start-up) with background characteristics and attitudes of a large sample of entrepreneurs. The popular press has also written extensively about the "special psychological characteristics of the entrepreneur," generally understood as someone who starts—somewhat successfully—his or her own business (Silver 1983).

An interesting twist in this trend is the study of the relationship between personal characteristics of entrepreneurs and the companies they set up. Smith and Miner (1983) analyzed the adequacy of different "types" of entrepreneurs along the different stages in the development of a firm, while Webster (1977) and Gartner (1985) focused on the kinds of firms set up by different kinds of entrepreneurs.

The second part of this "supply-side entrepreneurship" conceptualizes entrepreneurship "as a social role . . . that may be enacted by individuals in different social positions" (Wilken 1979, p. 58). It was pioneered by McClelland's famous *The Achieving Society* (1961). The essence of this approach is that entrepreneurial behavior is dependent upon personal motivations, which in turn are dependent on environmental characteristics. McClelland started from a psychosociological point of view, asking why some societies, at some points in time, had exhibited high economic and social growth. He attributed that growth to the "need for achievement (n-achievement)" present in the psychological makeup of large parts of the population in those societies. This point of view has been very fruitful in that it has brought all the theoretical resources of sociology to bear on the field of entrepreneurship. Its results have been well-detailed accounts of how the environment affects the practice of entrepreneurship (see, for instance, Kirzner 1973; Greenfield, Stricken, and Aubey 1979; Delacroix and Carrol 1983; Pennings 1982a, 1982b). The practical consequences for public policy are obvious, so much of the research undertaken with this "environment as motivator" approach has clear political overtones. In fact, much of what is being published right now falls into this advocacy approach (see, for instance, Backman 1983; Kent 1984).

Many criticisms have been leveled at this attempt to understand the *why* of entrepreneurship. First, it can be pointed out that general psychological or sociological traits may be difficult to link causally to outcomes, or may ultimately be irrelevant. It is a matter of common experience that effort is not wholly related to performance, nor performance to success. Thus, many difficulties creep up when something useful is to be learned from "patterns of success" (Cooper, Dunkleberg, and Woo 1988).

This focus on the *why* has also in many cases helped perpetuate the confusion between entrepreneurship and small-business management (Carland et al. 1984). In addition, this practice often precludes the clear differentiation between individuals and organizations. Yet the contribution of this whole stream of research is extremely important: apart from the possible social benefits that might have been obtained from the advocacy approach, it focuses the study of entrepreneurship on its protagonist: the individual entrepreneur, he or she who got "lost" in the previous analysis by economists. It adds the idea that since entrepreneurship is, in the final analysis, carried out by individuals, there must be some specific things that those individuals do. This approach makes it clear that certain skills will be essential to entrepreneurship, and that personal considerations (from environmental expectations to interpersonal relationships) cannot be forgotten.

By way of summary, we could say that this "causes-of-entrepreneurship" approach makes some contributions that cannot be forgotten in any serious attempt at understanding entrepreneurship: (1) it is individuals who carry out entrepreneurial activities, no matter how they are defined; (2) their characteristics (personality, background, skills, etc.) matter; and (3) environmental variables are also relevant, not only because they open up opportunities to exploit market inefficiencies, as in the "economists' approach," but also in the sense that different environments are more or less conducive to entrepreneurship and can be more favorable to the new venture's success.

Entrepreneurial Management

These two streams of research, which have been characterized as "the effects of entrepreneurship" and "the causes of entrepreneurship," deal with the *what* and the *why* of entrepreneurship. It is now left to study the *how*. Entrepreneurship can be considered from a practical point of view—what do entrepreneurs do, or normatively, "how to succeed at being an entrepreneur." It is, in fact, what is between the "causes" and the "results": the "managerial behavior" of the entrepreneur. Figure 12.1 represents the three major categories into which entrepreneurial studies can be classified.

There is a vast literature along these "how-to" lines, from functional studies on aspects of interest for small businesses, to works on how to foster innovation within the large, established corporation (see Burgelman 1983a, 1983b, 1984a, 1984b; Brandt 1986; Nielsen, Peters, and Hisrich 1985; Kanter 1983; MacMillan, Block, and Subba Narasimha 1986; Hisrich and Peters 1986; MacMillan and Day 1987; Stevenson and Jarillo 1986). In this area, we could include work on start-ups, venture capital, etc. (Timmons and Bygrave 1986; Roure and Maidique 1986; MacMillan, Zemann, and Subba Narasimha 1987), as well as many practical, functional studies on how to set up and run small businesses successfully (see, for instance, Silver 1983).

Two other important areas of research are those concerned with the different life cycles through which new ventures pass and the problems entrepreneurs face

Figure 12.1. **Classification of Entrepreneurial Studies**

CAUSES	BEHAVIOR	RESULTS
Psychology Sociology	Entrepreneurial Management	Economics
WHY	HOW	WHAT

as their companies mature (Gray and Ariss 1985; Quinn and Cameron 1983), and studies that try to find predictors of success for new ventures, generally by relating such success (or lack thereof) to (a) the entrepreneurs' background; (b) the chosen strategy; (c) environmental considerations; or (d) a mixture of some of these (Dollinger 1984; Miller 1983; Cooper and Bruno 1975).

It can be argued that this research on "how" is the most appropriate focus for a business school, since it focuses on understanding and improving managerial practice. An example of the importance of understanding "how" may help clarify this. The success in business of the overseas Chinese and other ethnic minority groups has been well documented (see Limlingan 1986, for an up-to-date analysis; Sowell 1983). This can be analyzed from the point of view of the "why," finding answers such as the traditional closeness of the Chinese family or the need for achievement of a barely tolerated minority. But the "how" can also be studied; there, a network of both strong and weak relationships is found (Larson 1988). That network enables its participants to work with much lower transaction costs (Williamson 1975), thus becoming much more efficient than larger, more formal competitors (Jarillo 1988). The first level of analysis provides little guidance for a would-be entrepreneur. The second gives a clue as to how a start-up company can structure itself in order to be more competitive.

A Basic Dilemma

Throughout this review, nothing has been done to address the basic disagreement on what an entrepreneur is: is it only those individuals who start a business who qualify as an entrepreneur? Or is an entrepreneur by definition an innovator, whether in a large or a small firm? If we take the first approach, then Ray Kroc of McDonald's or Thomas Watson of IBM would not qualify as entrepreneurs. The first definition excludes people who have been producers of all the "good things'' that entrepreneurs are supposed to create through the introduction of new products and services, such as jobs and wealth. At the same time, only a few of those researchers interested in entrepreneurial studies would consider the opening of a typical ''Mom and Pop'' store an entrepreneurial act worthy of much study. Studies by Reynolds, Van de Ven, Vesper, and Cooper have provided insights into the start-up process, but have not focused extensively on the difference between high-potential ventures and others.

This basic divergence spills over to the literature. Thus, some prominent researchers want the present explosion in interest to be diverted to nothing other than new venture creation (Vesper 1985), while others see entrepreneurship as something indistinguishable from innovation, which should therefore not be circumscribed to new ventures, but which would encompass the struggle of large firms to remain competitive (Kanter 1983). There is such a great divergence in perspectives that it has been said that even a ''unifying theme'' is lacking (Kirzner 1973, p. 281). Casson has pointed out that the task of reviewing the literature on entrepreneurship ''is rendered still more difficult by the fact that in most academic studies of entrepreneurs the word 'entrepreneur' does not appear in the title, whilst most of the literature with 'entrepreneur' in the title is either nonacademic or is not about entrepreneurs at all'' (1982, p. xiii).

We believe that attempts to pigeonhole entrepreneurship do not contribute very much to our understanding. Each of the aspects described above focuses on some important aspect of entrepreneurship: although risk bearing, for instance, is a critical element of entrepreneurial behavior, it is clear that many entrepreneurs bear risk grudgingly and only after they have made valiant attempts to get their capital sources and other resource providers to bear the risk. As one successful entrepreneur said: ''My idea of risk and reward is for me to get the reward and others to take the risks'' (personal communication). Creativity is clearly not an absolute prerequisite for entrepreneurship either. Many successful entrepreneurs have been good at copying others. They qualify as innovators and creators only if the definition is stretched beyond elastic limits.

Generally speaking, it does not appear useful, *in managerial terms*, to delimit entrepreneurship by defining those economic functions that are ''entrepreneurial'' and those that are not. Nor does it appear particularly helpful to decide which individuals are entrepreneurs and which are not. The first exercise appears to be rather more semantic than practical. The second appears to be fruitless in that individuals in our society may attempt entrepreneurship and often succeed even if they do not fit the standards of academic judges as to their entrepreneurial personality or sociological background.

Entrepreneurship as a Process

Entrepreneurship, from this managerial point of view, is most fruitfully understood as a process by which the vision of opportunity is pursued. This purely behavioral, situational definition fits well with the fact that the level of "entrepreneurship," however defined, often varies during the life of an individual, and/or among the different activities that an individual pursues at a given moment. This approach overcomes the dilemma of whether entrepreneurs are to be found only in start-up companies or can also be in large firms: whenever opportunity is being pursued that requires resources beyond those controlled at the start of the process, we assume we are viewing the phenomenon of entrepreneurship. The final advantage of this point of view is that it concentrates on practice, thus leading us to study (and then to teach) basic entrepreneurial skills. It is understood not as a trait of character (hardly transmittable in a classroom), but as knowledge that helps in problem solving. Entrepreneurial behavior is the result of training and experience that has been stored over the years. It is based on acquired abilities (Simon 1984). Thus, by concentrating on entrepreneurial behavior, and on trying to understand the "entrepreneurial process," we may be able to make use of all findings of previous research. Only then can we begin the cumulative process of gaining insights on a crucial issue: how to foster entrepreneurship by learning the nature of the entrepreneurial process.

This approach also allows us to deal with both individual and organizational entrepreneurship, and to make rational the decrease in entrepreneurship so often observed when people or organizations have succeeded in establishing a resource base sufficient to support their expectation of well-being.

Entrepreneurship and the Pursuit of Opportunity

Entrepreneurship can be understood as the process by which opportunity is pursued. An entrepreneur is someone engaged in the process of pursuing opportunity. "Opportunity" is defined here as a future situation that is deemed desirable and feasible. Thus, opportunity is a relativistic concept: opportunities vary among individuals and for individuals over time because individuals have different desires and they perceive themselves with different capabilities. Desires vary with current position and with future expectations. Capabilities vary depending upon innate skills, training, and the competitive environment. Perception of both desires and capabilities is only loosely connected to reality. In any case, the essence of entrepreneurship is the willingness to pursue opportunity regardless of the resources currently under control. It is typical of the entrepreneur to "find a way."

Business behavior can then be categorized in a *range* between two poles, according to the main strategic motivation: the exploitation of perceived opportunity at one extreme, and the exploitation of the resources already under control at the other. Those poles would be represented by the "promoter" and the "trustee." The promoter is the person whose basic mental attitude is "I can make it happen," while the trustee's approach is "I must guard what I have." Although not exactly the same ("trustee" and "promoter" are idealized ex-

Figure 12.2. **A Process Definition of Entrepreneurship: Strategic Orientation**

PROMOTER/ENTREPRENEUR	STRATEGIC ORIENTATION	MANAGER/TRUSTEE
OPPORTUNITY DRIVEN	⟵ ⟶	RESOURCE DRIVEN
DIMINISHING OPPORTUNITY STREAMS RAPIDLY CHANGING TECHNOLOGY ECONOMICS POLITICS CONSUMER		SOCIAL CONTRACTS MEASUREMENT SYSTEMS PLANNING SYSTEMS REWARDS

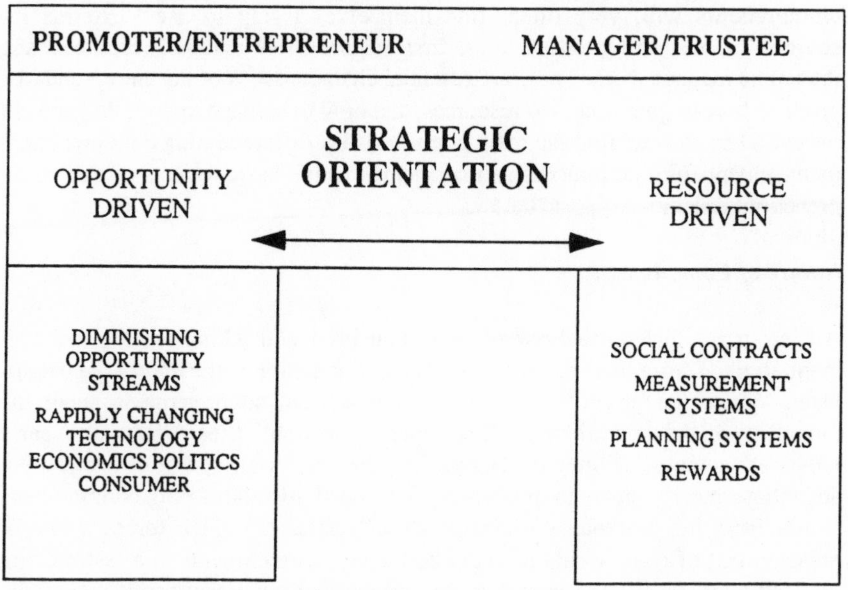

tremes), the "entrepreneur" would be someone close to the "promoter" pole on the spectrum, while the "administrator" would lie closer to the other end. Better yet, we should talk of *behavior* that is close to that of a prototypical "promoter" as "entrepreneurial behavior," and behavior that is close to that of a prototypical "trustee" as "administrative behavior" for, as we have already mentioned, individuals often exhibit different behavior at different points in their lives or even simultaneously with regard to different aspects of their lives. The distinction is not dichotomous, rather it is a spectrum. Figure 12.2 represents this spectrum.

Many factors drive businesspeople toward the trustee side: social contracts are developed within the firm (Walton and Lawrence 1985); planning systems and control cycles take this resource maximization approach (Lorange, Scott-Morton, and Ghoshal 1986), as do performance measurement systems (Johnson and Kaplan 1987).

This basic difference in strategic orientation between the promoter and the trustee may explain the commonly held belief that entrepreneurs are less risk averse than other businesspeople. Indeed, entrepreneurs are very often "out on a limb," trying to accomplish things beyond their means. But this is a very superficial analysis of risk: many entrepreneurs would argue that the fact that they are not using their own resources lowers their personal risk, tilting the risk/reward equation strongly in their favor. The very fact that others are willing and able to provide resources increases the opportunity.

The most important consequence, however, of this basic difference is that entrepreneurs will, very often, find themselves trying to use "external resources." Thus, entrepreneurs must first acquire these external resources, and then must manage them. These are essential characteristics of the entrepreneurial process: how to gain access to resources, and how to manage them if they are not owned. Here we can find the main characteristics differentiating entrepreneurial management from administrative management. Five basic aspects of this entrepreneurial task are explained below.

Nature of Commitment

An important difference between entrepreneurial and administrative management, derived from their respective strategic orientation, is the *nature of commitment*. Where the promoter is committed to action, doubt remains about the durability of the commitment. This "bias for action" tries to capture "early mover advantages" (Porter 1981), probably the only stable source of competitive advantage clearly open to promoters. The need for short-term commitments comes from the promoter's intrinsic lack of resources, which forces a careful management of risks, trying to avoid permanent commitments in a fast-moving world (Quinn 1980). The trustee is slow to act, but the commitment is durable. The need to recognize multiple constituencies (Lodge 1980, 1984) and to negotiate strategies with them (Dayer, Salter, and Webber 1987) pushes managers with substantial resources under their control toward the trustee side. There are, however, obvious advantages in coping with a rapidly changing environment when the commitment can be made quickly and dropped just as quickly, as illustrated in Figure 12.3.

Commitment of Resources

An important entrepreneurial skill is to deploy scarce resources in the most effective manner. The entrepreneur is known, as has been said, for doing more with less. Many entrepreneurs often start the pursuit of an opportunity with no resources other than the confidence that they have identified a "real opportunity." This is often based on the belief that they control one key resource such as technology, market access, or production skill. The administrator and the trustee have as their major preoccupation and as the source of their personal rewards the effective administration of the resources that they currently control. The result is a very different process by which resources get committed to the pursuit of an identified opportunity (Bower 1986). In many cases, the process may be directed toward *personal* risk reduction, regardless of the interest of the firm (Fama 1980). For the entrepreneur, it, perforce, is multistaged as necessary resources are acquired from others. The acquisition of resources is often dependent upon demonstration of success or accomplishment of milestones that lower the risk to

Figure 12.3. **A Process Definition of Entrepreneurship: Commitment to Opportunity**

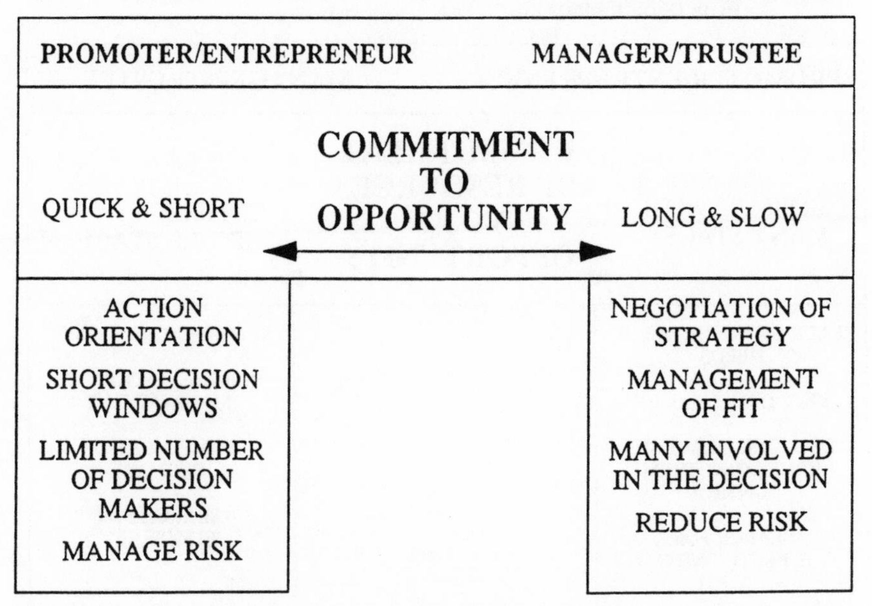

the provider of later-stage resources (Sahlman 1988). The entrepreneur is thus perceived as a gambler and as tentative. The trustee is often simply responding to the sources of the rewards offered. Reducing risk through careful study enhances one's image as a careful steward of resources. Abandonment of a well-laid plan comes at the cost of organizational credibility and thus power. It should not be shocking that the trustee is slow to commit and slow to abandon. The chart in Figure 12.4 shows this dimension.

The promoter is explicit about his lack of precise knowledge about which resources will be needed when. To be successful, he or she must be realistic about the impossibility of maintaining control over all the resources that will be used. This leads to another characteristic of successful promoters: their different notion of "control."

Control of Resources

The promoter is often horrified at "overhead" and at the inflexibility of encumbrances that owned resources and employed people imply. The trustee/administrator is often compensated on the basis of the amount of assets under his or her management and the number of people employed. These are totally different attitudes and evidence responsiveness to very different measurement schemes. Figure 12.5 illustrates the difference.

The issue here is the difference between ownership and control. Chandler

Figure 12.4. **A Process Definition of Entrepreneurship: Commitment of Resources to an Opportunity**

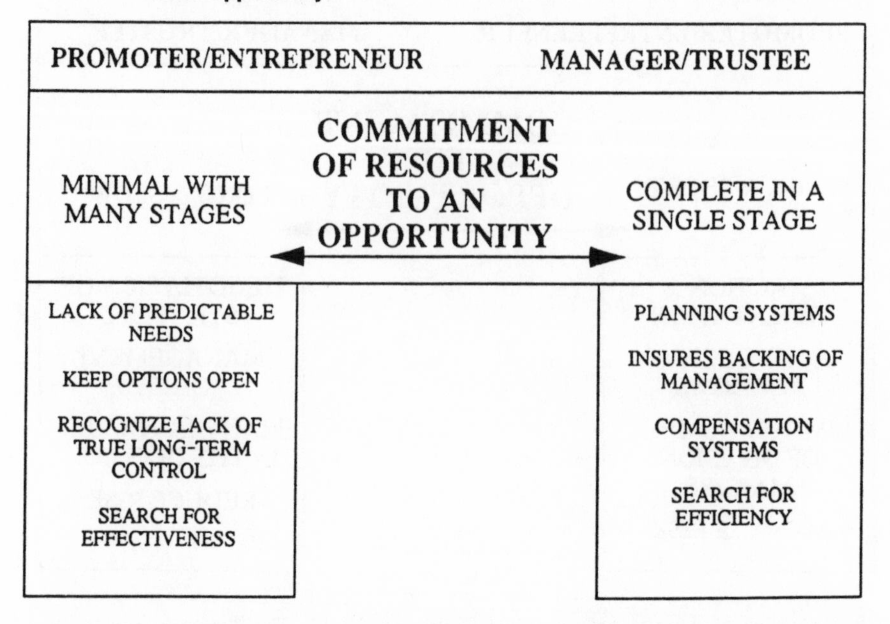

(1977) has illustrated how firms grew large in order to exploit economies of scale, and how they integrated in order to ensure efficient running of large investments. When a given process becomes large, with an important fixed investment, the need to control it becomes paramount. It has traditionally been assumed by administrators that the only—or at least, the best—way to control a given resource is to own it (or in the case of human resources, to hire it). Yet control is possible over resources that are not owned, as can be shown, for instance, in many franchise agreements. Traditional governance systems are not the only way to do business, and entrepreneurs find many ways to structure arrangements that avoid the need to own resources (Larson 1988), thus avoiding "hierarchies," with their attendant agency costs (Pratt and Zeckhauser 1985), and yet provide control and allow coordination (beyond "markets") (Williamson 1975). At the same time, the shortening cycles of products and technologies may make renting resources a far better alternative to outright investment (Hayes and Wheelwright 1984).

Concept of Management Structure

The strategic orientation toward opportunity, the quick commitment and decommitment, and the need to manage resources that are not owned all lead to the entrepreneur's preference for management structures that do not impede the

Figure 12.5. **A Process Definition of Entrepreneurship: Concept of Control**

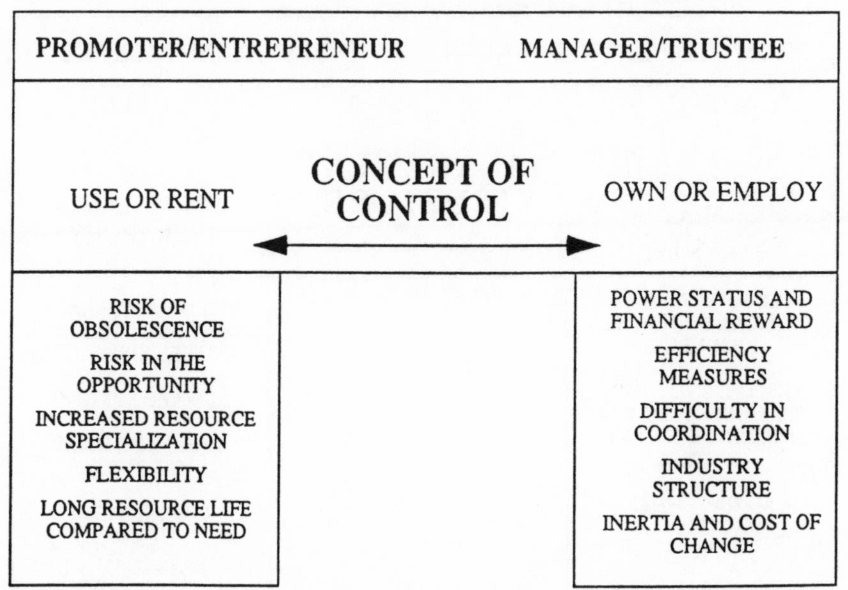

flexibility that is a precondition for pursuing rapidly developing and changing opportunities. The trustee/administrator often views organizations more formally. Responsibilities and authority should be well defined. Without such definition, differentiation, performance measurement, and subunit independence are difficult, if not impossible, to achieve, as the classic literature on management points out (Lawrence and Lorsch 1967; Gulick and Urwick 1937). The decision to use and to rent resources implies the necessity to manage in a different way. Figure 12.6 illustrates this distinction in management form.

Not incidentally, there are pressures toward the promoter's style of management structure that are exerted not only by its strategic characteristics, but also by environmental changes: people cannot be managed now as in the past (Mills 1987). This is another reason for the surge in public interest in the entrepreneurial phenomenon: entrepreneurial firms are often seen as a better place to work.

Compensation/Reward Systems

Finally, entrepreneurs must devise compensation systems that are different from traditional ones because of the higher uncertainty of the outcome. Entrepreneurial organizations thus base compensation on value creation and on team performance, while administrative organizations base compensation on individual responsibility level (e.g., assets or resources under control) and on performance relative to short-term accounting targets (e.g., profits or return on assets) and rely

Figure 12.6. **A Process Definition of Entrepreneurship: Management Structure**

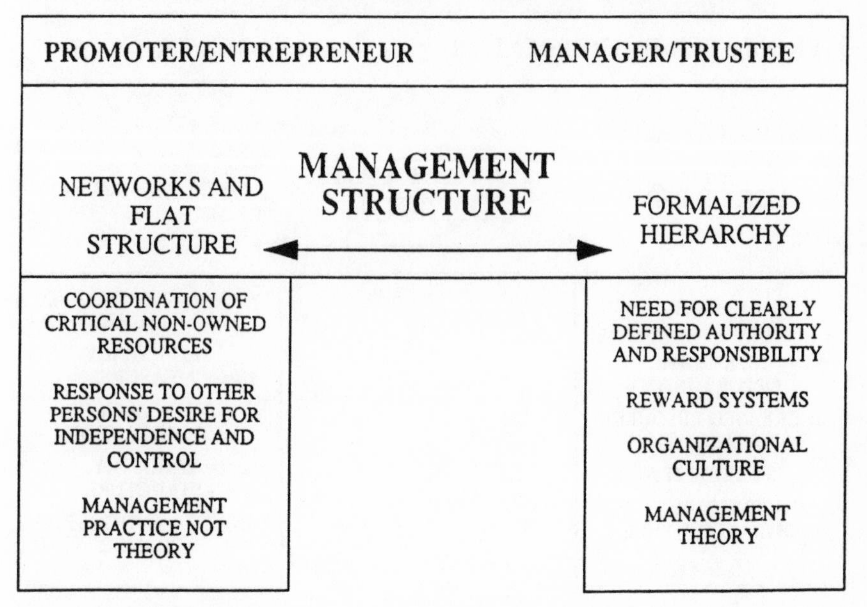

heavily on promotion as a means of reward (Baker 1986). The chart in Figure 12.7 shows these differences and lists some of the factors underlying each solution to the issue of how to measure and reward employees.

Conclusions

Entrepreneurship, from the managerial point of view that has been taken in this paper, is the process of doing more with less, of reaching for opportunities regardless of the resources already controlled. This poses clear research questions and teaching objectives: How is that done? How can entrepreneurs first marshal those resources needed to pursue the opportunity, and then manage them? Are there any particular interpersonal skills involved? Does game theory or negotiation theory help to develop skills in structuring "win/win" deals? From the analysis above, it is clear that these could be basic "entrepreneurial skills," for they clearly facilitate the entrepreneurial process. Some of the basic characteristics of this process have been outlined above, and are shown on Table 12.1, but many more are possible, and would be valuable to research and teaching.

The reader should keep in mind when reading this table that the authors do not intend to be judgmental in differentiating between entrepreneurial and administrative behavior. Each behavior mode has its place, and the degree to which a particular management style or process is appropriate will depend heavily on

Figure 12.7. **A Process Definition of Entrepreneurship: Compensation and Rewards**

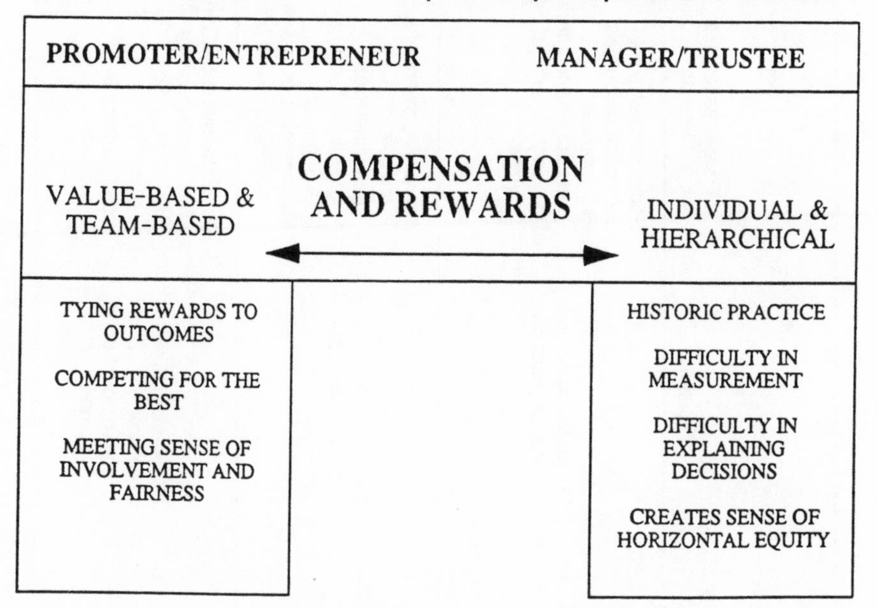

the opportunity, the company, the people involved, and the demands of the external environment. There are often equally strong reasons to be on the entrepreneurial side as on the administrative side. What is necessary is for management to know that there are choices and to act intelligently in making those choices. Nor should the reader infer that entrepreneurship is important and trusteeship is not. In fact, the goal of entrepreneurship is often the creation of value and wealth. Success in the pursuit of the entrepreneurial goal thus leads to the need for effective trusteeship.

In developing a behavioral theory of entrepreneurship, it becomes clear that entrepreneurship is more than an individual and different from a well-defined economic function, although it is both of these things. It is a cohesive pattern of behavior. The reason the authors believe that entrepreneurial behavior is critical now, particularly in larger companies, is simply that the world is experiencing change at a different scale and pace. The nature of the change suggests that managers must generally gravitate to the left of the scale introduced earlier. When analyzing Table 12.1, it is important to note that most of the skills taught at business schools emphasize elements on the right-hand side (Porter and McKibben 1988). Generally, MBAs are trained to become trustees, and management theory focuses on how to accomplish effective trusteeship.

Entrepreneurial behavior, that is, engaging in the entrepreneurial process of pursuing opportunities, requires the skills shown on the left-hand side. These skills bear little resemblance to the usual syllabus of an "entrepreneurial course"

Table 12.1

Two Modes of Management

Pressures toward this side	Promoter	**Key business dimension**	Trustee	Pressures toward this side
Diminishing resource-based opportunity streams Rapidly changing: Technology Consumer economics Social values and political rules	Driven by perception of opportunity	STRATEGIC ORIENTATION	Driven by resources currently controlled	Social contracts with existing resources Performance measurement criteria Planning systems and cycles
Action orientation Short decision windows Risk management Limited decision constituencies	Revolutionary, with short duration	COMMITMENT TO OPPORTUNITY	Evolutionary, of long duration Controlled	Acknowledgment of multiple constituencies Negotiation of strategy Risk reduction Management of fit with existing resource base
Lack of predictable resource needs Lack of long-term control Social needs for more opportunity per resource unit	Multistaged, with minimal exposure at each stage	NATURE OF COMMITMENT	Single-staged, with complete commitment upon decision	Personal risk reduction Managerial turnover Capital allocation systems Formal planning systems

Efficiency of resource specialization Long resource life compared to need Risk of resource obsolescence Risk inherent in any new venture Inflexibility of permanent commitment of resources	Episodic use or rent of required resources	CONTROL OF RESOURCES	Ownership or employment of required resources	Power, status, and financial rewards Coordination Efficiency measures Inertia and cost of change Industry structures of preemptive resource control
Coordination of key noncontrolled resources Employees challenge management control Employees' desire for independence	Flat, with multiple informal networks	MANAGEMENT STRUCTURE	Formalized hierarchy	Need for clearly defined authority and responsibility Organizational culture Reward system Management theory
Individual expectations of equity Competition for resource involvement Increased perception of personal wealth creation possibilities	Value-based Team-based	COMPENSATION & REWARD POLICY	Resource-based Promotion-oriented	Societal norms Tax regulation Impacted information Search for simple solutions to complex problems of equity Demands of public shareholders

in a business school. They have little to do with "how to start a firm" and everything to do with business policy, control, organizational behavior, etc. There is plenty of information for the former, and very little for the latter. In fact, research on entrepreneurship requires a rethinking of much of what is taught at our business schools. If we want to facilitate the pursuit of opportunity, thus increasing the economic level of our society, we must teach our students how to carry out the entrepreneurial process, teach them *how* opportunities can be pursued. Of course, opportunities must exist, and the students must want to pursue them. Those two conditions lie outside the limits of what a management researcher can do, but if students feel competent to pursue opportunities, they are much more likely to find them and to be motivated to pursue them. That is what it means to teach entrepreneurship.

References

Backman, J., ed. (1983) *Entrepreneurship and the Outlook for America.* New York: The Free Press.

Baker, G.P., III. (1986) "Management Compensation and Divisional Leveraged Buy-outs." Ph.D. diss., Harvard University, Cambridge, MA.

Birch, D.L. (1979) *The Job Generating Process.* Cambridge, MA: MIT.

———. (1987) *Job Creation in America: How Our Smallest Companies Put the Most People to Work.* New York: The Free Press.

Bower, J. (1986) *The Resource Allocation Process.* Boston: Harvard Business School Press.

Brandt, S.C. (1986) *Entrepreneuring in Established Companies.* Homewood, IL: Irwin.

Brockhaus, R.H. (1975) "I-E Locus of Control Scores as Predictors of Entrepreneurial Intentions." *Academy of Management, Proceedings of the 35th Annual Meeting,* August, pp. 433–35.

———. (1980) "Risk Taking Propensity of Entrepreneurs." *Academy of Management Journal* 23, 3:509–20.

Burgelman, R.A. (1983a) "Corporate Entrepreneurship and Strategic Management: Insights from a Process Study." *Management Science* 29, 12:1349–64.

———. (1983b) "A Process Model of Internal Corporate Venturing in the Diversified Major Firm." *Administrative Science Quarterly* 28:223–44.

———. (1984a) "Designs for Corporate Entrepreneurship in Established Firms." *California Management Review* 26, 3:154–66.

———. (1984b) "Managing the Internal Corporate Venturing Process." *Sloan Management Review* 25, 2:33–48.

Carland, J.W., F.H. Hoy, W.R. Boulton, and J.A.C. Carland. (1984) "Differentiating Entrepreneurs from Small Business Owners: A Conceptualization." *Academy of Management Review* 9, 2:354–59.

Casson, M.C. (1982) *The Entrepreneur.* Oxford: Martin Robertson.

Chandler, A.D., Jr. (1977) *The Visible Hand.* Cambridge, MA: Harvard University Press.

Churchill, N.C., and V.L. Lewis. (1985) "Entrepreneurship Research: Directions and Methods 1985." Paper presented at the 1st Babson Conference on Entrepreneurship, Philadelphia.

Cole, A.H. (1968) "The Entrepreneur: Introductory Remarks." *American Review of Economics,* May, pp. 60–63.

Collins, O.F., and D.G. Moore. (1964) *The Enterprising Man.* East Lansing: Michigan State University.
Cooper, A.C., and A.V. Bruno. (1975) "Predicting Performance in New High-Technology Firms." Academy of Management, Proceedings of the 35th Annual Meeting, August, pp. 426–28.
Cooper, A.C., and W.C. Dunkelberg. (1986) "Entrepreneurship and Paths to Business Ownership." *Strategic Management Journal* 7:53–68.
Cooper, A.C., W.C. Dunkelberg, and C.Y. Woo. (1988) "Survival and Failure: A Longitudinal Study." *Frontiers of Entrepreneurship Research 1988.* Babson Park, MA: Babson College, pp. 222–37.
Dayer, D., M. Salter, and A.M. Webber. (1987) *Changing Alliances.* Boston: Harvard Business School Press.
Delacroix, J., and G.R. Carrol. (1983) "Organizational Foundings." *Administrative Science Quarterly* 28, 2:351–68.
Dollinger, M.J. (1984) "Environmental Boundary Spanning and Information Processing Effects on Organizational Performance." *Academy of Management Journal* 27, 2:351–68.
Drucker, P. (1985) *Innovation and Entrepreneurship, Practice and Principles.* New York: Harper & Row.
Fama, E. (1980) "Agency Problems and the Theory of the Firm." *Journal of Political Economy* 88:132–45.
Gartner, W.B. (1985) "A Conceptual Framework for Describing the Phenomenon of New Venture Creation." *Academy of Management Review* 10, 4:696–706.
Gray, B., and S.S. Ariss (1985) "Politics and Strategic Change across Organizational Life Cycles." *Academy of Management Review* 10, 4:707–23.
Greenfield, S.M., A. Stricken, and R.T. Aubey, eds. (1979) *Entrepreneurs in Cultural Context.* Albuquerque: University of New Mexico Press.
Gulick, L., and L. Urwick, eds. (1937) *Papers on the Science of Administration.* New York: Institute of Public Administration.
Hayes, R.H., and S.C. Wheelwright. (1984) *Restoring Our Competitive Edge: Competing through Manufacturing.* New York: Wiley.
Hirschman, A.O. (1958) *The Strategy of Economic Development.* New Haven, CT: Yale University Press.
Hisrich, R.D., ed. (1986) *Entrepreneurship, Intrapreneurship, and Venture Capital.* Lexington, MA: Lexington Books.
Hisrich, R.D., and M.P. Peters. (1986) "Establishing a New Business Venture Unit within a Firm." *Journal of Business Venturing* 1, 3:307–26.
Hochner, A., and C.S. Granrose. (1985) "Sources of Motivation to Choose Employee Ownership as an Alternative to Job Loss." *Academy of Management Journal* 28:860–75.
Jarillo, J.C. (1988) "On Strategic Networks." *Strategic Management Journal* (UK) 9, 1:31–41.
———. (1989) "Entrepreneurship and Growth: The Strategic Use of External Resources." *Journal of Business Venturing* 4:133–47.
Jarillo, J.C., and J.E. Ricart. (1987) "Sustaining Networks." *Interfaces* 17:82–91.
Johnson, H. Thomas, and Robert S. Kaplan. (1987) *Relevance Lost: The Rise & Fall of Management Accounting.* New York: Harper & Row.
Kanter, R.M. (1983) *The Change Masters: Innovation and Entrepreneurship in the American Corporation.* New York: Simon & Schuster.
———. (1989) *When Giants Learn to Dance.* New York: Simon & Schuster.
Kent, C.A., ed. (1984) *The Environment for Entrepreneurship.* Lexington, MA: Lexington Books.

Kent, C.A., D.L. Sexton, and K.H. Vesper, eds. (1982) *Encyclopedia of Entrepreneurship*. Englewood Cliffs, NJ: Prentice-Hall.

Kilby, P., ed. (1971) *Entrepreneurship and Economic Development*. New York: The Free Press.

Kirzner, I.M. (1973) *Competition and Entrepreneurship*. Chicago: University of Chicago Press.

———. (1979) *Perception, Opportunity and Profit: Studies in the Theory of Entrepreneurship*. Chicago: University of Chicago Press.

Larson, A. (1988) "Networks as Social Systems." Ph.D. diss., Harvard Graduate School of Business Administration, Boston.

Lawrence, P.R., and R. Johnston. (1988) "Beyond Vertical Integration—The Rise of the Value Adding Partnership." *Harvard Business Review*, May–June, pp. 94–194.

Lawrence, P.R., and Jay W. Lorsch. (1967) *Organization and Environment*. Boston: Harvard Business School.

Leibenstein, H. (1968) "Entrepreneurship and Development." *American Review of Economics*, May, pp. 72–83.

Limlingan, V.S. (1986) *The Overseas Chinese: Business Strategies and Management Practices*. Manila: Vita Development Corp.

Lodge, G.C. (1980) *The New American Ideology*. New York: Alfred A. Knopf.

———. (1984) *The American Disease*. New York: Alfred A. Knopf.

Lorange, P., M. Scott-Morton, and S. Ghoshal. (1986) *Strategic Control Systems*. St. Paul, MN: West Publishing.

McClelland, D.C. (1961) *The Achieving Society*. Princeton, NJ: D. van Nostrand.

McClung, J.J., and J.A. Constantin. (1982) "Nonacademic Literature on Entrepreneurship: An Evaluation." In C.A. Kent, D.L. Sexton, and K.H. Vesper, eds., *Encyclopedia of Entrepreneurship*, pp. 103–25. Englewood Cliffs, NJ: Prentice-Hall.

MacMillan, I.C., Z. Block, and P.N. Subba Narasimha. (1986) "Corporate Venturing: Alternatives, Obstacles Encountered, and Experience Effects." *Journal of Business Venturing* 1, 2:177–89.

MacMillan, I.C., and D.L. Day (1987) "Corporate Ventures into Industrial Markets: Dynamics of Aggressive Entry." *Journal of Business Venturing* 2, 1:29–39.

MacMillan, I.C., L. Zemann, and P.N. Subba Narasimha. (1987) "Criteria Distinguishing Successful from Unsuccessful Ventures in the Venture Screening Process." *Journal of Business Venturing* 2, 2:123–37.

Marcin, E.R., and D.L. Cockrum. (1984) "A Psychological Comparison of Entrepreneurs and Small Business Managers in the United States, West Germany and Mexico in Respect to Achievement, Power, Affiliation Motivation as well as Locus of Control." Paper presented at the Eleventh International Small Business Conference, London.

Miller, D. (1983) "The Correlates of Entrepreneurship in Three Types of Firms." *Management Science* 29, 7:770–91.

Mills, D.Q. (1987) *Not Like Our Parents*. New York: William Morrow.

Nielsen, R.P., M.P. Peters, and R.D. Hisrich. (1985) "Intrapreneurship Strategy for Internal Markets—Corporate, Non-Profit and Government Institution Cases." *Strategic Management Journal* 6, 2:181–89.

Pennings, J.M. (1982a) "Organizational Birth Frequencies: An Empirical Investigation." *Administrative Science Quarterly* 27, 1:120–44.

———. (1982b) "The Urban Quality of Life and Entrepreneurship." *Academy of Management Journal* 25, 1:63–79.

Pinchot, G. (1985) *Intrapreneuring: Why You Don't Have to Leave the Corporation to Become an Entrepreneur*. New York: Harper & Row.

Porter, L.W., and L.E. McKibben. (1988) *Management Education and Development.* New York: McGraw-Hill.
Porter, M. (1981) "The Contributions of Industrial Organization to Strategic Management." *Academy of Management Review* 6, 4:609–20.
Pratt, J.W., and R.J. Zeckhauser, eds. (1985) *Principals and Agents: The Structure of Business.* Boston: Harvard Business School Press.
Quinn, J.B. (1980) *Strategies for Change.* Homewood, IL: Irwin.
Quinn, R.E., and K. Cameron. (1983) "Organizational Life Cycles and Shifting Criteria of Effectiveness." *Management Science* 29, 1:33–51.
Roure, J.B., and M.A. Maidique. (1986) "Linking Prefunding Factors and High Technology Venture Success: An Exploratory Study." *Journal of Business Venturing* 1, 3:295–306.
Rowen, D.D., and R.D. Hisrich. (1986) "The Female Entrepreneur: A Career Development Perspective." *Academy of Management Review* 11:393–407.
Sahlman, W.A. (1988) "Aspects of Financial Contracting in Venture Capital." *The Continental Bank Journal of Applied Corporate Finance* 1, 2:23–26.
Sahlman, W.A., and H.H. Stevenson. (1986) "Importance of Entrepreneurship in Economic Development." In R.D. Hisrich, ed., *Entrepreneurship, Intrapreneurship and Venture Capital.* Lexington, MA: Lexington Books.
Scherer, F.M., (1984) *Innovation and Growth: Schumpeterian Perspectives.* Cambridge, MA: MIT Press.
Scherer, F.M. and D. Ravenscraft. (1984) "Growth by Diversification: Entrepreneurial Behavior in Large-Scale United States Enterprises." Working Paper, Bureau of Economics, Federal Trade Commission, Washington, DC.
Schumpeter, J.A. (1934) *The Theory of Economic Development.* Cambridge, MA: Harvard University Press.
Silver, A.D. (1983) *The Entrepreneurial Life.* New York: Wiley.
Simon, H.A. (1984) "What We Know about the Creative Process." Paper presented at the Second International Conference on Creative and Innovative Management, Miami.
Smith, N.R., and J.B. Miner. (1983) "Type of Entrepreneur, Type of Firm, and Managerial Motivation: Implications for Organizational Life Cycle Theory." *Strategic Management Journal* 4:325–40.
Sowell, T. (1983) *The Economics and Politics of Race: An International Perspective.* New York: William Morrow.
Stevenson, H.H. (1983) "A Perspective on Entrepreneurship." Harvard Business School Working Paper #9–384–131, Boston.
Stevenson, H.H., and D.E. Gumpert. (1985) "The Heart of Entrepreneurship." *Harvard Business Review*, March–April, pp. 85–94.
Stevenson, H.H., and J.C. Jarillo. (1986) "Preserving Entrepreneurship as Companies Grow." *Journal of Business Strategy* 7:10–23.
———. (1990) "A Paradigm of Entrepreneurship: Entrepreneurial Management." In William D. Guth and Ari Ginsberg, eds., *Corporate Entrepreneurship. Strategic Management Journal*, special issue, vol. 11:17–27.
Stevenson, H.H., M.J. Roberts, and H.I. Grousbeck. (1989) *New Business Ventures and the Entrepreneur.* Homewood, IL: Irwin.
Timmons, J.A., and W.D. Bygrave. (1986) "Venture Capital's Role in Financing Innovation for Economic Growth." *Journal of Business Venturing* 1, 2:161–73.
Vesper, K.H. (1985) "A New Direction, or Just a New Label?" In J.J. Kao and H.H. Stevenson, eds., *Entrepreneurship: What It Is and How to Teach It.* Boston: Harvard Business School Press.

———. (1988) "Entrepreneurial Academics—How Can We Tell When the Field Is Getting Somewhere?" *Journal of Business Venturing* 3, 1:1–10.

Walton, R.E., and P.R. Lawrence, eds. (1985) *Human Resources Management: Trends and Challenges*. Boston: Harvard Business School Press.

Webster, F.A. (1977) "Entrepreneurs and Ventures: An Attempt at Classification and Clarification." *Academy of Management Review* 2, 1:54–61.

Wilken, P.H. (1979) *Entrepreneurship: A Comparative and Historical Study*. Norwood, NJ: ABLEX.

Williamson, O. (1975) *Markets and Hierarchies*. New York: The Free Press.

V

The Role of Institutions

13

MITCHEL Y. ABOLAFIA AND
NICOLE WOOLSEY BIGGART

Competition and Markets

An Institutional Perspective

Economic competition is widely believed to be a critical—even *the* critical—social process in market societies. From a market perspective, the competitive pursuit of gain by individuals and firms creates exchange conditions that result in allocative efficiency, the greatest good for the greatest number. This utilitarian ideology is the foundation of modern economics and, not coincidentally, of numerous legal and political institutions. Economic utilitarianism even achieves moral embodiment in an esteemed social role, the entrepreneur. Competition and its outcomes approach the status of natural law—an expected, even inevitable product of human interaction.

This paper is an attempt to create a framework for understanding economic competition as social action structured by political, economic, and cultural contexts. We propose a conceptualization of competition as an institutionally embedded and socially maintained form of mutual striving. Markets, we argue, are not merely the sum of the buying and selling activities of autonomous competitive individuals. Rather, we understand markets to be social arenas that structure competition according to legitimated organizing principles. Organization is manifest in the voluntary agreement of competitors to renounce certain practices and to abide by others. We will argue against the popular microsocial conceptualization of competition as the unboundedly antagonistic moves of independent actors. Rather, we believe that competition—no less than cooperation, obedience, and other forms of social action—is oriented toward others, has underlying norms, and is sustained by institutional arrangements.

Recent work in economic sociology and organization theory has questioned the view of the competitive market as an atomized, unorganized mass (White 1981; Baker 1984a, 1984b; Burns and Flam 1987; Abolafia and Kilduff 1988). An awareness that market competition is embedded in social relations is clearly emerging (Granovetter 1985; Schapiro 1987), yet little has been written about how competitive relations are structured or about the institutional means through which competitive action is maintained. Nor do most authors address the normative underpinnings of market arrangements (see, however, Orru, Biggart, and Hamilton, forthcoming).

In this paper we propose an institutional perspective on competition and markets. We argue that every market is an institutionalized system for the mediation of competition and that the structure of these systems varies by their historical and cultural context. The degree of organization in market systems varies greatly, however. At the lowest level of organization there is little more than a normative system, agreed-on business practices such as the meaning of a handshake. Formalized institutional systems are characterized by associations with rules and a division of labor whose purpose is to maintain market order. Moreover, market institutions vary from the transient and informal, such as a flea market, to the relatively more permanent and formalized organization of a stock exchange. Markets also vary in their enforcement of competitive norms—from weak trade and professional associations to powerful self-regulated sports leagues in football, baseball, and basketball. All markets, however, have normative underpinnings and institutionalized means for sustaining norms of competition.

Our discussion is organized in three parts. First, we review theories of economic competition, suggesting that they are mainly of two types: those that see competition as an asocial process, and those that describe competition as a political process. We briefly compare these two conceptualizations of competition, and argue for a political view that incorporates an institutional perspective. Second, we describe features of an institutional perspective on market competition. Third, we illustrate the utility of an institutional approach for understanding market competition by examining three very different competitive environments: a commodity futures market, Japanese business groups, and direct selling organizations. We demonstrate that each market setting has a substantive organizing principle that defines "appropriate" competition, and has institutionalized arrangements for maintaining competition in conformance with norms.

Theories of Economic Competition

Competition has been a central concept in both economics and sociology since their inceptions, and these disciplines have produced several conceptualizations. They can, however, be divided into two types: the asocial and the political. Asocial conceptualizations are those in which actors are isolated units and social relations are, as Granovetter (1985) describes it, "frictionless." The market is composed of actors who are independent and mindless of each other, or if they are strategically aware of competitors, this awareness is understood to be futile in altering competitive outcomes. In some asocial formulations, the market is an autonomous institution uninfluenced by other social institutions. We use the term "asocial" to emphasize that these formulations do not have a theory of social action, or assume that the process of meaningful interaction is unimportant to competitive outcomes, not that they posit no social consequences to competition.

In political conceptualizations of competition participants mutually orient their action toward each other. In this view competition is not the self-seeking abandon of isolated individuals, but the purposive acts of mutually aware rivals. Markets are political arenas that are often influenced by the state and other social institutions.

Competition as an Asocial Process

The idea of competition as an asocial process has achieved currency as part of the general domination of utilitarian thought in western society (Hamilton and Biggart 1985). There are three important variations of this model. The first two have their origin in economics, the third in sociology.

Classical and neoclassical economists use the term competition in two different ways (McNulty 1968). In the first usage—one employed by Adam Smith (1776/1976) but still current—competition refers to a regulatory force. Competition "forces" price to equal marginal cost, thereby assuring allocative efficiency in the use of resources. McNulty compares this notion of competition to gravity: "through competition, resources 'gravitate' toward their most productive uses, and through competition, price is 'forced' to the lowest level which is sustainable over the long run" (p. 643). Competition is analogous to a force of nature that assures order and stability in the economic world.

In the second usage of the term, competition refers to an idealized set of conditions or state of affairs, which although unrealizable, is a useful analytic device. In this sense, competition refers to a specific market structure. Perfect competition includes the following conditions (Stigler 1968):

1. The number of firms producing a commodity is sufficiently large for no single firm to make more than a negligible contribution to output.
2. The commodity is homogeneous, in the sense that consumers have no reason to prefer the commodity as produced by one firm against the commodity as produced by any other.
3. Firms are assumed to act independently. Rather than strong rivalry, perfect competition assumes utter dispersion of autonomous actors.
4. Participants possess complete knowledge of offers to buy and sell in the market.

What is striking about this definition is that competition is not a process, but is rather a state of the world under given conditions. Moreover, it is an equilibrium state. This contrasts to the "regulatory force" view of the classicists, which assumed disequilibrium. The great paradox is that in this definition of competition, there can be no competitive behavior. According to Frank Knight, a leading neoclassicist, perfect competition involves "no presumption of psychological competition, emulation, or rivalry" (quoted in McNulty 1968, p. 642). Hayek has gone even further in stating: "if the state of affairs assumed by the theory of perfect competition ever existed, it would not only deprive of their scope all the activities which the verb 'to compete' describes but would make them virtually impossible" (quoted in McNulty 1968, p. 649).

This model of a competitive market forms the basis of economic theorizing today. Economists recognize that the empirical world differs from the postulated ideal, of course, but the unrealized and unrealizable ideal is the point of theoretical reference: neoclassical scholars attempt to uncover those real-world "imperfections" that impede ideally competitive conditions, for example, cartels and tariffs.

A third model of asocial competition comes from sociological theory. This perspective, which views competition as a selection process, grew out of an ecological view of social institutions. As Carroll (1984) shows, early social ecologists such as Spencer and Hawley espoused developmental and adaptation-based theories. They saw organizational forms evolving to fit a changing environment better. These writers saw symbiosis and other adaptive responses, rather than competition, as the central processes of social life. A competition-based notion of the selection process, as Carroll notes (1984), did not emerge until Hannan and Freeman's (1977) influential paper on population ecology. Their selection perspective focuses on the birth and death rates of organizational forms; it posits that organizations are bound by inertia and are relatively unable to adapt to changing conditions. Rather, the environment selects those organizations that are most fit to survive. Births and deaths of firms and other institutions are the result of competitive pressures, with the better adapted surviving and the less fit dying. According to Hannan and Freeman (1988a, chap. 5), competition refers to the situation in which increases in the density of one population depress the growth rate of another. Firms that try to compete strategically have limited ability to affect outcomes because of limited information, established cognitive patterns and structural arrangements, commitment to contracts, and other sunk costs. Despite the best of strategic efforts, it is the environment, not actors, that determines competitive outcomes.

This view of competition as a selection mechanism is in some ways related to an economic view. Both views assume that an organization's survival is dependent on some kind of "fitness" for its environment. The economists express this fitness in terms of the efficiency of each firm, while the selection theorists refer to the relative success of organizational forms at the population level. Both efficiency and form are context-dependent, the former referring to the market, and the latter to a niche (which may be a market location). In both, the outcome of the competitive process is determined by competitors' positions relative to others in the market or niche.

A significant difference between most neoclassical economists and the selection theorists is the latter's emphasis on disequilibrium. The interaction of two populations is inherently unstable and the ecology model reflects this bias toward a dynamic formulation. In addition, according to economics, actors compete at the margin, while in the selection view competition is between populations with different structural characteristics.

Perhaps where the neoclassical and selection models differ most is in their purposes. While economists are interested in the optimal allocation of resources, the selection theorists are concerned with the development of variation in organizational forms (e.g., specialist organizations versus generalist organizations) and the distribution of those forms throughout society. In other words, the selection theorists are concerned with how environmental competition shapes social structure.

In sum, there is no rivalry, in fact, no social contact in the three asocial views of competition. Competition is either a force of nature, a structural condition, or the result of environmental conditions.

These asocial conceptualizations of competition have been extremely powerful devices for understanding, at the abstract and aggregate level where much economic and ecological inquiry takes place, the dynamics and organizational configurations of western market societies. We find asocial views inadequate, however, for two reasons. First, asocial models, as Mark Granovetter has argued, provide an undersocialized conceptualization of human agents who everywhere act alike, rationally pursuing unspecified interests (1985). Asocial models cannot account for the influence of social networks, gender, class, culture, religion—those factors of social life that influence what people want and how they choose to go about getting it. Important work in the area of behavioral decision theory (e.g., Tversky and Kahneman 1974; Kahneman, Knetsch, and Thaler 1986) has raised powerful questions about the limits to economic rationality, but its focus on individual decision making has not yet included the impact of norms, social groups, and institutions. Cognitive processes operate within social processes that are shaped by groups and by community (Etzioni 1988).

Neoclassical models assume an ideal state of the world and then explain deviations from the ideal; the neoclassical model of a competitive market is transhistoric and acultural. The ecological model, despite the inclusion of a temporal dimension, is also transhistoric and acultural. Recently, several ecologists have elaborated the model by including in their work institutional elements, such as ideology and conflict (e.g., Singh, Tucker, and House 1986; Carroll 1987; Hannan and Freeman 1988a, 1988b). This adds important context to population dynamics and suggests that institutional influence may be compatible with the ecological model. But the institutional reality incorporated in these studies is by needs in the attenuated form amenable to the variable-based methodology of ecological analysis. Institutional variables may be associated with varying rates of organizational birth and death, but ecologists can say little about how the process of competition varies or is transformed in differing institutional contexts.

In sum, asocial theories of both the neoclassical and ecological types tend to be transhistoric, assuming that all markets, in all places and times, operate according to the same logic. Economists and many ecologists, in an attempt to develop a general theory, envision a unitary competitive force that, like gravity, expresses itself the same way anywhere under given conditions.

It is equally possible, however, to hypothesize that competitive norms are socially constructed by actors in specific sociocultural contexts that shape and are shaped by competitive action. Rather than explaining market and competitive differences as corruptions or imperfections of an ideal, differences may reflect varied beliefs, orientations to materialism, and the relative weakness or strength of individualism as an ethic. Western norms, for example, should not be taken for granted in a culturally sensitive theory of competition. Clearly, this second hypothesis is consistent with those disciplines such as anthropology, history, and some forms of sociology that presume that social action is historically shaped and meaningful only within a cultural context. We would argue that while asocial models may be suited to phenomena adequately described by aggregated variable analysis, they are susceptible to a reductionist fallacy when examining intramarket relations.

A second major limitation of asocial views of competition, including those of population ecology, is that they are concerned only with the outcomes of competitive arrangements, not with competitive activity itself. We accept that neoclassical modeling of macrolevel supply and demand, and ecological analyses of population configurations, make significant contributions to our understanding of the collective consequences of competitive action. A focus on outcomes and consequences, however, allows economists and ecologists to ignore as unimportant the social relations that are crucial to an understanding of the competitive process. An institutional theory concerned with the structure, content, and maintenance of social action, in contrast, puts relationships at the center of inquiry.

Competition as a Political Process

In the ecological selection perspective, it is the environment that optimizes (Hannan and Freeman 1977); competitors are constrained by structural inertia. In the political perspective, competitors are active agents mobilizing scarce resources to shape their environment. Versions of this voluntarist view are found in conflict theory (Tilly 1978), social movement theory (McCarthy and Zald 1973, 1977; Jenkins and Perrow 1977), and some versions of strategic management (Henderson 1984; Harrigan 1985) and marketing (Kotler and Achrol 1984). Competitors attempt to shape their environment through such strategies as advertising, public relations, government lobbying, and campaign contributions. Weber (1978, p. 38) in this vein, defined competition as "a formally peaceful attempt to attain control over opportunities and advantages which are also desired by others."

In addition to seeing competitors as active agents who shape the competitive arena, the political perspective argues that actors have social orientations: actors recognize each other as contestants, although they may not be in actual contact. Selection, like competition, according to Weber, is a struggle for advantages and survival, but "without a meaningful orientation (toward others) in terms of conflict" (1978, p. 38). It is this social orientation that most clearly distinguishes the political from the asocial views of competition. Recently, for example, White (1988) has put mutual orientation at the center of a theory of markets. According to White (1988, p. 228):

> 1. Market actors, and many potential entrants into markets, are known to one another.
> 2. They take the perceived actions of others into account in formulating market strategies and in acting.
> 3. Market actors are keenly interested in one another and in how each producing firm relates to the buyers' side.
> 4. They normally share a great deal of information about the style of behavior each firm adopts vis-à-vis the others, that is, the social context in which they operate.

These four propositions may be usefully compared with Stigler's propositions quoted above. According to White, mutual orientation is the basis on which competitors adapt to each other's moves, as well as the means through which they are mobilized for collective action. The economist's assumption that only oligopolists are mutually oriented is questioned by recent work such as this in the sociology of markets (see Baker 1984a, 1984b; White 1988).

The political perspective, moreover, views competition less benignly than does the asocial perspective. While market forces and niche characteristics select winners and losers in asocial markets, in the political view it is actors who shape events. Weber, for example, sees competition leading to stratification along whatever dimension is contested. Dahrendorf (1959, p. 209) goes a step further than Weber, claiming that conflict will emerge around socially desired ends: "Despite terminological traditions, I can see no reason why a conceptual distinction between competition and conflict should be necessary, or indeed, desirable." In this view, as Etzioni (1988) explains, competition is a form of conflict. It assumes that the divergent interests of competitors are not automatically eliminated by a self-regulating market mechanism. Markets, like bureaucracies, have politics. There are wars, battles, coalitions, and truces. The battlefield analogy is common in business culture and the business strategy literature.

The empirical work of C. Wright Mills (1951, 1956) is in this tradition and argues for the emergence of a power structure in capitalist societies as a product of competition. Similarly, Mintz and Schwartz (1985) in *The Power Structure of American Business*, describe the self-maintenance strategies of a powerful corporate elite. A less political, but related view is inherent in resource dependency theory. Pfeffer and Salancik (1978) describe how organizations attempt to create stable environments for themselves by establishing ties with suppliers, customers, and others on whom they depend. Firms move away from impersonal market relations and toward long-term contracts, corporate interlocks, joint ventures, mergers, and other anticompetitive relations. These political process views come full circle: capitalist competition creates inequality, and powerful actors limit competition in an attempt to sustain their privileged status.

Political theories of competition may also be critiqued. First, in some formulations, particularly but not exclusively Marxist theories, the structure of the economy is seen to be the determining factor in the presence and shape of competitive relations. What should be an object of investigation is assumed a priori. Second, political theories also may suffer from oversocialized conceptualizations of actors, seeing actors mindlessly acting as agents of their class or interest group. Social action is depersonalized and stylized.

An Institutional Perspective on Competition

There is a tradition of thinking along the institutional lines we propose by both economists and sociologists. The sociologist Simmel, for example, recognized that in all but "the absolute competition of the animal struggle" (1955, p. 76) certain means of competition are renounced: "It is possible for competitors to agree in the very area of competition without thereby weakening it in any way." J.R. Commons, the noted economist, similarly explained that collective restraint was part of the process of competition (1959, p. 713):

> Competition is not Nature's "struggle for existence" but is an artificial arrangement supported by the moral, economic and physical sanctions of collective action. The theory of free competition developed by economists is not a natural tendency toward equilibrium of forces but is an ideal of public purpose adopted by the courts, to be attained by restraints upon the natural struggle for existence.

What links Simmel and Commons is their view that people and firms compete according to a socially constructed normative order. Competitors voluntarily renounce certain practices—e.g., violence—and abide by others. Asocial theories of competition have largely ignored the institutional system that develops in every competitive arena, the persistent network of beliefs, customs, and procedures that organize social action (White and White 1965). Methodological individualism combined with the assumption that the market is a natural system, a self-equilibrating organism, obscures the socially constructed nature of competitive arenas. Institutional systems in markets are usually manifest as tradition, language, and unspoken restraint, and therefore easily taken for granted.

We propose an institutional perspective that builds on the ideas of thinkers such as Simmel and Commons, a perspective that incorporates much from the political theories but goes beyond them by emphasizing the historically developed normative underpinnings of market behavior, in particular the system of mutual restraint that paradoxically emerges in institutionalized markets. The perspective we propose has three tenets. Like the political theorists, we first view competition as a form of social action, that is, action that is meaningfully oriented toward others (Weber 1978, pp. 22–24). Second, we believe that competitive action that takes place in relatively stable market settings will evidence discernible patterns with corresponding norms. Competitive action is normative action. Third, we believe that over time, market actors create institutional supports (or conversely will imitate existing institutional arrangements in the larger society) to regulate and sustain competition. Mutual restraint, not self-seeking autonomy, is the hallmark of an institutionalized market. Taken together, these tenets suggest that competition is socially constructed and maintained.

We argue these points by examining three market settings: the Chicago Board of Trade (CBOT), a commodity futures exchange; direct selling organizations (DSOs); and Japanese business groups. The CBOT has been described as a nearly "perfect" example of an auction market, closely conforming to the neoclassical ideal. The DSOs, which organize the selling activities of independent competitive agents, operate in the same socioeconomic context as the CBOT—the United States, whose regulatory and ideological underpinnings, probably more than anywhere in the world, favor free market conditions. Nonetheless, we show that the commodity futures exchange, far from being the unbridled free market of isolated, independent actors found in the neoclassical model, is highly organized. Moreover, DSOs, also operating in the American marketplace, have likewise developed arrangements to mediate and channel competitive behavior between agents. The CBOT and DSOs are both arenas in which individuals compete with each other, and both are located in the United States. Nonetheless, each has developed distinctive and extraordinarily different competitive norms and institutional arrangements for sustaining them.

The final example is taken from a nonwestern setting where the group, not the individual, is the significant social unit. We show how a group orientation leads to somewhat different competitive norms than one would expect in a western, individuated society.

Each example, including the "model" auction market, shows substantial deviation from the neoclassical ideal. Each has a different norm of competition and distinctive institutional means for regulating competition in conformity with norms.

The Chicago Board of Trade: Competitive Individualism

Eighteen hundred and forty-eight, the year the Chicago Board of Trade (CBOT) first met, was the same year the Illinois-Michigan Canal was finished. With the completion of the canal, Chicago was linked to midwestern trading centers all the way to New Orleans. In that same year, the first freight delivery of grain reached Chicago by rail. According to Hoffman (1932), the construction of the railroads, accomplished between 1845 and 1860, was the most significant element in making Chicago a terminal market. Prior to 1848, all grain reached Chicago by wagon. By 1855, 66 percent of grain receipts arrived by rail, 29 percent by canal, and less than 5 percent by wagon. These changes not only brought an increase in receipts, but they increased the risks and uncertainty of businesspeople. As the geographic barriers isolating markets were removed, the degree of uncertainty in markets increased dramatically. The informal normative system, first developed at medieval fairs and known as the law merchant, was unable to govern the newly developing forms of transaction.

The rapid growth of terminal markets in Chicago, New York, and Liverpool, and the new opportunities for trade brought by changes in transportation and communication could not easily go unnoticed. Coffeehouses in England and curbs in America were crowded with traders, and transactions were carried on well into the evening. The establishment of a Board of Trade in 1848 was initially an effort to centralize information and promote commerce. Over the next seventeen years the merchants mobilized to make the benefits of association more tangible. They formalized contract terms and developed a system for the arbitration of disputes. In 1856 they established standard grades for grain. By 1858 the CBOT had refined those standards and centralized inspection under a chief inspector (Hoffman 1932). The standardization and formalization of commodity contracts in the 1850s reflect the efforts of merchants to reduce uncertainty.

The development of standardized forward contracts at the CBOT attracted speculators who could buy and sell these contracts before the delivery date. These speculators helped merchants by increasing the liquidity in the market, but they also increased the rate of defaults and manipulations. The merchants responded by seeking the authority of the state to govern the market. The first step was to obtain a state charter in 1865. The charter not only gave the association the power to make rules, it gave an arbitration awarded by the CBOT the same authority "as if it were a judgment rendered in circuit court" (Chicago Board of Trade 1980). The CBOT was the first commodity exchange to establish a formalized system including procedures for recovery from default, provision of security deposit on all trades, and a rule providing for the suspension of any member not complying with contract terms. When the General Rules of the Board of Trade were adopted on October 13, 1865, this system was formally institutionalized. Individual members voluntarily yielded to the collectivity the power to restrain their behavior. This power was refined and strengthened over the next fifty years.

The institutionalization of market norms and constraints was not unique to the CBOT. It was matched in a wide variety of commodity and financial markets in the latter half of the nineteenth century. Trade associations were established by cotton manufacturers (1854), brewers (1862), and bankers (1876), among others.

These associations performed a number of functions, including public relations, collection of statistics, development of uniform standards, and arbitration of conflicts. These functions reflected the strategic goals of the associations: legitimation, cost reduction, and the restraint of some aspects of competition. As Stocking and Watkins (1951, pp. 233–34) note, each of these activities may be considered innocent or even wholesome, but when taken together, they tend to constitute a restraint of trade:

> Standardization of products and of cost accounting methods, for example, may eliminate waste and lower costs, but it may also help insure uniform prices among trade rivals. Exchange of information on the credit of customers may help reduce bad debts, but it may also serve as a basis for boycotting "undesirable" customers. Statistical reporting on prices, output, sales, shipment, stocks, and the like, may aid producers in independently formulating sound price and production policies, but it may also afford a basis for a tacit understanding to stabilize prices and curtail output.

We do not mean to suggest that all institutional systems are cartels, or that they would choose to be if the law permitted it. Rather, long-term market participants developed and agreed on means for maintaining the market. There is an apparent paradox here: in order to sustain their rivalry, competitors cooperate on the fundamental rules of the game. These rules not only reduce costs for all by reducing uncertainty and by creating predictable means for transacting, but offer selective benefits. The example of the CBOT's attempt to eliminate bucket shops illustrates this paradox.

Bucket shops first made their appearance around 1879, by which time futures trading was already thriving in Chicago. They were an attempt to profit from commodity speculation without playing by the rules of the exchange. In the practice of bucketing, the proprietor of the shop took the customer's bid or offer without ever executing it on the exchange. Bucket shops were storefronts where people gathered to speculate on the direction a commodity's price might take on the exchange.

At first the CBOT paid little attention. But as the shops grew and attracted more customers, opposition began to surface. There are three explanations for the opposition. First, the existence of the shops reduced trading on the exchange and thereby affected the efficiency of the market. Second, the shops provided competition for the exchange members who made their living from the commissions paid by customers. Third, the shops threatened the legitimacy of exchange trading by equating commodity speculation with storefront gambling in the minds of the public and its officials. These three explanations, which can be characterized as efficiency, cartel, and legitimation, respectively, are not mutually exclusive. Rather, somewhat paradoxically, the CBOT could not have efficiency without the quasi-cartel for which it sought state legitimation.

Four years after the appearance of bucket shops, the CBOT approved a provision for punishing those members who bucketed orders by the close vote of 281 to 251. Following this, the exchange attempted to deny telegraphic price quotes to the shops. The shop owners contrived ways to get the quotes, even using wire taps. In 1894 the directors of the exchange decided to put an end to bucketing within the exchange by suspending and expelling bucketers. A legal battle ensued culminating in a 1905 Supreme Court decision (*Chicago Board of Trade* v. *Christie Grain and Stock Co.*) in which the CBOT was found to have the right to deny access to quotations and that limiting market information served a public purpose.

It is clear that within even so "perfect" a market as a commodity futures exchange, the utilitarian norm of autonomous buyers and sellers required social rules of self-restraint and institutionalized means for enforcing the rules. The United States courts, perhaps the most dedicated in the world to the ideology of free competition, continue to recognize the legitimacy of "reasonable restraint of trade" for the purpose of sustaining competition.

Direct Selling Organizations: A Competitive "Family"

Direct selling organizations (DSOs) are companies that sell products to distributors for further resale to consumers (Biggart 1989). Selling usually takes place in a private home on either a distributor-to-consumer basis, or in a group at a "party." Amway, Shaklee, and Herbalife are DSOs that sell person-to-person; Mary Kay Cosmetics, Tupperware, and Home Interiors and Gifts are examples of "party plan" direct selling organizations. The headquarters of each of these companies is a bureaucratically organized firm. The distributors that buy and in turn sell the firm's products are independent contractors, not employees. They are autonomous agents who purchase products at a discount from the firm and are legally free to set their own prices and to sell when and how they choose.

From an economic perspective, as well as a legal one, distributors form a market for the firm's goods on the one hand, and form a marketplace of competitive sellers on the other, as they compete to sell identical goods to the public. Under these conditions one might conjecture that there would be rampant price competition and conflicting, or at best coolly impersonal, relations among distributors. In fact, neither of these is the case. Goods are almost universally sold at the price suggested by the firm, and relations are highly personal, even familial. These competitors applaud each other's success and are emotionally bound to each other and to the firm.

Market relations in these DSOs proceed through a distinct set of social relations that were constructed as a solution to a historically specific problem, the imposition of a minimum wage and employment taxes during the New Deal (Biggart 1989, pp. 32–41). Direct selling at that time was (and remains) an economically inefficient form of distribution compared to retailing and bureaucratically organized "outside" sales forces such as those maintained by companies like Xerox and IBM. Direct selling distributors of the 1930s typically sold part-time as a secondary source of income and were highly dispersed. Selling competed with other work and nonwork activities in distributors' lives and turnover was as much as 100 percent a year. Moreover, DSOs had little control over the quality and quantity of the selling behavior of even committed salespeople. A dispersed work force not tied to a salary evaded easy supervision.

Prior to New Deal social reforms, direct selling companies were content with inefficient distributors who sold "on the side." The logic of direct selling permitted even poorly skilled, less-than-committed workers to profit a company because of the low overhead involved: there were no salaries, no place of work to maintain, no supervisors to pay. Even a distributor who sold only a very small amount could profit a company because the overhead for achieving the sales was negligible. Large numbers of inefficient distributors could yield a handsome profit at the level of the firm.

This economic logic was threatened with New Deal proposals for the imposition of minimum wages and employment taxes; the overhead could not be justified given the selling conditions of direct sales. The industry responded to the threat of employment regulation by declaring distributors independent contractors and, therefore, outside the purview of federal protections.

The industry paid a price for this maneuver, however. By relinquishing the employment relation, they also relinquished the possibility of managerial authority and controls. Sales force management was a developing discipline in the 1930s and sales training, routing schedules, and other techniques that were coming into widespread use were placed beyond the legal reach of the industry.

Instead of bureaucratic controls, in the 1940s some DSOs innovated social and financial controls. Distributors who sponsored new recruits were given a percentage of the recruits' sales, and often of the sales of the people whom their recruits sponsored, and so on. These sponsorship chains became known as "lines" and resembled family trees. Individuals in a line had a financial interest in the selling success of people "downline" from them and spent a great deal of effort motivating recruits to sell and recruit yet others to the line. Over time these financial ties became the basis for intense social relations wherein people became interested, even obsessed, with the success of others. These financial and social ties have come to substitute for bureaucratic management in this $8.5 billion industry, and are crucial to recruiting distributors and sustaining sales under conditions of employment regulation.

A critical competitive balance must be maintained within a direct selling organization for it to work in the interests of both distributors and the firm. Distributors must compete in the marketplace to generate sales and profits for themselves and the firm, but it is equally crucial that competition not destroy the social relations that in another sense maintain selling activity. The individual's self-interested financial incentive must be met in a way that preserves social relations within the line.

Direct selling organizations have evolved a distinctive set of norms that maintain competition at a level that serves both the individual and the organization as a whole. Perhaps most important, DSOs typically espouse some version of a family ideology: the organization as a "family," "sisterhood," or group of "close friends."

"Family" provides an easily understood metaphor of social relations that guides social action, including competitive action, between distributors. One does not compete directly with a "sister" who is closely placed in a family line; rather, one helps her to achieve success. People who act autonomously and in disregard of competitive norms are socially isolated in DSOs and do not receive assistance in, for example, filling emergency orders when their product stores are depleted. "Good" competitors are given assistance in recruiting and training new downline members, and are invited to meetings for mutual inspiration and the sharing of selling techniques. Norms about competing do tend to be weaker when applied to members of other lines in the organization where the maintenance of social bonds is less important to a focal individual.

A number of practices have emerged within DSOs to direct competition outside the line, and sometimes outside the organization altogether. In Mary Kay Cosmetics, for example, a distributor is expected to ask a potential customer if she has ever used Mary Kay products. If the prospective customer says that she has, the distributor is expected to suppress her own financial self-interest by referring the consumer back to her original supplier. If a Mary Kay distributor moves away from her sponsor and into the geographic area of another sponsor, the new sponsor is expected to encourage and aid the distributor in her selling activities even though the original sponsor will continue to benefit financially from the distributor's sales. This selfless work is highly praised within the organization and may be rewarded with a "Miss Go-Give Award." This award is given for other-regarding, noncompetitive behavior, clearly an unusual honor in a profit-oriented capitalist enterprise.

Because top salespeople can profit a sponsor greatly, there is an incentive to attempt to steal a productive distributor away from one line to another. In Shaklee, a not untypical example, a distributor must quit for six months before being allowed to join a new line. This rule clearly limits interline competition that would threaten the overall harmony of the organization. Occasionally a line becomes inactive when most of its members give up selling. A distributor thus left without sponsors is called an "orphan" in the Shaklee "family" and may be "adopted" by another line under conditions that likewise limit internecine squabbling. In Shaklee, Mary Kay Cosmetics, and most other DSOs, there are expensive prizes such as cars and fur coats that may only be won by an individual who has a very successful downline. The individual's success is in this way tied to the overall success of the group.

Practices such as these create conditions that jointly optimize competition for the individual and the organization. Institutionalized norms, rules, and awards allow individuals to succeed, not at a theoretically maximal level, but at a level that preserves the continuity of social relations that are critical to the maintenance of the DSO under current regulatory conditions.

Japanese Business Groups: Firm Communitarianism

In the United States, the ideal of the autonomously competitive firm is maintained through multiple institutional means: laws, regulations, even business school education channels economic action in ways that maintain the essentially individualist pursuit of profit by firms. Clearly, there are exceptions to the ideal, but many exceptions such as price fixing and the hiring away of talented executives with inside knowledge are viewed as unfair and in fact are often illegal.

The American ideal of the autonomously competitive firm, and the social and political institutions that maintain that ideal, are largely absent in Japan. Instead, the Japanese economy is dominated by a number of large business groups that bind firms together in multiple social and financial ways. Business groups are composed of legally independent firms that consider themselves to be members of an economic "community." The community mutually plans, invests, trades, advises, and in other ways acts together for the good of the group. Numerous scholars have argued that the crucial economic actor in Japan is not the firm as in the West, but the business group (e.g., Futatsugi 1986; Kobayashi 1980; Okumura 1982). Institutionalized norms of restraint are established and maintained at this suprafirm level. Firms that are members of these large business groups must subordinate their interests to those of the group. In practice this means that each firm must tailor its business plan to the larger requirements of the community.

The most prominent type of Japanese business group is the intermarket or enterprise group, a network model that dates to the prewar *zaibatsu*, which in turn dated from preindustrial Tokugawa Japan (Clark 1979, pp. 42–43). (There are other business groups in Japan, including the "independent" or *keiretsu* group, for example Toyota and its subcontractors, and *gai* or small-business groups in neighborhoods that may mutually plan and invest.) The six enterprise groups are Sumitomo, Fuji, Sanwa, Dai-Ichi Kangyo, Mitsubishi, and Mitsui. Each is composed of an average of 112 medium-to-large companies that represent different market sectors. Most, for example, have member firms that are in chemicals, construction, electrical products, textiles, and glass and cement. Every business group has its own bank, insurance firm, and trading company to take care of the financial needs of the group. Business groups try to have at least one member representing each important area of the economy: it is as though General Electric, Ford Motor Company, Bechtel, Dow Chemical, Prudential, Coldwell Banker, and the Bank of America decided to affiliate informally for their mutual benefit.

Members of an enterprise group maintain communitarian, but not egalitarian relations. While every member firm, including the most powerful, is subordinate to the group, each has a ranked status location. The chief executives of the largest member firms meet, usually monthly, in a President's Club to strategize together for their mutual benefit. They may, for example, agree to joint research and development projects, exchange executives, or jointly invest in a promising industrial project. Although every firm is legally independent of the others, each typically owns a 2 to 7 percent share of other major members' stock. While no one firm has a controlling interest, the cumulative interest of all group firms' shares can be substantial. Their legal independence is further obscured by shared public relations, common logos and trademarks, and other institutionalized displays of their communal character.

Each member firm in the six enterprise groups in turn maintains relatively stable subcontracting relations with smaller firms that contribute to its finished products or services. Although not members of the intermarket groups, these smaller companies often consider themselves affiliates. Small firms are linked to large ones through vertical social and financial (but not legal) relations, and large ones are connected to each other through the horizontal bonds of mutual support.

The enterprise groups are business communities that maintain social relations that depart from the western economic ideal of the autonomously competitive firm (Hamilton and Biggart 1988). Intermarket groups compete fiercely with one another, but strive to maintain collaboration within their groups.

Social relations are typically the basis for economic relations in Japan, not the reverse. Within the group, and even with outside trading partners, the social precedes the economic. For example, where a neoclassical model would predict self-interested market action with customers and suppliers, profitable "spot" deals are typically subordinated to the desire to achieve a mutually beneficial outcome for all economic actors where a long-term relationship is possible. Price mechanisms do not determine trading partners: "In intercorporate trading corporations prefer, first, to select their trading partners and, second, to determine price. What works here is not the 'invisible hand,' but the 'visible hand' " (Okumura 1989, p. 4).

Social relations in the enterprise group community likewise dictate that a member firm submit to the collective will of the group, even if a given decision—for example, to enter a promising market sector—does not favor the firm's interests. Over time, however, the community will try jointly to maximize the financial welfare of all members. Groups maintain relations with each other (and with subcontractors) that are not self-interested in the short term. For example, even during economic downturns, large "parent" companies will try to sustain financially small subcontractors. They often aid their affiliate firms in gaining equipment loans and other types of business assistance.

The social norms that bind legally independent Japanese companies and channel their competitive and profit-seeking activity are embedded in multiple social and political institutions. Joint shareholding by firms is widespread throughout the Japanese economy and militates against the independence of any given firm.

Banks, in particular, are large investors, and play a substantial role in orchestrating the activities of business groups (in the United States the Glass-Steagall Act limits the role of banks to that of independent financial actors). Although the banks are legally independent, like all member firms, Flaherty and Hiroyuki (1984, p. 151) call their transactions "quasi-internal":

> The dealings between the banks and the firms in this complex are not arms'-length transactions. . . . Japanese firms borrow from the bank at the loss of some independence, with more information disclosures and the two-way demands of a long-term relationship. Sometimes this means that firms borrow even when they have no real investment needs.

The Japanese state is an economic collaborator, too, and encourages, often financially, the large business groups in research and investment projects. The U.S. state, in contrast, works to limit the size of mergers, prevent collusion, and maintain the independence of firms. What is seen as an impediment to capitalism in the West—community—is seen in Japan as the very means through which market activity can best take place. Indeed, the notion of community and group so pervades the Japanese economy (and Japanese society generally) that even fiercely competitive enterprise groups typically own symbolic amounts of stock in each other's banks or other important firms. The small shareholdings signal their mutual recognition as worthy opponents and joint acceptance of economic conventions. What would be described as inefficient "friction" by the neoclassical model of competition is the very social lubricant that sustains competitive action in Japan today.

Community norms are taken very seriously by the actors involved, as evidenced in 1987 when a Toshiba intermarket group company was accused by the U.S. government of secretly selling a strategic machine tool to the Soviet Union in violation of a United States–Japan agreement. The entire Toshiba group felt implicated in the shameful act of a community member, although none had shared in the firm's illegal decision. Indeed, the president of the largest Toshiba company resigned, even though his company had nothing at all to do with the sale. His resignation was a symbolic act publicly acknowledging the self-interested behavior of a member firm in breach of communitarian norms.

Conclusion

Each of the three examples given above illustrates economic competition as social action structured by political, economic, and cultural contexts. Direct selling companies have a "family" norm of limited competition within the line, even though adherence to such a norm limits an actor's short-term interests. Japanese business groups similarly have a "community" norm that requires individual firms to subordinate their interests to the interests of the group. Each of these two examples departs from the neoclassical assumption of utilitarian individualism; neither DSOs nor Japanese business groups recognize unbridled economic individualism as an ideal, much less as an approximation of reality. They both have alternative competitive ideologies and institutional means for sustaining them.

At the Chicago Board of Trade, where economic individualism is in fact the normative ideal, institutional arrangements have emerged to sustain it. Paradoxically, the "free market" can only be sustained by an elaborate institutional scaffolding. This scaffolding not only defines competitive limits but provides the basis for restraint when the limits are exceeded (Abolafia and Kilduff 1988).

Where do these norms come from? Clearly, our argument that market actors institutionalize competitive practices suggests that answers to questions of normative origins can only come about with close historical examination of particular market settings. It is not necessary, however, to follow a historicist logic, that is, arguing that every market has distinctive norms. Nor is it necessary to fall into a functionalist fallacy whereby each market somehow gets the norms it needs.

Rather, we believe that the institutional school of organizational analysis points in the right direction. Scott (1987, p. 495) describes institutionalism as a process of creating reality, a shared venture to construct meaningful social relations:

> Social order comes into being as individuals take action, interpret that action, and share with others their interpretations. . . . The process by which actions become repeated over time and are assigned similar meanings by self and others is defined as institutionalization.

This explanation for the development of structures of interaction can be applied to any type of social activity, including competition. We posit that as actors enter into repeated economic exchanges, they develop patterned ways of doing business. Over time, the patterns come to be taken-for-granted, socially accepted norms of business. Moreover, we believe that actors will draw on culturally available models of organization in trying to construct workable routines.

For example, the founders of the Chicago Board of Trade chose a pattern that became common in late nineteenth- and early twentieth-century America. The model was the membership association in which each dues-paying member had a vote in the establishment of rules and policies, itself a model taken from the American political sphere: direct democracy. The result was a federated structure in which each merchant operated independently of every other, except for those rules of trade that defined what commodity could be sold, when, and by whom. There was a continuous tension between the rights and autonomy of individual members and the benefits to be gained from mutual restraint. Likewise, the DSO draws from two models: American individual entrepreneurialism and the patriarchal family (Biggart 1989, pp. 70–91). The modern Japanese business group can be traced to the *ie,* or extended household organization of the preindustrial Japanese merchant class (Clark 1979, pp. 14–15).

An institutional explanation does not require us to assume that all market settings will exhibit different norms. On the contrary, we would hypothesize thatets in the same institutional arena would have similar norms of exchange or at least be able to draw upon the same socially available models. Even two so different markets, the Chicago Board of Trade and DSOs, both have competitive norms that are based on American individualism, although in the case of DSOs, individualism is subordinated to "family" norms.

An institutional explanation does not posit functional necessity as the source of competitive patterns. Indeed, there was nothing inevitable about the development of norms in each of the three markets we describe. The Japanese were exposed to and encouraged to adopt the western market system under the post–World War II American occupation. In the case of the CBOT, market practices were the outcome of political struggles between powerful interests. Although most DSOs exhibit some version of the family norms we describe, they are not universal throughout the industry.

Market structures, as with all forms of social order, are fundamentally structures of domination. They include insiders and outsiders, powerful and less powerful members (Abolafia 1985). They have ideologies of participation and exclusion, and institutionalized means for sustaining action in conformity with norms. Particular norms emerge in particular markets because of the choices and actions of historically and culturally embedded actors, and the power of some actors to impose their will on others cannot be ignored as part of the process.

In conclusion, competition, as we have argued, is not the self-seeking abandon of autonomous individuals, but the stylized acts of mutually aware competitors embedded in a social arena. People and firms compete according to social rules because sustaining norms is the best strategy for maintaining competitive relations and long-term profitability. Nor, we believe, is there a single set of market rules. Market order, like all forms of social order, has ideological underpinnings that are the result of historical experience and are institutionally maintained.

Note

This paper has benefited from the comments and suggestions of Fred Block, Mark Granovetter, Martin Kilduff, Victor Nee, and Charlotte Phelps, whose help we gratefully acknowledge. An earlier version of this paper was presented at the Socio-Economics Conference held at the Harvard Business School, March 31–April 2, 1989.

References

Abolafia, Mitchel Y. (1985) "Self-Regulation as Market Maintenance: An Organizational Perspective." In Roger Noll, ed., *Regulatory Policy and the Social Sciences.* Berkeley: University of California Press.

Abolafia, Mitchel Y., and Martin Kilduff. (1988) "Enacting Market Crisis: The Social Construction of a Speculative Bubble." *Administrative Science Quarterly* 33:177–93.

Baker, Wayne E. (1984a) "The Social Structure of a National Securities Market." *American Journal of Sociology* 89:775–811.

———. (1984b) "Floor Trading and Crowd Dynamics." In P. Adler and P. Adler, eds., *The Social Dynamics of Financial Markets*. Greenwich, CT: JAI Press.

Biggart, Nicole Woolsey. (1989) *Charismatic Capitalism: Direct Selling Organizations in America*. Chicago: University of Chicago Press.

Brown, F.E., and A.R. Oxenfeld. (1972) *Misperceptions of Economic Phenomena*. New York: Sperand Douth.

Burns, Tom R., and Helena Flam. (1987) *The Shaping of Social Organization*. London: Sage.

Carroll, Glenn R. (1984) "Organizational Ecology." *Annual Review of Sociology* 10:71–93.

———. (1987) *Publish and Perish: The Organizational Ecology of Newspaper Industries*. Greenwich, CT: JAI Press.

Chicago Board of Trade. (1980) *Rules and Regulations*. Chicago: Board of Trade of the City of Chicago.

Clark, Rodney. (1979) *The Japanese Company*. New Haven, CT: Yale University Press.

Commons, John R. (1959) *Institutional Economics*. Madison: University of Wisconsin Press.

Dahrendorf, Ralf. (1959) *Class and Class Conflict in Industrial Society*. Stanford, CA: Stanford University Press.

Etzioni, Amitai. (1988) *The Moral Dimension*. New York: The Free Press.

Flaherty, M. Therese, and Itami Hiroyuki. (1984) *Competitive Edge: The Semiconductor Industry in the United States and Japan*. Stanford, CA: Stanford University Press.

Futatsugi, Yusaku. (1986) *Japanese Enterprise Groups*. Monograph no. 4. Kobe, Japan: The School of Business Administration, Kobe University.

Granovetter, Mark. (1985) "Economic Action, Social Structure, and Embeddedness." *American Journal of Sociology* 91:481–510.

Hamilton, Gary, and Nicole Biggart. (1985) "Why People Obey: Theoretical Observations on Power and Obedience in Complex Organizations." *Sociological Perspectives* 28:3–28.

———. (1988) "Market, Culture and Authority: A Comparative Analysis of Management and Organization in the Far East." *American Journal of Sociology* 94S:S52–S94.

Hannan, Michael, and John Freeman. (1977) "The Population Ecology of Organizations." *American Journal of Sociology* 82:929–64.

———. (1988a) *The Ecology of Organizations*. Cambridge, MA: Harvard University Press.

———. (1988b) "The Ecology of Organizational Mortality: American Labor Unions, 1836–1985." *American Journal of Sociology* 94:25–52.

Harrigan, Kathryn. (1985) *Strategic Flexibility*. Lexington, MA: Lexington Books.

Henderson, Bruce D. (1984) "On Corporate Strategy." In Robert B. Lamb, ed., *Competitive Strategic Management*. Englewood Cliffs, NJ: Prentice-Hall.

Hoffman, G. Wright. (1932) *Futures Trading upon Organized Commodity Markets*. Philadelphia: University of Pennsylvania Press.

Jenkins, J. Craig, and Charles Perrow. (1977) "Insurgency of the Powerless." *American Sociological Review* 42:249–68.

Kahneman, Daniel, Jack L. Knetsch, and Richard Thaler. (1986) "Fairness as a Constraint on Profit Seeking: Entitlements in the Market." *American Economic Review* 76:728–41.

Kobayashi, Yoshihiro. (1980) *Kigro Shudan no Bunseki* (Analysis of Business Groups). Sapporo, Japan: Hokkaido Daigaku Tosho Kankokai.

Kotler, Phillip, and Ravi Singh Achrol. (1984) "Marketing Strategy and the Science of Warfare." In Robert B. Lamb, ed., *Competitive Strategic Management*. Englewood Cliffs, NJ: Prentice-Hall.
McCarthy, John D., and Mayer N. Zald. (1973) *The Trend of Social Movements*. Morristown, NJ: General Learning Press.
———. (1977) "Resource Mobilization and Social Movements." *American Journal of Sociology* 82:1212–41.
McNulty, Paul J. (1968) "Economic Theory and the Meaning of Competition." *Quarterly Journal of Economics* 82:639–56.
Mills, C. Wright. (1951) *White Collar*. New York: Oxford University Press.
———. (1956) *The Power Elite*. New York: Oxford University Press.
Mintz, Beth, and Michael Schwartz. (1985) *The Power Structure of American Business*. Chicago: University of Chicago Press.
Okumura, Hiroshi. (1982) *Gendai Nikon Shihon Shugi no Shihai Kozo* (The Structure of Domination in Modern Japanese Capitalism). Tokyo: Shimpyoron.
———. (1989) "Intercorporate Relations in Japan." Paper delivered at Conference on Japanese and U.S. Interfirm Relations, University of California, Davis, March.
Orru, Marco, Nicole Biggart, and Gary Hamilton. (Forthcoming) "Organizational Isomorphism in East Asia: Broadening the New Institutionalism." In Walter W. Powell and Paul J. DiMaggio, eds., *The New Institutionalism in Organizational Analysis*. Chicago: University of Chicago Press.
Pfeffer, Jeffrey, and Gerald R. Salancik. (1978) *The External Control of Organizations*. New York: Harper & Row.
Schapiro, Susan P. (1987) "The Social Control of Impersonal Trust." *American Journal of Sociology* 93:623–59.
Scott, W. Richard (1987) "The Adolescence of Institutional Theory." *Administrative Science Quarterly* 32:493–511.
Simmel, Georg. (1955) *Conflict and the Web of Group Affiliations*. New York: The Free Press.
Singh, Jitendra V., David Tucker, and Robert House. (1986) "Organizational Legitimacy and the Liability of Newness." *Administrative Science Quarterly* 31:171–93.
Smith, Adam. (1976 [1776]) *The Wealth of Nations*. New York: Modern Library.
Stigler, George J. (1968) "Competition." In David Sills, ed., *The International Encyclopedia of the Social Sciences*. New York: Macmillan.
Stocking, George W., and Myron Watkins. (1951) *Monopoly and Free Enterprise*. New York: Greenwood.
Tilly, Charles. (1978) *From Mobilization to Revolution*. New York: Random House.
Tversky, Amos, and Daniel Kahneman. (1974) "Judgement under Uncertainty: Heuristics and Biases." *Science* 185:1124–31.
Weber, Max. (1978) *Economy and Society*. Ed. by Guenther Roth and Claus Wittich. Berkeley: University of California Press.
White, Harrison C. (1981) "Where Do Markets Come From?" *American Journal of Sociology* 87:517–47.
———. (1988) "Varieties of Markets." In Barry Wellman and S.D. Berkowitz, eds., *Social Structures: A Network Approach*. Cambridge: Cambridge University Press.
White, Harrison C., and Cynthia A. White. (1965) *Canvasses and Careers*. New York: John Wiley.

14

John Oliver Wilson

Human Values and Economic Behavior

A Model of Moral Economy

Economists have long struggled with the issue of human values and economic behavior. The debate has ranged from those who deny that economics has anything to say about human values to those who argue that human values are the basic source from which an economic system derives its legitimacy. However, most economists tend to operate in the nebulous area that lies between these two extreme positions, clinging to the view that economics as a "science" is value-free, but not at all comfortable with this position for it denies a certain commonsense reality: economics deals with choices involving the production, distribution, and consumption of scarce resources and in that process it greatly impacts human life.

Philosophers and theologians have never suffered from such ambiguity. Economic arrangements "can be sources of fulfillment, of hope, of community—or of frustration, isolation, and even despair. They teach virtues—or vices—and day by day help mold our characters. They affect the quality of people's lives; at the extreme even determining whether people live or die. Serious economic choices go beyond purely technical issues to fundamental questions of values and human purpose" (National Conference of Catholic Bishops 1986, p. 3).

It is the contention of this study that human values have not been adequately integrated into a model of economic behavior, and the time for attempting such an integration is long overdue. Therefore, the purpose of this paper is to develop a theoretical model that integrates human values into the essential behavioral characteristics of an economic system. First, we will briefly summarize the general nature and major limitations of the traditional models of economic behavior; second, we will state the essential characteristics of a moral model of economic behavior, characteristics that are expressed in terms of seven basic postulates; and third, we will examine the nature of each of these seven postulates.

Conventional Models of Economic Behavior

The traditional view of economics is that human values and ethical considerations are on a different plane of discourse than are such economic behavioral issues as the production and distribution of commodities. This position was expressed some years ago by Lionel Robbins (1962) in his influential essay on the nature and significance of economic science: "Economics deals with ascertainable facts; ethics with valuations and obligations. The two fields of enquiry are not on the same plane of discourse" (p. 148).

This view has been deeply embedded into the conventional models of economic behavior. In particular, the neoclassical model, which dominates economic theory, is held to be a "positive" model that is solely concerned with explaining how individuals and institutions behave regarding economic matters. No consideration is given to such "normative" concerns as values, ethics, or moral behavior. Such normative considerations are relegated to a "social-welfare model" of economic behavior. However, the social-welfare model is quite narrow in its consideration of these matters, as we will soon discover.

In discussing the matter of human values and economic behavior, two major issues arise: First, what is the essential nature of individual motivation? Second, how do we assess social achievement in comparing one economic system with another?

The neoclassical model answers that the individual is motivated by considerations of rational behavior and maximization of self-interest. As a positive model, it does not address the second issue. The individual is assumed to confront a range of alternative socioeconomic choices, generally expressed in the narrow terms of consumer choice among alternative commodities. In making a choice, the individual will behave in a rational manner defined as follows: (1) for all pairs of alternative choice, *A* and *B*, the individual knows whether he or she prefers *A* to *B* or *B* to *A* or is indifferent between the two; (2) only one of the three possibilities is true for any pair of alternatives; and (3) if the individual prefers *A* to *B* and *B* to *C*, then that individual will prefer *A* to *C*.[1] Whether or not *A* is "better" than *B* or *C* is not an issue that the neoclassical model attempts to address. The only concern is that the individual express a "preference" for *A* or *B* or *C* that is internally consistent.

Furthermore, the individual is assumed to make his or her rational choices in such a manner as to maximize some goal that the individual holds. This goal may be the maximization of individual consumer utility, the profitability of the firm wherein the individual is engaged in earning an economic livelihood, or the provision of social goods by government where the individual is acting out his or her social or public desires through the political process. The important point of this condition of rational behavior is that there is "an external correspondence between the choices that a person makes and the self-interest of the person" (Sen

1982, p. 15). This means that the individual does not take into consideration any non-self-interested goals such as altruism or concern for others.

Since the neoclassical model is considered to be positive, it does not attempt to determine whether one economic state is better than another. It simply accepts the outcome of all individual choices and actions motivated by self-interest and economic efficiency in allocating scarce resources among competing ends. The outcome can just as readily be an economic system of great inequality—a few rich indulging their most extreme desires while the masses live in abject poverty—as well as that of greater equality—all persons able to enjoy a satisfactory standard of living.

For those who want to pass judgment upon such alternative economic systems, economic theory has provided another model of economic behavior. This is the "social-welfare model," so named because it introduces the concept of a social-welfare function as a means of judging social achievement. A social-welfare function is an ordinal index of society's welfare and is a function of the utility levels of all individuals. It is not unique; its form depends upon the value judgments of the persons for whom it is a desirable welfare function.

It can be stated mathematically as: $W = f(U_1, U_2, \ldots, U_n)$, where W is the total social welfare of a given economic system, and U_n is the utility level of the nth individual who lives in that economic system. The utility of the nth individual is expressed mathematically: $U_n = f(Q_{n1}, Q_{n2}, \ldots, Q_{nx}, r, s, t)$, where Q_{n1} through Q_{nx} is the quantity of all commodities consumed by individual n, and r, s, t are noneconomic factors.

The social-welfare function reflects the values of society, assumed to be determined through a political process. These values are traditionally assumed to reflect a desired distribution of income that may differ from that which results from the actions of the positive model of neoclassical theory. Therefore, the social-welfare model is viewed as a normative model of economic behavior.

Theoretically, it would be possible to aggregate all of the utility functions of individuals in economic system X and compare the value of that aggregation to that in economic system Y. If the sum is greater in X than in Y, we could say that economic system X is more socially desirable than economic system Y. This was the view of the early utilitarian theorists, but such cardinal objectivity was challenged by subsequent behavioral theorists. The validity of interpersonal comparisons of utility was denied, and therefore the ability to aggregate individual utilities into a social-welfare function for an entire economic system was eliminated. To answer the question of whether one economic system is better than another, we must rely upon Pareto optimality.

A given economic system is Pareto optimal—that is, it is socially desirable—if, and only if, it is impossible to increase the utility of one individual without reducing the utility of someone else. This rather narrow concept of social desirability means that in an economic system of great inequality, there can be no redistribution of wealth from the rich to the poor, for to do so would reduce the utility of the rich individual even though it might enable the poor individual to survive. As Amartya Sen (1982, p. 32) comments, ''Pareto optimality can, like 'Caesar's spirit,' 'come hot from hell.' ''

While the social-welfare model is normative, and thus represents an improvement upon the neoclassical model for purposes of our discussion, it is a normative model in a very limited sense. It is only concerned with matters of distributive justice, and as we will soon discuss, there are other forms of economic justice that are relevant to an economic system. The social-welfare model does not allow interpersonal utility comparisons, and so there is a great deal of disagreement as to whether and how individual utility functions can be aggregated into a meaningful social-welfare function.[2] It relies upon Pareto optimality as the only test of social desirability, but the conditions of optimality are so narrow that they can justify conditions of extreme poverty existing alongside opportunities of extreme profligacy. Finally, the social-welfare model is limited in that it adopts the same assumption of the maximization of self-interest that is found in the neoclassical model. This greatly narrows the scope of individual choice, ruling out many of the ethical considerations that impact the nature of such choice.

For those who desire a little less hell and a little more heaven in their economic system, we must turn to another model of economic behavior. This model will be termed ''the moral model''; it is expressed in the form of the following seven postulates:

> *Postulate One: In an economic system individuals confront a range of alternative socioeconomic actions, and in making a choice among these actions an individual will act upon a particular set of moral values.*
>
> *Postulate Two: Any set of moral values that satisfies the conditions of legitimacy consists of social values, and these values function to integrate individual self-interests into an economic system.*
>
> *Postulate Three: Associated with the social values of an economic system are appropriate sets of social goods that characterize how a particular economic system chooses to realize its social values. The dominant social goods in an economic system are individual happiness and economic justice.*
>
> *Postulate Four: The social goods of an economic system are interdependent. Given such interdependency, an economic system must determine how one social value and its associated goods will be traded off against other values and associated goods.*
>
> *Postulate Five: How an economic system integrates its values into rules of economic behavior, distributes the rewards from participation in the economy, and solves the trade-off problem between interdependent social values and associated goods is determined by the dominant ideology that prevails in the economic society. The two dominant ideologies are individualism and totality.*
>
> *Postulate Six: An economic system that adopts the ideology of individualism will institutionalize the following primary characteristics in its economic behavior: the autonomous individual as the primary unit within the economic system; optimization behavior regarding the role of the individual within the economic system; and conflict generation-resolution as the es-*

Figure 14.1. **Social Goods, Social Values, and Socioeconomic Outputs**

Social goods	Social values	Socioeconomic outputs
Individual happiness	Sustenance Quality of life Participation	Basic economic essentials Economic security Equal opportunities Respect, acknowledgment
Economic justice	Equity Fairness Human rights	Commutative justice Productive justice Distributive justice

sential nature of interaction between individuals and institutions within the economic system.

Postulate Seven: An economic system that adopts the ideology of totality will institutionalize the following primary characteristics in its economic behavior: the interdependent individual as the primary unit within the economic system; satisficing behavior regarding the role of the individual within the economic system; and consensus formation as the essential nature of interaction between individuals and institutions within the economic system.

Before we begin to examine the nature of each of these postulates, it is useful to distinguish clearly the relationship between human, moral, and social values, and social goods and associated outputs. Human values reflect those things that an individual desires, regards as worthy of achievement, or holds in high esteem. These human values are identical to moral values when the individual is confronted with a situation in which different desires promise opposed social goods and in which incompatible courses of action seem to be morally justified; that is, the individual must distinguish between what he or she thinks is a right or wrong choice. Social values are human-moral values that relate to interpersonal relationships and involve social externalities. (Note: social values will be defined more completely later in our discussion.) Social goods represent the basic outputs or goals of an economic system, such as consumer utility or happiness and economic justice. Specific socioeconomic outputs are associated with social values and social goods as shown in Figure 14.1, and they characterize how a particular economic system chooses to realize its social values and goods.

Postulate One: Human Values and Moral Choice

The first postulate states that in an economic system, individuals confront a range of alternative socioeconomic actions, and in making a choice among these actions an individual will act upon a particular set of moral values.

The role of moral values in affecting the choice of individuals has been identified by a number of economic theorists and philosophers in recent years.

For instance, John Harsanyi (1955) makes a distinction between what he terms "ethical preferences" and "subjective preferences" of an individual. Ethical preferences express the choice an individual would prefer on the basis of impersonal social considerations alone, and the latter expresses what he or she actually prefers, on the basis of personal interests or on any other basis. This distinction enables an individual to distinguish between what he or she thinks is good or ethical from a social point of view, and what that individual thinks is good or utility-enhancing from a personal point of view.

Harry G. Frankfurt (1971) makes a distinction between "desires of the first order" and "desires of the second order." First-order desires are simply desires to do or not to do one thing or another, and the source of these desires is nonreflective response to such stimuli as habit, social conditioning, or impulsive hedonism. Second-order desires are those where human will intervenes, causing the individual to undertake reflective self-evaluation and to determine preferences, and thereby to take actions different from those that result from first-order desires. Thus, an individual has the capacity of wanting to be different in his or her preferences and choice from what they may actually be.

Amartya Sen (1982) argues that the dichomotization between different levels of preferences—whether that dichomotization be characterized as ethical versus subjective preferences or first-order versus second-order desires—is too narrow in its conceptualization of human behavior. Rather, the individual acts upon a "meta-ranking of preference orderings."

Assume that the individual confronts a set $[X]$ consisting of n alternative actions: $[x_1, x_2, \ldots, x_n]$. In the traditional approach, the individual would rank order his or her preferences among these n, such as: $x_1 > x_2 > \ldots > x_n$. A given individual might believe that x_1 is morally or ethically preferred to x_2 through x_n, and thus is the most desirable outcome based upon an ethical preference function or second-order desires. But the actual choice may be the following: $x_2 > x_1 > x_3 > \ldots > x_n$, for the individual is acting upon subjective preferences or first-order desires.

The reason for the "inferior" actual choice, rather than the presumably more desirable or ethical choice, is generally attributed to weakness of the will, what philosophers term "akrasia." If only the individual had a stronger will, then he or she would have made the more ethical choice. But given human weakness, the lesser choice was made. It is this dichomotization and the assumption of akrasia that Sen finds too narrow.

Rather than an individual expressing a choice among a simple set of rank-ordered preferences, Sen suggests that orders of preference rankings will express the full range of our moral judgments. This full range of moral choice can be expressed as follows: let X be a set of all possible action choices: $X = [x_1, x_2, \ldots, x_n]$, and let Y be a set of all possible orderings of the elements of X.

$Y = [R_1, R_2, \ldots, R_m]$, where $m = n!$

A quasi-ordering of the elements of Y, or a "meta-ranking," allows for a range of moral or ethical considerations.

What distinguishes these theories of individual choice is the existence of a set of moral values that shape an alternative preference function to the one that is traditionally assumed in neoclassical theory. That set of values may create a dichomotization between ethical preferences and subjective preferences (Harsanyi) or first-order and second-order desires (Frankfurt). If so, the preference ranking of the alternative actions in set X is an "either-or" choice. Alternatively, if that set of values expresses a range of moral judgments (Sen), then the individual confronts a set Y, consisting of a ranking of preference rankings of individual actions in set X.

However a given individual reflects his or her choice among alternative socioeconomic actions, that choice involves moral values. In making a choice between two alternatives, the individual reveals that one alternative is *better* than a second alternative. This is a choice of a quite different order than simply to reveal that one alternative is *preferred* to a second alternative. The latter does not require any knowledge about individual preference functions. This is not the case for the former choice. To select one alternative as better than another is to act upon a particular set of values that define a moral or ethical preference function for the individual. Whether or not these moral values are common or social values is quite another matter.

Postulate Two: Individual Moral Values as Social Values

The second postulate states that any set of moral values that satisfies the conditions of legitimacy consists of social values, and these values function to integrate individual self-interests into an economic system.

It is not at all self-evident that the set of moral values adopted by an individual will be identical to a set of common or social values. It is quite possible to formulate a model of human behavior that is morally based, but each individual determines for himself or herself what is or is not moral behavior. The source of this determination may be either metaphysical (emanating from natural law) or religious (emanating from God). In either case, the individual forms a particular metapreference function based on a personal understanding of the nature of God or natural law or some other source.

Yet to assume a personally based morality without relating such values to a set of relevant social values begs the issue, for then economics could be treated as dealing with only ascertainable facts regarding economic choices and ethics or morality with personal valuations. If this were true, then our study of human values and economic behavior would have to cease. But to postulate that there is a set of social values that are acceptable as integrative values in an economic system forces us to enter an arena of debate that has raged for centuries.

Since antiquity, philosophers have struggled to define an absolutely correct standard of human behavior, and from such a standard, to develop a set of values that are both universal and absolute. The values would be universal in that they would be applicable for all people, all societies, and for all time. They would be absolute in that they would define with finite certitude certain conditions of human behavior and would derive their legitimacy from a source that is of a higher order than any given ruler, legislative body, or law-making process of a particular economic system.

The fact that we cannot discern an absolute set of values from rational cognition has several major implications for our second postulate. First, we can accept the reality that absolute values can only be revealed through metaphysics or religion, and postulate a set of reasonable values that will be used in comparing one economic system to another. Such a set of values would be assumed to be relevant to both individual behavior and social behavior, so that individual values and social values are identical and are assumed to be absolute. However, this approach means that my set of assumed values is no more legitimate than those of John Smith or Sue Jones.

Second, we can develop a model that accepts that values are relative, but we can postulate that there is an underlying sense of morality that influences human behavior regarding what is right or what is wrong. Such an individualistic morality may be revealed to human beings through metaphysics, religion, or some other means. However, the specific source of that morality is not critical, for our analysis of individual behavior would be ordinal rather than cardinal. But such an individualistic morality solution to the problem raises the difficult issue that if our choices are defined by our preferences, but those preferences are arbitrary, "then each self constitutes its own moral universe, and there is finally no way to reconcile conflicting claims about what is good in itself" (Bellah et al. 1985, p. 76).

Third, we can pursue "the extremely delicate task of seeking out what there is in common between the various conceptions of justice" or any other moral value and allow for variation in how a given economic system integrates a common or universal understanding of that value.[3] The basis of this third approach is that there are certain conditions that must be satisfied by any set of moral values that make these values legitimate as common or social values. These conditions are that moral values must function as: (1) social values; (2) shared values; and (3) integrative values.

Social values are defined as those values that relate to interpersonal relationships and involve social externalities. Thus, the value must involve more than a single isolated individual and the fulfillment of that value must create some form of externality that affects other individuals.

Shared values means that a set of moral values must be shared by all individuals living in a given economic system as representing those attributes or things that human beings desire, regard as worthy of achievement, or hold in high esteem. The values must be on the order of a system of beliefs so pervasive that they express the harmonizing sentiments of the individuals of a given economic system.

Integrative values means that a given set of moral values functions to sanction economic relationships between individuals, and between individuals and the institutions that are created to form a particular economic system; that is, they serve to integrate individual self-interests into an economic system.

Postulate Three: Social Values and Social Goods

The third postulate states that associated with the social values of an economic system are appropriate sets of social goods that characterize how a particular economic system chooses to realize its social values. The dominant social goods are individual happiness and economic justice.

Economists generally address the question of happiness through the concept of utility, defined as the ability of a good or a service to satisfy human wants. This association of utility happiness with the consumption of economic commodities has been criticized by many observers who argue that economics is far too narrow in its understanding and interpretation of human behavior. Nor does the narrow definition of utility happiness do justice to the much broader framework out of which the concept has evolved. A survey of the intellectual thought on happiness provides two major views on the meaning of this social good.

The first view is that happiness is purely subjective—it is determined by the psychological state or mental attitude of a given individual. Such an interpretation means that the human desires that determine happiness are purely individualistic and internalized. Those desires do not relate to the external economic and social environment, and there is no relationship between the economic system and the attainment of happiness of those persons who comprise that system.

The alternative view of happiness is that it is objective. Such a view was well expressed by Hegel: There is "a system of complete interdependence, wherein the livelihood, happiness, and legal status of one man is interwoven with the livelihood, happiness of all" (1942, p. 183). On this system individual happiness depends, and only in this connected system can happiness be actualized and secured.

Given this broader view of utility happiness, what are the outputs associated with this social good? These are not difficult to discern; a careful reading of the intellectual thinking on the subject reveals a number of relevant socioeconomic outputs. Aristotle defined happiness as "the active exercise of the mind in conformity with perfect goodness or virtue" (1943, p. 28; quoted in Jones 1966, p. 67). William James suggested that happiness is derived from the ability of the individual to reach an adjustment between inner experience and the outer world. For Ralph Waldo Emerson, happiness is achieved through work. According to Sigmund Freud, work provides us with a sense of reality. To St. Thomas

Aquinas, work is a natural right and a duty—a source of grace along with learning and contemplation.

Human behavior psychologists are the latest to identify the socioeconomic outputs associated with happiness. Kurt Goldstein argues that the dominant driving force in human development is "to actualize the individual capacities as fully as possible" (quoted in McGill 1967, p. 323). Yet it is Abraham Maslow who spells out most clearly the characteristics that are generally identified with self-actualization happiness.[4] These needs begin with the most basic physiological needs for food, sleep, and shelter, and move up through a hierarchy of safety and security needs, love and belonging needs, esteem needs, and finally growth needs such as truth, goodness, justice, and meaningfulness.

As shown in Figure 14.2, the specific socioeconomic outputs that are associated with happiness fall into four major areas: (1) economic needs; (2) communal needs; (3) human development needs; and (4) self-fulfillment needs. For example, in the general area of economic needs, the outputs would be x_1 (basic economic essentials that provide for human self-preservation), x_2 (economic security in the form of stability, safety, freedom from anxiety and chaos, and the desire for orderly structure), and x_3 (economic growth, which implies opportunities for the individual to improve his or her economic and social status within the economic system). Most of these outputs are related to objective happiness.

Yet not all outputs are objective. For example, the outputs associated with the general areas of human development needs and self-fulfillment needs are far more subjective in nature. Love and belongingness, pleasure and enjoyment, and sense of totality, oneness, completeness are outputs that are highly personal and largely internalized within the individual.

We can consider individual happiness as defined by a matrix $[H]$ of relevant outputs: $[x_1, \ldots, x_{12}]$. Each individual will attempt to attain those particular outputs that he or she desires in order to realize happiness. Individual A may choose as a set of outputs: $H_a = [x_1, x_3, x_7, x_{12}]$. Such an individual might be characterized as a risk taker who, having satisfied a basic need for economic essentials, wants to live in an economic system that offers maximum individual freedom for economic activity.

Alternatively, we can postulate individual B who might choose the following set of outputs: $H_b = [x_1, x_2, x_4, x_9, x_{11}]$. Such an individual might be characterized as risk-averse, preferring to attain happiness in an economic system that enables this individual to attain economic security, stability, a sense of belongingness, and to enjoy the quality of life that accompanies this particular set of goods.

We cannot state that the choice of outputs of individual A is better or worse than that of individual B in any normative sense. This does not mean, however, that there are no normative value assumptions implicit in our formulation of consumer behavior. We have not included any outputs in the matrix that one might infer as being less ethical or moral than those that have been included. For instance, a complete matrix of outputs might include such conditions as freedom

Figure 14.2. **Individual Happiness and Associated Outputs**

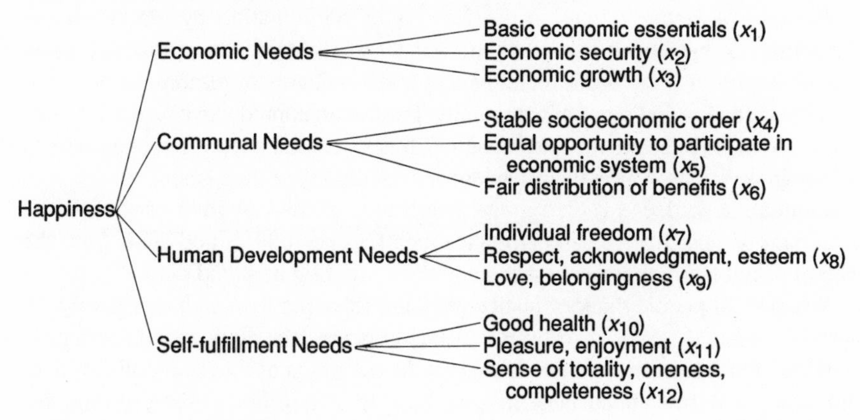

to engage in sadistic behavior, to take by force the property of others, or to enslave others. Clearly, the definition of the particular socioeconomic outputs imposes value judgments by society on what is acceptable and unacceptable behavior in the attainment of individual happiness.

Economists have traditionally equated justice with distributional issues. The primary problem is one of distributive justice, in particular a question of the ideal or desirable distribution of income. Yet, when it comes to defining what is a desirable degree of equality in the distribution of income, or an acceptable degree of inequality, economic theory is woefully inadequate.

The issue is viewed as a trade-off between efficiency and equality, a problem of determining the appropriate distribution of income through the political system and then allowing the economic system to achieve maximum efficiency in the production and consumption of commodities. Given the limitations of the traditional economic understanding of justice, we must turn to the literature of philosophers and others who have dealt with this issue in far more depth. We begin with the meaning of commutative justice, then examine productive or social justice, and conclude with distributive justice.

The concept of *commutative justice* is rooted in the fundamental moral prohibition against harm, and in economic exchange, harm is avoided when there is equivalence of exchange. Therefore, the issue of commutative justice is to determine the meaning of equivalence of exchange. Adam Smith argued that a competitive market will determine a just or fair market price for all exchanges, but implicit in such a market is a world of shared meanings and mutual knowledgeability. It is a world that involves trust and credibility. In one of the more current statements on the issue, the National Conference of Catholic Bishops (1986, pp. 35–36) states that commutative justice "calls for fundamental fairness in all agreements and exchanges between individuals or private social groups. It demands respect for the equal human dignity of all persons in economic transactions, contracts, or promises."

Productive justice relates to the fairness of participation by individuals in the economic system. It considers the impact of the methods of production on the fulfillment of basic needs, employment levels, patterns of discrimination, environmental quality, and sense of community. Furthermore, productive justice includes a duty to organize economic and social institutions so that people can contribute to society in ways that respect their freedom and the dignity of their labor.

Productive justice is rooted in the acceptance of the essentially social nature of human beings. Justice can be neither specified nor understood apart from the web of social interdependence that entails mutual obligation and duty.

When most people think of justice, they are referring to *distributive justice.* In the most general terms, distributive justice concerns the issue of allocating the benefits of an economic system among all the members of that economic system. But how to define those benefits and how to determine a just criterion for allocation are highly debatable issues. A survey of the vast literature on distributive justice suggests that there are four primary criteria that contend with each other in these regards: (1) to each according to merit; (2) to each according to rank; (3) to each according to essential needs; and (4) to each the same.[5]

To each according to his or her merit is generally interpreted to mean work or labor effort. Therefore, distributive justice is achieved when the benefits of an economic system accrue to individuals in proportion to their own efforts. If one individual works longer and harder than another individual, then that individual should receive a greater portion of the benefits available in an economic system.

To each according to his or her rank requires that the members of a society or economic system be divided into different classes, and that the members of each class be treated according to some notion of equality while those in different classes may not be accorded equal treatment. Rank-ordered justice has a long tradition, and is most frequently associated with a view of society that rank has its privileges up to such a point that this creates stability and certainty in the nature of things. Rank may be viewed as the best means of achieving equity in the treatment of individuals within an institutional setting, such as where rank-ordered justice is applied to the principle of seniority in employment: many American corporations and government institutions practice the principle of "last hired, first fired," particularly where labor unions are strong. This is clearly a case of rank-ordered justice.

To each according to his or her essential needs requires that an economic system determine a certain level of basic human needs that must be satisfied, either through direct participation in the economic system (productive justice) or through a redistribution of resources sufficient to satisfy those needs (distributive justice). Traditionally, essential needs are defined in terms of certain basic requirements to sustain life and enable the individual to live at some minimal standard of living. That standard could be expressed in terms of income (a minimum guaranteed income of $15,000 for an urban family of four) or certain

Figure 14.3. **Economic Justice and Associated Outputs**

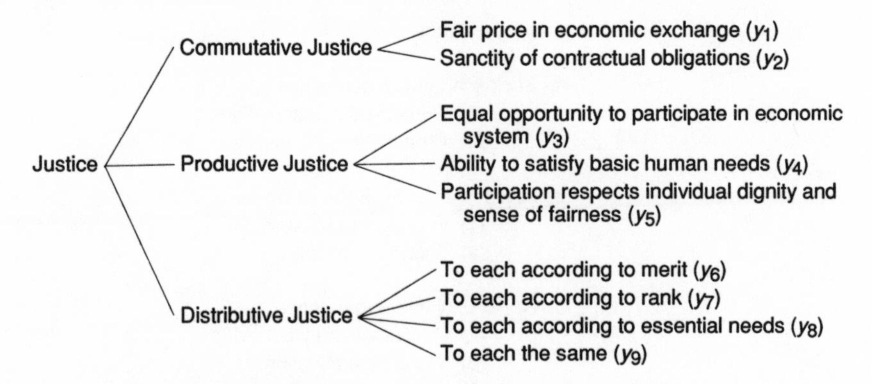

levels of food consumption, housing standards, and legal, day care, and other family support services. Clearly, the difficulty with this approach is how to define essential needs.

To each the same thing is the final concept of distributive justice. When the same thing is defined in terms of income, and it is assumed that every individual has an identical and known marginal utility function of income, then this concept requires equality in the distribution of income. Such an extreme position has never been achieved by any economic system, but there are less absolute versions that fall into this general concept of distributive justice.

As shown in Figure 14.3, we can consider economic justice as consisting of three different concepts: commutative justice, productive justice, and distributive justice. Justice is defined by a matrix $[J]$ of relevant socioeconomic outputs $[y_1, \ldots, y_9]$, and a particular economic system can be characterized by those outputs that are dominant in that society.

For instance, Economic System I might integrate the following outputs into its legal system and institutional structure: $J_I = [y_1, y_2, y_3, y_6]$. Such an economic system would reward all individuals on the basis of merit, while ensuring that all individuals have an equal opportunity to participate in the economic system. Alternatively, Economic System II might integrate a different set of outputs: $J_{II} = [y_1, y_2, y_4, y_5, y_7]$. This economic system would attempt to maintain equality in access to social practices through rank-ordered justice, while structuring its public and private institutions to ensure that the basic needs and sense of dignity and fairness of each individual are satisfied.

Whether or not Economic System I is better or worse than Economic System II cannot be determined by simply comparing the two matrices of outputs. There is no absolute definition of economic justice, and therefore the issue can only be resolved by analyzing the impact of a given system of economic justice upon the happiness of the individual. This means that justice and happiness are interdependent, an issue to which we now turn our attention.

Figure 14.4. **Continuum of Interdependency**

I. Absolute Independence

A. Socioeconomic Externalities
(1) Consumption externalities
(2) Production externalities

B. Interdependence of Social Goods
(1) Individual happiness
(2) Economic justice

C. Communal Interdependence
(1) Consumer-utility behavior
(2) Wage determination
(3) Production interdependence

II. Absolute Interdependence

Postulate Four: Interdependence of Social Goods

The fourth postulate states that the social goods of an economic system are interdependent. Given such interdependency, an economic system must determine how one social value and its associated goods will be traded off against other social values and associated goods.

The issue of interdependency can be expressed in its most extreme alternatives as that of absolute independence versus absolute interdependence. However, neither absolute independence nor absolute interdependence exists in the real world. These are not models of reality, but rather basic ideologies that define how the real world is perceived by a particular economic system. As ideologies, they define the extreme points on a continuum of interdependent relationships. This continuum can be expressed as shown in Figure 14.4.

The form of interdependence that is closest to the extreme of absolute independence is that of socioeconomic externalities. These externalities can be consumption externalities where the nature of consumption of one individual has a positive or negative impact upon the consumer utility level of another individual. The external social benefits associated with education (better citizens, less likelihood of going on welfare) or the social costs associated with neighbors (loud stereo usage or unsightly junk in the yard) are examples of such externalities. Production externalities occur when the nature of the output of a firm impacts the utility function of an individual; an example is pollution of the environment.

These consumption and production externalities are well recognized and have been incorporated into traditional neoclassical models of economic behavior. The essential point is that they are treated as anomalies to a "perfect" model of economic behavior, and their incorporation into the neoclassical models of consumer and firm behavior does not significantly alter the basic assumptions of absolute independence.

The second degree of interdependence on our continuum is that of social values and social goods. This is true by definition, for the condition imposed upon a moral value to qualify as a social value is that of social externalities. Such interdependence is clearly present in our example of happiness and justice. For instance, the outputs associated with economic needs (basic economic essentials and economic security) are very similar to those outputs associated with productive justice (ability to satisfy basic human needs) and distributive justice (to each according to essential needs).

Clearly, this form of interdependence begins to challenge the basic assumptions of absolute independence and moves closer to those of absolute interdependence. An individual's actions in attaining happiness are strongly influenced by agencies or causes outside that individual's control, such as the nature and degree to which an economic system promotes economic justice. The preference functions of the individual are significantly shaped by the environment in which that individual lives.

The final form of interdependence on our continuum is that of communal interdependence. This comes closest to absolute interdependence, for it essentially assumes that happiness and justice can be neither specified nor understood apart from the web of social interdependence. This level of interdependence extends to three major areas of economic behavior: consumer behavior, wage determination, and the production function of the firm.

By definition, the utility function of the individual consists of the matrices of socioeconomic outputs associated with happiness and justice, along with the level of utility of other individuals. Such interdependence can be stated mathematically as: $U_i = f(H_i, J_i, U_o)$, where U_i is the utility function of individual i, H_i, and J_i are the matrices of outputs associated with individual happiness and economic justice, and U_o is the utility of other individuals.

This broadened definition of consumer utility integrates the individual into the community both through the interdependencies inherent in the outputs associated with happiness and justice and in its inclusion of the utility of other individuals. The latter condition means that the individual holds a view of reality that his or her level of utility is dependent upon the overall level of utility of the broader community. It is a view of reality that comes close to the characteristics of absolute interdependence: the community is a living organism of interdependent entities, the true existence of each entity lies more in its fundamental interrelationships than in its discreteness, and no single entity can live in isolation from all others.

Wage determination in our expanded model integrates the individual worker with the firm as well as with all other firms in the economic system. Stated mathematically: $W_i = f(P, S_i)$, where W_i is the wage received by individual i and that wage is a function of the price at which the firm is able to sell its product, P, and the economic value associated with the social practice of individual i by the particular firm, S_i, where that individual works.

P is a matrix of market conditions, including the market-determined price for the product (degree of competition in the market), the different goals of the firm that will influence price (profit maximization, market share, voluntary price and market share agreements with other firms and/or government), and external sources of financial support (relationship to banks, membership in industrial groups, and government industrial policy).

S_i is a matrix of economic benefits (income, bonuses, economic security), personal benefits (self-esteem, participation, contribution), and social benefits (offices and positions with their rights, duties, powers, and immunities) that are associated with a particular position within a given institution. The economic value associated with this social practice will only in part be determined by the skill level, experience of the individual, and directly measurable contribution to the goals of the firm as assumed in neoclassical theory.

To a large extent the economic value will be determined by the "perceived" contribution of the individual to the goals of the firm, and this perceived value is highly subjective. It will be strongly conditioned by the relative position of power and influence that the individual has in the firm and the community, the importance attached to that particular social practice by those who control the distribution of the economic rewards, and the firm's prevailing form of economic justice.

For instance, if the firm adheres to a concept of "to each according to merit" and the individual is assumed to be autonomous and to possess the capacity to affect the outcome of the firm, then that individual is likely to be paid a great deal more than if the firm adheres to a concept of "to each according to rank" and the individual is assumed to be interdependent with all other employees of the firm in affecting the outcome. The former condition to a large extent characterizes the attitude in U.S. corporations, while the latter is typical of Japanese corporations. And it is well known that the senior corporate executive in an American firm is paid a great deal more than his counterpart in the Japanese firm.

The production function of the firm is defined as $Q = f(K, E_i, Q_o)$, where Q is the output of the firm, K is the total capital factor input, E_i is the effective labor factor input provided by individual i, and Q_o is the output of other firms. Effective labor factor input is defined as $E_i = f(L_i, J_i)$, where L_i is the labor input of individual i measured in terms of hours worked, skill level, experience, and so on, as in traditional neoclassical theory. J_i is the effect of productive and distributive justice upon the labor input of individual i. Thus, if the economic system operates with a high degree of productive justice so that there are no sex, race, age, or other barriers to the utilization of the skills and experience of individual i, the labor input will be higher. And if the specific social practices within the firm are rewarded with wages and other perquisites that individual i perceives to satisfy his or her concept of distributive justice, then the labor input will be higher. In essence, the distribution of job-related benefits is not perceived to be unfair or unjust to such a point that the effectiveness of the worker is diminished.

Q_o is the output of other firms, and this argument in the production function carries much the same meaning as did U_o in the consumer utility function of the individual. The firm will view that it is part of a broader community, and that the future success of one firm cannot be isolated from what happens to all other firms within the community. This view of reality does not necessarily diminish competition between firms, but competition is accepted as a desirable condition so long as it advances the output and welfare of all who participate in the economic system. Constructive competition is desired rather than destructive competition.

In sum, communal interdependence is far more complex and pervasive throughout the economic system than are simple socioeconomic externalities. To what extent a given economic system recognizes the degree of interdependence that exists, and particularly, how that economic system chooses to resolve the trade-off issues that such interdependencies create, will be determined by the dominant ideology that prevails in the society.

Postulate Five: The Role of Ideology

The fifth postulate states that how an economic system integrates its values into rules of economic behavior, distributes the rewards from participation in the economy, and solves the trade-off problem between interdependent social values and associated socioeconomic outputs is determined by the primary ideology that prevails in the economic society. The two dominant ideologies are individualism and totality.

The ideology of individualism has three major theses that are particularly relevant to our analysis of economic behavior: individual autonomy, individual dignity, and individual self-development.

The concept of individual autonomy has been traced back to Epicurus (342?–270 B.C.) who argued that: "There is no such thing as human society. Every man is concerned for himself" (quoted in *Encyclopaedia of the Social Sciences* 1942, p. 675). Throughout subsequent centuries of intellectual thought, this initial concept has been extended into its more modern version: an individual's thought and action are his or her own, and are not determined by agencies or causes outside that individual's control.

The true nature of the individual is not shaped and formed by the pressures and norms of society, but we have within ourselves the inherent capability of independent thought and rational reflection. This frees us from the binds of superior commands as those commands are expressed in social structure. Such autonomy comes from several sources.

To the theologians, the individual's autonomy arises from the independent relationship between that individual and God. Appealing to scripture, Martin Luther espoused his famous conclusion that "each and all of us are priests because we all have the one faith, the one gospel, and the same sacrament; why then should we not be entitled to taste or test, and to judge what is right or wrong in the faith?" (quoted in Woolf 1952, p. 112).

Philosophers looked to other sources for our individual autonomy, primarily within the mind or will of the human being. Our autonomy arises from the active exercise of our power of thought, and through this power of thought we are able to derive self-evident truths. This frees us from servitude or enslavement to desires, obsessions, and fantasies that are in response to the environment in which we live. "As a rational being, and consequently as belonging to the intelligible world," stated Immanuel Kant, "man can never conceive the causality of his own will except under the Idea of freedom; for to be independent of determination by causes in this sensible world is to be free. To the Idea of freedom there is inseparably attached the concept of autonomy" (1967, p. 113).

The concept of individual dignity refers to the ultimate moral principle of the supreme and intrinsic value, or dignity, of the individual human being. It is a concept that embraces a number of different theses, including: (1) all men and women are equally children of and under God, each with his or her own unique purpose; (2) all individuals exist as an end in themselves, never merely as a means for arbitrary use by this or that will or power; (3) the primary function of society is the advancement of the welfare of the individual, and any legitimate society must recognize the inherent dignity and the equal and inalienable rights of all members of the human family.

Individual self-development is a fairly recent addition to the ideology of individualism. Its origin is generally attributed to Goethe, who appealed to the theory of the right and duty of self-development. But it was given its most eloquent and well-known expression by John Stuart Mill (1956). According to Mill, it is an inherent right and duty of all individuals to pursue their own self-development, and this self-development can take the form of increased power and diversity, creative originality, and unrestricted pursuit of opportunities so long as that pursuit does no injury to another individual.

The ideology of totality has three major concepts that explain a universe seen as one living organism of identical and interdependent parts: absolute emptiness, mutual identity, and universal intercausality.[6]

Absolute emptiness is defined as the relationship between entities, which is expressed as the "law of interdependent originations."[7] This law means that an entity exists in its relations to other entities, and does not have a true reality independent of those other entities.

To clarify this rather esoteric concept (at least to a western philosophical mind), we can use the example of a chair. What is the true essence of a chair? Does a chair exist as a completely independent entity? We might quickly answer that a chair is something that we use to sit. But in making this statement, we are defining the chair in relationship to an individual. Without the individual who desires to use the chair in order to sit down, does the chair exist? We could just as readily answer that the chair is an ornamental object that exists as an entity of art. But again, its existence as an object of art depends upon the perception of the beholder and the location of the chair in a given spatial context.[8]

The concept of mutual identity follows rather routinely once we accept the meaning of emptiness. The logic can be stated as follows: existence means that an entity exists as a result of conditionality. Emptiness refers to the fact that what exists in dependence on conditions has no ultimate being in and of itself. If we examine the relationship between a single entity conceived as a cause and the many other entities that are the result of that cause, we will discover that despite the apparent differences in each entity, there is no essential difference between one entity and the many entities. There is a fundamental identity among all entities.[9]

We can apply this concept to that of an economic system. An economic system is defined as a collection of individuals and institutions, laws, codes, and traditions that establishes acceptable behavior, and so on. The totality of any given economic system is dependent on the existence of each of these entities. Each individual and institution, law, or tradition, is empty, for their true essence is defined by the interdependencies and conditionalities that exist within the entire economic system.

Furthermore, each entity is identical in defining the nature of that economic system. Remove one individual, institution, or other entity and that economic system is different from the one that existed previously. Each entity is mutually identical in defining the totality of the entire economic system. However, this is a static concept of totality, or an economic system. To complete our understanding, we must consider the dynamics of totality. This involves the concept of universal intercausality.

Intercausality is the condition of interpenetration, which results from a situation in which the cause includes the conditions within itself while at the same time, since it is a result of other causes, its qualities are being absorbed into the other. The part includes the whole while the whole includes the part. This means that an entity considered to be the cause includes within itself, by a kind of borrowing or usurpation, the qualities possessed by the contributing conditions to that causality.

This rather abstract concept has great implications for an understanding of the dynamics of an economic system. Rather than dynamics representing a linear flow of cause and effect, a movement from one static equilibrium position to another, the dynamics of intercausality mean that all entities both are the cause for the totality and are caused by that totality. This is a far more powerful concept of dynamics. We can think of dynamics as existing with both "vertical" and "horizontal" causal interdependencies, or even more appropriately, we can think of a "matrix" of interdependencies in *n*-dimensional space. In this matrix of interdependence, there is no one center of causation. Causality cannot be isolated apart from the economic system itself, for the dynamics of intercausality *are* the system.

In sum, it is the contention of Postulate Five that the true nature of an economic system is primarily shaped by the particular ideology that is adopted by the society from which that economic system is formed, and that the ideologies of individualism and totality are far more pervasive in shaping an economic system than are the political ideologies of capitalism, communism, socialism, or any others. The ideologies of individualism and totality establish the most basic conceptualization of reality held by an economic system, and that conceptualization defines the essential nature of economic behavior prevalent within a given economic system.

This postulate concludes what might be viewed as the basic structure of our moral model, and we now turn to the final postulates, which are in some sense more applied. The sixth postulate defines the essential nature of economic behavior that dominates in an economic system that derives its source of understanding of the general environment in terms of the ideology of individualism. The final postulate defines economic behavior for an economic system in which the dominant ideology is one of totality.

Postulate Six: Ideology of Individualism and Economic Behavior

Postulate Six states that an economic system that adopts the ideology of individualism will institutionalize the following dominant characteristics in its economic behavior: the autonomous individual as the primary unit within the economic system; optimization behavior regarding the role of the individual within the economic system; and conflict generation-resolution as the essential nature of interaction between individuals and institutions within the economic system.

The individualism model, as we will characterize the economic system that adheres to the ideology of individualism, is built upon the base of an autonomous individual who has the inherent capacity to be the causality of his or her own will. In expressing this will, the individual will strive to attain self-development, where the nature of self-development is individually defined and largely self-determined. For instance, self-development could be defined as achieving as high a level of hedonistic consumption as possible, or alternatively as living life as a mendicant friar.

In the individualism model, the institutions of the economic system are viewed essentially as aggregations of individuals, and the basic function of a given institution is to satisfy individual desires. Thus, the corporation, as the primary economic institution, functions to convert factor inputs of labor, capital, and technology into commodities, and in that process generates income for employees, and dividends and profits for shareholders. The role of the corporation as a socioeconomic institution where the distribution of social practices affects individual esteem, positions of relative power, and personal feelings of dignity, is given secondary consideration.

The primary function of the institution of the family or household is to provide a secure environment for achieving individual self-development of its members, for rearing and educating children, and for passing a set of human values from one generation to another. The members of the family must define relative positions of power and responsibility within the structure of the family institution, but these positions are largely defined in individualistic terms as necessitated by the condition of individual autonomy.

Government is viewed as the aggregation of individuals into a public institution whose primary purpose is to provide for the common defense and security of all, establish an orderly environment in which individuals can pursue their independent goals, provide for certain minimal public goods and services, and achieve justice. This latter function gives government a unique institutional role within the economic system, for economic justice is not deeply integrated into the institutionalized behavior of family, corporation, or community. This follows from the individualized nature of the economic system, for it is difficult for autonomous individuals, each pursuing his or her self-interests, to incorporate into their behavior the conditions of justice.

The institution of community is something of an anomaly in the individualistic model. It is essentially a collection of individuals who live within a common geographic area, and therefore these individuals must resolve certain issues of interdependence. But these issues are largely viewed in terms of socioeconomic externalities rather than the more pervasive communal interdependencies. Therefore, communities tend to become what is commonly termed "life style enclaves" where individuals seek to live among like-minded peers. Such like-minded peers mean that the existence of socioeconomic externalities will be minimal and readily resolved. The community will provide a secure haven for protecting the values of person and property, will minimize social conflict, and will support the pursuit of self-fulfillment and the self-development goals of its individual residents.

Given individual autonomy, and the assumption that each individual has the inherent capacity for the causality of his or her own will, how will the individual behave in the various institutional settings discussed above? The answer as clearly given in neoclassical economic theory is optimization behavior.

The individual in the role of consumer is assumed to maximize consumer utility, allocating a given income among all available commodity choices in such a manner as to attain the highest possible level of consumer utility. To the extent that those choices affect communal, human development and self-fulfillment needs as well as the traditional economic needs, then the individual will behave in such a manner as to maximize his or her happiness.

The role of the individual in the corporation is to contribute to the maximization of the profitability of the corporation, and in the process, to achieve maximum return in terms of income and other benefits for that individual's particular social practice within the firm. Finally, the role of government regarding the individual is to provide a general environment in which each individual's opportunity to maximize his or her own welfare is not inefficiently constrained by the existence of government.

The individualistic model will be characterized by conflict generation-resolution. Conflict generation begins with the individual acting as a utility maximizing consumer. Given limited resources, an efficient solution to the consumer choice problem creates what Boulding (1952, p. 17) has characterized as the "conflict curve." This curve exemplifies the fact that an efficient solution to the production and consumption of economic commodities can generate both a highly equal as well as a highly unequal distribution of commodities. Therefore, individual consumers are in conflict with one another over the "equitable" distribution of commodities, for an increase in total consumption by one individual can only be achieved by a reduction in consumption by another.

If the meaning of economic commodities is extended to incorporate the elements of happiness and justice discussed in this study, then a conflict is generated in the distribution of relative positions of power, esteem, and responsibility within the family and the corporation. For instance, the role of one individual family member is seen as conflicting with the role of another family member (relative positions of power and responsibility between husband and wife), and the role of one individual employee in the corporation is seen as conflicting with the role of another employee (management positions based on presumed individualistic merit considerations). Furthermore, the role of the individual within the family is frequently seen as conflicting with the role of that individual within the corporation (conflict between the desire for family-community stability and corporate-career mobility). Or the role of the individual within the corporation is seen as conflicting with the role of government regarding that individual (the ability of the corporation to provide for the economic security of the individual employee versus the desire of government to regulate and control the behavior of the corporation to achieve economic security for all individuals). In sum, conflict generation is inherent in an economic system in which the individual is seen as an autonomous, self-development-oriented, and individual-welfare-maximizing human being.

Given this inherent conflict generation, the economic system must develop means of resolving conflict. In an individualistic model, it is not surprising that conflict resolution is primarily defined in individualistic-legal terms and is not resolved through social-institutional means. Individuals seek a redress to perceived injustice, whether that injustice occurs within the family or within the corporation, through legal action. And the legal action represents an attempt to determine the validity of the case for each individual treated autonomously.

Nor is it surprising that conflict resolution between institutions is resolved through a legal-political process rather than through social-institutional means. The conflict between the family, the corporation, and government is resolved legalistically-politically where each individual and each institution attempts to influence the outcome of that resolution process to achieve maximum benefits for each party to the conflict. Little effort is made to resolve the conflict for the mutual benefit of all entities, that is, for the broader social community. This is to be expected, since the broader community is viewed as little more than a collection of individual entities, and therefore an individualistic process of conflict resolution is assumed to advance the social welfare of the community by definition.

Postulate Seven: Ideology of Totality and Economic Behavior

Postulate Seven states that an economic system that adopts the ideology of totality will institutionalize the following dominant characteristics in its economic behavior: the interdependent individual as the primary unit within the economic system; satisficing behavior regarding the role of the individual within the economic system; and consensus formation as the essential nature of interaction between individuals and institutions within the economic system.

The totality model is built upon the base of an individual whose very existence is defined in terms of his or her relationship to other entities (individuals, institutions, laws, regulations, codes of behavior, etc.) that characterize the entire economic system. The individual does not exist in autonomous isolation from other entities, nor does he or she possess the inherent capacity to be the causality of his or her own will. Rather, the true essence of the individual is defined by the interdependencies and conditionalities that exist among all entities within the economic system.

In terms of economic behavior, this understanding of true essence means that the individual will attempt to achieve self-fulfillment and self-development, but the ability to do so exists within the context of the institutions that define the economic system. Thus, within the institution of the firm, the individual has a particular role that establishes relative positions of power and responsibility. To a large extent these relative positions will be institutionalized; each individual within the firm knows and accepts his or her role. But this acceptance is not a matter of passive compliance; rather, it is a recognition of the communal interdependencies that exist within the structure of the firm. Given these interdependencies, each member of the firm knows that both total firm welfare and individual welfare will be greater when there is cooperative behavior than when there is autonomous and independent behavior. The same conditions define the role of the individual in all other institutions as well: family, community, and government.

We now turn to the issue of satisficing economic behavior. Given the complexity of economic reality, it is naive to postulate that economic entities are able to behave as maximizers. A single-focused objective function cannot be defined, sufficient knowledge is not available to enable an individual or firm to know that it is selecting the best alternative, and uncertainty is too great to assume that maximization is feasible. Rather, the economic institutions are socioeconomic entities that will attempt to satisfy a matrix of goals or objectives. Individuals and institutions will adopt a set of rules or routines that make the decision process expedient. These routines, according to Nelson and Winter (1982), "range from well-specified technical routines for producing things, through procedures for hiring and firing, ordering new inventory, or stepping up production of items in high demand" (p. 14).[10] These routines are a persistent feature of the economic entity, whether that entity be a firm, an individual consumer, or a government agency. They are heritable in the sense that tomorrow's economic institutions and entities that evolve from today's have much the same characteristics. And they are selectable in the sense that entities with certain routines may do better than others, and if so, their relative importance in the economic system is augmented over time.

Furthermore, in satisficing behavior, the future is viewed as an entity that shapes the current reality. It is as much an entity as all past and current entities. Whatever perception of the future that a given economic entity or the economic system as a whole adopts is an element that defines the current reality and hence economic behavior in that reality. For instance, if the prevailing view of the future is one of great uncertainty, economic behavior is likely to be dominated by concerns for security, survival, and minimal risk. The individual will not likely accumulate large debt obligations. Firms will invest in projects that offer short-term returns. And government will finance those public goods that provide economic security to individuals and to firms. But if the prevailing view of the future were to change to one of expanded opportunities as the result of a new technological advancement, the current reality would be greatly altered.

With a view of a future that offers unique opportunities for growth and development, individuals, firms, and government would behave quite differently. Investments would be made that might enable the individual to realize a higher level of individual happiness or economic justice, perhaps through new and better rewarded social practices in expanding institutions. Firms would make investments in projects that might lead to new markets and greater profits. And government might increase expenditures on research and development, education, and other areas that would enhance the ability of the economic system to realize the expected returns from an expansion of economic opportunities. Whether or not the new opportunities materialize is not relevant for current economic behavior. It is the expectation of such opportunities that is the relevant entity in defining the current economic system, and the behavior within that new economic system.

The final behavioral characteristic of the totality model is consensus formation, which is defined as the concerted effort to engage the broadest possible group of participants in the decision process in order: (1) to consider a large range of intelligence regarding the likely effect of any decision; (2) to build a base of political support within the institution for an eventual decision; and (3) to make the implementation of the decision more efficient.

The process of consensus formation will likely be far more lengthy in the intelligence-gathering and political-support-building phases than is true in the individualistic model of conflict generation-resolution. In the individualistic model, the decision maker can make a decision quite independently from other entities, and can impose this decision on all those entities. In this respect it is a more efficient decision-making system. But in implementation (in which conflict is generated and must be resolved), the individualistic model is likely to be far less efficient than the consensus-formation process of the totality model. Once a consensus is reached, all entities party to that consensus will embrace the final decision and quickly integrate that decision into their own behavior.

In the totality model, the means of resolving potential areas of conflict will be institutionalized within the economic system rather than being resolved through an external legal-political process, as in the individualistic model. As the consensus is formed, areas of potential conflict will be negotiated and resolved. However, the process of institutionalized conflict resolution extends far beyond that of decisions that are internal to a specific institution. Compromises will be worked out between institutions that are viewed as equally important and interdependent. Thus, government does not operate in a contentious relationship with corporations (the public versus private dichotomization so prevalent in an individualistic economic system). As coequal institutions within the totality of the economic system, government and corporations recognize their interdependent relationship and realize that the welfare of both institutions will be increased through cooperation rather than conflict.

Conclusion

In concluding our study of a moral economy, we must observe that in reality no economic system is a pure model of individualism or totality behavior. Rather, there is a range of alternative economic systems involving the institutionalization of individualism and totality, and the choice among these alternative systems will determine the nature both of economic behavior and of moral choice that prevails in an economic system.

For example, the individualistic model is commonly associated with the United States while the totality model is frequently associated with economic behavior in Japan. In reality, neither the United States nor Japan is a perfect case of these two extremes. Elements of interdependence are found within the United States, a fact that is increasingly being recognized in economic theory. Elements of autonomy are evident within Japan, a fact that is being recognized in actual practice. Most other countries fall between these two countries, with economic systems that combine characteristics of individualism and totality to differing degrees.

Notes

1. These conditions of rationality are paraphrased from Henderson and Quandt (1971), p. 8.

2. Kenneth Arrow, *Social Choice and Individual Values* (1951), is the classic statement of this problem. Since Arrow's seminal work in 1951, there has developed an enormous literature concerning the conditions under which individual preferences can be aggregated into a social welfare function. For an excellent listing of this literature, see Sen (1982), p. 34, n. 5.

3. This approach is adopted from Perelman (1963).

4. The principle works of Abraham Maslow in which the hierarchy of human needs is developed are *Toward a Psychology of Being* (Maslow 1968), *New Knowledge in Human Values* (Maslow 1959), and *Motivation and Personality* (Maslow 1970).

5. This categorization of distributive justice is from Perelman (1963), pp. 1–29.

6. Several good references to this philosophy are Chang (1971); Cook (1977); and Cleary (1983).

7. A good statement of this concept is Abe (1985), pp. 152–54.

8. The chair example was first used by Alfred North Whitehead (1929), pp. 97–98, and more recently by Cleary (1983), p. 21.

9. This paragraph is paraphrased from Cook (1977), p. 64.

10. The remainder of this paragraph is paraphrased from Nelson and Winter as well.

References

Abe, Masao. (1985) *Zen and Western Thought*. Honolulu: University of Hawaii Press.

Aristotle. (1943) *Aristotle's Ethics for English Readers: Rendered from the Greek of the Nichomachean Ethics*. Trans. by H. Rackham. Oxford: Basil Blackwell.

Arrow, Kenneth J. (1951) *Social Choice and Individual Values*. New York: John Wiley.

Bellah, Robert N., Richard Madsen, William M. Sullivan, Ann Swindler, and Steven M. Tipton. (1985) *Habits of the Heart, Individualism and Commitment in American Life*. Berkeley: University of California Press.

Boulding, Kenneth. (1952) "Welfare Economics." In Bernard F. Haley, ed., *A Survey of Contemporary Economics*. Homewood, IL: Irwin.

Chang, Garma C.C. (1971) *The Buddhist Teaching of Totality: The Philosophy of Hwa Yen Buddhism*. University Park, PA: Pennsylvania State University Press.

Cleary, Thomas. (1983) *Entry into the Inconceivable: An Introduction to Hua-yen Buddhism*. Honolulu: University of Hawaii Press.

Cook, Francis H. (1977) *Hua-yen Buddhism: The Jewel Net of Indra*. University Park, PA: Pennsylvania State University Press.

Encyclopaedia of the Social Sciences. (1942) "Individualism." *Encyclopaedia of the Social Sciences*. Vol. 7. New York: Macmillan.

Frankfurt, Harry G. (1971) "Freedom of the Will and the Concept of a Person." *Journal of Philosophy* 68, 1:5–20.

Harsanyi, John. (1955) "Cardinal Welfare, Individualistic Ethics, and Interpersonal Comparisons of Utility." *Journal of Political Economy* 63:309–21.

Hegel, Georg W.F. (1942) *The Philosophy of Right*. Trans. by T.M. Knox. Oxford: Clarendon Press.

Henderson, James H., and Richard E. Quandt. (1971) *Microeconomic Theory: A Mathematical Approach*. 2d ed. New York: McGraw-Hill.

Jones, Lewis Mumford. (1966) *The Pursuit of Happiness*. Ithaca, NY: Cornell University Press.

Kant, Immanuel. (1967) *The Moral Law: Kant's Groundwork of the Metaphysic of Morals*. Trans. by H.J. Paton. New York: Barnes & Noble.

McGill, V.J. (1967) *The Idea of Happiness*. New York: Frederick Praeger.

Maslow, Abraham H. (1968) *Toward a Psychology of Being*. New York: D. Van Nostrand.

———. (1970) *Motivation and Personality*. 2d ed. New York: Harper & Row.

———, ed. (1959) *New Knowledge in Human Values*. New York: Harper and Brothers.

Mill, John Stuart. (1956) *On Liberty*. Indianapolis, IN: Bobbs-Merrill. (Originally published in 1859.)

National Conference of Catholic Bishops. (1986) *Economic Justice for All*. Washington, DC: National Conference of Catholic Bishops.

Nelson, Richard R., and Sidney G. Winter. (1982) *An Evolutionary Theory of Economic Change*. Cambridge, MA: Belknap Press, Harvard University Press.

Perelman, Chaim. (1963) *The Idea of Justice and the Problem of Argument*. Trans. by John Petrie. London: Routledge & Kegan Paul.

Robbins, Lionel. (1962) *An Essay on the Nature and Significance of Economic Science*. London: Macmillan. (Originally published in 1932.)

Sen, Amartya K. (1982) "Choice, Orderings and Morality" and "Rational Fools: A Critique of the Behavioural Foundations of Economic Theory." In *Choice, Welfare and Measurement*. Cambridge, MA: MIT Press.

———. (1987) *On Ethics and Economics*. Oxford: Basil Blackwell.

Whitehead, Alfred North. (1929) *Process and Reality*. New York: Macmillan.

Woolf, Bertran Lee, trans. (1952) *Reformation Writings of Martin Luther*. Vol. 1. *The Basis of the Protestant Reformation*. London: Butterworth Press.

VI

Corporate Culture

15

Daniel R. Denison

Organizational Culture and "Collective" Human Capital

This essay begins by briefly describing a line of research carried out over the past decade that has attempted to draw a link between the cultural characteristics of individual business organizations and their economic performance and effectiveness.[1] At the core of this research is the idea that the nature of the bond between an individual and a social organization, and the resulting character of the interaction among individuals with an organization, are important determinants of the economic performance of the firm. I have pursued this both as a theoretical issue in organizational behavior and organizational theory, and as a topic of empirical research through extensive field work applying both quantitative and qualitative methods.

Within my own field of organizational theory and organizational behavior, it is important to note that this work has been both criticized and praised: criticized for having the temerity to cloak one of the most potent social constructionist concepts of the decade (culture) in the trappings of logical positivism; and praised because of the attempt to draw together an academic literature and a popular literature and lend some empirical evidence to the debate.

After a brief review of my past and current research on organizational culture and effectiveness, I would like to use this occasion to attempt to expand the implications of this research beyond the bounds of organizational theory and organizational research and begin to explore what this research means for human capital theory and socio-economics.

Research on Organizational Culture and Effectiveness

I began this research as a frustrated graduate student studying organizational psychology. Nearly all of the theories that I studied implied that a particular internal process, structure, or dynamic had a positive impact on organizational performance. Unfortunately, there was so little evidence on the topic, that it was difficult to be persuaded that organizational behavior was actually linked to organizational performance. More research was needed.

Thus, for a dissertation, I studied the literature on organizational culture and organizational climate, and assembled enough survey data to study thirty-five firms, using these behavioral data to predict financial performance ratios drawn from Standard and Poors (Denison 1982, 1984). The results showed that:

- Survey indicators could distinguish quite well between high and low performing firms;
- The results were time dependent—survey measures were often a better predictor of future performance than of current performance;
- "High-involvement" organizations outperformed low-involvement firms, often by a factor of 2:1;
- "High leadership ideals" were a better predictor of performance than were actual leadership behaviors.

At the encouragement of several of my mentors,[2] I then began a set of case studies designed to develop a better understanding of the process by which culture influenced effectiveness. These case studies included firms that fit the involvement/effectiveness finding described above, as well as firms that seemed directly to contradict it. These case studies are presented by Denison (1990) and briefly summarized by Denison and Mishra (1990).

The outcome of this inductive case research was a model of organizational culture and effectiveness (Denison 1990). The model emphasized four dimensions of culture: involvement, consistency, adaptability, and mission. The influence of these four cultural dimensions on effectiveness can be described as follows:

Involvement: High levels of involvement and participation create a sense of ownership and responsibility. Out of this sense of ownership grows a greater commitment to an organization, and a growing capacity to operate under conditions of autonomy. Increasing the input of organizational members is also seen as increasing the quality of decisions and their implementation.

Consistency: A shared system of beliefs, values, and symbols, widely understood by an organization's members, has a positive impact on the members' ability to reach consensus and carry out coordinated actions. Implicit control systems, based upon internalized values, are a more effective means of achieving coordination than external control systems, which rely on explicit rules and regulations.

Adaptability: The capacity of an organization to receive and interpret signals from its environment and to translate those signals into changes in internal processes and behavior increases the organization's chances for survival and growth. The capacity continually to restructure and reinstitutionalize allows for adaptation.

Figure 15.1. **The Culture and Effectiveness Model**

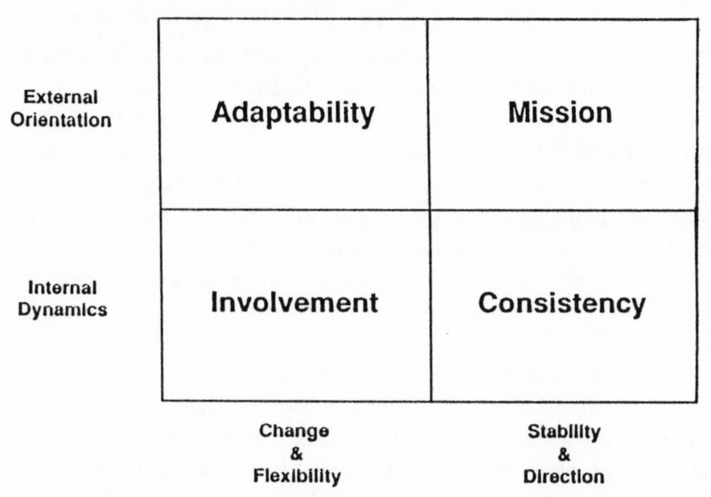

Mission: A mission provides purpose and meaning to work, and often gives a host of noneconomic reasons why the work of an organization is important. A mission also provides clarity of direction and goals to define an appropriate course of action.

As shown in Figure 15.1, there is a clear relationship among these four dimensions. Two of these dimensions, involvement and consistency, can be seen as characteristics of the internal integration and governance of an organization. The other two characteristics, adaptability and mission, refer to the organization's external adaptation and orientation toward its environment. Consistency and mission may also be seen as characteristics that enhance stability and predictability, whereas involvement and adaptability are seen as sources of change and flexibility.

Despite the fact that this model was derived from inductive field work, a review of the organizational culture literature, and quantitative analysis, it nonetheless bears a clear resemblance to several prior models of the functioning of social systems (Parsons 1951; Katz and Kahn 1978; Quinn 1988). This model and its development are discussed in greater detail elsewhere (Denison 1990; Denison and Mishra 1989, 1990).

A more recent study attempted to test this model in a large-scale investigation of nearly 1,000 firms (Denison and Mishra 1989, 1990), using CEO perceptions of culture and effectiveness as a means to begin testing the theory. The study showed that each of the four cultural characteristics could differentiate between high, medium, and low performing firms. Involvement and mission proved to be the most powerful of the four predictors in this study.

Other authors have also made important contributions to this line of research. Gordon (1985), for example, showed that high and low performing companies in the utility, manufacturing, and financial industries showed differences in areas such as openness of conflict and action orientation. Kravetz (1988) found that such progressive human resource practices as participation, communication, creativity, and decentralization were closely related to both growth in sales and growth in profits. Hansen and Wernerfelt (1989), working from a strategy perspective, compared the financial impacts of external factors such as market share with organizational factors such as human resources. They found that the two factors had independent effects on performance, but that the organizational factors were the stronger predictors. Several reviews of the culture and effectiveness literature also have helped to highlight some of the important issues regarding research in this area (Barney 1986; Siehl and Martin 1988; Camerer and Vepsalainen 1988).

Taken together, these findings support the idea that the normative structure of a social organization has considerable value, *even when viewed in purely economic terms.* Even though most culture studies have focused on aspects of culture that are less directly related to performance, such as the formation of culture or the transmission of culture to new organizational members, it is encouraging to note that the few studies that have addressed this issue explicitly have generated some significant findings. Several other observations also help to support the general notion that a strong normative system, based on networks of human interdependence, is a key organizational asset.

First, similar findings can also be found at the level of international competition. Lodge and Vogel (1987), for example, in a study of nine nations, found a close linkage between the presence of a "strong communitarian ideology" and growth in GNP, exports, and share of GNP that went to investment.[3] Hofstede and Bond (1988) also draw similar conclusions about the impacts of culture on the growth and development of national economies, citing "Confucian dynamism" as a key to the economic development of many Pacific Rim nations.

Second, in my own research, I am struck by the fact that American firms in industries that are high in capital intensity and low in demands for human-based coordination (e.g., paper, petroleum) thus far seem to have faced far less threat from international competition than industries such as manufacturing, banking, or electronics, where there is greater labor intensity and greater demand for human-based coordination. While there is clearly a different set of resources and entry barriers in each of these industries that may account for some of these differences (Porter 1980), this observation may nonetheless imply that American firms are competing most poorly in industries that require the most in the way of human coordination. This is, of course, exactly the type of situation that can be managed best through a normative, rather than an exclusively economic, system.

Third, the events of 1989 assure that this trend toward competition based on organizational capacity, ability at human-based coordination, and the normative regulation of the firm will continue. Freer global markets for technology and capital will tend to increase the importance of human capital as a source of competitive advantage. As Fukuyama (1989) has noted, the future will be one of global managerialism. Or, in Lester Thurow's words:

> If you aren't better educated than a Korean, if you don't have more capital equipment to work with than a Korean, if you don't have better technology than a Korean, you will work for Korean wages because it is possible for anybody to build anything in Korea and service the American market. [Thurow 1989]

To this I would add, however, that if the managers of this enterprise, which manufactures in Korea and sells in the United States, are to remain American, they have to demonstrate a superior ability to coordinate and develop both individual and collective human capital within the firm. "Factor price equalization" (the economist's term for the process Thurow describes above) will influence choices about corporate governance as well.

On a lighter note, while attempting to explain to a student the concept of "collective human capital" as *an organization-specific asset rooted in the interactive coordination among multiple organizational members*, I used the illustration of a double play in baseball—an inherent act of teamwork in a relatively individualistic game. We began speculating about what evidence might be available to test this idea, and eventually produced the simple analysis presented in Figure 15.2.

Figure 15.2 presents the number of double plays produced by two teams as a function of the number of years that the shortstop/second base dyad played together.[4] Interestingly enough, very few teams had much stability in this pair—only one other pair was stable for more than three years, and that dyad produced an essentially random pattern. The results for these two teams, however, show an improving trend that declines somewhat in the second case, presumably toward the end of the players' careers.

Few of these findings would be anticipated by a conventional economic analysis of firms, groups, and individuals. This is because each of these findings focuses on the economic results of the interactive capacity of groups, teams, and organizations; they produce results that are difficult to capture by focusing only on the firm or the individual as a rational actor. Furthermore, this asset of collective human capital, one might argue, is highly important in a strategic sense because it is among the most difficult to imitate (Barney 1986; Ulrich 1986; Camerer and Vapsalainen 1988). Thus, it is likely to remain an increasingly important element in competition.

Potential Implications for Socio-Economics

One of the first implications of this research for a theory of socio-economics is that the area of human capital deserves reconsideration. A two-stage framework is necessary to provide a more complete model of the impact that human effort

Figure 15.2. **Double Plays as a Function of Tenure**

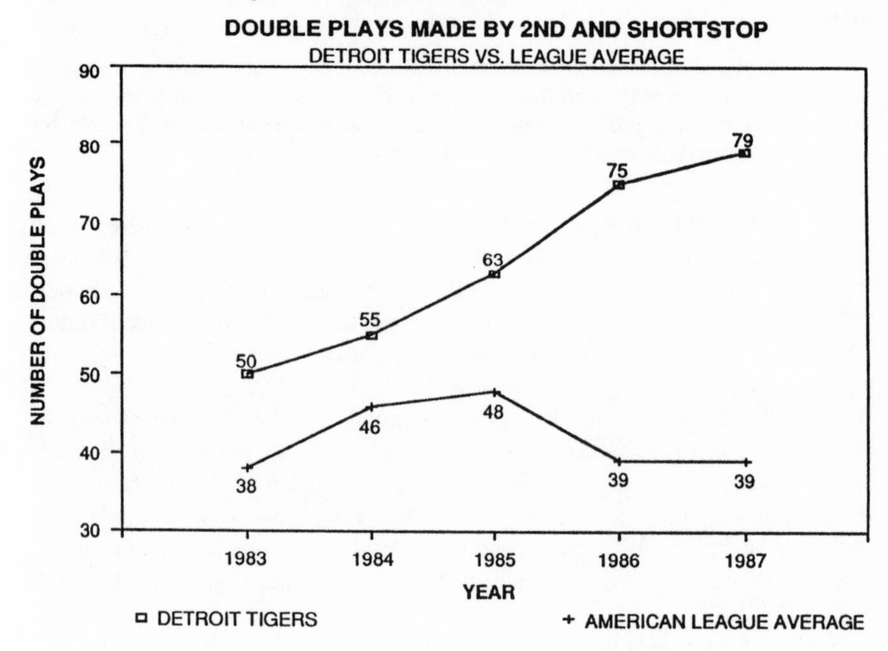

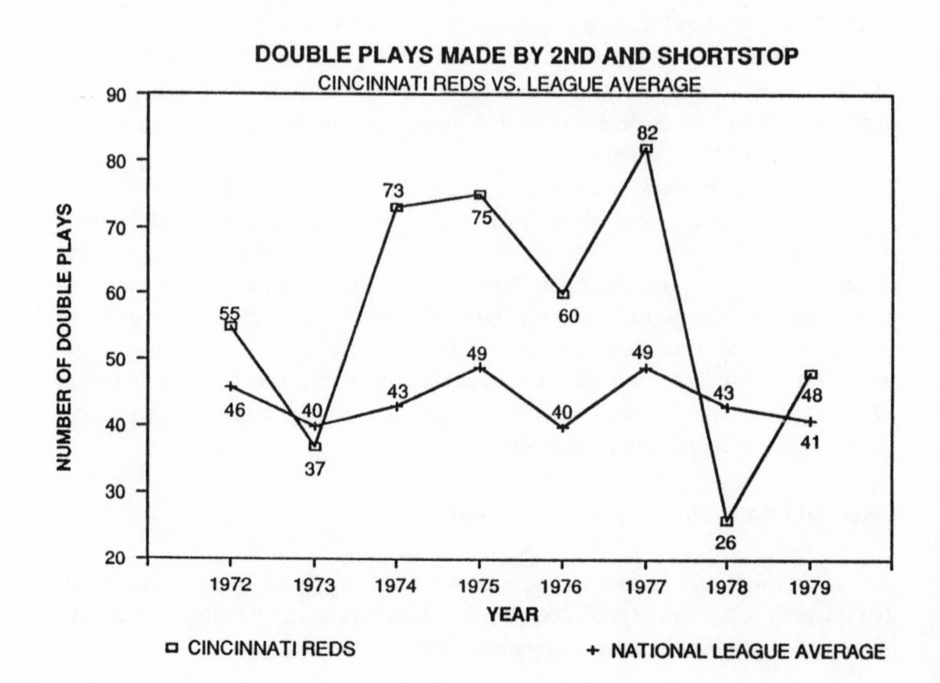

has on the performance of a firm. The first stage, individual human capital (Becker 1964), is well developed and is more important to an understanding of competitive advantage today than ever before (Johnson 1987; Thurow 1989). A second stage of human capital theory, however, must begin to emphasize collective human capital and must focus on interaction, coordination, and the relationship of the individual to the organization. This second stage must develop and build upon a more systematic way to attribute economic value to integrative normative structures. The problem can perhaps be treated as one of the creation of specialized assets, but the assets are fundamentally *collective and interactive* assets, rather than individually held assets. Examples include the organizational capacity to develop new products, create high-involvement work systems, and create social institutions that provide meaning for members.

It is still unclear, to me at least, just how useful existing economic theory is for solving these problems. Very few authors have treated the issue of the intersection of organization theory and economics in any detail (see Barney and Ouchi 1986, or Camerer and Vepsalainen 1988, for exceptions). Even a classic like Alchian and Demsetz (1972), which attempts to analyze "teamwork" from a transaction costs perspective (Williamson 1975), has a very difficult time explaining why team members would ever cooperate. In fact, it does a far better job of explaining why what looks like cooperation is, in reality, rational self-interest.

For example, Alchian and Demsetz, in recognition of the fact that much of the work in organizations is done more efficiently by teams than by individuals, begin by assuming that an organization is a "centralized contracting agent in a team productive process" (p. 778). They focus first on the "metering" problem, or the difficulties in assuring that the payment of rewards is in accord with the productivity of individual group members. These authors conclude that efficient metering requires "cheap" monitoring, and that obstacles to cheap monitoring, such as difficulties in correlating behavior directly with productivity, require the creation of firms. Monitoring is expensive, and in some situations it may actually cost more than it saves. Such costs must be deducted from the "residual" and thus act like a tax on work results.

The dilemma is that in an effort to prevent "shirking"—the main barrier (they argue) to productivity-based reward in team tasks—the role of the "monitor" (manager) must be created. Furthermore, they argue that the manager will be efficient in this role to the degree that he or she is the "sole expropriator" of the group's residual productivity. If this residual is distributed more widely, this dilution will result in increased "shirking" by the monitor. Thus, they conclude that:

> general sharing in the residual results in losses from enhanced shirking by the monitor that exceed the gains from reduced shirking by residual-sharing employees. If this were not so, profit sharing with employees should have occurred more frequently in Western societies where such organizations are neither banned nor preferred politically. [p. 787]

They also comment briefly on the opposite of shirking, "hyperactivity," and argue that it creates instability, implying that teams function best when team members neither under- nor overinvest their efforts. As to "team spirit" or "loyalty," they conclude that:

> Obviously the team is better, with team spirit and loyalty, because of the reduced shirking—not because of some feature inherent in loyalty or spirit as such. [p. 790]

As one might expect, there are several aspects of Alchian and Demsetz's theoretical analysis of team-based production that do not square well with a model of effective organization that has been developed from studying culture and effectiveness. Some of these differences are summarized briefly as a way of commenting on some of the problems associated with explaining a phenomenon such as organizational culture through neoclassical economic analysis.

The Role of the Manager

The role of the manager in this analysis is to ensure rationality and equity. The primary roles are described as monitoring and metering the marginal productivity of individual inputs to team outputs. Clearly, this creates a short-term environment not conducive to risk taking, and does not take into account the losses associated with a manager who conceives of his or her task as monitoring and metering rather than directing and leading a group or organization.

"Best Practice"

The more pressing problem, however, is the relevance of this frame of reference for defining "best practice," "competitive advantage," or "organizational effectiveness." Or to put it more simply, "What does an effective work group look like?" Rather than argue that an effective group is one in which inputs and rewards reach equilibrium, one might argue that the most effective group is likely to be one composed of hyperactive overinvestors who recognize that the market-driven feedback loops that would allow for their rewards to be accurately "metered" are in fact far too long to allow for much meaningful calculation of the economic returns of immediate cooperation. Groups (or organizations) whose members consistently err on the side of overinvestment are the most likely to survive. He who estimates is lost.

Simplistic Examples

An equally serious problem is the attempt to deal only with the most rudimentary examples of coordination ("Two men jointly lift heavy cargo into trucks . . . " [p. 779]). In doing so, it ignores the possibility of complex synergy as a normative expectation. Alchian and Demsetz's conclusions about profit sharing, for example, seem almost quaint by today's standards.

By the same token, the expectation that individuals in all cultures will estimate under- and overinvestment in similar ways seems outmoded. Terrorists with car bombs and cultures in which individuals make sacrifices for the collective that violate our "western equilibrium" are all an integral part of the global terrain, despite the fact that they seem to violate the assumptions of neoclassical economics. Organizations are ill equipped to cope with these conditions without a thorough understanding of the impact of normative and ideological systems on global competition.

Homo economicus, then, must be seen as a normative statement in itself, based in values, with a particular logical structure. The questions that must be answered are, "*which situations are these norms most useful in understanding?*" and "*which situations require an application of a different normative system?*"

Conclusion

In the end, the greatest contribution of Etzioni's (1988) argument for socio-economics may be parsimony. By proposing an economics based on both rational self-interest and obligation (or normative control), the door may have been opened for a quicker way to understand the impact that a firm's culture can have on its performance. Conventional neoclassical or transaction-cost economics might conceivably lead us down a path to an understanding of the normative and ideological structure of business organizations and their impact on effectiveness and survival. But it will not be a short path. Maybe there is not enough time to take the longer path. People join organizations that provide meaning and direction, and they value their membership far beyond the economic benefits the organizations provide. At some point it seems easier to accept this as an emergent assumption rather than continue the innumerable permutations of *homo economicus* in an attempt to dissect what, for a moment, may have looked like cooperation, obligation, or normative control.

Notes

1. Rather than redefining organizational culture, I will rely on one of my favorite definitions, originally provided by Elliot Jaques. Other useful definitions and discussion of the concept of organizational culture are provided by Schein (1985, 1990).

> The culture of the factory is its customary and traditional way of thinking and of doing things, which is shared to a greater or lesser degree by all its members, and which new members must learn, and at least partially accept, in order to be accepted into service in the firm. Culture in this sense covers a wide range of behaviour: the methods of production; job skills and technical knowledge; attitudes towards discipline and punishment; the customs and habits of managerial behaviour; the objectives of the concern; its way of doing business; the methods of payment; the values placed on different types of work;

beliefs in democratic living and joint consultation; and the less conscious conventions and taboos. Culture is part of second nature to those who have been with the firm for some time. Ignorance of culture marks out the newcomers, while maladjusted members are recognized as those who reject or are otherwise unable to use the culture of the firm. In short, the making of relationships requires the taking up of roles within a social structure; the quality of these relationships is governed by the extent to which the individuals concerned have each absorbed the culture of the organization so as to be able to operate within the same general code. The culture of the factory consists of the means or techniques which lie at the disposal of the individual for handling his relationships, and on which he depends for making his way among, and with, other members and groups. [Jaques 1951, p. 251]

2. I am especially indebted to J. Richard Hackman and Stanley Seashore for their valuable contributions to this research.

3. Lodge and Vogel (1987) define a strong communitarian ideology as a consistency in how people in a country see and respond to their environment, based on five dimensions:

1. Equality of result
2. Rights and duties of membership
3. Community need
4. The active, planning state
5. Holism.

4. One source of potential error in this analysis is that the total number of double plays per year was available only for the entire team, rather than for the particular combination of shortstop/second base.

References

Alchian, A.A., and H. Demsetz. (1972) "Production, Information Costs, and Economic Organization." *American Economic Review* 62:777–95.

Barney, J.B. (1986) "Organizational Culture: Can It Be a Source of Sustained Competitive Advantage?" *Academy of Management Review* 11, 3:656–65.

Barney, J.B., and W.G. Ouchi. (1986) *Organizational Economics*. San Francisco: Jossey-Bass.

Becker, G.S. (1964) *Human Capital*. New York: Columbia University Press.

Camerer, C., and A. Vepsalainen. (1988) "The Economic Efficiency of Corporate Culture." *Strategic Management Journal* 9:115–26.

Denison, D.R. (1982) "The Climate, Culture, and Effectiveness of Work Organizations: A Study of Organizational Behavior and Financial Performance." Ph.D. diss. University of Michigan.

———. (1984) "Bringing Corporate Culture to the Bottom Line." *Organizational Dynamics* 13 2:4–22.

———. (1990) *Corporate Culture and Organizational Effectiveness*. New York: John Wiley.

Denison, D.R., and A.K. Mishra. (1989) "Organizational Culture and Organizational Effectiveness: A Theory and Some Preliminary Empirical Evidence." *Proceedings of the Academy of Management*, pp. 168–72.

———. (1990) "A Theory of Organizational Culture and Effectiveness." Working paper, University of Michigan.

Etzioni, A. (1988) *Moral Dimension: Toward a New Economics*. New York: The Free Press.

Fukuyama, F. (1989) "The End of History?" *National Interest* 16 (Summer: 3–18).

Gordon, G.G. (1985) "The Relationship of Corporate Culture to Industry Sector and Corporate Performance." In R.H. Kilman and M.J. Saxton, eds., *Gaining Control of the Corporate Culture*. San Francisco: Jossey-Bass.

Hansen, G.S., and B. Wernerfelt. (1989) "Determinants of Firm Performance: The Relative Importance of Economic and Organizational Factors." *Strategic Management Journal* 10, 5:399–412.

Hofstede, G., and M. Bond. (1988) "The Confucius Connections from Cultural Roots to Economic Growth." *Organizational Dynamics* 16, 4:4–21.

Jaques, E. (1951) *The Changing Culture of a Factory*. London: Tavistock.

Johnson, W.B. (1987) *Workforce 2000: Work and Workers for the 21st Century*. Indianapolis: The Hudson Institute.

Katz, D., and R.L. Kahn. (1978) *The Social Psychology of Organizations*. 2d ed. New York: John Wiley.

Kravetz, D.J. (1988) *The Human Resources Revolution: Implementing Progressive Management Practices for Bottom-Line Success*. San Francisco: Jossey-Bass.

Lodge, G., and E. Vogel. (1987) *Ideology and National Competitiveness*. Boston: Harvard Business School Press.

Martin, J., C. Anterasian, and C. Siehl. (1988) "Externally Espoused Values and the Legitimation of Financial Performance." Working paper, Stanford University.

Parsons, T. (1951) *The Social System*. Glencoe, IL: Free Press.

Porter, M. (1980) *Competitive Strategy*. New York: The Free Press.

Quinn, R.E. (1988) *Beyond Rational Management*. San Francisco: Jossey-Bass.

Schein, E. (1985) *Organizational Culture and Leadership*. San Francisco: Jossey-Bass.

———. (1990) "Organizational Culture." *American Psychologist* 45, 2:109–19.

Siehl, C., and J. Martin. (1988) "Organizational Culture: A Key to Financial Performance?" In B. Schneider, ed., *Organizational Culture and Climate*. San Francisco: Jossey-Bass.

Thurow, L. (1989) Remarks to the Governor's Conference on Science and Engineering Education, Research, and Development. Boston, December 4.

Ulrich, D. (1986) "Human Resource Planning as a Competitive Edge." *Human Resource Planning* 9, 2:41–50.

Williamson, O. (1975) *Markets and Hierarchies: Analysis and Antitrust Implications: A Study in the Economics of Internal Organization*. New York: The Free Press.

16

NANCY DITOMASO, GEORGE G. GORDON, AND TED H. SZATROWSKI

Corporate Culture and Financial Performance

A Preliminary Investigation

Previous conceptual work on corporate culture leads to the question, "So what?" or more elegantly, "To what effect?" Despite the often insular way corporate culture is sometimes discussed in the literature, we recognize, as would any sensible person, that all organizations are embedded within a culture, and thus a large part of what corporate culture is said to be is undoubtedly a reflection of the larger societal culture. Also, organizational participants, as Charles Perrow notes (1979), track mud in from the outside, so they bring their cultures with them.

Beyond the micro- and macro-influences of culture on organizations, the critical question is whether there is enough difference among organizations that can be identified and defined as "cultural" to make a difference in anything of importance that can be said about how organizations function, or behave, or perform (take your pick). In this paper, we discuss how one would address such a question, and specifically investigate the relationship between aspects of corporate culture and the financial performance of organizations. Although our analysis is preliminary, we feel that it can contribute to a clarification of the relationship between corporate culture and organizational consequences.

If there are cultural differences among organizations, from where would such culture come? Is it only the mud tracked in by critical participants who make a difference, or is there a collective effect from organizational properties themselves?

Culture: Form versus Content

The corporate—or organizational—culture literature is clearly divided into two arenas: an academic one, where the language is often esoteric and the direction more like a circle than a line, and the practitioner one, where the concerns are very everyday. By and large, we would suggest that the academic literature on corporate culture has concentrated more on the forms or elements of culture as applied to organizations, whereas the practitioner literature has been more concerned with the content of corporate culture. Although we would like to think of our work as fitting into the academic arena, we feel that it is necessary to think about the content of corporate culture if one is to answer questions about either its causes or its consequences. Thus, our work on corporate culture presented here addresses content more than form. In fact, given our purposes, which are to compare cultures across organizations, we are limiting our discussion of corporate culture to one cultural element, namely, the values held by organizations as reflected in the survey responses of the management of the organization.

The sources of our data limit what we can say about corporate culture: we are using surveys and publicly available data. At the same time, the virtue of this kind of data is that it allows us to compare variability across organizations, and hence to answer questions about causes and consequences, rather than leading us to write one more paper on the conceptualization and form of corporate culture. We accept and agree with the corporate culture literature that culture is primarily about symbolic processes, but we argue that the values reflected in our data are no less symbolic than those that would be uncovered from other forms of data collection, whether participant observation, interviews, or ethnography.

Culture versus Climate

The main body of our data set comes from surveys of "management climate" collected on several hundred organizations by the Hay Group (a major human resources consulting firm). This raises the obvious question of whether a "climate" survey is appropriate for developing a study of corporate culture. Our answer is obviously yes, but we know that we need to defend that conclusion and hope that we can do so persuasively. The core of our argument is that this particular climate survey, in both its development and its conceptualization, is more reflective of what is currently discussed as corporate culture in the literature than the body of work on what is called organizational climate.

According to Payne and Pugh (1976, p. 1126), the organizational climate literature grew out of the desire to discover "how the organization is a psychologically meaningful environment for individual organization members." In other words, organizational climate provided measurement of the context of individual psychology. The constructs most frequently included in climate surveys include (Payne and Pugh 1976, p. 1127):

- the progressiveness and development of the organization
- risk taking
- warmth
- support
- control.

Questions on climate surveys are often about the work group and the characteristics of and interactions with one's immediate supervisor. Although there is disagreement in the literature about whether climate should be a dependent, independent, or intervening variable, the consequences primarily indicated for organizational climate in the "climate" literature are individual behaviors, whether performance, satisfaction, or some other aspect.

Clearly, some of the organizational culture literature discusses culture in a way that overlaps in meaning with the concept of organizational climate (see Denison 1988), but others have argued that the two are very distinct concepts (Trice, Beyer, and Morand 1985). It has been claimed, for example, that the two are epistemologically different, and even that the nature of the methods appropriate for the study are distinct, with surveys being suitable for climate research and ethnographic studies appropriate for culture studies.

We reject such claims and argue that the concepts are method-neutral, but we do feel that there is a distinction to be made between the two. Organizational climate is the psychological environment of individual behaviors. As such, its primary focus has been on such issues as morale and satisfaction. In our view, corporate culture is the distinct embodiment of values that are relatively stable and transmitted from old members to new, and that shape and guide the use of discretion within an organization. It is symbolic in the sense that it provides meaning for organizational members to interpret their actions and those around them, but it can be transmitted and communicated through any number of elements, from structure, to artifacts, to legends, and to rituals. Importantly, corporate culture is an organizational property, and not solely the expression of the individual values of a particular management.

Whether strong initial leaders are able to establish an identifiable culture is problematic; it depends on their ability to manage the symbolic life of the organization in such a way that their own values "take hold" in the use of discretion made by their subordinates and successors. Whether subsequent leaders are able to change an established culture is also problematic and dependent on the same ability to manage successfully the symbolic life of the organization. Whatever the cultural forms utilized to manage the symbolic messages of the organization, and however identifiable or distinct the organization's culture, the content—if not the form—of the culture can still, in our view, be revealed in the responses to questions about how things are done around here and what things are of importance in this organization.

The questionnaire used by Hay and made available to us was developed by George Gordon when he worked as research director for Hay. Although it has been labeled a survey of management climate, it was neither an extension nor an adaptation of the climate surveys available in the management literature. Instead, it grew out of extensive interviews in a number of organizations (approximately thirty to forty), designed to identify those managerial issues pertinent to the sustained performance of those organizations. Each of the surveys done by Hay at that point followed extensive unstructured interviewing and was customized to the organization. Only after it was determined that the same sorts of issues were emerging repeatedly, was the questionnaire standardized and used across many types of organizations. Although, of course, there were modifications over the years as new organizations were contacted and new issues became apparent, the basic questionnaire has remained relatively stable since about 1974. In other words, these quantitative data grew out of qualitative field work, which the literature on corporate culture seems to imply is a necessary precursor to the measurement of corporate culture.

There are several important things about this questionnaire that make it different from the academic literature on organizational climate:

- All of the questions are intended to measure organizational, not individual, properties. The questions, with few exceptions, are asked in the third person, e.g., "To what extent do the people in this organization do such and such . . . ?"
- The content of the questions is primarily about organizational practices: the quality of decision making, cooperation, goal setting, innovation, etc. The assumption underlying the questionnaire is that the collective responses are a measure of the behaviors of the organization which, in turn, reflect what is valued in the organization by its management over time.
- In most cases, the respondents include all of top management and several levels down. Although there are known biases in the views of management compared to lower-level employees—namely, that management almost always views their organization more positively than other employees—for our purposes, this is not a major problem. Because the survey is not about attitudes of employees (e.g., morale, satisfaction) but about organizational properties, and because management is said to be key to the development of culture in the culture literature, it seems appropriate that the description of the relative extent to which different practices are followed in the organization come from those who have the broadest view.
- The content of the questionnaire, for the most part, does not focus on either job design (challenge of an individual's job) or the work group (supportiveness of peers).
- The content of the questionnaire, for the most part, does not overlap with measures of organizational structure. For example, it does not measure the centralization or decentralization of decision making, but rather the extent to which decision making is done at the appropriate level.

In other words, if one were developing a questionnaire to tap how an organization's practices reflected its values on how to manage, one would probably develop it in this way and the questionnaire would probably look something like the one we have used here. This, we think, is a good instrument for a comparative study of corporate or organizational culture. Further, it is quite distinct from much of what is emphasized in the organizational climate literature. It is much less about the psychological climate in which organization members behave than it is about what values management thinks are embodied in their organization. At the same time, it is limited, if one were to use the terminology developed by Davis (1984), to values about how to manage, to the exclusion of values about how to compete.

Corporate Culture and Financial Performance of Firms

To define culture in terms of the values held by the corporation makes it necessary to specify what values we mean. As noted above, the academic literature on organizational or corporate culture has focused more on the form than on the content of corporate culture, whereas the practitioner literature has done the opposite. Even the latter, however, is not always very specific about what corporate culture, as opposed to societal culture, entails. For example, much of the early literature on corporate culture grew out of the comparison between companies in the United States and Japan. The culture said to be characteristic of Japanese firms never described all or even most Japanese companies, but only the largest one-third. Similarly, the culture of what was called the "excellent" U.S. firms was evidently not stable enough to weather recent economic downturns in several industries, nor strongly valued enough in many companies to forestall the changes wrought by mergers, acquisitions, and downsizing (*Business Week* 1984). Nevertheless, such success-inducing culture was said to include such things as an action-oriented management style (bias for action), a clear orientation regarding the company's mission (sticking to the knitting), and so on (Peters and Waterman 1982). Although the literature on what a successful corporate culture entails has proliferated, to say the least, in the last several years, it seems to include the kinds of dimensions listed in column 1 of Table 16.1. Although the survey that we are using here was not designed for the purpose of measuring "culture"—successful or otherwise—another indication that this survey is really tapping much of the same kind of content can be seen by column 2 of Table 16.1. The survey includes many items that address similar areas of concern.

To ask questions about culture and performance implies that we have some idea of what kind of culture leads to what kind of performance for what kinds of companies in what kinds of situations. Probably the most relevant discussion in the literature in this area is that regarding "strong" and "weak" cultures (see Saffold 1988). Effective companies are said to have strong—or identifiable—cultures, whereas less effective companies are said to have weak—or nonspecific—cultures. Again, the practitioner literature is more of a guide, but there are similar referents in the academic literature.

There is ambiguity about the meaning of a "strong" culture versus a "weak" culture in the literature, because of two implications often found in discussions of strong culture:

Table 16.1

Content of Corporate Cultures

In the literature	In our surveys
Values about how to compete	
• Service (to the customer)	
• Quality, high standards, doing what's right	Quality/favorable image (some companies only)
Values about how to manage	
• Participation, involvement in decisions, decision making at level of competence	Integration/communication
• Integration, cooperation	
• Innovation, being on the cutting edge, meeting challenges	Innovation/risk taking
• Shared goals, organizational goals consistent with individual goals	Clarity of strategy/shared goals
• Action, getting things done, winning	Accountability
• Rewards commensurate with contributions	Rewards
• Mutual regard, family feeling	Morale/belief in competence of co-workers
• Opportunities for growth and challenge	Opportunities for promotion and challenge
• Job security/lifetime employment	Long-term orientation

1. A company must have an identifiable set of values that shape the uses of discretion in the company in order for all organizational members to work together toward common goals in which all believe, but the exact nature of those values is immaterial.

2. A strong culture may imply stability and hence lack of adaptability. Thus, if culture is not to bind the organization to an anachronistic set of values, strength must be of guiding beliefs, the application of which changes with the environment, and not of specific goals (see DiTomaso 1987).

Using some preliminary analysis from the Hay climate surveys, we want to present some evidence regarding the content of corporate culture and the financial performance of companies. (The authors are in the process of updating and

Figure 16.1. **Correlations of Culture Profiles between and within Companies**

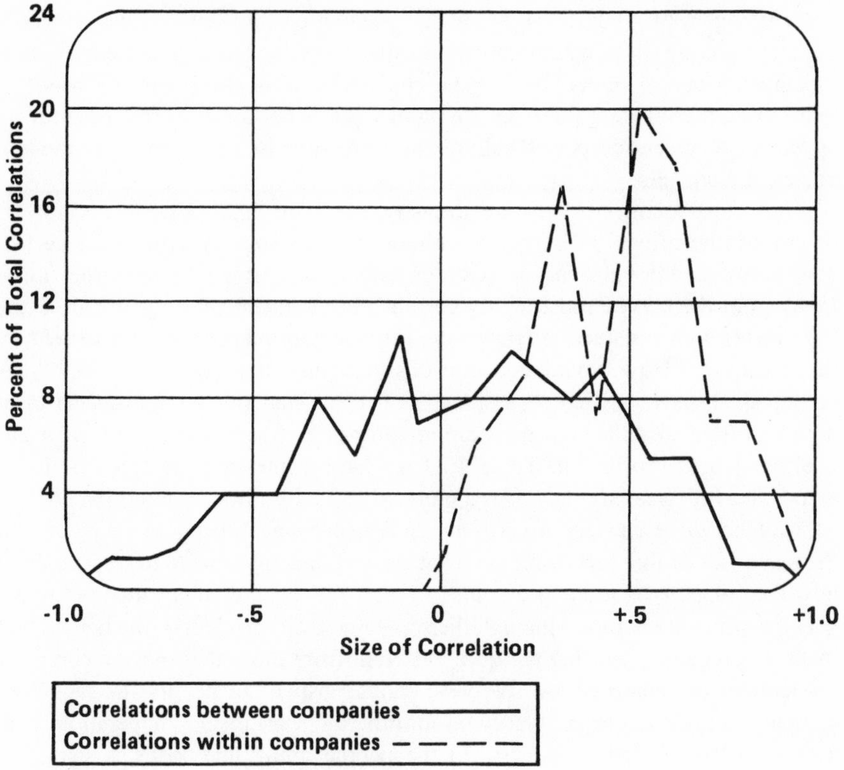

Source: Gordon and Goldberg (1977), p. 39.

enhancing this data set for future analyses on culture and performance.) The data reported here include surveys of the top four or five levels of management from approximately 100 companies that had used the same survey questions. The surveys were conducted beginning in 1974. Although we cannot claim that these companies had "strong" cultures as discussed above, there was nevertheless some consistency in the responses of their managers on a variety of questions. Despite the claims of some researchers that company cultures vary so much from group to group that there are likely to be greater differences between subgroups within the same company than between similar subgroups in different companies, these data suggest that there are indeed pervasive corporate cultures. In a previous analysis of the same data, Gordon and Goldberg (1977) computed all possible correlations among departments and divisions within companies and also computed all possible correlations between pairs of companies. Figure 16.1 shows the two distributions. The distribution of correlations between companies approximates a random normal distribution, with values ranging from –0.88 to

+0.97, with a median of +0.05. In contrast, correlations among units within companies show a very striking departure from a random distribution, with values ranging from –0.04 to +0.84, with a median of +0.54. Obviously, there is variation among units within companies, but there is also a great deal of commonality, a commonality that can be characterized as companywide belief or value systems. Whether these are strong or weak is not for us to say, but they do appear to represent corporate cultures in a broad sense, as opposed to random values of managers.

The primary concern we have in analyzing these data, however, is how to determine the effects of corporate culture on the company's financial performance. An additional analysis (Gordon and Cummins 1979) identified those items from the survey most highly correlated (all statistically significant at the 0.01 level) with satisfaction among the management respondents (measured by the question, "How would you rate this company as a place to work?"). A second analysis identified those items (again all statistically significant) most highly correlated with high performing companies (measured by five-year annual growth in profits). In Table 16.2 we have contrasted the types of items associated with a satisfying versus a productive (i.e., profitable) environment.

We label these clusters of items as "beliefs or values" because we claim that the responses of this survey reflect what the respondents believe to be true about how the company is run and that this, in turn, reflects the values inherent in the way the company is run. Although there is some overlap, clearly, the beliefs that make a company satisfying are quite different from those that make a company productive, as measured by five-year annual growth in profits. In satisfying companies, high values are placed on information sharing and cooperation, with a very orderly decision process. In the people arena, the focus is upon the importance of people development. Contrast this with productive companies in which information sharing and cooperation are highly valued, but more importantly, values are placed on knowing where you are going and measuring and rewarding performance, which implies that the abilities of people to impact the business rather than the importance of their professional development are what is important.

Not surprisingly, where beliefs about how to manage focus on things that enhance people's status (including them and developing them), people report high satisfaction with their environment. On the other hand, where beliefs on how to manage focus more on setting objectives, making objectives difficult, and holding people accountable for measured performance, the firm is likely to be more productive. In other words, the beliefs that relate most closely to bottom-line performance as measured by five-year annual growth in profits is some combination of these beliefs from both kinds of environments. Consistent with the previous literature on the subject, the values related to participation and cooperation do relate to performance as well as to satisfaction, but it is also important to value having objectives, plans for meeting and measuring them, and

Table 16.2

Survey Items Correlated with Satisfying and Productive Cultural Values

Satisfying	Productive
Information sharing	Information sharing
Good overall communications	Good overall communications
Information available for decisions	Information available for decisions
High interunit cooperation	Good lateral communications
	Information used for decisions
Logical, systematic management	Knowing where you want to go
Decisions made at appropriate levels	Clear organizational goals
Decisions implemented effectively	Defined plans to meet the goals
Few problems with internal management	Formal planning system
	Comprehensive planning system
People development	Measuring and rewarding performance
Opportunities for personal growth	Clear measures of managerial performance
Emphasis placed on development from within	Managers clear about results expected
Talents matched to jobs	Compensation is related to performance
	Benefits are competitive

Source: G. Gordon and B. Goldberg (1977), "Is There a Climate for Success?" *Management Review* (May): 39.

rewarding their accomplishment. This combination of concerns for people and concerns for performance is clearly consistent with the leadership literature. This study suggests that beliefs about how to manage underlie such leadership styles and create organizational or corporate environments that produce or fail to produce the profits sought by the company.

Although these data do not in any way provide a definitive test of the effects of different types of cultures for the financial performance of companies, they do suggest that there are differences that should be further investigated. (We hope to do just that with an updated and expanded version of these data.) Corporate culture does seem to be important for what happens within companies, as well as for how they fare. And, it appears—as the leadership literature has for a long time claimed—that there is an important distinction to be made between people versus production orientation. Further, leadership and management style have usually been looked at as a people issue or as part of a situational analysis oriented to a very micro-level. These data suggest that the people versus production distinction may be influenced by the cultural values of the firm and that these permeate the company. These issues clearly warrant further study. Corporate culture is too important a concept to be allowed to rest on endless variations in conceptualization, rather than examining its consequences under different circumstances and in different types of environments.

References

Administrative Science Quarterly. (1983) Special Issue on Organizational Culture, 28, 3.

Allaire, Y., and M.E. Firsirotu. (1984) "Theories of Organizational Culture." *Organization Studies* 5:193–226.

Althusser, L. (1971) *Lenin and Philosophy and Other Essays*. London: New Left Books.

Alvesson, M. (1987) "Organizations, Culture, and Ideology." *International Studies of Management and Organization* 17:4–18.

Amsa, P. (1986) "Organizational Culture and Work Group Behavior: An Empirical Study." *Journal of Management Studies* 23:347–62.

Andriaansens, H.P.M. (1980) *Talcott Parsons and the Conceptual Dilemma*. London: Routledge & Kegan Paul.

Baird, D., D. Baker, G. Gordon, R. Smoker, and R. Whitney. (1981) "Managing for Performance." Unpublished manuscript. Philadelphia: The Hay Group.

Baker, E.L. (1980) "Managing Organizational Culture." *Management Review* (July): 8–13.

Barley, S.R. (1983) "Semiotics and the Study of Occupational and Organizational Cultures." *Administrative Science Quarterly* 28:393–413.

Barley, S.R., and M.R. Lewis. (1983) "Many in One: Organizations as Multi-cultural Entities." Paper presented at the Annual Meeting of the Academy of Management, Dallas, Texas.

Barnard, C. (1968) *The Functions of the Executive*. Cambridge, MA: Harvard University Press.

Barney, J.B. (1986) "Organizational Culture: Can It Be a Source of Sustained Competitive Advantage?" *Academy of Management Review* 11:656–65.

Bate, P. (1984) "The Impact of Organizational Culture on Approaches to Problem Solving." *Organization Studies* 5, 1:43–66.

Becker, H.S. (1982) "Culture: A Sociological View." *Yale Review* 71:513–27.

Bendix, R. (1956) *Work and Authority in Industry*. Berkeley: University of California Press.

———. (1964) *Nation-building and Citizenship*. New York: Wiley.

Bennis, W., and B. Nanus. (1985) *Leaders: Strategies for Taking Charge*. New York: Harper & Row.

Broms, H., and H. Gahmberg. (1983) "Communication to Self in Organizations and Cultures." *Administrative Science Quarterly* 28:482–95.

Business Week. (1980) "Corporate Culture: The Hard to Change Values That Spell Success or Failure." October 27, pp. 148–60.

———. (1984) "Who's Excellent Now?" November 5.

Carter, P., and N. Jackson. (1987) "Management, Myth, and Metatheory: From Scarcity to Postscarcity." *International Studies of Management and Organization* 17, 3:64–89.

Child, J. (1981) "Culture, Contingency, and Capitalism in the Cross-national Study of Organizations." In L.L. Cummings and B.M. Staw, eds., *Research in Organizational Behavior*, vol. 3, pp. 303–56. Greenwich, CT: JAI Press.

Clark, B. (1972) "The Organizational Saga in Higher Education." *Administrative Science Quarterly* 17:178–84.

Dandridge, T.C., I.I. Mitroff, and W.F. Joyce. (1980) "Organizational Symbolism: A Topic to Expand Organizational Analysis." *Academy of Management Review* (January): 77–82.

Davis, S.M. (1984) *Managing Corporate Culture*. Cambridge, MA: Ballinger.

Deal, T.E., and A. Kennedy. (1982) *Corporate Cultures: The Rites and Rituals of Corporate Life*. Reading, MA: Addison-Wesley.

Denison, D.R. (1984) "Bringing Corporate Culture to the Bottom Line." *Organizational Behavior* 13, 2:5–22.

———. (1988) "Corporate Culture and Organizational Effectiveness." Unpublished manuscript.

DiMaggio, P.J., and W.W. Powell. (1983) "The Iron Cage Revisited: Institutional Isomorphism and Collective Rationality in Organizational Fields." *American Sociological Review* 48, 2:147–60.

DiTomaso, N. (1982) "Sociological Reductionism from Parsons to Althusser: Linking Action and Structure in Social Theory." *American Sociological Review* 47 (February): 14–28.

———. (1985) "The Managed State: Governmental Reorganization in the First Year of the Reagan Administration." In R.G. Braungart and M.M. Braungart, eds., *Research in Political Sociology*, vol. 1, pp. 141–66. Greenwich, CT: JAI Press.

———. (1987) "Symbolic Media and Social Solidarity: The Foundations of Corporate Culture." In S.B. Bacharach and N. DiTomaso, eds., *Research in the Sociology of Organizations*, vol. 5, pp. 105–34. Greenwich, CT: JAI Press.

Drexel, J.A., Jr. (1977) "Organizational Climate: Its Homogeneity within Organizations." *Journal of Applied Psychology* 62, 1:38–42.

Dunn, M.G., D. Norburn, and S. Birley. (1985) "Corporate Culture." *International Journal of Advertising* 4:67–73.

Durkheim, E. (1956) *The Division of Labor in Society*. New York: The Free Press.

Dyer, W.B., Jr. (1982a) "Culture in Organizations: A Case Study and Analysis." Cambridge, MA: Sloan School of Management, MIT, Working Paper #1279–82.

———. (1982b) "Patterns and Assumptions: The Keys to Understanding Organizational Cultures." Report no. TR-ONR–7. Arlington, VA: Office of Naval Research.

———. (1985) "The Cycle of Cultural Evolution in Organizations." In R.H. Kilmann, M.J. Saxton, R. Serpa, et al., eds., *Gaining Control of the Corporate Culture*, pp. 200–29. San Francisco: Jossey-Bass.

Edwards, R.D. (1983) "The Cultural Crisis in Banking." *United States Banker* 94:12–16, 90.

Evered, R. (1983) "The Language of Organizations: The Case of the Navy." In L.R. Pondy, P.J. Frost, G. Morgan, and T.C. Dandridge, eds., *Organizational Symbolism*, vol. 1, pp. 125–43. Greenwich, CT: JAI Press.

Fischer, W., and P. Lundgreen. (1975) "The Recruitment and Training of Administrative and Technical Personnel." In C. Tilly, ed., *The Formation of National States in Western Europe*, pp. 456–561. Princeton, NJ: Princeton University Press.

Fligstein, N. (1985) "The Spread of the Multidivisional Form among Large Firms, 1919–79." *American Sociological Review* 50:377–91.

Fombrum, C.J. (1983) "Corporate Culture, Environment, and Strategy." *Human Resource Management* 22:139–52.

Gagliardi, P. (1986) "The Creation and Change of Organizational Cultures: A Conceptual Framework." *Organization Studies* 7:117–34.

Gerth, H., and C.W. Mills. (1953) *Character and Social Structure*. New York: Harcourt, Brace & World.

Giddens, A. (1979) *Central Problems in Social Theory*. Berkeley: University of California Press.

Glaser, S.R. (1983) "Accessing Organizational Cultures: An Interpretive Approach." Paper presented at the Annual Meeting of the Speech Communication Association, Washington, DC.

Gordon, G.G. (1984) "Corporate Culture in Financial Services." *Bankers Monthly* 10, 12:16–18.

———. (1985) "The Relationship of Corporate Culture to Industry Sector and Corporate Performance." In R.H. Kilmann, M.J. Saxton, R. Serpa, et al., eds., *Gaining Control of the Corporate Culture*, pp. 103–25. San Francisco: Jossey-Bass.

Gordon, G.G., and W. Cummins. (1979) *Managing Management Climate*. Lexington, MA: Lexington Books.

Gordon, G.G., and B. Goldberg. (1977) "Is There a Climate for Success?" *Management Review* 66 (May): 37–44.

Gregory, K.L. (1983) "Native-view Paradigms: Multiple Cultures and Culture Conflicts in Organizations." *Administrative Science Quarterly* 28, 3:359–76.

Handy, C. (1976) *Understanding Organizations*. New York: Penguin.

Harrison, R. (1972) "Understanding Your Organization's Character." *Harvard Business Review* 5, 3:119–28.

Hebden, J.E. (1986) "Adopting an Organization's Culture: The Socialization of Graduate Trainees." *Organizational Dynamics* 15, 1:54–72.

Hitt, M.A., and W.G. Zikmund. (1977) "Organizational Climate: An Empirical Approach to the Perceptual Consensus Question." *Review of Business and Economic Research* 13, 1:59–67.

Holland, J.L. (1985) *Making Vocational Choices: A Theory of Careers*. Englewood Cliffs, NJ: Prentice-Hall.

Jelinek, M., L. Smircich, and P. Hirsch. (1983) "Introduction: A Code of Many Colors." *Administrative Science Quarterly* 28, 3:331–38.

Jenster, P.V., and W.R. Bigler, Jr. (1986) "Organizational Culture in Different Strategic Contexts: A Study in the Banking Industry." Paper presented at the Strategic Management Society Conference on Strategies for Financial Institutions, London.

Johnston, R.H. (1976) "A New Conceptualization of Source of Organizational Climate." *Administrative Science Quarterly* 21:95–103.

Kanter, R. M. (1977) *Men and Women of the Corporation*. New York: Basic Books.

Karpik, L. (1972) "Le Capitalisme Technologique." *Sociologie due Travail* 13 (January–March):2–34.

Kilmann, R.H., M.J. Saxton, R. Serpa, et al., eds. (1985) *Gaining Control of the Corporate Culture*. San Francisco: Jossey-Bass.

Kroeber, A.L., and C. Kluckhohn. (1952) *Culture: A Critical Review of Concepts and Definitions*. Cambridge, MA: Peabody Museum of American Archaeology and Ethnology, Harvard University.

Kroeber, A.L., and T. Parsons. (1958) "The Concepts of Culture and of Social Systems." *American Sociological Review* 23:582–83.

LaFollette, W.R., and H.P. Sims, Jr. (1975) "Is Satisfaction Redundant with Organizational Climate?" *Organizational Behavior and Human Performance* 13:257–78.

Lipsky, M. (1980) *Street-level Bureaucracy*. New York: Russell Sage.

Louis, M.R. (1981) "A Cultural Perspective on Organizations." *Human Systems Management* 2:246–58.

McGoldrick, B. (1984) "Inside the Goldman Sachs Culture." *Institutional Investor* 18, 1:53–67.

Martin, J., M.S. Feldman, M.J. Hatch, and S.B. Sitkin. (1983) "The Uniqueness Paradox in Organizational Stories." *Administrative Science Quarterly* 28:438–53.

Martin, J. and C. Siehl. (1983) "Organizational Culture and Counter-culture: An Uneasy Symbiosis." *Organization Dynamics* 12, 2:52–64.

Mayo, E. (1945) *The Social Problems of an Industrial Civilization.* Cambridge, MA: Harvard University Press.

Meyer, J.W., and B. Rowan. (1977) "Institutionalized Organizations: Formal Structure as Myth and Ceremony." *American Journal of Sociology* 83, 2:340–63.

Muchinsky, P.M. (1976) "An Assessment of the Litwin and Stringer Organizational Climate Questionnaire: An Empirical and Theoretical Extension of the Sims and La-Follette Study." *Personnel Psychology* 29:371–92.

Myerson, D., and J. Martin. (1987) "Cultural Change: An Integration of Three Different Views." *Journal of Management Studies* 24:623–47.

Nathanson, D.A., and J.S. Cassano. (1982) "Organization, Diversity, and Performance." *Wharton Magazine* 6, 4:19–26.

O'Reilly, C. (1983) "Corporations, Culture and Organizational Culture: Lessons from Silicon Valley Firms." Paper presented at the Annual Meetings of the Academy of Management, Dallas, Texas.

Ouchi, W.G., (1982) *Theory Z: How American Business Can Meet the Japanese Challenge.* New York: Avon Books.

Ouchi, W.G. and A. Jaeger. (1978) "Types of Organizations: Stability in the Midst of Mobility." *Academy of Management Review* 2:305–14.

Ouchi, W.G., and J. Johnson. (1978) "Types of Organizational Control and Their Relationship to Emotional Well-being." *Administrative Science Quarterly* 23:293–317.

Parsons, T. (1951) *The Social System.* Glencoe, IL: The Free Press.

———. (1960) *Structure and Process in Modern Societies.* New York: The Free Press.

———. (1968) "On the Concept of Value-commitments." *Sociological Inquiry* 28 (Spring): 135–60.

———. (1968 [1937]) *The Structure of Social Action.* New York: McGraw-Hill.

———. (1973) "Culture and Social System Revisited." In L. Schneider and C.M. Bonjean, eds., *The Idea of Culture in the Social Sciences*, pp. 33–46. Cambridge: Cambridge University Press.

———. (1977) *Social Systems and the Evolution of Action Theory.* New York: The Free Press.

———. (1978) *Action Theory and the Human Condition.* New York: The Free Press.

Pascale, R. (1985) "The Paradox of 'Corporate Culture': Reconciling Ourselves to Socialization." *California Management Review* 27, 2:26–41.

Pascale, R., and A. Athos. (1982) *The Art of Japanese Management: Applications for American Executives.* New York: Warner Books.

Payne, R., S. Fineman, and T.D. Wall. (1976) "Organizational Climate and Job Satisfaction: A Conceptual Synthesis." *Organizational Behavior and Human Performance* 16:45–62.

Payne, R., and R. Mansfield. (1978) "Relationships of Perceptions of Organizational Climate to Organizational Structure, Context, and Hierarchical Position." *Administrative Science Quarterly* 18:515–26.

Payne, R., and D.S. Pugh. (1976) "Organizational Structure and Climate." In M.D. Dunnette, ed., *Handbook of Industrial and Organizational Psychology*, pp. 1125–74. Chicago: Rand McNally.

Pennings, J.M., and G.G. Gresov. (1986) "Technoeconomic and Structural Correlates of Organizational Culture: An Integrative Framework." *Organization Studies* 7:317–34.

Perrow, C. (1979) *Complex Organizations: A Critical Essay.* 2d ed. Glenview, IL: Scott, Foresman.

Peters, L.H., and J.R. Terborg. (1975) "The Effects of Temporal Placement of Unfavorable Information and of Attitude Similarity on Personnel Selection Decisions.'' *Organizational Behavior and Human Performance* 13:279–93.

Peters, T.J. (1978) ''Symbols, Patterns, and Settings: An Optimistic Case for Getting Things Done.'' *Organizational Dynamics* (Autumn):3–23.

Peters, T.J., and R.H. Waterman, Jr. (1982) *In Search of Excellence: Lessons from American's Best-run Companies*. New York: Harper & Row.

Pettigrew, A.M. (1979) ''On Studying Organizational Cultures.'' *Administrative Science Quarterly* 24:570–81.

Pfeffer, J. (1981) ''Management as Symbolic Action: The Creation and Maintenance of Organizational Paradigms.'' In L.L. Cummings and B.M. Staw, eds., *Research in Organizational Behavior*, vol. 3, pp. 1–52. Greenwich, CT: JAI Press.

Pondy, L.R., P.J. Frost, G. Morgan, and T.C. Dandridge, eds. (1983) *Organizational Symbolism*. Vol. 1. Greenwich, CT: JAI Press.

Posner, B.Z., J.M. Kouzes, and W.H. Schmidt. (1985) ''Shared Values Make a Difference: An Empirical Test of Corporate Culture.'' *Human Resource Management* 24:293–309.

Rand, T.M., and K.N. Wexley. (1975) ''Demonstration of the Effect 'Similar to Me' in Simulated Employment Interviews.'' *Psychological Reports* 36:535–44.

Reynierse, J.H., and J.B. Harker. (1986) ''Measuring and Managing Organizational Culture.'' *Human Resource Planning* 9:1–8.

Reynolds, P.D. (1986) ''Organizational Culture as Related to Industry, Position, and Performance: A Preliminary Report.'' *Journal of Management Studies* 23:333–45.

Riley, P. (1983) ''A Structurationist Account of Political Cultures.'' *Administrative Science Quarterly* 28, 3:414–37.

Rogers, E.D., W.G. Miles, Jr., and B.D. Biggs. (1980) ''The Factor Reliability of the Litwin and Stringer Organizational Climate Questionnaire: An Inter- and Intra-organizational Assessment.'' *Journal of Management* 6, 1:65–78.

Saffold, G.S., III. (1988) ''Culture Traits, Strength, and Organizational Performance.'' *Academy of Management Review* 13, 4:546–58.

Sanday, P.R. (1979) ''The Ethnographic Paradigm(s).'' *Administrative Science Quarterly* 24:527–38.

Sapienza, A.M. (1985) ''Believing Is Seeing: How Culture Influences the Decisions Top Managers Make.'' In R.H. Kilmann, M.J. Saxton, R. Serpa, et al., eds., *Gaining Control of the Corporate Culture*, pp. 66–83. San Francisco: Jossey-Bass.

Schein, E.H. (1981) ''Does Japanese Management Style Have a Message for American Managers?'' *Sloan Management Review* 23:55–68.

———. (1983a) ''Organizational Culture: A Dynamic Model.'' Office of Naval Research, Technical Report No. 13, March.

———. (1983b) ''The Role of the Founder in Creating Organizational Culture.'' *Organizational Dynamics* 12, 1:13–28.

———. (1986) *Organizational Culture and Leadership*. San Francisco: Jossey-Bass.

Schneider, B. (1975) ''Organizational Climates: An Essay.'' *Personnel Psychology* 28:447–79.

Schneider, L., and C. Bonjean, eds. (1973) *The Idea of Culture in the Social Sciences*. Cambridge: Cambridge University Press.

Schwartz, H., and S.M. Davis. (1981) ''Matching Corporate Culture and Business Strategy.'' *Organizational Dynamics* (Summer):30–48.

Selznick, P. (1957) *Leadership in Administration*. New York: Harper & Row.

Silverzweig, S., and R.F. Allen. (1976) ''Changing the Corporate Culture.'' *Sloan Management Review* 17:33–49.

Simon, H. (1976 [1945]) *Administrative Behavior*. 3d ed. New York: The Free Press.

Sims, H.P., Jr., and W. LaFollette. (1975) "An Assessment of the Litwin and Stringer Organization Climate Questionnaire." *Personnel Psychology* 28:19–38.

Singer, M. (1968) "The Concept of Culture." In David L. Sills, ed., *International Encyclopedia of the Social Sciences*, vol. 3, pp. 527–43. New York: Macmillan, The Free Press.

Smircich, L. (1983) "Concepts of Culture and Organizational Analysis." *Administrative Science Quarterly* 28:339–58.

Smith, K.K., and V.M. Simmons. (1983) "A Rumpelstiltskin Organization: Metaphors on Metaphors in Field Research." *Administrative Science Quarterly* 28:377–92.

Thompson, J.D. (1967) *Organizations in Action*. New York: McGraw-Hill.

Tilly, C., ed. (1975) *The Formation of National States in Western Europe*. Princeton, NJ: Princeton University Press.

Trice, H.M. (1985) "Rites and Ceremonials in Organizational Culture." In S.B. Bacharach, ed., *Research in the Sociology of Organizations*, vol. 4, pp. 221–70. Greenwich, CT: JAI Press.

Trice, H.M., and J.M. Beyer. (1984) "Studying Organizational Culture through Rites and Ceremonials." *Academy of Management Review* 9:653–69.

Trice, H.M., J.M. Beyer, and D. Morand. (1985) "Climate and Culture: Mutually Exclusive Concepts and Data." Paper presented at the Academy of Management Meetings, Boston.

Tunstall, W.B. (1985) *Disconnecting Parties: Managing the Bell System Break-up—An Inside View*. New York: McGraw-Hill.

Tylor, E.B. (1958 [1871]) *Primitive Culture: Researches into the Development of Mythology, Philosophy, Religion, Art and Custom*. 2 vols. Gloucester, MA: Smith.

Vancil, R.F. (1978) *Decentralization: Ambiguity by Design*. Homewood, IL: Dow Jones-Irwin.

Van Maanen, J. (1979) "The Fact or Fiction of Organizational Ethnography." *Administrative Science Quarterly* 24:539–50.

Vroom, V.R. (1966) "Organizational Choice: A Study of Pre- and Post-decision Processes." *Organizational Behavior and Human Performance* 1:212–26.

Walden, J.C., T.N. Taylor, and J.F. Watkins. (1975) "Organizational Climate: Changes over Time." *Educational Forum* 40:87–93.

Weick, K.E. (1979) *The Social Psychology of Organizing*. 2d ed. Reading, MA: Addison-Wesley.

Wiener, Yoash. (1988) "Forms of Value Systems: A Focus on Organizational Effectiveness and Cultural Change and Maintenance." *Academy of Management Review* 13, 4:522–33.

Wilkins, A.L. (1983) "Organizational Stories as Symbols which Control the Organization." In L.R. Pondy, P.J. Frost, G. Morgan, and T.C. Dandridge, eds., *Organizational Symbolism*, vol. 1, pp. 81–92. Greenwich, CT: JAI Press.

Wilkins, A.L., and W.G. Dyer, Jr. (1988) "Toward Culturally Sensitive Theories of Cultural Change." *Academy of Management Review* 13, 4:534–45.

Wilkins, A.L., and W.G. Ouchi. (1983) "Efficient Cultures: Exploring the Relationship between Culture and Organizational Performance." *Administrative Science Quarterly* 28, 3:468–81.

Wilkins, A.L., and K.J. Patterson. (1985) "You Can't Get There from Here: What Will Make Culture-change Projects Fail?" In R.H. Kilmann, M.J. Saxton, R. Serpa, et al., eds., *Gaining Control of the Corporate Culture*, pp. 262–91. San Francisco: Jossey-Bass.

Woodman, R.W., and D.C. King. (1978) "Organizational Climate: Science or Folklore?" *Academy of Management Review* 3:816–26.

Wrong, D. (1961) ''The Oversocialized Conception of Man in Modern Sociology.'' *American Sociological Review* 26:187–93.

Zucker, L.G. (1983) ''Organizations as Institutions.'' In S.B. Bacharach, ed., *Research in the Sociology of Organizations*, vol. 2, pp. 1–47. Greenwich, CT: JAI Press.

VII

Boundaries

17

JOSEPH L. BADARACCO, JR.

The Boundaries of the Firm

Do firms have boundaries? In one sense, the answer is: not really. Nations, states, and backyards have boundaries, the skin is more or less the boundary of the body, but no one ever sees or touches or steps across the boundaries of a firm. The phrase "the boundaries of the firm" does appear in many articles and books, but only in a loose, figurative way. It simply conveys the commonsense notion that government bodies, competitors, and markets are somehow "outside" a firm, while managers, employees, equipment, and inventory are more or less "inside" it.

Why then write (or read) an essay, like this one, dealing exclusively and systematically with the boundaries of the firm? Three propositions give the answer. First, the classic literatures of economics, organization theory, and business administration have made a vital but tacit assumption: that firms do have boundaries, that these boundaries are fairly well defined and sometimes quite sharp, and that they should be this way. Second, this assumption cannot remain tacit, and therefore unexamined, because it is inaccurate and misleading, sometimes profoundly so. Third, efforts to explore the boundaries of firms may significantly alter our thinking about firms, management, economics, and the social role of business organizations.

Recently, scholars in several disciplines have begun to explore the peripheral regions of firms, and they have drawn partial maps of this territory. But these sketches are not like familiar modern maps that meticulously display cities, topography, roads, political divisions, and that present each part of a territory in realistic relationship to the whole. Instead, they resemble pictures of the earth drawn in the middle ages, before the voyages of discovery and exploration. These showed the earth as a flat disk surrounded by water. Land areas around the Mediterranean and in eastern and central Asia were accurately represented, but territories nearer the periphery were only partially charted. Our modern picture of the world emerged in the following centuries as new technology, such as the compass and instruments of astronomy, and voyages of discovery led to knowledge that mapmakers integrated into ever more precise pictures of the earth.

Like early cartography, thinking in economics, organization theory, and business administration is changing as new intellectual tools and recent studies examine the boundaries of firms. Law, international relations, and game theory have also suggested important new perspectives. But each of these is a special-purpose map: no overarching general map of the boundary regions has emerged. Nevertheless, one broad trend stands out: the realization that this territory is a broad, complex, and important sphere of social, economic, organizational, and managerial activity. And, since conceptions of firms' boundaries are difficult to separate from conceptions of the firm itself, the newer maps invite reexamination of familiar ideas about the core of the firm, the traditional managerial domain generally thought to have been accurately charted.

This essay examines the leading works in the literatures mentioned in the last paragraph, concentrating on what they have said and what they now say, not about firms and markets or about firms and their environments, but about the region in between. The first section presents what I call the classic map of the firm. This is a constellation of powerful, deeply rooted ideas about firms and their boundaries. The second section explains why the classic map must be redrawn, and the third section sketches a way of doing so that draws upon both classic and recent ideas about the firm and its boundaries. The last section discusses the implications of this new map.

The Classic Map of the Firm and Its Boundaries

The familiar and intellectually dominant way of thinking about firms is to distinguish firms and markets or, following Oliver Williamson (1975), to distinguish markets and hierarchies. More vividly, firms have been described as islands of planned coordination surrounded by a sea of market relations (Richardson 1972, p. 883). Firms' boundaries play no role in any of these familiar characterizations. Yet, if one approaches various literatures with two questions in mind—do firms have boundaries, and do those boundaries matter?—a long, full, complex answer emerges, and one discovers the importance of tacit assumptions about boundaries to our familiar ways of thinking and theorizing about firms, their behavior, and their management. The answer to the two questions is that firms do have boundaries, that these boundaries do matter, and that they should be sharp. But the importance of these questions and answers cannot be fully grasped without understanding the origins, the intellectual and practical power, the protean versatility, and the complexity of the ostensibly simple idea that a firm is a sphere of activity whose bounds are demarcated fairly sharply.

I have called this idea the classic map of the firm. Like a map, it communicates by highlighting essential features and stripping away detail, and it also provides guidance, in this case to managers and public-policy makers. The map is classic in the sense that it represents old, enduring, powerful ideas.

On this conceptual map, firms' boundaries demarcate a sphere characterized by managerial discretion, ownership, property rights, hierarchical organization structure, common purpose, norms and values, and concentrated political and economic power. These features define the core of the firm. Boundaries separate the firm, not only from other firms, but from government agencies, labor unions, universities, and the other organizations within a society. They also separate the firm from its environment. After all, if there were no separation, then our familiar, working distinctions between firms and markets and between firms and environments would be ambiguous if not meaningless. The same literatures also answer the question of whether boundaries matter. Well-defined boundaries encourage risk taking, support efficient allocation of society's resources, encourage the efficient management of firms' resources, protect society against the economic and political abuses that can arise when firms—especially large ones—band together, protect owners and managers from infringement on their rights by outside groups, and clarify legal, moral, and economic responsibilities within society.

The twin assumptions that firms have boundaries and that they should be kept sharp is perhaps the most important *tacit* assumption in our conventional thinking about firms. Even though this view of the firm seems to be mainly a matter of economics, its power and its deep, almost intuitive familiarity arise from its roots in ideas and experiences that are the wellsprings of Anglo-American political philosophy. Its origins precede modern economic thought and have almost nothing to do with the notion of a firm as a sphere of coordination surrounded by competitive markets.

The deepest layer of ideas rests in Roman law and political life. Roman law recognized the existence of bodies called *collegia,* which correspond to our modern corporations in two fundamental ways. First, they had rights and duties of their own that were separate from those of their members. In this way, a *collegium* was treated as a person with its own identity. Second, unlike a person, the *collegium* could exist in perpetuity, even if all its members changed. These two characteristics created legal and conceptual boundaries that separated the *collegia* from their members and from other bodies in society. Some Roman *collegia*, called trade societies, were precursors of modern business firms, but the most important were public governing bodies, religious societies, and official societies, such as the scribes employed by the state. Thus, the earliest stratum of thinking about business firms or, more precisely, about their early forerunners, was a broad way of depicting civil, religious, as well as economic activity, and one that drew a legal boundary line around organizations and set them off as spheres of special rights and duties.[1]

Another way of drawing boundaries around spheres of commercial activity appeared more than half a millennium after the fall of Rome, when money reappeared and trade slowly reemerged within the Mediterranean. During the ninth and tenth centuries, in a few coastal Italian cities, small trading companies appeared. They were soon followed, in inland areas, by other commercial groups called *compagnie* in Italian. Their name, which literally means a group that breaks bread together, reflects the fact that these were usually family enterprises. Moreover, the members of the trading firms and *compagnie* shared full liability for the enterprise—all their worldly belongings were at risk. Hence, two dimensions came to distinguish members of ''businesses'' from nonmembers: family ties and a share in an enterprise's liabilities (Braudel 1986, pp. 434–37).

The next stratum of ideas about firms' boundaries originated in Britain, not the Mediterranean, and was political rather than commercial. In the centuries after the Norman conquest, the Anglo-Saxons had struggled to regain control over their land. They ultimately gained the right to buy, hold, and sell their land, and later the right to meet their feudal obligations through payments in cash. The possession of property came to be associated with security against external force: in William Pitts's phrase, ''The poorest man in his cottage may bid defiance to all the force of the Crown.'' In a fundamental sense, ownership of property defined a boundary around a sphere of political and personal security. Only later, in the fourteenth and fifteenth centuries, did property come to be associated with economic opportunity, as commoners sought ways, especially through commerce, to improve their lot and shake off the constraints of guilds, government, and the church. Ultimately, under Elizabeth I, the descendants of these early entrepreneurs succeeded in securing the Statute of Monopolies of 1623 that limited conspiracies, combinations, and other monopolies of trade. Thus, 200 years before the birth of Adam Smith, the English had associated individual commercial initiative, control of property, freedom from external intervention, and limits on the monopolization of trade.

Later, the classical economists—Adam Smith, David Ricardo, and John Stuart Mill—added yet another layer of thinking about firms and their boundaries, but they did so implicitly, almost accidentally. This is because the classical economists developed a theory of markets, not a theory of firms or their boundaries. Their preoccupation with markets reflected the revolutionary economic transformation underway while they wrote. The Industrial Revolution in Great Britain was accompanied by the creation of a self-regulating market in which small economic units, run and owned by their managers, coordinated their dealings with each other through market transactions, rather than the rules and norms of guilds, social or village custom, family ties, or the power of royalty and nobility. These burgeoning marketplace transactions captivated economists, a preoccupation reflected today in economics textbook descriptions of a firm as a black box or a production function.

Firms, the atomic units of competitive markets, were small, familiar, and uninteresting. In *The Wealth of Nations*, Adam Smith (1976) discusses the economics of land, money, value, and capital; he ranges widely to discuss government, taxes, trade, and colonies; but in nearly 600 pages he treats firms only in passing references to farms, collieries, and apothecaries. In general, organizations of almost any kind remain invisible, with the exception of the Bank of

England, the British government, and its royally chartered trading companies. Similarly, in *The Principles of Political Economy and Taxation*, David Ricardo (1926, p. 49) mentions clothiers, hat makers, mines, and farms; the largest firm to which he refers, solely as a brief illustration, is a manufacturer with 100 employees. Firms and organizations also languish unnoticed in the 600 pages of John Stuart Mill's *Principles of Political Economy* written in 1848 (Mill 1871). The question of how to organize and manage these small units was too simple to merit attention. They were run, generally by their owners, on a hands-on, day-to-day basis.

Boundaries around firms did matter, however, to the classical economists. They demarcated the boundary of the firm—not through legal rights and duties, family membership and liability, ownership of property, or freedom from external intervention, but in terms of managerial discretion. Outside the firm, markets set prices and allocated resources. Inside the firm, the owner-managers of mills, hat makers, and apothecaries made decisions about how to respond to market forces. The firm "stopped" at the point where managers' discretion to make decisions stopped and where market allocation began. Through their ideas, the classical economists transformed thinking about firms' boundaries from a mainly legal and political question into an economic one as they worked out the powerful view that firms were competing, bounded spheres of managerial control disciplined by surrounding markets. In this way, classic economic theory made the classic map of the firm and its boundaries enormously more persuasive.

Neoclassical economics did so as well. In *Principles of Economics*, first published in 1890, Alfred Marshall does discuss firms at length: he explicitly distinguishes large firms from small ones, presents the advantages of large-scale operations, and devotes an entire chapter to "business management" in which he discusses leadership, the separation of ownership from management, and company financial policies (Marshall 1961, pp. 291–313). He also treats the German cartels, profit-sharing cooperatives, and the trusts in the United States, but he does not comment on the ways in which joint management and joint ownership distinguish these forms of organization and economic enterprise from ordinary sharply bounded businesses (pp. 282, 304, 306). Marshall seems to suppose, although he never states it in so many words, that ownership of property and management control define the boundary line between what is inside a firm and what is outside.

Just as Marshall was writing, firms' boundaries became an urgent practical concern for politicians, government officials, and business executives. The watershed was the rise of truly large business firms during the last part of the nineteenth century. In the United States, these firms, initially the interstate railroads, sought to cooperate with each other to limit capacity and maintain prices. These efforts took various forms: tacit collusion, cartels, pools, and trusts, and coordination through industry associations.[2] Through these arrangements, business managers often agreed to *share authority* over strategic decisions, pricing, capital investment, and other critical areas. In the view of economists, this blurring of firms' boundaries destroyed market discipline. For small business and many small towns, it led to abuse of economic and political power.

The Sherman, Clayton, and other antitrust acts aimed to pare back the power and influence of large firms and sharpen their boundaries. Separate businesses, of course, remained free to contract with each other, so long as they did not combine in a conspiracy against trade. Keeping the boundaries of large firms sharp became a vital social, political, and economic issue. Samuel Eliot Morison portrays this perspective vividly:

> The Federal Government was at the summit of a pyramid of corruption in the Northern States. . . . Jim Fisk and Jay Gould polluting the Erie Railroad by stock watering. . . . Collis P. Huntington buying the California legislature and bribing the Congressmen to promote transcontinental railroad interests; Peter Widener, obtaining street railway franchises by bribing aldermen; John D. Rockefeller, using strong-arm methods when chicanery failed to build his Standard Oil empire. These were the conspicuous examples in the middle tier of this indecent pyramid, the lower courses of which were built by a sordid alliance between liquor, prostitution, and city police. [Morison 1965, p. 732]

But these social, ethical, and political concerns about firms' boundaries were not simply a return to earlier perspectives. In Elizabethan England, boundaries defined by property protected its owners against the power of kings and prelates. Now, sharp boundaries were needed to rein in the aggregations of economic and political power in giant firms and to protect the rest of society against the actions of the owners of these giant private properties. As on early navigational maps, which marked the uncharted periphery of the earth with zephyrs, monsters, and lions, the boundary regions of firms were now marked for public-policy makers as regions of hazard.

This perspective drew upon deep ideological wellsprings in the United States, a nation whose political institutions and traditions reflected deep fears of collusion among large units, whether economic or political. The sweep of U.S. antitrust policy ultimately grew much broader and targeted not only trusts and cartels, but also joint ventures, licensing arrangements, retail price maintenance, signaling, tie-ins, and many other practices that diminished or replaced arm's length relations among firms (Brodley 1982). Fear of the power of giant business organizations also motivated the creation of independent regulatory agencies. In principle, these were intended to protect the public interest from private interests of powerful firms through arm's length, independent, nonpartisan regulation.[3]

During the twentieth century, the classic map of the firm became a dominating intellectual paradigm. Two literatures, those of organization theory and business administration, evolved new ways of defining firms' boundaries and explaining the merits of keeping them sharp.

The path of exploration taken in the organizational literature has been the opposite of that of economists whose preoccupation was markets, not firms. The organizational literature originated in studies of the inner regions of firms, and only later did it examine firms' external relations and their environments. The starting point of this evolution is the description of bureaucracy developed by Max Weber, the modern intellectual pioneer of organizational theory. His ideal organizational type was independent of its environment and defined exclusively in terms of internal features: specialization, roles assigned by technical competence, a hierarchy of authority, standard operating procedures, and clear specification of the duties and authority of each member of an organization.[4] During the 1920s, writing on organizations stressed the so-called principles of management. These gave executives straightforward advice on running their companies—through sharp lines of authority, tight control systems, and clearly defined responsibilities. An almost exclusively internal perspective, preoccupied with hierarchical control and formal accountability, dominated this era of thinking about organizations.

The idea that firms had boundaries and that these should be sharp lay implicit, but just barely so, in this line of thinking. Its tacit definition of a firm's boundaries was formal and organizational, rather than political, economic, or legal. A person was "inside" an organization when he or she had an assigned role in its formal structure, was explicitly accountable to someone else, and behaved according to the organization's standard procedures. The firm stopped at the point where formal, hierarchical structures stopped. An organization chart displayed a firm's boundaries.

The importance of boundaries defined by hierarchical control was apparent in both the literature of organization theory and the literature of business administration. The latter includes the reports of business managers, consultants, business school academics, and business historians. Their principal aim has been descriptive. They have not sought, through abstraction and parsimony, to theorize about firms or markets or boundaries. Rather, they have aimed to chronicle important developments, tell accurate stories of their work as executives, give cautious advice, or suggest modest, middle-level generalizations. *My Years with General Motors* by Alfred P. Sloan (1972) typifies much of the American literature of business administration. It presents the actions, reflections, and implicit recommendations of one of the most important business executives of this century.

The book also displays the logic of hierarchical control. In describing his pathbreaking 1920 plan for reorganizing General Motors, Sloan wrote: "The responsibility of the chief executive of each operation shall in no way be limited. Each such organization headed by its chief executive shall be complete in every necessary function and able to exercise its full initiative and logical development" (p. 57). Putting a "boss" in charge of an operation, giving him the power to secure information and implement decisions, and holding him accountable for results proved to be a powerful way to accomplish many economic tasks.

Hierarchical control mattered at the shop-floor level of organization as well as in executive offices. Frederick W. Taylor, in effect, coupled Weber's principles with the techniques of time and motion studies and sought to transform the factory into a carefully controlled and monitored continuous processing operation. In 1911, in the *Principles of Scientific Management*, Taylor wrote: "In the past, the man has been first; in the future the system must be first."[5] At the Ford Motor Company, Henry Ford applied both the managerial and shop-floor approaches to hierarchical control and created an industrial engine that awed the world.

The logic of marking off a firm as a sphere of hierarchical control is not a cultural artifact peculiar to America or to western nations. Managerial control through a clearly defined hierarchy of authority has a rationale of its own. It rests upon the need to control the high-volume throughput of manufactured goods that was made possible by technological developments and the emergence of large national markets at the end of the nineteenth century. Management hierarchies, sophisticated cost accounting and scheduling systems, and clear reporting responsibilities enabled the "visible hand" of management to be more efficient than the invisible hand of markets in certain industries. This occurred in the same capital-intensive industries in other countries, albeit at different times, indicating the advantages of strict hierarchical controls in certain industries (Chandler 1986).

A second set of ideas, embedded in the classic map of the firm, also originates in the literatures of organization theory and business administration—but as an act of rebellion against the notion of the firm as a formal, rational, technology-driven hierarchy. The alternative depicts firms as communities, bound together by shared values, social norms, and common purpose. These ideas originate in the writings of Ferdinand Tonnies, the German sociologist who distinguished between two fundamentally different social entities. One he called a *gesellschaft*. This group is formed consciously and is fundamentally a mechanism designed to achieve a specific objective. Its value depends on how well it does so. The other kind of group, a *gemeinschaft*, arises from habit, mutual sympathy, or common belief, and it is valued as an end in itself. Neighborhoods, religious bodies, and towns are examples of *gemeinschaft* (Tonnies 1957, pp. 16–28). Philip Selznick (1957) applied these ideas to firms and other bodies in *Leadership in Administration* in 1957, contrasting the view of an organization as an "expendable tool" or technical-economic instrument with viewing it as a "valued source of personal satisfaction" for its members (pp. 17, 93–94). Many others have mined these themes. The most popular versions are the descriptions of Japanese companies and certain of their practices, such as lifetime employment, that bind members of these firms into tight, social communities. A Japanese scholar recently described his nation's firms as "capsules" to emphasize that, as social units, they are closed societies that provide full ways of life for their members (Tsuchiya 1979). Running through all of these perspectives is the clear, though tacit, premise that firms do have boundaries and that they are social, defined not by actual family ties as in the Italian *compagnie*, but by shared norms and values, common purpose, and long, familiar association.

The final stratum underlying the classic map of firms' boundaries lies in American contract law. As such, its roots reach back to the early Roman *collegia*, which had the right to contract with others; to the classic economists, such as John Stuart Mill, who recognized the right of owners to acquire and dispose of assets through contracts; and to the antitrust-minded guardians of giant firms' boundaries, who sought to distinguish acceptable contracts among firms from unacceptable ones that restrained trade. Classical contract law aims to facilitate exchanges among separate parties (Macneil 1978). It does so through the creation of formal, legal documents that clearly specify the rights and obligations of the parties and that state explicitly what remedies will apply in the event that a party fails to perform according to the terms of the contract. What matters in classic contracting is a discrete transaction between two parties, not broader personal, social, or political relationships. As such, classical contracting is analogous to the sorts of exchanges that take place between firms or between firms and employees under laissez faire or free markets. And as such, classical contracting draws another boundary around a firm, one defined by clear, precise, discrete agreements that specify obligations sharply and leave the parties free to act as they please, outside the limits of the contract.

Such contracting clearly demarcates spheres of rights and autonomy. Within these contractually specified limits, managers can respond to market forces, exercise discretion, manage their hierarchies, develop the social cohesiveness of their firms, exercise their rights, and perform their duties as officers of their corporations. Precisely crafted legal rules delineate relationships, not only between firms, but also between firms and government bodies, labor unions, employees, managers, and others. They specify what activities firm managers have the right to coordinate. For example, postwar labor relations in the auto, steel, and coal industries in the United States developed within the interstices of long, elaborate, formal agreements on wages, conditions, and work rules negotiated by company and union hierarchies.[6]

The classical map of the firm and its boundaries is, of course, an ideal type. Like a map, and unlike an aerial photograph, it presents a stylized version of reality. But this map accurately describes wide stretches of the economic landscape; if it did not, then it would be much more difficult to account for the intellectual and practical hegemony it has exercised over thinking about firms in the United States. The classic map of the firm portrays economic reality for the millions of small businesses and sole proprietorships that have, for nearly two centuries, been the most common (though not the largest or most powerful) economic units in developed countries. The map has also described many large firms accurately. During the 1960s, both General Motors and IBM were vast, independent citadels—spheres of managerial discretion and hierarchical control buffered against external intervention by their vast economic, political, technical, and market power.

Because the classic map is realistic, and because its roots are intertwined with our social, political, and legal heritage, it is an utterly familiar and natural part of our way of thinking about firms, about markets, and, implicitly, about the boundaries that separate firms from other organizations, economic and noneconomic, in society. Boundaries matter because they demarcate a peculiar sphere—defined by some constellation of ownership, property rights, financial liabilities, managerial discretion, hierarchical control, concentrated economic and political power, communal norms and values, and rights and obligations defined by law and contract. Moreover, when this core area of the firm is set off by well-defined boundaries, a wide range of economic, social, political, and ethical ends are well served.

The Rationale for a New Map

During the next decade or so, a new map of the firm will replace the old one. What will distinguish the new map from its predecessors will be its attention to firms' boundaries. The new map of the firm will emerge for precisely the reasons why new maps of the earth began to appear half a millennium ago: powerful intellectual tools (counterparts of the compass and new instruments of astronomy) and recent empirical explorations have provided important new information. The intellectual tools have been the open system theory of the firm and institutional economics. The empirical studies have taken researchers first to Japan and then, ironically, back to the United States. In both cases, they have made important discoveries about firms' boundaries.

The new intellectual tools and the empirical studies undermine both the descriptive accuracy and the prescriptive guidelines of the classic map of the firm. Modern organization theory treats firms as open systems, in particular as open social and political systems. Hence, firms' boundaries cannot be viewed as sharp, for a firm, as a system, is deeply embedded in other, broader systems. It depends upon them, their influences penetrate deeply into the "core" of the firm, and the firm and its members extend their influence far outside the boundaries drawn by the classic map. The empirical studies of Japan and the United States demonstrate that firms' boundaries are often quite blurry. Moreover, evidence indicates that the boundaries of many U.S. firms are becoming even more complex, rendering the classic map less and less accurate. Finally, the studies of Japan and the new institutional economics attack the prescriptive guidelines embedded in the classic map of the firm. Institutional economics helps to explain theoretically what the Japanese economic miracle has demonstrated in practice: that sharp boundaries around firms are not necessarily the most efficient or the most competitive form of industrial organization.

Hence, the assault on the classic map of the firm is massive. It is theoretical as well as practical. It does not originate simply from one line of theory or the experience of a single country. Above all, as the rest of this section shows, the new intellectual tools and empirical studies reexamine, transform, and sometimes completely abandon each of the powerful ideas underlying the classic map of the firm.

Firms as Open Social Systems

The open system theory of the firm has overthrown the simple notion of a firm as a sphere of activity sheltered from external influence and intervention, and defined by formal, hierarchical arrangements, shared norms and values, and an aggregation of economic and political power deployed by a firm's executives. This attack on the received notions about the firm falls into two phases.

The first attack issued from a single, central, seminal idea: the idea that organizations, including firms, are open social systems. This conceptualization parts company with the classic notions of the firm at the level of first principles. It does not start with firms and markets as givens. Rather, it supposes that all organizations actually consist of subunits, that relationships link these units into systems (some of which we call firms), and—most importantly for our purposes—that organizations are deeply enmeshed through these relationships in many broader systems—social, economic, technical, informational, symbolic, and political. By conceptualizing firms as bundles of relationships, the open system theory of the firm invites researchers and theory builders to specify just what these relationships are. This challenge, implicit in the writings of Talcott Parsons during the 1950s and early 1960s, has ramified outward, like force spreading from the center of a powerful earthquake, to transform a vast body of literature.[7]

The literature of organization theory has been directly and profoundly influenced by Parsons's ideas.[8] And it is this literature, taken as a whole, that forms the second powerful attack on the classic map of the firm. Modern organizational theory is extraordinarily capacious. It draws upon economics, political science, sociology, social psychology, and other disciplines to buttress its concepts. Its intellectual leaders have aimed to describe and explain phenomena affecting all organizations, not just firms. Their units of analysis include individuals, small groups, formal organization structures, power, and culture. Through dozens of books and hundreds of articles, organizational theorists had taken Parsons's broad, sweeping, abstract conceptualization of firms as open social systems and specified it, operationalized it, tested it, and extended it on a vast scale. By the 1980s, this protean body of ideas and writings suggested a powerful, central idea: *that firms' boundary regions are, in effect, full-fledged forms of organization, just as complex and important as the core areas of the firm.*

In describing the complex links between firms and other, broader systems, the organizational literature loosens or utterly abandons three of the classic ways of distinguishing firms from their broader environments. These are the views that the firm is a unit whose boundaries are marked off by formal, hierarchical control, by social systems, and the aggregations of economic and political power.

Instead of using hierarchical control and formal organization to define an organization and its boundaries, recent books and articles have drawn maps of firms' boundaries as networks of formal and informal relationships. The literature on organizations now provides many analytical schemes for specifying, or even measuring, the many mechanisms linking organizations. These include homogeneity (the similarity of the linked organizations), stability, the length of time the parties have been linked, the distribution of resources among the parties, the size of the network, and "domain consensus," the degree to which the linked organizations shared common goals. Other approaches include the degree of formalization of the exchanges between the parties; the intensity of the involvement, as defined by the resources each party spends on linkages; reciprocity, the degree to which the exchanges are based on mutual agreement or are dominated unilaterally by one of the parties; and the degree to which the exchanges have been standardized.[9]

Second, the modern literature on organizations moves beyond the classic notion of a firm as a social capsule, demarcated by shared norms, values, and goals. The literature does not reject this conceptualization, but rather argues for a much broader, more inclusive perspective. All open social systems—families, towns, societies, and so forth—influence their environment or are influenced by it, and engage in social exchanges with it. The literature of organization theory has interpreted the boundaries of open social systems in terms of membership, behavior, and social exchange. None of these approaches leaves the classical notion of firms' social boundaries undisturbed. For example, in their analysis of membership as a way of defining firms' boundaries, Daniel Katz and Robert Kahn (1966, p. 122) conclude bluntly:

> Some organizations are characterized by sharply defined, rigid boundaries. Entrance into such systems and exit from them are not the decisions of the individuals who seek admittance or who seek to leave. The U.S. Army represents one extreme of a closed organization. At the other extreme would be the major political parties in the U.S. . . . Between these extremes . . . exist many degrees of openness and tightness . . . an industrial organization is a semi-voluntary system.

Two other theorists, Jeffrey Pfeffer and Gerald Salancik, have used behavior rather than membership as the way of thinking about firms' boundaries. They acknowledge that, abstractly, "the organization ends where its discretion (ability to initiate, maintain, or end behavior) ends and another begins." But, in practice, they describe an organization as essentially a system of "interlocked behavior" and stress that organizations influence or control only some of the behavior of their members, even when these are full-time, long-term employees. Early childhood experience, families, labor unions, communities, and the political allegiances of members also influence behavior (Pfeffer and Salancik 1978, p. 31).

Finally, obligations derived from social exchange blur the boundaries of firms. This matters because social exchange, unlike the economic exchange on which the classic map of the firm is based, can create a complex social fabric linking separate organizations. Peter Blau, in *Exchange in Power and Social Life*, writes:

> The basic and most crucial distinction is that social exchange entails unspecified obligations. The prototype of an economic transaction rests upon a formal contract that stipulates the exact quantities to be exchanged. . . . Social exchange involves favors that create diffuse future obligations, not precisely specified ones and the nature of the return cannot be bargained about but must be left to the discretion of the one who makes it. . . . Only social exchange tends to engender feelings of personal obligation, gratitude, and trust; purely economic exchange does not . . . the benefits involved in social exchange do not have an exact price in terms of a single quantitative medium of exchange. . . . Since social benefits have no exact price, and since the utility of a given benefit cannot be clearly separated from that of other rewards derived from a social association, it seems difficult to apply the economic principles of maximizing utility to social exchange. [Blau 1964, pp. 91–92]

As spheres of social exchange, organizations' boundaries may grow so complex that they become social systems of their own with norms, obligations, and influences that may rival those of the organizations to which individuals belong. Employees of a joint venture may become more loyal to the venture itself than to the parent organizations.

Finally, modern organizational literature does not treat firms simply as separate spheres of economic and political power. It recognizes that firms and their managers do seek autonomy, aim to control critical resources, and prefer to pursue their own aims. Sociologist James Thompson writes that firms "seek to place their boundaries around those activities which if left to the task environment would be crucial contingencies" (1967, p. 132). Mass production firms that need to operate near full capacity use vertical integration to control a crucial contingency, the supply of raw materials. Inevitably, however, many activities will fall outside the boundaries of firms. Hence, they must adopt a second set of tactics to reduce dependency and control uncertainty. Some of these are internal: they plan, forecast, create buffer inventories, and schedule in anticipation of external shocks.

Other approaches blur the boundaries of the firm—through efforts to coopt other parties, develop coalitions, bargain with other parties, or create a negotiated environment. These arrangements do not create interdependence;[10] they acknowledge its existence. Interdependence is the base condition, proceeding and explaining formal mechanisms and social devices intended to buffer uncertainty and expand a firm's power. Fundamentally and inescapably, firms are dependent upon other organizations and immersed in wide-reaching webs of interdependence.[11]

Japan

The idea that firms' boundary regions are often full-fledged, complex forms of organization is confirmed by the industrial landscape of postwar Japan. The classic map of the firm does not describe this terrain; the view of the firm as an open social system does. Richard Caves and Masu Uekusa (1976, p. 495) describe Japanese firms as enmeshed in a "thick and complex skein of relations matched in no other country."

Complex relationships link Japanese firms with other firms, with labor unions, and with government agencies.[12] Industrial policy has linked important Japanese firms with the Ministry of Finance, the Economic Planning Agency, and the Ministry of International Trade and Industry. In the 1950s and 1960s, these agencies intervened systematically in the strategic decisions and financing of important firms through explicit controls on credit, foreign exchange, technology licensing, and exports and imports as well as gentle administrative guidance. During the last ten years, as Japanese firms have grown more successful and powerful, and as Japan has acceded to international pressures to liberalize its economy, these "strong" forms of industrial policy have given way to subtler, gentler ways of harmonizing company decisions with government economic goals.

Japanese firms have been closely enmeshed with their suppliers of capital in two ways: until recently, their debt equity ratios have been extremely high by U.S. standards, and banks often hold shares in firms that they finance. Japanese firms and their labor unions have genuinely symbiotic relationships. Under the system of enterprise unionism, Japanese workers organize themselves on a company-by-company basis. Relations between firms and their unions are close, generally very cooperative, and often paternalistic. James Abegglen has written, "The trade union and the kaisha [the Japanese firm] are coterminous . . . the union does not exist as an entity separate from, or with an adversarial relationship to the company" (Abegglen and Stalk 1985, p. 205).

Finally, exploration of Japanese industrial organization has revealed an extraordinary form of collective industrial endeavor known as enterprise groups or *keiretsu.* These pervade Japanese economic life: keiretsu firms control roughly a third of Japan's industrial assets. There are two sorts of keiretsu in contemporary Japan. One is a successor to the *zaibatsu,* the giant conglomerates that dominated Japanese industrial life for most of the first half of this century. Mitsui, Sumitomo, and Mitsubishi were the most famous and powerful of these. Their member firms included banks, insurance companies, light and heavy industrial firms, and overseas trading companies. The U.S. occupation broke up the zaibatsu to disperse their economic and political power, but many of the original groups later reemerged, although with much looser and more informal ties among members. Presidents of member companies meet regularly, often monthly; the boards of directors of member firms interlock; and firms own small fractions of each other's shares. They rely more heavily on banks and other financial institutions within their groups for loans, and they buy and sell goods from each other more frequently than from firms outside their groups. Long-established keiretsu such as Mitsui, whose origins may be traced to the early seventeenth century, also bind their member firms together through deep social ties.[13]

The second kind of keiretsu is represented by large manufacturing firms like Toyota and Hitachi. These manufacturers stand at the apex of a hierarchy of primary, secondary, and tertiary suppliers. The firms in each tier remain legally separate, but they are linked through semipermanent arrangements, such as minority equity ownership, interlocking directorates, financial aid in the form of trade credits, loans, and credit guarantees that the parent gives its subsidiaries, and the provision of personnel and technological guidance by the peak firm. Above all, each tier of the hierarchy purchases a high fraction of the outputs from its subordinate suppliers.[14]

The complex networks around Japanese firms subvert our conventional ways of thinking about firms and their boundaries *because of Japan's economic success.* A historian has called the Japanese postwar economic miracle "the most remarkable economic progress in the history of the world" (McCraw 1986, p. viii). The constellation of institutional arrangements linking firms, labor unions, government agencies, and other institutions of Japanese life helped the nation adapt to the postwar explosion of technology, to the oil shocks of the 1970s, and in the last two years, to the intense pressures created by the rising value of the yen. Japan's *success* matters to our thinking about firms because, in and of themselves, the complex links between Japanese firms and other institutions of Japanese society are hardly novel. Large, powerful business groups, like the keiretsu, are found in Mexico, Colombia, India, the Philippines, and many other countries (Strachan 1976). Throughout their histories, many European countries have promoted economic activity through state ownership, subsidies, cartels, protection, and administrative guidance—all of which obscure the boundaries between states and firms and between public and private enterprise.

Japan's success matters because it has been achieved at the expense of so much of our conventional economic thinking. The theory of comparative advantage (which originated at the same time and among the same thinkers as some of the central ideas in the classic map of the firm) dictated that Japan, after World War II, should have concentrated on textiles and light manufacturing rather than seek to become a world-scale industrial giant. Its firms do not compete for funds in deep, arm's length capital markets. Above all, in the second most important economy in the world, the boundaries of firms have been blurred rather than sharp. The result, in part, seems to have been extraordinary economic success, rather than infringement upon the rights of property, intrusion in managerial decision making, erosion of hierarchical control, and inefficiency arising from collusion among giant firms.

The Blurring Boundaries of U.S. Firms

The third challenge to the classic map of the firm is ironic: it springs from the discovery that the classic map no longer describes many American firms. More and more U.S. firms are blurring their boundaries through complex relationships with other organizations.

Some firms doing this are giants that operated for decades as independent citadels. In 1966, General Motors stated that "unified ownership for coordinated policy control of all of its operations throughout the world is essential for its effective performance as a worldwide corporation" (General Motors Corporation 1966, p. 3). Twenty years later, GM had formed a joint venture with Toyota, its most formidable Japanese adversary, and owned shares in two other Japanese car firms, Suzuki and Isuzu. It had three joint ventures with Daewoo, a Korean conglomerate; close relations with ten robotics makers around the world, including a joint venture with Fanuc, the world's dominant numerical controls company; and a range of other linkups with Nissan and Hitachi. Through pathbreaking agreements with the United Auto Workers, GM had begun a new era of cooperation, an abrupt shift from decades of adversarial clashes. At GM's new Saturn subsidiary, UAW members participated directly in strategic planning, long the exclusive prerogative of GM executives. The IBM story is similar. During the early 1960s, it undertook entirely on its own the staggering colossal and technological risks of developing its 360 series of computers.[15] Two decades later, IBM had formed relationships with Intel, MCI, Rolm, and scores of Japanese and European partners.

Many smaller firms have taken similar steps. Since the early 1980s, domestic joint ventures have become much more common in service industries, such as advertising, financial services, and communications systems, and among high-tech manufacturers of electrical equipment, consumer electronics, computer peripherals, and software.[16] Some of these links are very complex. For example, Advent International is a Boston-based network of fourteen independent venture capital firms around the world. Its chairman sits on the boards of these firms and actively supervises their principal deals; computers link all of them to Advent's U.S. headquarters. One of Advent's largest investments is in a consortium of European microchip makers, called European Silicon Structures. In short, a network of small firms has linked itself through active ownership to still another network of small firms. Quite recently, researchers have begun to map the dense networks that link any small, entrepreneurial firms to their suppliers, customers, and financiers. Other forms of collaboration link firms and universities; in biotechnology, these links have recently been dubbed "the university-industrial complex" (Jarillo 1986; Kenney 1987).

Underlying all these diverse arrangements are three simple choices. More and more frequently, American executives are choosing among a variety of *partners* (other firms, government agencies, labor unions, universities) to accomplish a wide range of *tasks*: marketing, manufacturing, and the other traditional business functions, as well as strategic decision making; and are doing so through a *variety of arrangements* that range from formal, explicit, legal structures like joint ventures to a wide variety of tacit, informal linkups. As they make these three choices, U.S. firms are creating an endless variety of new organizational arrangements.

The forces driving these changes are varied and powerful: the spread of technology around the world, the attack by Asian firms on U.S. markets, maturity or saturation in many industries, shortening life spans and rising R&D costs, overcapacity and intensifying global competition, and the high costs and risks of building facilities and organizations that can compete on a global scale. Over time, some of these forces will wax and others will wane. But the likelihood that they will all subside is slender. Consequently, more and more U.S. firms will blur their boundaries through complex networks of relationships. And, as a result, the classic map of the firm will grow increasingly inaccurate.

Institutional Economics

The fourth attack on the classic map of the firm, institutional economics, emerged during the 1970s, principally in the writings of Oliver Williamson.[17] It does not wholly reject the notion that property rights, hierarchical control, communal social systems, discrete contracting, and other characteristics can define the boundaries of the firm. However, like the open system theory of the firm, institutional economics argues that these are only partial concepts, not universal traits. It also argues that the classic map of the firm gives poor guidance to public-policy makers, steering them away from complex arrangements that blur firms' boundaries. Institutional economists rebelled against the received wisdom about firms and their boundaries for the same reasons that fourteenth-century mapmakers rejected the Christian maps of the world, which placed the Holy City of Jerusalem at the center of the earth and the universe and were criticized as misleading oversimplifications dominated by unexamined assumptions and sometimes by dogma.

For institutional economics, the basic unit of analysis is the transaction, not the firm or the market. In a transaction, parties exchange goods, services, money, and other things of economic value. These transactions must somehow be governed. Markets are one way of doing this. Firms are another. The notion of an economy as a vast web of transactions, governed either by firms or by markets, lay implicit in a pathbreaking article written in 1937 by Ronald Coase called

"The Nature of the Firm" (1937/1952). Coase asked why some transactions are performed inside firms while others are performed outside them in markets. His answer was that firms arise when they can perform transactions at lower costs than markets.

Market-governed transactions involve many costs. Parties must write a contract setting out their agreement. This involves costs and risks because the future is uncertain, because the rationality of the parties is bounded, because others will sometimes behave in self-interested opportunistic ways, and because of the cost of monitoring and enforcing contracts and modifying them when circumstances change. When the costs of market relationships grow too great, it becomes more efficient to govern transactions through a firm. The firm's executives have advantages that markets do not. They may have more information than either party to an exchange. They can resolve disputes by fiat if necessary; they can work with incomplete contracts knowing the details can be taken care of later; they can audit for compliance with contracts and punish opportunists; and they can change the terms of an agreement when new circumstances make that necessary.

But firm-governed transactions can also be costly. At some point administrative failure sets in. As firms grow larger, the entrepreneurial incentives of their members weaken. Owner-managers of smaller firms have powerful, direct, personal motives to respond quickly and efficiently to market pressures and to limit internal politicking. Large firms can attempt this through reward systems, monitoring, organization by profit center, and other means. However, as a firm does so on a wider and wider scale, the costs and administrative entanglements of the effort grow. If this didn't happen, firms—or perhaps even one giant, all-encompassing firm—would replace all market transactions.

In short, markets and firms (or hierarchies) are alternate ways of governing transactions. Each has advantages and disadvantages. Given at least some competition, a kind of natural selection will work itself out so that transactions will be governed inside firms when that is more efficient and outside firms when market governance is more efficient. But what then separates the "inside" of a firm from the "outside"?

For institutional economists, the answer is that a wide, varied, and complex region often falls between firms and markets. That is, firms have not made a simple, black and white choice between governing transactions within a firm or through markets. Rather, they have spawned a vast range of complex governance arrangements. These hybrid arrangements involve bilateral or even multilateral ways of governing transactions. Firms create them because they are sometimes more efficient ways to govern transactions than either markets or firms.

Consider, for example, a common kind of transaction between a buyer and a supplier. Assume that the buyer relied upon arm's length market bidding to select a supplier that will provide customized equipment from time to time over several years. During this period, their relationship may evolve dramatically and its arm's length character may attenuate almost completely. The supplier may invest in specialized equipment to meet the buyer's needs. The two parties may learn a great deal about each other's capabilities as a result of working together. Managers in both companies may develop personal relationships of trust with each other. Training and experience may create specialized ''human assets'' that facilitate the dealings between the two parties. As this happens, the relationship between the two parties changes. The classic economist's map, based on arm's length, explicit contractual dealings between independent parties, no longer accurately describes their relationship. The boundary between the two parties is blurred, not sharp.

In situations like this, the classic map of the firm is not accurate. Moreover, its implicit hostility toward cooperative relationships among firms may actually lead to inefficiency. Parties involved in hybrid relationships may be able to govern transactions more efficiently than through market or hierarchical arrangements. The economies gained from specialized human and physical assets may reduce transaction costs more than enough to offset whatever losses result from weakened market discipline. In this way, institutional economics rejects both the descriptive and normative elements of the classic map of the firm. It refuses to theorize away, or condemn as presumptive deviants, joint ventures, industry associations, joint R&D efforts, trusts, industrial policy, enterprise union, state-owned enterprises, industry norms, and other hybrid forms of economic life. Institutional economics acknowledges the protean diversity of economic and organizational forms, and evenhandedly acknowledges that markets can fail, as can firms or hybrid relationships.

Institutional economics has also rejected the notion that property rights always distinguish what is inside from what is outside. The reason is that ownership has several meanings, not just one. Ownership can refer to the right to determine the use of property, the right to the returns generated by the property, the right to change the form of an asset, and the right to exchange any of these first three rights. In some cases, such as franchising arrangements, these separate components of property rights are broken apart and then assigned to separate parties (Rubin 1978). Given competition, these rights tend to fall into the hands of parties, either inside or outside the firm, that can use them more efficiently. Furthermore, parties sometimes cannot find ways to allocate a property right—such as the right to the return generated by a property—among themselves. In these cases, some arrangement must be created to enable parties to share this right. This would happen in the case of the buyer and supplier that have each invested in specialized assets but cannot find a way to determine precisely what return each should get on its investment. In either case, a simple, fairly sharp boundary defined by ownership and property rights cannot be used to define in all cases what is inside and what is outside the firm.[18]

Finally, institutional economics casts aside as incomplete the traditional notion of classical contracting. Firms do write clear, precise, contracts specifying their rights and obligations and those of the external parties with which they are dealing. But at other times they rely upon "relational contracting" and do not draw sharp lines demarcating the rights and obligations of each party. Under relational contracts, parties guide their behavior on the basis of their entire relationship, as it has developed over time and with reference to how they expect it to develop in the future. Their whole relationship is the fundamental reference point of the contract, rather than the precise specifications of some original agreement. In fact, there may be no original agreement. The context of the parties' dealings with each other may be a "mini society with a vast array of norms beyond the norms centered on exchange and its immediate processes" (Macneil 1978, p. 901). The concept of relational contracting allies institutional economics quite explicitly with the open social system view of the firm, for it says that contracts are often inextricably embedded in complex social and political processes connecting firms with other organizations.

In summary, institutional economics breaks away from the received notions of firms and markets by starting out its analysis at a completely different point of departure, the elemental transaction. It does not suppose that there is just one way or two ways or even only a dozen ways to govern transactions efficiently. Rather, the most efficient way to govern a transaction depends on its particular characteristics. Sometimes this will be arm's length market dealings, sometimes this will be a traditional firm relationship, but in a vast range of cases it will be one of many complicated arrangements, found in Japan and more and more frequently in the contemporary United States, that blur the boundaries of firms.

Sketching a New Map

The first two sections of this essay, taken together, pose a serious problem: reconciling the classic map of the firm with the ideas and findings described in the last section.

One approach would be to abandon the classic map and forswear efforts to describe or analyze the boundaries of firms. Several scholars have suggested just this. Economists Michael Jensen and William Meckling have written that

> it makes little or no sense to try to distinguish those things which are "inside" the firm (or any other organization) from those things that are "outside" of it. There is in a very real sense only a multitude of complex relationships (i.e., contracts) between the legal fiction (the firm) and the owners of labor, material and capital inputs and the consumers of output. [Jensen and Meckling 1976, p. 311]

In the same vein, organizational theorists Daniel Katz and Robert Kahn (1966, p. 122) have compared organizations to primitive forms of animal life made up of "globular masses of protoplasm through which flow the fluids of their watery environment and from which they cannot be easily distinguished."

At these high levels of abstraction, the problem vanishes. But these conceptualizations—however imaginative, provocative, or profound they may be—succeed at a very high cost. They simplify away the familiar empirical universe of managerial life that pervades the literatures of organization theory and business administration. "Inside" firms, managers do exercise discretion, work through hierarchical control, and build organizations that share norms, values, and purpose. From the high summit of abstraction, the vexing issues of firms, boundaries, and broader environments may vanish, but only at the risk of irrelevance and implausibility. The situation can be compared to Samuel Johnson's reaction to Bishop Berkeley's idea that none of reality actually existed, but rather was an idea in the mind of God: Johnson stood up, kicked a stone, and said, "I refute it thus."

Even Chester Barnard, the business executive turned organization theorist who stressed the open, fluid nature of the firm and described it by analogy to a field of magnetic forces, described a "zone of discretion" within firms in which managers' decisions could be made and executed. Because of his management experience, Barnard knew there was a difference between what is inside and outside firms. Hence, he defined the "periphery of an organization" as the point at which firms and other organizations exchange outputs and funds. Within the periphery, executives coordinate activity, control exchanges, maintain communication, and promote understanding of the firm's purpose. From this managerial perspective, firms' boundaries are not airtight; there are no organizational equivalents of the Berlin Wall. But boundaries matter because they do distinguish, protect, and enhance certain activities inside the firm (Barnard 1968, pp. 138–60).

The other problem with relying upon abstraction to resolve the problem of boundaries is that it fails to address the almost bewildering heterogeneity of activities on firms' boundaries and the profusion of ideas intended to explain or describe them. Keiretsu, consortia, industrial policy, Defense Department contracting, industry standards, rate setting in regulated industries, networks of social relations among employees working for Silicon Valley firms, and literally dozens of other activities fall into the broad category of activities that are neither inside or outside firms. Without some way of ordering these many activities and relating them to each other and to firms, one is left facing what William James, in describing an infant's experience of the world, called "a buzzing, blooming confusion."

There is no simple solution to the conflict between the old map and the new facts and ideas, or to the nearly chaotic variety of boundary-blurring phenomena. Individual bodies of literature provide only special-purpose maps, sometimes in embryonic form, of the territories around firms. Like specialized maps, which present detailed information about political divisions, geological formations, or the habitats of wildlife, these maps cannot be aggregated simply into a general map.

A step forward, I believe, is to work with a rough sketch of the boundary territories around firms. This sketch, presented below, shows how the findings and ideas of many ostensibly disparate literatures relate to each other, how the new organizational forms mentioned in the last section relate to the classic map of the firm, and how rewarding and challenging further studies of firms' boundaries are likely to be.

This sketch displays no sharp dividing lines separating the inside of the firm from the outside. Rather, it shows the firm as a dense network at the center of a web of relationships. These relationships are defined by ownership, hierarchical control, centralized power, managerial discretion, social bonds of membership, loyalty, and shared purpose, and formal, legal contractual arrangements—all of the powerful ideas underlying the classic map of the firm. This dense intersection of relationships is the *central domain* of the firm.

No sharp dividing lines set it off from a surrounding environment. It does not display the firm as a medieval citadel surrounded by walls, or as an island bounded by the sea. Rather, the central domain of the firm blends slowly into its surrounding environment. This happens as ownership, hierarchy, control, power, social bonds, classic contracting, and other boundary-defining devices diminish in significance or are shared with other organizations. Ultimately, the gradual attenuation of these relationships reaches a point at which the firm exercises neither power nor influence. Here, the genuinely external environment of the firm begins.

Although it does not show any boundaries, this sketch does display four different territories. I have already mentioned two of these, the central domain, or core, of the firm, the area characterized by the most intricate intertwining of relationships, and the external environment. The third territory, lying outside the central domain of the firm is a *sphere of alliances.* Here, firms join forces with other organizations through formal, overt arrangements in which they share authority and jointly perform important activities. Further on is the fourth territory, a *sphere of influence.* Here lie the obscure frontiers of the firm. Through interactions that are tacit, subtle, and elusive, firms and other organizations influence each other. No sharp boundaries separate these spheres from each other or from the surrounding environment. They overlap, their boundaries are blurred, and so inevitably are the boundaries of the firm.

This sketch, like the territory it describes, is nearly amorphous. Hence, it is necessary to state much more precisely the main characteristics of the central domain of the firm, the sphere of alliances, the sphere of influence, and the external environment. There are important differences between the spheres, and the ideas and phenomena that each of them encompasses have more in common with each other than with the ideas and phenomena in adjacent spheres. That is why this sketch of the firm displays a rough division between these four overlapping, interpenetrating territories.

The central domain of the firm and the external environment of the firm are by far the most familiar parts of this map. The central domain is the classic core of the firm. It is Barnard's "zone of discretion," the area managed through what Williamson calls "unilateral governance"; it is the firm as a social "capsule," as a black box or a production function, as a legal fiction with perpetual life and carefully defined liabilities, rights, and duties.

In contrast, the external environment of the firm is *genuinely* external. Here firms and other organizations stand at arm's length to each other. Firms are price takers. In the economist's phrase, there are no nonmarket interdependencies among firms. They operate within spheres of autonomy carefully defined by law and regulation. Their voluntary relationships with other organizations are governed by classical, discrete contracting. For economists, the external environment of the firm is the competitive market, not oligopoly or cartel. For political scientists, it is the arena of pluralistic competition, rather than corporatist cooperation. At the extreme, this external environment is the economist's pure market or the Hobbesian state of nature, the war of all against all. If one concentrates solely on the sphere of control and the external environment, and ignores the rest of the sketch, one is looking at the classic map of the firm. The central domain of the firm and its market environment have been the preoccupation of the practical literature on strategy and business management. For example, neither Kenneth Andrews's classic work, *The Concept of Corporate Strategy*, nor Michael Porter's recent *Competitive Strategy* treats the boundary regions of firms.[19]

Hence, the novel aspects of this sketch of the firm and its boundaries are the corridor of alliances and the sphere of influence. Each of these requires a detailed explanation.

The Sphere of Alliances

Activities fall in the sphere of alliances when the managers responsible for them share authority with other organizations through explicit arrangements. Examples of this kind of activity include joint ventures, collaborative arrangements with a firm's labor unions (like those at GM's Saturn plant), equity purchases by "active investors," the franchise agreements, "strong" forms of industrial policy, consortia like MCC and Sematech or the Fifth Generation project in Japan, and pools, trusts, and cartels. Powerful regulatory agencies and elaborate contractual arrangements that serve as surrogates for hierarchical control also fall within this sphere.[20] What all these different organizational arrangements have in common is that they link firms to other, separate organizations in relationships that are explicit, formal, and involve shared authority.

Shared authority means simply that the parties in these relationships make some important decisions jointly. Unless both parties play an important role in the decision making, their effort is not genuinely cooperative and does not fall within this sphere of activity. When a victim obeys an armed kidnapper, they are not really engaged in a partnership and do not have a genuinely cooperative relationship. When a supplier, albeit legally independent, depends wholly upon a single customer for its livelihood and has little influence on the customer's decisions, little if any genuine cooperation occurs. On the other hand, organizations may blur their boundaries without operating any joint facilities or sharing ownership. This happens, for example, when members of a cartel make joint decisions about pricing or capacity. Hence, shared decision making is the central defining characteristic of activities that fall in the sphere of alliances.

However, shared authority is usually accompanied by complicated formal or semiformal relationships that link a firm with other organizations. These arrangements blur the dividing lines that distinguish what is inside the firm from what is on the outside of the classic map of the firm. For example, partners in a joint venture own assets in common, and they share the venture's liabilities. Managerial control is not divided neatly into autonomous spheres but rather is shared in the joint decision making, usually through a board of directors that jointly represents the venture's parents. Organizational structures and systems for hierarchical control no longer distinguish what is inside and outside a firm when the venture's parents create both formal and informal organizational mechanisms (task forces, joint boards of directors, integrated accounting systems or reporting systems, or management information systems, and so forth) to facilitate their joint decision making and to implement the decisions they make. Two parties linked in a close collaborative effort may no longer remain separate, social "capsules." In fact, some joint activities are created precisely in order to enable one organization to learn practices, attitudes, and values from another. General Motors, for example, created its joint venture with Toyota in order to learn the technical, social, and managerial aspects of the Toyota production system. When firms join together in explicit alliances, they may create aggregations of economic and political power that are not delimited simply by the boundaries of any of the separate organizations. Finally, these firms may no longer be engaged in discrete, classical contracting. Rather, in the language of institutional economics, they are engaged in relational contracting and the management of bilateral or multilateral governance structures. In all these respects, the classic ways of demarcating the boundaries of the firm no longer hold when its activities fall within the sphere of alliances.

The Sphere of Influence

The sphere of influence is easier to illustrate than to define. It is also easier to say what this sphere is not than to define precisely what it is. Activities in this sphere are not characterized by hierarchical structures, contracts, defined rights, and duties. Nor are they simply arm's length market arrangements. The activities within this sphere are subtle and diverse. They are the least charted territory on the boundaries of the firm.

What activities and phenomena fall within the sphere of influence? One example is the "rules of the game" that shape the decisions of firms that are long-term players in stable, oligopolistic industries. Another is the many forms of deference that small suppliers show to large powerful buyers (Blois 1972; Adelman 1949). In Japan, the recent, subtler forms of industrial policy described in the last section and the administrative guidance through which Japanese government agencies sometimes act are another form of informal, noncontractual, nonhierarchical harmonization. So are the many devices through which member firms in the Japanese keiretsu harmonize their decisions and activities. Another tacit kind of mutual accommodation takes a form that the French call the "rule of anticipated reactions." This happens when American firms shape decisions about mergers and acquisitions in view of the likely reactions of U.S. antitrust authorities, or when firms modify decisions—on outsourcing, for example—because of the reaction they expect from labor unions.

The sphere of influence also encompasses subtle social interactions. Some firms operate more successfully because they are located within larger, geographically based networks of firms and institutions—such as Silicon Valley, the greater Tokyo area, and Wall Street—as a result of informal, social webs of relationships that link members of these firms and encourage the commingling of talent, technology, and information. In the United States, a few peculiarly fertile areas produce new jobs at a rate ten times faster than other regions (Birch 1987, pp. 135–65). Historical examples of economically fecund social communities include the cities in the north of England that nurtured the British textile firms that led the Industrial Revolution (Landes 1969, pp. 60–75).[21] Finally, gentle forms of influence are at work when managers in an industry make decisions with ethical or quasi-ethical overtones by saying something along the lines of, "That's not how we do business in this industry." They are responding to norms of behavior and tacit obligations that are not specified in contracts, and are not enforceable in court or through other formal means of adjudication, and that they may not even be able to articulate clearly and precisely. Yet expectations about trust, reliability, credibility, honor, and commitment permeate much behavior on firms' boundaries in the United States and in other nations (Shimokawa 1985; Macaulay 1963).

What do all these examples have in common? The parties are involved in processes of mutual adjustment and influence that are informal rather than formal and tacit rather than explicit. These gentle influences work in several ways. Sometimes the parties have had long experience operating together in a similar environment, and so they share a common body of facts and assumptions about how the world works. Because the parties are familiar with each other's past behavior, they can practice "the rule of anticipated reactions." Other unwritten norms and obligations inevitably arise from national culture, from the shared historical experience of firms and families in the same region, or from critical events that profoundly affect the evolution of an industry and the thinking of all the parties—firms, suppliers, unions, and governments—involved with the industry. Finally, subtle forms of coordination can grow out of and eventually pervade formal alliances between firms and other organizations. Public and private parties involved with an industry may meet and work out a set of rules that define how a cartel or an industrial policy will work. Then, as the parties proceed with their affairs within this negotiated environment, they evolve the shared expectations, norms, and webs of social linkage that coordinate their behavior in countless subtle, unmeasurable, often unnoticed ways.

The sphere of influence is the counterpart of the Far East for fifteenth-century European explorers and mapmakers. It is the least charted territory on the periphery of firms. As the examples given in the last two paragraphs suggest, it is a vast and heterogeneous region. Above all, it may prove the most challenging and rewarding of the areas on the boundaries of the firm that are open for research and conceptualization. These challenges and rewards are the subject of the next section.

Implications

The implications of creating a new map of the firm, one that shows its boundary regions to be fully as complex and important as the traditional core of the firm, are profound. This section briefly describes some of these implications.

First of all, efforts to map the boundary regions of particular firms or classes of firms may be an important new avenue of research. The representation of the firm and its boundaries given in the last section is, after all, only a sketch. It needs to be specified—through efforts to map the boundaries of *individual firms*—rather than those of firms in general. Mapping the boundaries of a particular firm will mean examining the constellation of *all* of its relationships, not just its joint ventures or alliances, or its industrial relations. The exercise must be holistic.

Comprehensive maps of the boundaries of individual firms will vary greatly from company to company. Some will display relationships that resemble the classic map of the firm: the firm will be sharply bounded and surrounded by a sphere of arm's length market dealings. In other cases, the maps will display arrangements like those of the Japanese keiretsu and show firms deeply embedded in elaborate webs of relationships. Other firms may present lopsided pictures showing some of their activities enmeshed in alliances and complex frontiers while others are sharply demarcated by ownership, control, and other classic traits.

The most difficult part of this mapping exercise will be finding ways to characterize the sphere of influence surrounding particular firms. The literatures that treat firms' boundaries concentrate heavily on the formal organizational characteristics of these regions. They commonly examine complicated hierarchical arrangements, contracts, and fairly explicit forms of authority sharing (see, e.g., Child 1987; Powell 1987; Thorelli 1986). However, when a firm's activities are embedded in subtler, informal webs of social, personal, and economic arrangements, the task of description and conceptualization will be much more difficult. By their very nature, these informal, elusive interactions will slip through a net designed to catch hard, quantifiable data.

Rich, empirical descriptions rather than large sample, quantitative studies may prove much more effective in exploring the boundaries of individual firms. This is certainly true for the distant, outer sphere of tacit influences. Even activities that fall within the sphere of alliances and whose formal characteristics render them quantifiable require careful qualitative evaluation. For example, many of the studies and articles cited above on joint ventures and other forms of cooperation describe the frequency with which licensing agreements, joint ventures, or consortia are announced. Unfortunately, the studies do not examine the importance of these activities. Hence, the announcement of a $500,000 tie-up between small manufacturers can count as heavily as the creation of Aramco, the consortium of giant oil firms that developed the Saudi Arabian fields and has acted, over decades, as both an instrument and shaper of U.S. foreign policy. The strategic importance of any particular boundary arrangement can only be judged in the context of the firm's history, its strategy and competitive position, its capabilities and weaknesses, and its other boundary arrangements.

In time, as concepts that help to explain the boundary regions of firms are clarified and operationalized, more formal methods of study may prove successful. However, before it becomes clear precisely what it is that is being studied, rich descriptions are a more promising avenue. These need not be isolated case studies or monographs. The wide array of phenomena that fall within either the sphere of alliances or the sphere of influence provide many opportunities for comparative work: across countries or industries, across firms in the same industry, or over periods of time for the same firm.

Mapping the boundaries of firms will inevitably raise a host of important questions. Are there recurring, basic patterns of boundary arrangements in certain industries, in firms of certain sizes, or at particular points in firms' development? What explains why a firm's boundaries take one form rather than another: industry structure, the pace of technological change in the industry, the size or age of the firm, the laws of the firm's home government, or other factors?

Questions about the competitiveness of firms and industries will also arise. How important are a firm's boundary arrangements to its ability to compete? Is global competition an arena of combat among individual firms, or is the battle joined (at least in some industries) between complexes of firms and other institutions linked formally and tacitly? The commonplace notion that American firms often compete against a larger, amorphous adversary called "Japan Incorporated" suggests that international competition is sometimes a battle of industrial networks rather than of individual firms.

Concepts of corporate social responsibility and governance will also have to be recast for firms whose boundary regions are broad and complex. Consider how simple, at least in relative terms, the issues of responsibility and governance were for the firms portrayed by the classic map. Its executives controlled the firm; the owners owned it completely; the firm was a sphere of discretion within which managers, acting for owners, gave instructions that were then carried out and monitored through hierarchical control by full-time employees. The line of responsibility passed down clearly through the "chain of command." But if a firm is only the central ganglion in a complex network within which authority, influence, and operations are shared with other institutions, it is much more difficult to say precisely who is responsible for what.

Work on firms' boundaries need not always be new empirical work. The classic map of the firm has been such a powerful paradigm that it has diverted attention away from the areas of the U.S. industrial landscape, both now and in the past, in which firms have been immersed in complex relationships, both overt and tacit. For decades, joint ventures and consortia have been a standard industry practice in the oil industry, in other extractive industries, and in the chemical industry. American multinationals have decades of experience with various co-operative arrangements that they have used to gain access to overseas markets and to build positions in them (see Vernon 1972; Stopford and Wells 1972; Franko 1973; Gomez-Casseres 1985). Agribusiness and defense contracting are two giant industries pervaded by complex links among firms and between firms and government agencies. During the 1920s and 1930s, Du Pont created an international network—almost a "Du Pont keiretsu"—linking it with dozens of other chemical firms around the world. In the early 1930s, General Motors toyed with entering the infant airline industry through a series of minority equity investments in airline firms. And, during the first decade of GM's history under William Durant, the firm was a loose affiliation of automobile companies and parts companies rather than the decentralized hierarchy created by Alfred Sloan during the 1920s. Finally, one hundred years ago, U.S. firms experimented widely with collaborative arrangements that took the form of pools, trusts, powerful industry associations, and other arrangements. Any of these well-documented phenomena may prove to be valuable sources of ideas and data, if they are approached with hypotheses and questions about the nature of firms' boundaries and their management.[22]

What will be effective ways of developing concepts to address these many issues? The answer lies partly in searching for useful concepts within adjacent literatures, that is, bodies of work that have studied and conceptualized these issues but not through examination of firms and their boundaries. Adjacent literatures will provide rich arrays of hypotheses, theories, and concepts. Some may prove immediately useful; others, more distantly analogous, may provoke new ideas.

Two of the most promising adjacent literatures are those of international relations and game theory. During the last twelve years, international relations has developed a concept of "regimes," a close analogy to what I have called the sphere of influence. Later, a collective definition of a regime[23] emerged; it is:

> Sets of implicit or explicit principles, norms, rules and decision-making procedures around which actors' expectations converge in a given area of international relations. Principles are beliefs of fact, causation, and rectitude. Norms are standards of behavior defined in terms of rights and obligations. Rules are specific prescriptions or proscriptions for actions. [Krasner 1983, p. 2]

Another adjacent literature is game theory, particularly *The Evolution of Cooperation* by Robert Axelrod (1984) and the stream of subsequent research and commentary this book has generated. These ideas may also illuminate the spheres of influence around firms. Axelrod's book reports the results of a series of computer tournaments in which participants compete to win a simple game called the Prisoner's Dilemma.[24]

The winning strategy, called tit for tat, is simple and cooperative. It starts playing by offering to cooperate. Afterwards, it does whatever the other player did on the previous move. If the other player cooperates, tit for tat cooperates. Axelrod concluded that this strategy won out because it was "nice, retaliatory, forgiving, and clear." It offers cooperation and clearly develops a track record biased toward cooperation. This clear, credible precedent elicited cooperation from other parties. The bias toward cooperation was so effective that it succeeded even in tournaments that were rigged against it.

What is striking about the success of tit for tat is the circumstances in which it occurred. There were no hierarchical elements to coordinate the activities of the competitors in the tournament: they could not each go separately to a "boss" and ask for advice or direction. There were no cultural or social norms that reinforced cooperative behavior. Rather, cooperation emerged in conditions bereft of "friendship or foresight." Nevertheless, a clear, simple, credible strategy of cooperation emerged in triumph, suggesting the power of a bias toward cooperation and the power of precedent and mutual expectation.

The efforts to explore, conceptualize, and map firms' boundaries will be paralleled by new studies of the role of business managers. Nowhere in the vast literature of business management has anyone argued that managing firms' boundaries is a central task for business executives. Yet, if the boundary regions of firms are as complex and as important as the new conceptual tools and empirical studies suggest, then this task will demand extended examination. Moreover, thinking about the new task of managing firms' boundaries is likely to lead to rethinking about the classic tasks of setting strategy, allocating resources, designing and modifying the organization, etc. Strategy, for example, may no longer be viewed as the result of internal deliberations in response to external problems and opportunities. The reason is simple: the terms "external" and "internal" often do not apply. Broadly speaking, the strategies of many firms will be negotiated, formally and tacitly, within the network of a firm's relationships. But what does it mean to "negotiate" a strategy under these circumstances? Furthermore, at the heart of the task of managing the firm's boundaries lies the conflict between open and closed boundaries. Open boundaries are, first of all, inevitable and, second, often helpful. But they also create vulnerabilities and, as a result, strong pressure for caution, proprietary efforts, and other ways of defending, protecting, and safeguarding activities and technology that a firm considers vital to its future.

Refining and applying the concept of power is likely to be one of the most important ways of illuminating the managerial task and dilemmas of managing firms' boundaries. If one accepts the sketch presented in the last section and views firms as embedded in spheres of overt cooperation and tacit influence, then it is clear that a firm's power and influence do not start and stop at any definable or defensible boundary. Firms do secure benefits because they are enmeshed in webs of alliances and influences, but by the same token they are also vulnerable: to external shocks, to self-interested behavior by outsiders or quasi outsiders, and to inefficiencies and costs arising from the need to negotiate and maneuver within these complex relationships. Power, like social responsibility, was a simpler issue, less vexing and therefore less prominent, when firms were viewed as closed spheres in which power and authority were vested in senior management. To be sure, practical and conceptual difficulties arose when power and authority were decentralized *within* firms. However, the new map of the firm will show that power and authority are dispersed widely, inside and outside the firm, and not simply decentralized. When firms and managers are enmeshed in webs of relationships, what are the various sources of their power? What is power? What are the fundamental alternative ways of deploying it? Who is to be held accountable for its deployment? To whom are they accountable? The new map of the firm is likely to take the issue of power from the background and place it at stage center where it will compete with strategy, organization, governance, and other classic issues for the time, energy, and imagination of researchers.

A final implication is implicit in all the others. The boundary regions of firms are ripe for further exploration and analysis. Many of the problems and questions about the core areas of the firm have been deeply explored. Boundaries, in contrast, are an open intellectual terrain. Their detailed exploration by economists, organization theorists, and students of business management has begun only in the last decade or so. Given the breadth and complexity of these boundary regions, and the various forms that they have taken in different countries and during different historical periods, further study will likely pay high rewards.

Notes

1. Overviews of the history of the corporation include Chayes (1959) and Groening (1981); brief summaries of Roman and early British ideas about corporations, along with notes citing the classic works on these subjects, are Hurst (1970), pp. 1–8, and Van Cise (1970), pp. 4–12.

2. In general, these arrangements failed. They were administratively unwieldy, and the agreements upon which they were based did not have the binding power of legal con-

tracts and so could not be enforced in court. Member firms often cheated, and the management of the cartels and confederations did not have power over investment decisions or operating decisions of member firms. See Chandler (1977), especially pp. 315–44.

3. For an overview of the debate between the "public interest" and the "capture" perspectives on U.S. regulation, see McCraw (1975).

4. Early organization theorists did not, of course, ignore the firm's environment completely. Weber is perhaps best known for using the Protestant work ethic to account for the success of capitalism. Henri Fayol, writing in 1916, assigned to management the tasks of planning and forecasting that involve analysis of the environment. See Fayol (1930). Mary Parker Follett (1965) drew upon her experience as a social worker and political scientist and rejected Weber's abstract, formal, mechanistic view of organizations. She stressed the importance of "horizontal," as opposed to hierarchical relations within an organization, and advocated involving individuals affected by a decision in decision making; and she was skeptical about relying solely upon formal authority to explain decision making, when so many factors, inside and outside organizations, interact to make decisions. In these ways, Follett anticipated the open system view of organizations, discussed below, an important way station on the road to contemporary ideas about firms and their boundaries.

5. This quotation appears in Beniger (1986), p. 294; this book is a broad, sophisticated, historical account of the rise of control systems for large-scale enterprises.

6. This approach to labor relations, the "New Deal system," is described in Kochan, Katz, and McKersie (1986), chaps. 2 and 4. Disputes between labor and management were resolved through arbitration and grievance procedures, sometimes called "neoclassical" contracting. See Macneil (1978), p. 888.

7. See, for example, Parsons (1960), pp. 132–70.

8. In the early 1960s, a handful of organization theorists and sociologists quickly and imaginatively anticipated many of the ideas that would emerge in the organizational theory literature over the next twenty years from the starting point of Parsons's original ideas. See for example, Guetzkow (1966); Blau and Scott (1962), pp. 214–21; and Evan (1965).

9. An overview of these approaches is Van de Ven, Emmett, and Koening (1975).

10. This argument is developed in Pfeffer (1972) and Pfeffer and Nowak (1976).

11. The most comprehensive presentation of the organization theory literature on firms, boundaries, and power is Aldrich (1979), pp. 219–322; another broad overview, whose bibliography displays the vast array of organizational theory articles on firms and their environments is Pfeffer and Salancik (1978).

12. The most recent, systematic, and comprehensive comparison of Japanese industrial practices with those in the United States is McCraw (1986). More specialized recent works include Johnson (1982) on the history of Japanese industrial policy from the 1920s to the 1980s; Abegglen and Stalk (1985) on the competitive strategies and practices of Japanese firms; and Prindl (1981) on the Japanese financial system. Japanese industrial relations are described in detail in Japan Institute of Labor (1980), and in Shirai (1983).

13. The history of Mitsui, up to the late 1960s, is presented in rich detail in Roberts (1973).

14. The classic study of the zaibatsu is Hadley (1970). Other works include Caves and Uekusa (1976); on auto industry keiretsu, see Cusumano (1985). Recent, focused studies of collaboration and competition among keiretsu members include Shimokawa (1985); Imai (1978); Goto (1982); Futatsugi (1986).

15. The magnitude of the risks that IBM faced and the intensity of its zeal for autonomy are described in Fisher, McKie, and Mancke (1983), pp. 101–68, and in Sobel (1981), pp. 210–24.

16. One study that does not find an aggregate increase in cooperative activities among firms is Ghemawat, Porter, and Rawlinson (1986); studies documenting the increase in cooperative endeavors include Hladik (1985); Alster (1986); and Harrigan (1985).

17. The fullest exposition of Williamson's views is *The Economic Institutions of Capitalism* (1985).

18. A recent overview of the connections between the transactions cost literature and complex views of property rights is De Alessi (1983).

19. The exception to this generalization is Porter (1980), chap. 4. Andrews (1980, pp. 87–104) connects firms' strategy to the boundary activities described in this essay principally in his discussion of social responsibility and ethical values.

20. See McCraw (1975). Richard Posner (1974) has expanded the notion of capture and the ways in which it links firms and government agencies, arguing that regulation is a substitute for private cartelization in situations where there are so many firms that cartels are not practical. Contractual surrogates for hierarchy include what Robert Eccles (1981) calls "quasi-firms," dealings between contractors and subcontractors in the construction industry, based upon long-term and fairly exclusive relationships, governed by contracts rather than any hierarchical organization. And the complex contractual arrangements that serve the functions ordinarily performed by hierarchy in large-scale projects are described in Stinchcombe and Heimer (1985), pp. 121–71.

21. Similar communities on the Continent are described in Piore and Sabel (1984), pp. 28–54.

22. An example of an effort to test and refine a theory of complex contractual relationships using historical data is Casson (1987), pp. 121–52.

23. In 1975 John Ruggie (1965) proposed the concept of international regimes.

24. The game is based on a simple problem: two people have committed a crime together; they have been captured; and they are imprisoned separately and cannot communicate with each other; but neither has admitted guilt. The police offer each prisoner a choice, saying that if he pleads guilty and implicates his colleague, he will go free while the other will serve a long prison sentence. However, if both maintain their innocence, then they will both go free for there is no other evidence against them. If both plead guilty, then both will serve moderate prison sentences.

References

Abegglen, James C., and George Stalk. (1985) *Kaisha.* New York: Basic Books.

Adelman, M.A. (1949) "The Large Firm and Its Suppliers." *Review of Economics and Statistics* 31(May):113–18.

Aldrich, Howard E. (1979) *Organizations and Environments.* Englewood Cliffs, NJ: Prentice-Hall.

Alster, Norm. (1986) "Electronics Firms Find Strength in Numbers." *Electronic Business*, March 1, pp. 102–8.

Andrews, Kenneth R. (1980) *The Concept of Corporate Strategy.* Homewood, IL: Irwin.

Axelrod, Robert. (1984) *The Evolution of Cooperation.* New York: Basic Books.

Barnard, Chester I. (1968) *The Functions of the Executive.* Cambridge, MA: Harvard University Press.

Beniger, James R. (1986) *The Control Revolution.* Cambridge, MA: Harvard University Press.

Birch, David. (1987) *Job Creation in America.* New York: The Free Press.

Blau, Peter M. (1964) *Exchange and Power in Social Life.* New York: Wiley.

Blau, Peter M., and W. Richard Scott. (1962) *Formal Organizations: A Comparative Approach.* San Francisco: Chandler.

Blois, K.J. (1972) "Vertical Quasi-Integration." *Journal of Industrial Economics* 20(Summer):253–72.

Braudel, Fernand. (1986) *The Wheels of Commerce*. New York: Harper & Row.

Brodley, Joseph F. (1982) "Joint Ventures and Anti-trust Policy." *Harvard Law Review* 95:1523–90.

Casson, Mark. (1987) *The Firm and the Market*. Cambridge, MA: MIT Press.

Caves, Richard E., and Masu Uekusa, eds. (1976) "Industrial Organization in Japan." *Asia's New Giant*. Washington, DC: The Brookings Institution.

Chandler, Alfred D., Jr. (1977) *The Visible Hand*. Cambridge, MA: Harvard University Press.

———. (1986) "The Evolution of Modern Global Competition." In Michael E. Porter, ed., *Competition in Global Industries*, pp. 405–48. Boston: Harvard Business School Press.

Chayes, Abram. (1959) "The Modern Corporation and the Rule of Law." In Edward S. Mason, ed., *The Corporation in Modern Society*. Cambridge, MA: Harvard University Press.

Child, John. (1987) "Information Technology, Organization, and Response to Strategic Challenges." *California Management Review* 30(Fall):33–50.

Coase, Ronald H. (1937/1952) "The Nature of the Firm." *Economica* 4(1937):386–405. Reprinted in George C. Stigler and Kenneth E. Boulding, eds., *Readings in Price Theory*, pp. 331–51. Homewood, IL: Irwin.

Cusumano, Michael A. (1985) *The Japanese Auto Industry*. Cambridge, MA: Council on East Asian Studies, Harvard University.

De Alessi, Louis. (1983) "Property Rights, Transaction Costs, and X-Efficiency." *American Economic Review* 73(March):64–81.

Eccles, Robert. (1981) "The Quasi-Firm in the Construction Industry." *Journal of Economic Behavior and Organization* 12(December):335–57.

Evan, William M. (1965) "Toward a Theory of Inter-Organizational Relations." *Management Science* 11(August):B217–30.

Fayol, Henri. (1930) *Industrial General Administration*. London: Pitman.

Fisher, Franklin M., James W. McKie, and Richard B. Mancke. (1983) *IBM and the U.S. Data Processing Industry*. New York: Praeger.

Follett, Mary P. (1965) *Dynamic Administration*. Ed. by Henry C. Metcalf. London: Pitman.

Franko, Lawrence G. (1973) *Joint Venture Survival in Multinational Corporations*. New York: Praeger.

Futatsugi, Yusaku. (1986) *Japanese Enterprise Groups*. Tokyo: School of Business Administration, Kobe University.

General Motors Corporation. (1966) "General Motors' Position on United Control of Foreign Operations." February 11.

Ghemawat, Pankaj, Michael E. Porter, and Richard A. Rawlinson. (1986) "Patterns of International Coalition Activity." In Michael E. Porter, ed., *Competition in Global Industries*, pp. 345–67. Boston: Harvard Business School Press.

Gomez-Casseres, Benjamin. (1985) *Multinational Ownership Strategies*. Ph.D. diss., Graduate School of Business Administration, Harvard University.

Goto, Akira. (1982) "Business Groups in a Market Economy." *European Economic Review* 19(Summer):53–70.

Groening, William A. (1981) *The Modern Corporate Manager: Responsibility and Regulation*. New York: McGraw-Hill.

Guetzkow, Harold. (1966) "Relations among Organizations." In *Studies on Behavior in Organizations*, pp. 13–44. Athens: University of Georgia Press.

Hadley, Eleanor M. (1970) *Anti-trust in Japan*. Princeton, NJ: Princeton University Press.

Harrigan, Kathryn R. (1985) *Strategies for Joint Ventures*. Lexington, MA: Lexington Books.

Hladik, Karen J. (1985) *International Joint Ventures*. Lexington, MA: Lexington Books.

Hurst, James W. (1970) *The Legitimacy of the Business Corporation and the Law of the United States*. Charlottesville, VA: University Press of Virginia.

Imai, Ken'ichi. (1978) "Japan's Industrial Organization." *Japanese Economic Studies* 7(Summer):3–67.

Japanese Institute of Labor. (1980) *The Japanese Employment System*. Tokyo: Japanese Institute of Labor.

Jarillo, J. Carlos. (1986) "Entrepreneurship and Growth." Ph.D diss., Harvard Business School.

Jensen, Michael C., and William H. Meckling. (1976) "Theory of the Firm: Managerial Behavior, Agency Costs and Ownership Structure." *Journal of Financial Economics* 3(Fall):305–60.

Johnson, Chalmers. (1982) *MITI and the Japanese Miracle*. Stanford, CA: Stanford University Press.

Katz, Daniel, and Robert L. Kahn. (1966) *The Social Psychology of Organizations*. New York: Wiley.

Kenney, Martin. (1987) *Biotechnology: The University-Industrial Complex*. New Haven, CT: Yale University Press.

Kochan, Thomas A., Harry C. Katz, and Robert B. McKersie. (1986) *The Transformation of American Industrial Relations*. New York: Basic Books.

Krasner, Steven D., ed. (1983) *International Regimes*. Ithaca, NY: Cornell University Press.

Landes, David S. (1969) *The Unbound Prometheus*. Cambridge: Cambridge University Press.

Macauley, Stewart. (1963) "Non-Contractual Relations in Business: A Preliminary Study." *American Sociological Review* 28(Spring):55–69.

McCraw, Thomas K. (1975) "Regulation in America: A Review Article." *Business History Review* 49(Summer):159–83.

———, ed. (1986) *America vs. Japan*. Boston: Harvard Business School Press.

Macneil, Ian R. (1978) "Contracts: Adjustment of Long-term Economic Relations under Classical, Neoclassical, and Relational Contract Law." *Northwestern University Law Review* 72:854–905.

Marshall, Alfred. (1961) *Principles of Economics*. New York: Macmillan.

Mill, John Stuart. (1871) *Principles of Political Economy*. London: Longmans, Green, Reeder & Dyer.

Morison, Samuel Eliot. (1965) *The Oxford History of the American People*. New York: Oxford University Press.

Parsons, Talcott. (1960) *Structure and Process in Modern Societies*. Glencoe, IL: The Free Press.

Pfeffer, Jeffrey. (1972) "Merger as a Response to Organizational Interdependence." *Administrative Science Quarterly* 17:382–94.

Pfeffer, Jeffrey, and Phillip Nowak. (1976) "Joint Venture and Interorganizational Interdependence." *Administrative Science Quarterly* 21:398–418.

Pfeffer, Jeffrey, and Gerald R. Salancik. (1978) *The External Control of Organizations*. New York: Harper & Row.

Piore, Michael J., and Charles F. Sabel. (1984) *The Second Industrial Divide*. New York: Basic Books.

Porter, Michael E. (1980) *Competitive Strategy*. New York: The Free Press.
Posner, Richard A. (1974) "Theories of Economic Regulation." *Bell Journal of Economics and Management Science* 5(Autumn):335–58.
Powell, Walter W. (1987) "Hybrid Organizational Arrangements." *California Management Review* 30(Fall):67–87.
Prindl, Andreas R. (1981) *Japanese Finance*. New York: John Wiley.
Ricardo, David. (1926) *The Principles of Political Economy and Taxation*. New York: E.P. Dutton.
Richardson, G.B. (1972) "The Organization of Industry." *Economic Journal* 82:883.
Roberts, John G. (1973) *Mitsui: Three Centuries of Japanese Business*. New York: Weatherhill.
Rubin, Paul H. (1978) "The Theory of the Firm and the Structure of the Franchise Contract." *Journal of Law and Economics* 21(April):223–33.
Ruggie, John G. (1985) "International Responses to Technology: Concepts and Trends." *International Organization* 39:557–84.
Selznick, Philip. (1957) *Leadership in Administration*. New York: Harper & Row.
Shimokawa, Koichi. (1985) "Japan's Keiretsu System: The Case of the Automobile Industry." *Japanese Economic Studies* 14(Summer):3–32.
Shirai, Taishiro, ed. (1983) *Contemporary Industrial Relations in Japan*. Madison: University of Wisconsin Press.
Sloan, Alfred P., Jr. (1972) *My Years with General Motors*. Garden City, NY: Doubleday.
Smith, Adam. (1976) *The Wealth of Nations*. Chicago: University of Chicago Press.
Sobel, Robert. (1981) *IBM*. New York: Times Books.
Stinchcombe, Arthur L., and Carol A. Heimer. (1985) *Organization Theory and Project Management*. Oslo: Norwegian University Press.
Stopford, John M., and Louis T. Wells, Jr. (1972) *Managing the Multinational Enterprise: Organization of the Firms and Ownership of Subsidiaries*. New York: Basic Books.
Strachan, Harry W. (1976) *Family and Other Business Groups in Economic Development*. New York: Praeger.
Thompson, James D. (1967) *Organizations in Action*. New York: McGraw-Hill.
Thorelli, Hans B. (1986) "Networks: Between Markets and Hierarchies." *Strategic Management Journal* 7(Spring):37–51.
Tonnies, Ferdinand. (1957) *Community and Society*. East Lansing, MI: Michigan State University Press.
Tsuchiya, Moriaki. (1979) "The Japanese Business as 'Capsule.' " *Japanese Economic Studies* 8(Fall):8–41.
Van Cise, Jerold G. (1970) *Understanding the Antitrust Laws*. New York: Practicing Law Institute.
Van de Ven, A.H., D.C. Emmett, and R. Koening. (1975) "Frameworks for Interorganizational Analysis." In A.R. Negandhi, ed., *Interorganizational Theory*, pp. 19–38. Kent, OH: Kent State University Press.
Vernon, Raymond. (1972) *Sovereignty at Bay*. New York: Basic Books.
Williamson, Oliver E. (1975) *Markets and Hierarchies*. New York: The Free Press.
———. (1985) *The Economic Institutions of Capitalism*. New York: The Free Press.

18

ROSABETH MOSS KANTER
AND PAUL S. MYERS

Interorganizational Bonds and Intraorganizational Behavior

How Alliances and Partnerships Change the Organizations Forming Them

In response to rapid technological change and the globalization of markets and competition, American companies are increasingly forming coalitions with other organizations as part of their business strategy (see Johnston and Lawrence 1988; Powell 1987; Harrigan 1985; Porter 1985; Kanter 1989b). Such strategic alliances and partnerships are considered a form of leverage. They allow firms to increase their reach without adding fixed capacity, for example, or to gain a measure of stability in a turbulent environment by planning jointly with organizations on different points on the value chain. Besides the direct financial benefits of sharing costs and gaining economies of scale, partnerships lead to improved time to market for new products (Clark and Fujimoto 1989) and more opportunities for innovation. Business organizations are accomplishing these gains by *pooling* resources with similar companies in pursuit of a similar end (via consortia), by *allying* with other firms to pursue an opportunity for which they lack the full competence (via joint ventures), and by *linking* systems and processes with suppliers, customers, and other stakeholder organizations.

Kanter (1989b) identified the key success factors of partnerships. In successful alliances, managers regard the relationship as strategically important (see also Porter and Fuller 1986), and therefore provide it with adequate resources, management attention, and sponsorship. The partners share a long-term view of their investment in the relationship, which tends to help equalize benefits to each over time. The

Copyright © 1990 by Rosabeth Moss Kanter and Paul S. Myers. Reprinted with permission.

interdependence that often leads to the partnerships in the first place helps keep power balanced. Partnership managers work to integrate the two organizations to maintain communication at the appropriate points of contact. This means that both parties know about the plans and future directions of the other. Finally, successful partnerships become institutionalized, or bolstered by a framework of supporting mechanisms ranging from legal requirements to social ties to shared values.

These success factors imply a significant degree of intraorganizational change on the part of both partners in order to accommodate to the existence of the partnership and to manage it so that it brings benefits to all partners. While many analysts have described the conditions giving rise to alliances and the problems they entail, few have considered their impact on the internal structure and dynamics of the partners' home organizations. This paper attempts to fill that gap by drawing on field observations of partnerships. We present a series of grounded, testable propositions on the intraorganizational impact of alliances on power, roles, and relationships.

From Interorganizational Relationships to Hybrid Forms

Our approach is an attempt to extend the growing literature on interorganizational relationships into an important but as yet underexplored domain. Galaskiewicz (1985) pointed out that one stream of this research focuses on resource procurement and allocation. Work in this tradition has argued that organizations engage in relations with other organizations to manage power dependencies (e.g., Levine and White 1961; Pfeffer and Salancik 1978) or to reduce uncertainty (e.g., Thompson 1967; Aldrich 1979). This approach takes the organization as its level of analysis, and studies have examined standard, largely contractual, exchange relationships.

Moving away from explaining why interorganizational relationships emerge, Bradach and Eccles (1989) reviewed recent developments in economic approaches to the interorganizational arrangements themselves. They claimed that the markets versus hierarchies distinction advocated most notably by Williamson (1975) is more an array than a dichotomy. They focused on the governance mechanisms of price, authority, and trust that mediate transactions between (and within) firms to explain different organizational forms. Noting a growth in the appearance of these nonmarket, nonhierarchical relations between firms, Powell (1987) called such arrangements "hybrid forms." This transaction-focused stream of analysis discusses the emergence of trust, reciprocity, and cooperation in interorganizational relationships; Dore's (1983) work on relational contracting is a prime example. However, most studies or models in this tradition tend to examine the partnership or alliance itself as the unit of analysis, rather than the organizations entering into the relationship. While enlarging our conceptions of the kinds of relationships that can exist among firms, they do not help much in clarifying what this might mean for the firm itself. Issues of structure, governance, or behavior are considered for the partnership rather than for the rest of the partner firms' operations.

Because of an apparent growth in the number of interorganizational alliances and the increasing scope and strategic significance of these relationships, there has been a great deal of recent research on partnerships and alliances in the strategy and business policy fields, much of it with an economic orientation (e.g., Harrigan 1985). For the most part, this literature has focused on the rationale for choice of partners and partnership forms (the "input" side) and the factors associated with success or failure (the "output" side) more than on either alliance management itself (the "throughput" side) or the implications for the structure and behavior of the partner firms. Thus, there are studies of the industry conditions favoring coalitions, the conditions under which an equity stake is sought (Pisano 1989), or the reasons alliances dissolve (see Gomes-Casseres 1987). But despite a growing "popular advice to managers" literature on managing strategic alliances, there has been remarkably little scholarly attention in the business policy area to the organizational behavior implications that ensue when a firm conducts more—and more significant—activities in collaboration with another firm.

For all this recent attention to the emerging explosion of partnerships, then, little has been written that addresses the impact they have on the organizations and their members. While some of the resource dependency studies focus on power dynamics within a focal organization (e.g., Pfeffer and Salancik 1978), other internal implications of these relations are not explored, except for a pervasive classic (and somewhat self-evident) assumption in organizational sociology that organizations with long-term dealings with one another become more isomorphic in structure and behavior.

But if alliances and partnerships open a new sphere of cooperation between organizations, through which partner organizations carry out some of the work done independently and under their own control prior to the formation of the coalition, then the existence of this relationship must have implications for the flow of resources and information within the partner firms as well as for the points of contact among them. Thus, we contend that new interorganizational arrangements among companies produce shifts in the way the people who work for those firms view their roles and perform their work. We can theorize that changes in structure, roles, power dynamics, and behavior will occur within the firm when interorganizational relationships go from arm's length exchanges to closer, more cooperative, and more strategic interactions. The development of explicit alliances with "external" parties should change "internal" organizational dynamics for the firms in such a relationship.

Alliances and Partnerships

Before we discuss these intraorganizational changes we first must identify the specific kinds of arrangements our propositions address. Business organizations engage in a variety of transactions with other firms. We are not talking about these routine, arm's length market transactions. Rather, we examined particular kinds of interorganizational bonds—alliances—that emphasize the relationship aspect of the exchange as much as the goods or services being exchanged.

There are three major types of alliances. Multiorganization services alliances, or consortia, are groups of firms that band together to create a new entity to fill a need shared by all of them. They are generally limited in purpose, such as research and development, and offer the benefits of larger scale through resource pooling. The second type of alliance is the "opportunistic" joint venture, which is sought in order to gain quickly some competitive advantage. The partners exploit some opportunity to a greater extent than would have been possible by either firm alone. Each side makes a distinctive contribution, typically either technology or market access. Commitment beyond earning the initial expected return is uncertain and often depends on whether one of the firms has developed internally the capacity for which it had originally sought a partner. The third kind of alliance is the complementary, or stakeholder, partnership. These are defined by some preexisting interdependency, usually created because each party is on a different position in the value chain (see Porter 1985; Johnston and Lawrence 1988). These partnerships are vertical relations among organizations with complementary capacities.

These three kinds of alliances can be plotted on one axis by the degree of investment made by the partners (e.g., of people, money, time, and other resources), and on the other by their degree of commitment to the partnership (e.g., stake in or need for the output of the relationship). Consortia tend to be the weakest on both dimensions, limited in both investment and commitment. Joint ventures cover a wide range of intermediate investment and commitment, including on the one hand stand-alone ventures (the creation of a new organization under independent management) in which the partners' investment is largely financial and there is no overlap with any partner's own operations, and on the other hand, ventures with clear strategic significance and operations that overlap those of the partners' core businesses. Of the three types of alliances, stakeholder partnerships are entered into least lightly. The desire of a firm to create such an alliance demonstrates a willingness to give up some autonomy and control in exchange for partnerships benefits, to change its systems to match someone else's. While we would expect to see these changes in all kinds of alliances, their effects are most profound in partnerships with stakeholders. These relationships represent the greatest shift in the nature of the external relationship to benefit the company's core businesses, the largest sphere of cooperation, and the greatest potential overlap between the partners' operations; and the interdependence involved makes them likely to be the most enduring, even though they may vary in formalization. This type of alliance, therefore, is most likely to be associated with change in structure and behavior within each of the partner firms.

We would expect the greatest internal change to occur in the wake of relationships with the highest investment and the highest commitment. The data for our propositions thus come largely from stakeholder alliances—partnerships with suppliers or customers.

Intraorganizational Implications: Some Propositions

The intraorganizational implications of interorganizational relationships can be seen by comparing pre- and postpartnership conditions in the same organization as well as by comparing conditions in companies with and without significant partnerships. Exploratory field research from 1986 to 1989 on firms with newly developed partnerships permits the development of propositions about these implications, propositions that can be tested in more systematic research. Cases include the key supplier alliances at Digital Equipment Corporation; Pacific Telesis's union-management partnership; a pseudonymous high-tech joint venture (see Kanter 1988, 1989b for further description of the first three); NCR's stakeholder relations approach, including both supplier and customer partnerships; joint ventures at Banc One; and other examples encountered in the course of research on new venture investments by eight companies (Kanter 1989b).

For the most part, interviews and observations were conducted after the partnerships had already been established; but in all cases, subjects were asked for comparisons of "how it was before" as well as "what is different now," and observations of the most problematic or conflict-ridden issues within the organizations helped point to the changes taking place. While comparative data were retrospective, the consistency of findings across different settings indicates that they provided valid insight, especially for an exploratory field study. Other field research, on companies without significant partnerships, helped provide another, albeit more impressionistic basis for comparison.

As the "baseline" for the propositions we set forth, we posit an "ideal type" of prepartnership organization structure that is an extension of the paradigmatic closed system, hierarchical, bureaucratic corporation often described in the sociological literature on formal organizations (and assumed as Williamson's "hierarchy"). In this idealized prepartnership condition, for example, suppliers and customers are dealt with by specialized staffs with a limited role in strategy formulation (linked to the strategic level only by the head of their staff organization), confined to execution of policies defined elsewhere, and measured on the efficiency of ongoing operations (sales volume, reductions in purchase price, number of orders executed, etc.). These staffs serve as gatekeepers controlling the access of others within the organization to their external constituencies, and in turn, they have limited contact with other organizational functions, receiving inputs or passing on outputs in linear, arm's length fashion. When a new, closer relationship is established with suppliers, customers, or other partners, however, these classic, ideal-typical bureaucratic conditions change.

While we are confident about our comparative basis for advancing a set of propositions, we should also note that we are not asserting unilateral causality. The changes in structure and dynamics observed within partnership firms were not wholly (or in some cases even primarily) attributable to their partnership arrangements. Other strategic considerations, such as a desire to reduce costs, to improve technology sourcing to increase innovation, to reduce product development time, or to enter new markets, often drove changes in organization structure and roles including the very formation of partnerships in the first place. In each case studied, the creation of partnerships was one of a number of new strategic choices made by the organizations in response to changing competitive conditions. In short, cause and effect are difficult to entangle in the study of organizational change. Strategic alliances and partnerships are simultaneously effects and causes of other changes, all in the service of overall strategic choices for the organization.

Power

The most important degree of change from the prepartnership state is in power—both "outside" and "inside" the firm. By power, we mean increased centrality in the flow of, and ability to mobilize, resources, information, and support (Kanter 1983).

The redefinition of power begins with a rethinking of the company's role vis-à-vis its stakeholders to give them more influence over internal choices in the interest of greater control or influence over the portion of the environment represented by the stakeholder. The very notion of "strategic partnership" entails such a reexamination of power relations. "Partners" are welcome allies, not manipulated adversaries. Any enhanced benefits (in cost or innovation or market access) from partnering means enhanced roles for allies in internal decision making (either actually, or because they are now taken into account in a different way), and this can be accomplished only through a sincere acknowledgment that such influence is warranted. This requires a new attitude among those who might be prone to feel that kind gestures toward stakeholders are a gift offered in order to obtain some gain and thus something that equally can be withdrawn at will. Such a paternalistic attitude can undermine the essential core of the partnership effort and its future potential. The new power must be real.

As partners gain power in their dealings with the firm, power shifts also begin to occur inside the organization itself. Those closest to the firm's partners in terms of knowledge and contact come to play a more powerful role in their own organization—because they represent a key strategic relationship for the firm, and because they must be able to mobilize resources in service of the partnership. As the power of partners grows, so does the power of those dealing with the partners.

Proposition One. As those in closer contact with the organization's partners become more central to the strategic communication flow, their power inside the organization increases.

This is largely self-evident, but it is an important starting point for the rest of the propositions. The decision to rely more heavily on partners for "goods" or services of value to the organization changes the position of those who manage the interface from peripheral boundary-spanning roles to more central strategic roles. The purchasing department in a computer company, for example, is now the conduit for information about new technology, which has great value for the resource allocation decisions made by top managers as well as for the product design decisions made by other functional departments. But in order for purchasing staff to be able to flag important data they get from and on suppliers, they must be better informed about the issues and concerns of top management and related professional functions (engineering, manufacturing), and they must have an open channel of communication through which information passes in both directions. Even if a field sales staff gathers important customer intelligence in the course of its routine work, such data have no value for the firm unless there is an open communication channel and acknowledgment of the legitimacy and validity of data from that source; customer alliances tend to produce greater legitimacy and communication as field salespeople become part of the "key relationship management" team.

For many of the managers and professions involved in partnership dealings, we observed that empowerment through greater access to information is clear and direct. After partnerships are established with the external constituencies with which they are in contact, they tend to have increased access to top management, whereas previously they were not included in strategic deliberations. They tend to receive more information and data to understand better what drives business decisions, and they can get questions answered with a single phone call to a previously inaccessible executive. Because they may now interact with people in a number of functional areas who need their information, they become a central conduit in the communications channel. In some cases, these middle-level people may increasingly know things before the rest of company management does, even becoming a source of information and influence for others in middle as well as top management.

As partners become important sources of valuable information in other ways, beyond their centrality in strategic decisions and ongoing operations, those in contact with the partners have more valuable information to convey. When partners contribute their own market analyses and other results of their monitoring of environmental conditions that complement the scanning of their ally, or when partners consult each other on matters of business significance before decisions are made, the power of those in contact with the partner is enhanced. Those people have earlier access to key information and become a source of education for others inside the firm. NCR, which has a Vice President of Stakeholder Relations, assigns all of its key managers, regardless of formal responsibilities, to meet with five major customers at least twice a year to discuss future product plans, the effect on them of changing market conditions, and what NCR can do to help them deal with these issues, in an open-ended company-to-company information exchange. The legal counsel and the head of personnel thus become almost as qualified as the senior marketing executive to provide information and contribute to decisions about market trends.

Empowerment through centrality in the communication flow is further enhanced when those in contact with the partners are expected to become active champions for them. NCR has appointed internal "advocates" for each key supplier whose role is to facilitate new developments and to handle any issues arising out of the relationship. The NCR Intel advocate is an NCR employee, yet the expectation that this employee speak for Intel enables the advocate to speak up on the basis of his information in a more powerful way than existed before the partnership was established. People in such advocacy roles experience an independence that also augments their power.

> *Proposition Two. As a partnership develops greater strategic importance, the power of the subunit or department responsible for managing that relationship increases.*

As resource dependency theory would predict, the power of the managers in key strategic units increases since their duties are now viewed as more critical to the company's success. The empowerment of Digital's purchasing department was a clear outgrowth of the shift to a partnership orientation. Senior management held a higher expectation of the roles Purchasing could play in the financial and customer service performance of the company. Purchasing "controlled" billions of dollars of company resources; executives seeking to leverage these funds turned to Purchasing for discussions about how to do so. Concurrently, plant managers began to get involved in reviewing supplier performance, which had previously been relegated to a lone lower-level buyer. The participation of plant and senior management in such activities reflected the growing importance of Purchasing's strategic role. One Purchasing manager commented:

> Management at Digital now looks at Purchasing and asks us, "Which companies will we be working with in the future?" They want to know from both technical and cost points of view. They wonder, "Does management need to give more time to championing relationships with these companies?" What often happens is a top manager will say, "I will give Purchasing thirty hours of my time this year which you can use to schedule meetings with top-level people from supplier companies." If he feels Purchasing has used his time wisely, next year he might give us fifty hours. Each year, people at higher and higher levels of sponsorship are getting involved in building these new strategic relationships.

In one case, a purchasing manager accompanied a senior executive and some professionals on a tour of more than fifty suppliers around the world, meeting with their senior management. They explained the new strategy, including Digital's desire for "an equal relationship where we tell each other what we are doing right and what we are doing wrong."

Proposition Three. Partnerships decrease the monopoly power of staff gatekeepers on managing external relationships.

An ironic consequence of the increased power for the unit with operating responsibility for the partnership is that that same group loses its monopoly power over its area of expertise. A single point of contact between one organization and its external constituencies characterized the traditional mode. For example, the purchasing department managed procurement, the sales department dealt with customers, the labor relations department handled the union. These departments acted as gatekeepers, monitoring the boundaries and deciding, or at least influencing, what resources could come in and what would be sent out. All information flowed through that gate, and the gatekeepers monopolized the management of the relationship.

Partnerships, in contrast, simultaneously make the activities involved in external relationships more important and reduce the former gatekeepers' monopoly over them. At Pacific Telesis, the labor relations department no longer had sole responsibility for union relations, since union leaders met on a regular basis in joint committees with company executives. Started to facilitate and improve its data processing department, Banc One's alliance with EDS soon involved representatives from marketing and finance in the formerly exclusive bailiwick of the computer experts. Nearly 100 people drawn from many places in the organization served on a series of task forces to plan the computer system of the future.

Proposition Four. Empowerment is accompanied by greater responsibility, thus entailing greater career risk for those with enhanced power. Their personal success is increasingly dependent on partner performance.

While cooperative relationships empower some groups, they impose their burdens, too. With the power comes responsibility. Arm's length, adversarial relationships make it easy for people to complain, to cast blame on the outside organization "over whom we have no control," or to withdraw without having to play any role in improving the situation. But a partnership orientation means that those working with the partners are expected to work things out, and their own success depends on their ability to deliver performance from the partner (with only modest actual control).

If prepartnership Digital did not like what a particular supplier did, the company could complain vociferously or simply shift its business elsewhere. Now, with the spirit of partnership prevailing, Digital staff must first work with the supplier to solve the problem. If they cannot solve it, they must take the blame;

yet they do not have full control over the actions of a supplier. More time is spent, then, trying to influence suppliers to meet Digital standards; the purchasing organization is developing an elaborate series of supplier training programs and may even send consultants into supplier firms. Similarly, both the Pacific Telesis managers and the union presidents involved in the PacTel/Communications Workers of America union-management partnership expressed a sense of great career risks when their peers expected them to be able to influence the partners in the "right" way, to meet their own organization's standards. One manager reported great difficulty in shifting from blaming the union attitudes to an expectation that he could easily get the company's "partner" to see things the company's way; and his lack of success under the new expectations caused him to be moved out of the promotion mainstream.

> *Proposition Five. While enhancing the power of some, partnerships may disempower others (e.g., by displacing them in the communication channel or decreasing their strategic importance).*

Partnerships often mean a reduction in power for those not involved. Stronger links tying organizations together in a cooperative fashion pose dilemmas for the remaining hierarchies inside each partner's home organization. A variety of political problems develops. First, in some cases, partner representatives agreed that it could be difficult or dangerous to report much to others of partnership deliberations. They could report *outcomes* to their "home team," but not the *process* by which the decision was made. Sometimes the issue was purely procedural: why the discussions of various issues took so long, and concerns that attempts to share information about the process could create more confusion or misunderstanding. In other instances, representatives needed to maintain the partner's confidences or show commitment to the partnership, especially at times of delicate negotiations; this required that they mask the actual process. The effect of withholding such details was to make those left out of the partnership sphere, with middle managers foremost among them, feel isolated and disempowered.

The people involved in a partnership, then, face the problem of selling those around them and below them on partnership decisions—decisions that by definition can involve some deviation from the pure pursuit of the home company's short-term interest. Partners had to contend with intensely political considerations. They tried to convince members of their own organization that they were not "selling out" when their decisions appeared to offer benefits to the partner, while at the same time trying to persuade the partner that they were not caving in to parochial organizational interests when they advocated their company's position. One joint venture manager deliberately fought hard on symbolic issues of importance to the people below him, even though the fight put the partnership at risk, because he felt that the people reporting to him needed to see him win a few victories in order to support his leadership, and by extension, the partnership itself.

Structure and Roles

Because they have both strategic and operational significance, complementary or stakeholder partnerships tend to involve linkages, often cross-functional, between several levels of the partnering firms: joint goal setting at the strategic level, joint planning and technical data exchange at the professional level, and direct real-time data links at the operational level. Each of these linkages in and of itself may represent a major departure from previous practice; together they may constitute a new set of structural ties within the firm.

Overall, partnerships tend to involve line managers more directly in external relationships; they tend to involve more people from more areas of the firm; and they tend to be associated with greater cross-functional cooperation (although partnerships are not always the sole direct cause of the latter shift). More line manager and senior manager involvement in partnerships does not necessarily mean a *diminished* role for the former staff gatekeepers, but does mean a *different* role.

> *Proposition Six. Partnerships increase the number of functions and the number of people involved in the new external relationships. The staff function changes to include integration and coordination, rather than solely task initiation.*

Partnerships can increase the number of functions and people involved in external relationships. For example, where strong customer alliances prevail, both product designers and production workers get directly involved with customers. NCR has involved outside experts, including software developers, to provide solutions to customers that it cannot provide with internal resources alone. The staff members who have lost their monopoly power must change how they operate; they must be willing to share information and work together with others from different functional backgrounds. If they do not, they risk being bypassed altogether.

The interaction between functional areas takes place in at least three ways. The first area of contact involves strategic, long-term issues. At an intermediate level are activities such as planning for specific events; an example is contract negotiations between labor and management. The third arena is actual day-to-day tasks, such as data exchanges between customers and suppliers. Top management is likely to be involved at all levels. In the NCR supplier partnership case, for example, the CEO visits the CEOs of key suppliers regularly—a dramatic change in his use of time, and, he reported, the first time that any of them had been visited by the CEO of a customer firm—to discuss overall business goals. He began this practice when he realized that there were a number of suppliers of tremendous importance to NCR whose CEOs he did not know on a first-name basis. "This struck me as absurd," he commented, "so I immediately set out to visit them regularly, to cultivate a relationship that would let them make a greater contribution to our business." By 1989 he was visiting regularly with at least six major suppliers, discussing strategic matters as well as monitoring operations. At the same time, a cross-functional team of professionals from NCR as well as supplier organizations works together on product development and manufacturing planning. Then, when products become operational, NCR and supplier factories have direct communication to ensure a smooth, timely, and cost-effective flow of inventory.

This cross-functional interaction changes the task of staff departments in a partnership to one of integration and coordination rather than domination. With multiple ties connecting partners, communication can be unmanageable or inefficient unless each partner is well integrated itself. The intertwining of partnership interests with many aspects of the business also creates a need for early consultation across functions, and for closer working relationships. For departments to work in isolation could mean negative reverberations of their actions on the partnership. Furthermore, decisions may require the knowledge or expertise brought by those in touch with the partners. For example, one marketing manager at Digital commented:

> In the areas where we are doing a lot of work in building relationships with third-party suppliers, various marketing groups use our folks to help them select the supplier, to decide how good their product is, and to see how it should be positioned.

Similar joint efforts developed between Purchasing and both Engineering and Manufacturing. Clearly, the shift to supplier partnerships meant that the purchasing department was getting more involved in discussions and collaboration with other functions.

Proposition Seven. Staff positions become less routinized and less tightly controlled, allowing and encouraging more autonomous decision making.

Traditionally, staff roles are circumscribed, with bureaucratic policy manuals delineating who has accountability for what tasks and how those tasks are to be performed. Managing alliance relationships, though, calls for staff members to be flexible and responsive to stakeholder needs. The actions that such problem-solving situations require cannot be codified or routinized. Staff members of partner organizations gain autonomy, in part because their behavior—sometimes consisting of making soothing phone calls to upset customers or suppliers—cannot be measured and evaluated. It is results that count; staff members are left to their own best devices for making the partnership work.

The change in traditional staff roles is apparent in Digital's purchasing department. Jobs are being upgraded, as routine administration and an emphasis on meeting specifications are replaced by a need for more experienced people who can be involved in every aspect of a business process and can handle complex negotiations. While previously staff members were rewarded for never running out of parts, the department now emphasizes meeting broader time-to-market and profitability goals. Instead of using the purchasing staff as an opportunity to promote less sophisticated clerical personnel, the department seeks people who could effectively take more complete business responsibility for their decisions, represent the company in strategy discussions with partners, and even carry out such specialized professional tasks as writing contracts without using lawyers. While these would be more significant tasks, fewer people would do them as advanced electronic data transmission technology replaces purely routine paperwork. Orders can now be sent to vendors, and shipped by the vendor, with a few strokes on a computer keyboard. Purchasing staffers' time is now freed up, allowing them to concentrate on building a better relationship with the suppliers.

Proposition Eight. The staff role changes from control to consultation.

Partnerships require a new set of behaviors: cooperative problem solving replaces adversarial bargaining. Threats to cut off a customer's shipment or cancel a supplier's order or similar acts of brinkmanship are no longer a tactical alternative. Managers learn to resolve points of contention and deal with real issues instead of taking the easy option of exiting. Partnership is a commitment not to end the relationship abruptly, and subsequent investments reinforce that commitment.

Skills and Behavior

Regardless of personal preference or organizational style, behavior in a partnership cannot take a command-and-control form, since the relationship is not hierarchically governed. There is no decision-making autonomy when an alliance between firms is involved; decisions must involve a degree of consultation. Not only does the possibility of unilateral action decrease, but the number of forums for cooperative decision making may increase (e.g., the number of task forces or planning groups linking the partners). Thus, the skills of the individuals involved in partnership dealings would tend to become more important, and more participative, collaborative behavior would be associated with partnership activity.

Proposition Nine. Partnerships make individual personalities and competencies more important than in traditional arm's length relationships, and interactions become more relational and less formal as formal authority gives way to individual influence.

Overall, the development of strategic alliances is one more force toward politicizing the role of managers, making it essential for them to be able to juggle a set of constituencies rather than control a set of subordinates or contracted agents. Alliances and partnerships multiply the complexity of performing leadership tasks. For example, after leading Tecknowledge, Inc., producer of expert systems software, in development alliances with six major corporations, including General Motors, Procter & Gamble, and FMC, President Lee Jecht told a *Business Week* reporter that he feels "like the mayor of a small city. I have a constituency that won't quit. It takes a hell of a lot of balancing."

That balancing act was not required in the traditional corporation. Whatever its shortcomings in practice, the traditional managerial style had one advantage for control-conscious managers: it preserved the illusion of decision-making autonomy for the corporation as a whole. Executives could move quickly and even make unilateral decisions without consulting any of the other organizations that would be affected by the decisions. There might be negative consequences later—for example, a labor union calling a strike after an unpalatable management announcement, or customers switching to another manufacturer after a price rise—but at least there were few apparent constraints on action. It might be smarter management to consult with stakeholders and take their interests into account in making decisions, but it was not required.

Partnerships, in contrast, require this kind of consultation as a matter of routine. The illusion of autonomy is lost and unilateral action decreases. The number of forums for cooperative decision making increases.

> *Proposition Ten. Partnerships increase the importance of having participative skills.*

The shift from simple market exchanges to more intimate partnerships thus requires a different set of skills, especially for those working closely with a component of the partnership. These include gathering information, resisting preconceived ideas, testing assumptions, and seeking consensus. Partners need to be good listeners, to stop and see a problem situation from the other partner's perspective. Consensus building and involvement replace fiat announcements and exclusion. Digital recognizes the importance of this skill building. It conducts in-house training for its own employees and those of its suppliers. Both sets of managers learn the same communication and team-building skills. In the process, they learn how to work better with the other.

> *Proposition Eleven. Because relationships between partners will be more egalitarian and less hierarchical in terms of social roles, expectations, and behaviors, the expectation for more egalitarian relationships within the firm will also grow.*

Unlike relationships in a hierarchy, relationships in a partnership are ostensibly more egalitarian. Representatives of one organization cannot command those in the other to do anything the way they could issue directives to subordinate divisions or employees. Discussions of goals and a search for consensus become more important than who has the upper hand. Indeed, even when one partner has the power to make its will prevail over the other, it is considered very dangerous and damaging to the relationship to try.

This change in the relationships between the partners often has a counterpart internal to the partners as well. As more people are involved in decision making through cross-functional activity, power centers within the firm diminish. Power does not remain concentrated, and new staff areas are empowered by their increased strategic importance. More levels and more departments are exposed to the outside environment and are engaging in boundary-spanning activities that before were the province of monopoly gatekeepers. Internal distinctions about who is responsible for dealing with customers or suppliers break down when it becomes part of everyone's job.

Conclusions

We hypothesize that these changes in power, roles, and relationships come about because they facilitate the partnership and enable them to succeed. This functionalist, and seemingly tautological argument is based on analyses of successful partnerships. A better test would be to look at failures and see if there is an association between failure and absence of these changes. Of course, one difficulty in identifying the sources of these changes and linking them to venture success is that many firms entering into these relationships are undergoing internal shifts in many ways already. Seeking a venture or alliance partner is often driven by a shift in strategy. Firms undergoing such change frequently are changing the nature of their staff roles anyway. Acknowledging these other factors, we qualify our claims by saying only that we identify the intraorganizational changes that tend to be associated with alliances, although they may not be a sole or a direct result of the partnership itself.

Future research is needed to validate, amend, and add to these propositions. We do not have a complete understanding of the processes by which these changes occur. Nor do we know the long-term impact of partnerships, particularly whether these changes are stable or if traditional patterns will eventually regain prominence. We can say that alliances spawn a new way of thinking about the management and organizational tasks of a modern corporation. The internal changes we point to may help companies seeking to gain the benefits of allying with other organizations to understand what they may be in for and to prepare to deal with it.

References

Aldrich, H.A. (1979) *Organizations and Environments*. Englewood Cliffs, NJ: Prentice-Hall.

Bradach, J.L., and R.G. Eccles. (1989) "Price, Authority, and Trust: From Ideal Types to Plural Forms." *Annual Review of Sociology* 15:97–115.

Business Week. (1986) "Corporate Odd Couples." July 21, pp. 100–105.

Clark, K.B., and T. Fugimoto. (1989) "Lead Time in Automobile Product Development: Explaining the Japanese Advantage." Harvard Business School Working Paper no. 89–033.

Dore, R. (1983) "Goodwill and the Spirit of Market Capitalism." *British Journal of Sociology* 34:459–82.

Galaskiewicz, J. (1985) "Interorganizational Relations." *Annual Review of Sociology* 11:281–304.

Gomes-Casseres, B. (1987) "Joint Venture Instability: Is It a Problem?" *Columbia Journal of World Business* 22(Summer):97–102.

Harrigan, K. (1985) *Managing Joint Ventures.* Lexington, MA: Lexington Books.

Johnston, R., and P.R. Lawrence. (1988) "Beyond Vertical Integration: The Rise of the Value-adding Partnership." *Harvard Business Review* 66(July–August):94–104.

Kanter, R.M. (1983) *The Change Masters.* New York: Simon & Schuster.

———. (1988) "The New Alliances: How Strategic Partnerships Are Reshaping American Business." In H.L. Sawyer, ed., *Business in the Contemporary World.* Lanham, MD: University Press of America.

———. (1989a) "Mastering Innovation Dilemmas." *California Management Review* 31(Summer):45–69.

———. (1989b) *When Giants Learn to Dance: Mastering the Challenges of Strategy, Management, and Careers in the 1990s.* New York: Simon & Schuster.

Levine, S., and P. White. (1981) "Exchange as a Conceptual Framework for the Study of Interorganizational Relationships." *Administrative Science Quarterly* 5:583–601.

Pfeffer, J., and G. Salancik. (1978) *The External Control of Organizations: A Resource Dependence Perspective.* New York: Harper & Row.

Pisano, G. (1989) "Using Equity Participation to Support Exchange: Evidence from the Biotechnology Industry." *Journal of Law, Economics, and Organization* 5(Spring):109–26.

Porter, M.E. (1985) *Competitive Advantage.* New York: The Free Press.

Porter, M.E., and M.B. Fuller. (1986) "Coalitions and Global Strategy." In M.E. Porter, ed., *Competition in Global Industries*, pp. 315–44. Boston: Harvard Business School Press.

Powell, W.W. (1987) "Hybrid Organizational Arrangements: New Forms or Transitional Development?" *California Management Review* 30(1):67–87.

Thompson, J.A. (1967) *Organizations in Action.* New York: McGraw-Hill.

Williamson, O.E. (1975) *Markets and Hierarchies: Analysis and Antitrust Implications.* New York: The Free Press.

VIII

The Next Steps

19

AMITAI ETZIONI

Socio-Economics

The Next Steps

Socio-economists should not act like shoemakers who have no time to make shoes for themselves. It is time to apply socio-economics to the condition and dynamics of socio-economics. This entails recognizing that a change in paradigms is not merely an intellectual and social-philosophical matter; paradigms have infrastructures that affect their dynamics. Presently, socio-economics lacks institutions to train socio-economists to serve both in the community at large (as managers instead of MBAs, as policy analysts instead of neoclassical economists, and so on), and as educators (in business and management schools as well as undergraduate and high school social science departments). Socio-economics has rapidly advanced many of the elements that are necessary for a grand-scale paradigm shift to occur. Now, to complete the transformation, educational practices and job structures must be modified.

We should begin by briefly reviewing the elements that are already in place or are rapidly developing. Within a year of its founding at the Harvard Business School in March 1989, the International Society for the Advancement of Socio-Economics (SASE) grew to encompass more than 600 members, and created the tools of a cross-disciplinary society: executive council, elected officials, annual meetings (1990 in Washington, DC; 1991 at the Stockholm School of Economics; 1992 in California), representative fellows in eighteen countries. Other components are falling into place as numerous publications are in the works. In addition to the present collection, M.E. Sharpe will publish several volumes of socioeconomic papers, including one edited by Richard Coughlin, planned for 1991. A reader in socio-economics is also being prepared. Special issues of scholarly journals devoted to socio-economics are on their way (e.g., *Journal of Behavioral Economics*, Summer 1990; *Journal of Economic Psychology*; and *Human Relations*), and the *Journal of Socio-Economics* is to begin publication in 1991.

There is also broad consensus on the basic substance of the new paradigm.

This is reflected in the "minimum platform" of the Society for the Advancement of Socio-Economics, cited here in part:

> (a) The *independent variables* in any proposition member of socio-economic theory have to include *at least one non-economic variable and one economic one.* Thus if we study productivity rates (as a dependent variable), independent variables may include capital per worker, levels of pay and other such economic variables but must also include at least one variable from another social science (for example, level of commitment to work ethic), to qualify. Without it, the proposition would be a proposition of economic theory. Similarly, if all independent variables are non-economic, say they include commitment to work ethic, degree of self-esteem, and size of social groups at work, we are dealing with sociological, psychological, or socio-psychological propositions but not in socio-economics.
>
> (b) Core *substantive assumptions*: (i) *Competition is a sub-system* embedded within a societal context that contains values, power relations, and social relations. The societal context both enables and restrains competition. That is, socio-economics assumes that self-interests are not necessarily or automatically complementary and harmonious; societal source of order is necessary. (ii) *Individual choices* are shaped by values, emotions, and knowledge. There is no prior assumption that people act rationally, or that they pursue only or largely self-interest or pleasure.
>
> (c) *Methodological approach: Inductive studies are coequal in their methodological standing with deductive ones.* E.g., a study of how firms actually behave has the same basic merit as treating the firm as an analytic concept or mathematical model. Inductive inputs and deductive derivations are assumed to correct, and thus balance one another.
>
> (d) Socio-economics is both a *positive* and *normative* science. I.e., it openly recognizes its policy relevance and seeks to be self-aware of its normative implications rather than maintain a mantle of an exclusively positive science.
>
> (e) Socio-economics does not entail a commitment to any one ideological position, implied in terms such as political economy and social-economics, but is open to a range of positions that share a view of treating economic behavior as involving the whole person and all facets of society.
>
> To reiterate, rather than discuss what is socio-economics, the preceding statement attempts to draw the confines of socio-economics.

A large variety of viewpoints and perspectives exist within these confines, just as there is variety within the neoclassical paradigm. A new approach does not require a detailed agreement on all, or even most, concepts and theorems; it requires shared conceptual, philosophical, and ethical foundations. Socio-economics already has such foundations. They allow numerous individual scholars who have long been working in complementary directions (including Kenneth Boulding, Ronald Dore, Mary Douglas, Albert Hirschman, Paul Lawrence, Harvey Leibenstein, Leon Lindberg, Gunnar Myrdal, Fritz Scharpf, David Sears, Amartya Sen, Herbert Simon, Neil Smelser, Michael Useem, and many others) to join together. Moreover, socio-economics builds on the efforts of preceding groups including institutional economists, social economists, behavioral economists, and evolutionary economists.

In short, rather than starting from scratch, socio-economics provides a community and shared framework for much of this work. Hirschman best captured the situation when he commented during a dinner in his honor at the founding meeting of the SASE: "I have been doing this work for thirty years, but it was so lonely."[1]

If there is any particular reason why socio-economics seems to be taking off more rapidly than previous groups, aside from the fact that it stands on their shoulders, it is that unlike its forerunners, most of which were hindered in their ability to evolve a new paradigm by the mixing of both neoclassical economists and potential socio-economists, the SASE is openly and deliberately dedicated to the new paradigm. The SASE counts very few neoclassicists among its members, and as a result, avoids much sterile debate between loyalists of the two paradigms. Thus, the new community can focus on developing alternative conceptions, findings, and methodologies.

Socio-economics has already reached the stage where its predictive and explanatory power would lead many to choose this approach, were such power the main test leading people to choose paradigms. Socio-economic studies show: tax compliance is encouraged by social sanctions and moral commitments (disapproval of friends, value of honesty) as well as sanctions; energy use is affected by attitudes toward conservation as well as price incentives (Stern 1984); job turnover is explained as much by social commitment as by economic factors such as pay opportunities (Price and Mueller 1981); both deterrence and moral commitments significantly affect people's predispositions to commit crime (Grasmick and Green 1981); voting behavior is more strongly determined by a sense of civic duty than by self-interest (Sears et al. 1980); and so on. These studies are more powerful, by both predictive and explanatory criteria, than neoclassical attempts to deal with the same phenomena.

Among recent, highly specific predictions, note that after the crash of the stock market in October 1987, nine out of ten neoclassical economists predicted a major recession in 1988, based on their argument that as people's sense of wealth declines, so too will their purchases. Drawing on studies of slow learning and low rationality, however, this socio-economist predicted, as recorded in the *New York Times* business section, January 3, 1988, that no recession would follow—and none did. More recently, Poland is urged, on the basis of neoclassical theory, to "jump" into a market economy, to move rapidly from a command and control economy to a free market system. On the other hand, socio-economics predicts that unless Poland slows down, it will face a severe crisis leading to rejection of the economic program and the endangerment of democracy. Why? Because social, cultural, and institutional adjustments necessary to transform the economy take much more time and resources than neoclassicists assume.[2] We will see which prediction/prescription holds.

All this does not mean that there is no further need for extensive empirical, conceptual, and other forms of scientific and scholarly work in this area. It is only intended to suggest that this work is already relatively well attended to.

What is most sorely lacking now is the training of more hands. There is a great demand for socio-economists, but almost no new supply.

This demand is most strongly expressed by managers of corporations, non-profit institutions, and federal, local, and state governments. As one interviews those in charge, one soon discovers a nagging frustration. Most of the trainees they face, graduates of 700 or more business and management schools, and various programs in public administration and public policy, are trained in the "number crunching," individualistic, rationalist tradition of neoclassical economics. These graduates tend to have little training, understanding, or sensitivity for human relations, culture, community, "statecraft" (the skills of coalition building and developing bases of support for policies), or managing under partial information. True, many of these schools offer some courses in these non-neoclassical subjects, but such courses are often considered secondary if not marginal, and above all, are not integrated into a curriculum or paradigm because most of these schools are dominated by neoclassical thinking and teaching. Thus, the availability of some courses in human relations, ethics, psychology, sociology, or political science has little effect on students who spend most of their time learning to watch balance sheets, to make decisions on the basis of highly mathematical models that are denuded of information, sensibility, or sensitivity, or to shuffle assets.

To advance the paradigm, what is needed are series of courses in socioeconomic management in which the whole fabric of an organization's existence, including its societal, cultural, and political contexts, provides the core of the curriculum, and economic analysis finds its place *within* this context. There are very few institutions that explicitly train this way, and rather few that approximate it implicitly (the Wallace E. Carroll Graduate School of Management at Boston College is one of the few). Hence, those who retain managers have no choice but to "buy" what the market offers and then try, on the job, to correct what the existing schools have wrought. The final test of the proposition that corporations, hospitals, schools, government agencies, international bodies such as the World Bank and AID, churches, and many others, would much rather hire managers trained in socio-economics, will come as some entrepreneuring schools put together such a program and their graduates are eagerly sought.

Next, socio-economics needs graduate departments that will train socioeconomic Ph.D.s for teaching and research. There is more at stake here than meets the eye. Obviously, if the scholarly, intellectual, and empirical work of socio-economics is to grow, it requires that more people be systematically trained in it. But paradigms rest on more than philosophical assumptions; they have institutional underpinnings, ranging from job markets to grant-giving committees. Indeed, control of these institutions is one major force keeping neoclassical economics as powerful as it still is. As a consequence, for example, after Tom Jester presented powerful findings that contradicted neoclassical economics and supported socio-economics (he stated that people prefer a work/leisure mix over leisure; they care about nominal wages and not merely real wages; and so on), he added that he would still urge his students to study neoclassical economics because "that's where the jobs are." In another case, a graduate of the Harvard economics department, teaching at the School of Public Affairs at the University of Maryland, exclaimed, "I do not believe a single word I am teaching, but this is what I was hired to teach." National Science Foundation committees have only recently begun to consider applications by socio-economists, and are still dominated by the neoclassical paradigm. Some exceptions exist, such as the Russell Sage Foundation, which has a small program in behavioral economics (that supports both kinds of economists), but most foundations still support only the old kind. It follows that in order for the new paradigm to continue to grow, it will need to acquire all these institutional underpinnings (programs, divisions within professional schools, and departments) to gain both the collegiality and the jobs needed to create a critical mass and a market for socioeconomic faculty, who could in turn generate the teaching material and research to sustain the growth of socio-economics and train a steady stream of graduates to serve within the community.

There is also an important mission for socio-economics within undergraduate and high school curricula—a mission to provide not only a view of economic, and more generally choice behavior, that is more realistic, empirically grounded, and valid than neoclassical economics, but one that relies on much sounder ethical foundations. The messages of the neoclassical paradigm are reflected in textbooks that teach that you ought to give as little as possible and take as much as you can; that people are driven by self-interest; that those who do not attempt to get a free ride, or those who volunteer, are irrational; that morality is but a facade; and so on.[3] This perspective needs to be changed by teaching that emphasizes that people have, and ought to have, a nobler side; that they are inclined to serve others and the community; that cooperation is as important as competition; and that moral causes are, and ought to be, a major fact of life.

This corrected teaching is significant not only in shaping the education of future generations, but also for our current generation. There are powerful parallel world views in the community at large that are a corollary to the neoclassical one, namely, laissez faire conservatism and libertarianism. (I say parallel and corollary because these world views feed into the neoclassical paradigm and it feeds into them, but each has its own sources of support and dynamics.) These world views need correcting. For instance, when the market is celebrated as a cure-all, and idealogues call for the abolition of social security, when asset shuffling is destroying the economic bases of the economy, and when matters of safety and environment are subject to narrow and faulty cost-benefit analysis, there is an urgent need for a perspective that will encompass other factors, as well as economic ones. Thus, socio-economics stresses the role of social justice next to economic efficiency; the significance of psychological "income" and emotional security for a productive labor force; the importance of protecting institutional integrity (and various stakeholders) versus corporate raiding; and the significance of moral foundations, not merely for the family and community, but also for the market itself, which ultimately rests on trust and integrity.

Notes

1. On the history of socio-economics, see Swedberg (1990), Lutz (1990), and *Harvard Business School Bulletin* (1989).
2. See Etzioni (1990a) and Etzioni (1990b).
3. See Etzioni (1988), chap. 14.

References

Etzioni, Amitai. (1988) *The Moral Dimension: Toward a New Economics*. New York: The Free Press.

———. (1990a) "New Hopes, Old Habits." *National Interest*, no. 19(Spring):12–14.

———. (1990b) "Is Poland Getting Bad Advice?" *New York Times*, June 12.

Grasmick, Harold G., and Donald E. Green. (1981) "Deterrence and the Morally Committed." *Sociological Quarterly* 22 (1):1–14.

Jackson, Nancy. (1989) "Socio-Economics: Stirring the Neoclassical Pot." *Harvard Business School Bulletin* (June):56–64.

Lutz, Mark. (1990) "Emphasizing the Social: Social Economics and Socio-Economics." Paper presented at the Society for the Advancement of Socio-Economics Conference, March, Washington, DC.

Price, James L., and Charles W. Mueller. (1981) "A Causal Model of Turnover for Nurses." *Academy of Management Journal* 24 (3):543–65.

Roth, Jeffrey, John Scholz, and Ann Dryden White, eds. (1989) *Taxpayer Compliance*. Philadelphia: Univ. of Pennsylvania Press.

Sears, David O., Richard R. Lau, Tom R. Tyler, Harris M. Allen, Jr. (1980) "Self-Interest vs. Symbolic Politics in Policy Attitudes and Presidential Voting." *American Political Science Review* 74:670–84.

Stern, Paul C. (1984) *Improving Energy Demand Analysis*. National Academy Press: Washington, DC.

Swedberg, Richard. (1990) "The New 'Battle of Methods.' " *Challenge* (January/February):33–38.

Index